THE HOUSE
ON LEMON STREET

THE GEORGE AND SAKAYE ARATANI NIKKEI IN THE AMERICAS SERIES

The House on Lemon Street is the first book in the George and Sakaye Aratani Nikkei in the Americas Series. This series endeavors to capture the best scholarship available illustrating the evolving nature of contemporary Japanese American culture and community.

THE GOAL OF THE SERIES

This is an "occasional series" that aims to publish ten to twenty innovative books in Japanese American Studies over the next five years. By stretching the boundaries of the field to the limit (whether at a substantive, theoretical, or comparative level) these books aspire to influence future scholarship in this area specifically, and Asian American Studies, more generally.

THE HOUSE ON LEMON STREET

JAPANESE PIONEERS AND THE AMERICAN DREAM

MARK HOWLAND RAWITSCH

AFTERWORD BY LANE RYO HIRABAYASHI

UNIVERSITY PRESS OF COLORADO

Boulder

Published by University Press of Colorado
5589 Arapahoe Avenue, Suite 206C
Boulder, Colorado 80303

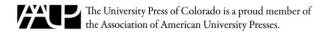 The University Press of Colorado is a proud member of
the Association of American University Presses.

The University Press of Colorado is a cooperative publishing enterprise supported, in part, by
Adams State College, Colorado State University, Fort Lewis College, Metropolitan State College of
Denver, Regis University, University of Colorado, University of Northern Colorado, Utah State University,
and Western State College of Colorado.

Library of Congress Cataloging-in-Publication Data

Rawitsch, Mark Howland, 1950–
  The house on Lemon Street : Japanese pioneers and the American dream / Mark Howland Rawitsch.
    p. cm.
  Includes bibliographical references and index.
  ISBN 978-1-60732-165-1 (cloth : alk. paper) — ISBN 978-1-60732-166-8 (e-book) —
ISBN 978-1-60732-271-9 (pbk. : alk. paper)
    1. Harada, Jukichi, 1875–1944. 2. Harada, Ken, 1881–1943. 3. Harada, Jukichi—Family. 4. Harada,
Jukichi—Trials, litigation, etc. 5. Japanese Americans—California—Riverside—Biography.
6. Immigrants—California—Riverside—Biography. 7. Riverside (Calif.)—Biography. 8. Riverside
(Calif.)—Race relations—History—20th century. 9. Japanese Americans—Civil rights—Case studies.
10. Immigrants—Civil rights—United States—Case studies. I. Title.
  F869.R6R29 2012
  973'.04956—dc23   2012011912

Design by Daniel Pratt

22 21 20 19 18 17 16 15 14 13   10 9 8 7 6 5 4 3 2 1

This publication was made possible with the support of Naomi, Kathleen, Ken, and Paul Harada, who
donated funds in memory of their father, Harold Shigetaka Harada, honoring his quest for justice
and civil rights. Additional support for this publication was also provided, in part, by UCLA's Aratani
Endowed Chair, as well as Wallace T. Kido, Joel B. Klein, Elizabeth A. Uno, and Rosalind K. Uno.

To
My love and muse, dancer Sandra Joy Metzler

CONTENTS

ACKNOWLEDGMENTS

Were it not for Sumi Harada's patience, inventive good humor, and frank assessment of my work, this book would never have been completed. To Sumi and the many members of the extended Harada family who have, over many years, supported my efforts to tell their story, I offer my warmest and most heartfelt appreciation.

In the early years, Mine Harada Kido and Clark Kohei Harada added generously to Sumi's stories of Harada family history. Decades later, their youngest brother, Dr. Harold Shigetaka Harada, and his wife, Chiye, helped to gather more family information and research materials. Shig also worked closely with the City of Riverside Harada House Project and many interested friends in Riverside and beyond to ensure public ownership of the Harada House and the Harada Family Archival and Artifact Collections of the Riverside Metropolitan Museum. Shig and Chiye's daughter, Naomi Harada, has served many as a family liaison and has maintained consistent communication with me for more than a decade. Along with her inquisitive menagerie of border collies, Naomi has also become a generous family friend in Northern California. Roy Hashimura worked with nephew Wally Kido, daughter Margo Hashimura Brower, and other family members to provide additional perspectives and oral history interviews. The families of Dr. Masa Atsu Harada and Dr. Yoshizo Harada have also provided essential information and support. Numerous Harada descendants and their families, including Rosalind Kido Uno, Kathleen Harada, Rosemary Hayashi, Dr. Kimi Klein, Dr. Ken Harada, Paul Harada, Warren and Patty Harada, Lily Ann Inouye, and Dr. Valerie Harada, offered additional support, information, referrals, or their personal perspectives about family history. Valerie, great-granddaughter of Jukichi and Ken Harada, obtained the previously unknown Harada and Indo family *koseki* records with help from hosts in Aichi prefecture during a trip to Japan. Joel Klein, Dr. Judy Seto, Terry Glazier, Dr. Alvin Hayashi, Jane Harada, and Dr. Don Harada also provided support to other family members as we worked together on family history research and the preservation of the landmark Harada House and family collections.

Ever since we began this project in the 1970s, a large community of supporters has been working with the City of Riverside to ensure the preservation and interpretation of the National Historic Landmark Harada House. Staff past and present at the Riverside Metropolitan Museum—including current staff Ennette Morton, director; Dr. Brenda Buller Focht, museum curator of collections and exhibitions; Kevin Hallaran, archivist; Lynn Voorheis, museum curator of historic structures and collections; and Teresa Woodard, curator of education—continue their enthusiastic professional and personal dedication to the project. Former museum staff involved with the project included Denise Brennan, Allison Campbell, Dana Neitzel, Ron Pidot, Warren Schweitzer, Wendy Sparks, John Wear, and museum directors Dr. H. Vincent Moses, Richard Esparza, and Charles Hice.

Other key contributors to the early success of my research include Dr. Ronald Tobey and the Department of History at the University of California, Riverside; Dr. Edna Bonacich and Dr. Morrison Wong, co-advisors for the Japanese Americans in Riverside Research Project; the members of the Riverside Chapter of the Japanese American Citizens League; the City of Riverside Cultural Heritage Board; the National Endowment for the Humanities; the dean of the College of Humanities and Social Sciences, University of California, Riverside; columnist Harry Honda of the *Pacific Citizen* newspaper, Japanese American Citizens League; and the staff at the California Office of Historic Preservation.

The Harada House National Historic Landmark Ad Hoc Advisory Council of the City of Riverside—including Naomi Harada, selected staff from the Riverside Metropolitan Museum mentioned above, Dr. Anthea Hartig, Dr. Knox Mellon, Eugene Itogawa, Peyton Hall, Dr. Lane Ryo Hirabayashi, Elaine Jackson-Retonda, Venita Jorgensen, Irene Ogata, Malcolm Margolin, Erin Gettis, Janet Hansen, former members David Look and Tonya Sorrel, and the author—have continued to develop long-range plans for the project.

The Harada House Strategic Visioning Workshop in 2004 prompted new research directions and topics explored in the present volume. The few participants in the workshop not already recognized in the acknowledgments included facilitators Tomi Nagai-Rothe and Kayia Kirsch of Grove Consultants International, Chuck Beaty, David Bristow, Marcia Choo, Bill Gardner, Marion Mitchell-Wilson, Joyce Nako, Tonya Rathbun, Anthony Veerkamp, Hiromi Ueha, Clyde Wilson, and Michiko Yoshimura.

The following colleagues, research associates, friends, and members of my own family also made significant contributions or offered generous encouragement during many years of research: Suzanne Abel, Mike Adams, Charley Adiano, Jiromaru Akira, Paulette Arnold, Dr. Eiichiro Azuma, Skip Beal and Kort Pettersen, Ross Beck, Steve and Bev Becker, Jane Beckwith, Kathleen Bowman, Dr. Hal Bridges, Dr. Sylvia Broadbent, Kevin Burtness, David Charlebois, Frank Chuman, David Cocke, Bob Comings and Linda MacDonald, Kathleen Correia, Darian Daries, Oscar De Haro, Dr. James Delgado, Dr. Gail Dubrow, Ellen Endo, Maria Fleming, Tom Frye, Linda Garvey, Bruce Ghent, Mona Gnader and family, Sue Goff, Paula Gray, William Greene, Virginia Guleff, Doug Haberman, Alan Hadley, Kelly Haigh, Dr. Nathan Hale, Joan Hall, Dr. Alayne Harris, Susan Hasegawa, Frank Hays, Sue Hebard, Cindy Heitzman, Dr. Robert Hine, Chris Hirano, Mary Holcomb, Warren Hower, Jessica Huey, the Inaba family, Martha Iseda, Anna Jackson, Evan Johnson, Linda Johnson, David Kessler, Kathleen and Dr. Bob Kirkpatrick, Esther Klotz, John Koetzner, Philip Krueger, Robert Lang, Harry Lawton, Dr. Thomas Layton, Kathy Lehner, Kayo Kaname Levenson and Monty Levenson, Eileen Lucas, Corey Madden, Kate Babcock Magruder, Diane Matsuda, Ruth McCormick, Shannon McCulley, Fred and Pattie Metzler, Kurt and Marjorie Metzler and family, Kaori Mizoguchi, Mark Mollan, Cate Moses, Eric Muller, B. J. Mylne, Daniel Nay, Laurel Near, Akiko Nomura, Doug Nomura, Beata Obydzinski, Takashi Oda, Irene Ogata, Mine Okubo, Kouhei Okuda, Lynne Otis, Hope Patterson, Tom Patterson, Dr. Victoria Patterson, Arlene Peters, Art Pick, Kim Pinson, Elizabeth Pridmore, Carolyn Pryor, Dr. Carroll Purcell, Meridith Randall, Peggy Randrup, Jim Rawitsch and Helen Rahder, Nick and Ezra Rawitsch, Melvin and Priscilla Rawitsch, Dr. Greg Robinson, Louis Rohlicek, Lua Safwenberg, Seth Metzler Smith, Susan Snyder, Denice Solgat, Steve Spiller, Dr. Sarah Stage, Gene and Carly Stewart, Karen and Dr. Jerry Strelitz, Seiji Sugawara and family, Tsutsui Tadashi, Gerry Takano, Mark Takano, Carol Taylor and Art Korngiebel, Sue Thompson, Joyce Carter Vickery, Sandy Wake, Barbara Wanderer, C. Malcolm and Joan Pearson Watkins, Kathleen Webber-Plank, David Weitzman, Chuck Wilson, Karen Wilson, Beverly Wingate Maloof, Cyndi Woskow, Irene McGroarty Wright, Dr. Deborah Wong, Connie Young, Doug Zimmerman and Nick Diorio, and Mabel Fujimoto Zinc.

Staff at the following archives, museums, libraries, schools, cultural institutions, and independent project consultants also provided research information or other support: City of Riverside, including Mayor Ronald O. Loveridge, the Riverside City Council, and City Administrative Office; California State Archives;

the Bancroft Library, University of California, Berkeley; National Archives and Records Administration; Kariya City Hall, Aichi Prefecture, Japan; Archive Centre at King's College, Cambridge; Victoria and Albert Museum, London; the Mission Inn Foundation and Museum; Riverside Polytechnic High School Library; Office of the Consulate General of Japan; Nagoya University Library; National Trust for Historic Preservation; Historic Resources Group; Riverside Public Library; Mendocino College Library; Monterey County Free Libraries; Monterey County Historical Society; California Preservation Foundation; California Cultural and Historical Endowment; Southern Poverty Law Center; Topaz Museum; Tai Hei Shakuhachi, Willits; School of Performing Arts and Cultural Education, S.P.A.C.E., Ukiah; Getty Foundation, a philanthropic division of the J. Paul Getty Trust; California Civil Liberties Public Education Program, California State Library; Public History Graduate Program and International Education Programs, University of California, Riverside; Reading the Walls: Riverside Stories of Internment and Return Project; Phillip M. Stokoe Elementary School, Innovative Teaching and Learning Center, Alvord Unified School District, Riverside; Magnolia Elementary School, Riverside; A. K. Smiley Public Library, Redlands; Institute of Museum and Library Services; California State Historical Resources Commission; National Historic Landmarks Program, National Park Service; Sendai/Riverside Sister City Association; Redlands Sister Cities Association; University of California, Los Angeles; Mendocino College; California Council for the Humanities; Riverside Unified School District; California Cultural and Historical Endowment Fund, State of California; Japanese American National Museum; California Restoration and Waterproofing; Coastline Roofing, Inc.; Plymouth Tower Retirement Home and Convalescent Facility; Williams Art Conservation; Structural Focus, Inc.; and Frederick L. Walters.

The University Press of Colorado, Darrin Pratt, Jessica d'Arbonne, Laura Furney, Daniel Pratt, and Beth Svinarich produced this publication with dedication and distinction.

Dr. Arthur A. Hansen, Professor Emeritus of History at California State University, Fullerton, along with a second anonymous manuscript reviewer engaged by the University Press of Colorado, offered keen analysis, enthusiastic support, and excellent suggestions for improvements inching me ever closer to a finished manuscript.

In addition to his afterword in this volume, Lane Ryo Hirabayashi, PhD, professor of Asian American Studies and the first holder of the George and Sakaye Aratani Professor of Japanese American Incarceration, Redress, and Community at the University of California, Los Angeles, is also a member of the Harada House Project team. Ever since we first met in Riverside at the Harada House Strategic Visioning Workshop in 2004, when Lane was a professor at the University of

California campus there, he has offered steady encouragement and guidance, solid advice, challenging conversations, scores of e-mail messages, and numerous structural improvements to several versions of the manuscript. Naomi Harada and Jim Rawitsch provided perceptive assessments of early manuscript drafts; Skip Beale helped create the notes and sources.

Finally, this book is dedicated to my love and muse, dancer Sandra Joy Metzler. Thank you, Sandy!

MARK H. RAWITSCH

THE HOUSE ON
LEMON STREET

INTRODUCTION

And yet words on a parchment would not
be enough to deliver slaves from bondage,
or provide men and women of every color
and creed their full rights and obligations as
citizens of the United States. What would
be needed were Americans in successive
generations who were willing to do their
part—through protests and struggles, on the
streets and in the courts, through a civil war
and civil disobedience and always at great
risk—to narrow that gap between the promise of our ideals and the reality of their time.

. . . I believe deeply that we cannot solve the
challenges of our time unless we solve them
together—unless we perfect our union by
understanding that we may have different
stories, but we hold common hopes; we may
not look the same and may not have come
from the same place, but we all want to move
in the same direction—towards a better future for our children and our grandchildren.

Barack Obama, "A More Perfect Union," March 18, 2008

Sumi Harada's old house on Lemon Street is now a National Historic Landmark
with an American story to tell. For much of the twentieth century, members of the
Harada family, Americans of Japanese ancestry, lived in this modest California
house on Lemon Street in Riverside, working to realize the American Dream of
aspiring to happiness and fulfillment by owning a home of their own. Like some
of the more familiar landmarks representing the experiences of Americans with
an immigrant heritage—Ellis Island and the Statue of Liberty come to mind—or
other places in our country where people of color took their struggle to the streets,

this American home tells the story of a fight for the rights of immigrants and their citizen children facing long-established attitudes and legal actions questioning their participation in American life.

In the early 1900s, father Jukichi, mother Ken, and their firstborn son came across the Pacific to the United States from their ancestral home in Japan. The young family settled in Riverside, a place of promise where hundreds of other Japanese immigrants were finding work in California's burgeoning citrus industry. As more children were born, the Haradas supported their growing family with small profits from their Washington Restaurant and a rooming house where they lived in Riverside's downtown commercial district. Because of the untimely passing of their second son in 1913, Jukichi and Ken vowed to move their surviving children from the stuffy and crowded rooming-house lodgings to a better home of their own in a good neighborhood just as soon as possible.

Two years later, Mr. Harada finally found an affordable thirty-year-old six-room house for sale, freshly painted and conveniently located in a white middle-class neighborhood on Lemon Street. The little house was less than a ten-minute walk from the Haradas' downtown restaurant and close to the family's church and the children's school. Jukichi and Ken decided to purchase the property because they believed it would provide a safe and healthy place for their children to live. However, just as the sale neared completion, white neighbors objected to the Haradas' move to the new neighborhood because of their Japanese ancestry.

When the Harada family decided to move to Lemon Street, California's Alien Land Law of 1913, later described in the US Supreme Court case *Oyama v. California* as "the first official act of discrimination aimed at the Japanese," denied real estate ownership to aliens ineligible for citizenship. According to the new law, because they had come from Asia and were not allowed to become citizens of the United States, young fathers and mothers like Jukichi and Ken Harada from Japan could never own real estate in California. For those who believed the Golden State had been and should always be "White Man's Country," the prohibition of real estate ownership by those who could never become citizens was desirable, because it was hoped that these immigrants should only be in California temporarily to harvest oranges or hoe weeds between the row crops.

Thinking of the future of his youngest children and aware of their rights as native-born citizens of the United States, Jukichi attempted to circumvent the new law. He bought the house on Lemon Street by recording ownership of the property in the names of the three American citizens in his family, his two young daughters and an infant son. Mr. Harada knew his three youngest children were citizens because they had been born on American soil, but most did not care that some in the Harada family were American citizens. Regardless of the Haradas' citizenship status, many people in town were more concerned that the parents and their children had Japanese faces. When the Haradas bought the house on

Lemon Street in 1915, many Americans across the nation still believed that any immigrant from Asia and all the other people of color already living within its borders should never be allowed to take part in the American Dream.

Within days of the Haradas' purchase of their new house, local newspapers printed the alarming news that a Japanese family was moving to Lemon Street. The Haradas' white neighbors quickly formed a committee and asked Jukichi to accept a small profit on the sale and move to another part of town. Harada refused. The anxious neighbors and other concerned citizens soon convinced California's attorney general to file suit against Harada to oust his family from the house on Lemon Street, charging he had violated the Alien Land Law. Before too much longer, with some prominent white people in town taking his side in the battle, Mr. Harada was seated in the witness chair at the Riverside County Courthouse, defending himself and his family against the State of California in the first Japanese American court case testing the 1913 Alien Land Law, *The People of California v. Jukichi Harada*.

By the time Harada's trial began, interest in the house on Lemon Street had expanded far beyond Riverside. Reports of the case were published in big-city newspapers on both coasts. It was also claimed that the proceedings against Mr. Harada had even aroused the concern of the Japanese government. Whatever the outcome of their court trial and the rest of their family's American journey, when they would, one day, find themselves exiled behind the barbed-wire fences of an American concentration camp, the Haradas and others like them soon understood that despite hard work, perseverance, and good behavior, the American Dream would not always be easy to come by.

In 2008, when presidential hopeful Barack Obama was struggling to maintain his political future with his speech "A More Perfect Union," delivered not far from the Liberty Bell and Independence Hall at Constitution Center in Philadelphia, he spoke of the "successive generations" of Americans willing to do their part to narrow the distance "between the promise of our ideals and the reality of their time." The tall son of a mother from Kansas and a father from Kenya said we all had the same hopes, and even though we all do not look the same and have not come from the same place, "we all want to move in the same direction—towards a better future for our children and our grandchildren."

Despite candidate Obama's optimism about the overarching good intentions of the American people, change has often been difficult to accept. As too many children and grandchildren experienced, for some in our divided land at the time of the Civil War it had been far too soon for anyone to deliver slaves from bondage. In 1915 it was impossible for others to imagine that a Japanese family might be coming to live next door. In another generation, more thought it was simply unacceptable for Rosa Parks to take a seat on a bus in Montgomery or to have nine well-dressed young men and women ascend the steps of Little Rock's Central

High School. Within our borders in our own time it has been difficult for some of our neighbors to believe that babies born to migrant workers who have come here without permission should become American citizens by virtue of our Constitution's Fourteenth Amendment. And it has not been all that long since many more among us refused to accept an Islamic community center rising too close to the ashes of Ground Zero.

If, as Barack Obama had said in Philadelphia, "words on a parchment" alone have not always been sufficient to "provide men and women of every color and creed their full rights and obligations as citizens of the United States," then the risky protests and struggles accompanying the story of our country, and the often confrontational practices of citizenship exercised in pursuit of the American Dream, have always been essential ingredients for the progress and success of the American people. For immigrants from Japan, their early efforts to purchase homes of their own in what they believed to be decent neighborhoods of respectable families were met with open hostility and challenges to their desire to become permanent residents of the United States and to join others in the country as equals. Those in authority who urged the government's forced removal of Japanese Americans from the West Coast during World War II, implemented by President Franklin Roosevelt's Executive Order 9066 in 1942 in response to advice that the removal was a military necessity, ignored official information saying that the Japanese Americans living on the West Coast were of little threat. Instead of a wartime action required by immediate concerns over national security, the expulsion was, as others in authority would one day recognize, a culmination of nearly fifty years of discrimination and legal harassment aimed at Japanese immigrants and their American citizen children. The story of the house on Lemon Street and the Harada family's quest for acceptance illuminates the deep underpinnings of anti-Asian animus setting the stage for Executive Order 9066 and recognizes fundamental elements of our nation's anti-immigrant history that continue to shape the American story today.

Candidate Obama's words resonated for many who know that the fight for the American Dream cannot be taken for granted. Some of them closest to the struggle in time and living memory remember the family stories of confrontation lived by the pioneers among us who faced their neighbors to take our country's promises out into the open air from their workingmen's shacks or migrant camps on the other side of the railroad tracks. With children and grandchildren on their minds, the most courageous ones among us marched into the daylight across our bridges, up and away from the hot fields and factories, onto our streets and into our jails and courtrooms. Some made inspiring speeches to defend the dream; others were lynched. Some were removed from their homes and forced to live beneath the guard towers of America's concentration camps, and some lived long enough to see a family of color move into the White House. However, despite the years of struggle and victories accomplished in pursuit and defense of the American Dream, some people around us today still know little of these patriotic efforts. And others who have learned nothing from the many lessons of this quest are already repeating some of the mistakes of our past.

ONE

HERE IS YOUR CHANCE

Yukihi Harada came to California . . .
with one suit of clothes and two hands.
Now he has a restaurant, a wife, three
children, a house and a law suit.

"The Japanese Cloud," *Sunset*, Holiday Number 1916

RIVERSIDE, CALIFORNIA, CHRISTMAS 1915

Still living in a crowded rooming house with yet another baby on the way, Jukichi and Ken Harada were determined to move into their first real home as soon as they possibly could. The Haradas had moved to Riverside in 1905 and, after ten years of hard work building a business, raising their children, and saving their pennies, by Christmas 1915 they were finally ready to make their move.

Like others in his extended family, Jukichi had been educated to be a schoolteacher back home in Japan. However, independent and restless for change, he only worked a year in his first teaching assignment before his thoughts turned to making his way elsewhere in the world. As soon as he made the acquaintance of Ken Indo, the beautiful fifteen-year-old sister of one of his friends from an old samurai family in Kariya-shi, he began thinking they both might make something more of themselves together in some other place.

In contrast to many of their contemporaries in the land of their ancestors, young men and women whose marriages would be arranged by elders with little say from future husband and wife, from their first meeting Jukichi and Ken approached life in ways that would make their story different from what would have been expected had they remained close to home. When they started their family and left Japan to come to the United States of America, they were driven by

7

optimism and the promise of new beginnings. Setting up housekeeping in a shabby rented rooming house in California, they had no idea it would take twenty years of struggle to even begin to see some financial stability, and half that long just to find a home of their own. By the time they finally bought a house in sunny Riverside they had no way of knowing how many years they would live there together or how their American story would end. Indeed, as soon as their new neighbors heard that a Japanese family was planning to live nearby, Jukichi and Ken Harada had no time to spend dreaming about the future. They had other more urgent matters to face as they fought to keep their house on Lemon Street.

With a baby due in just a few months, Jukichi had been busy nearly every day, taking time from his work at the restaurant to ask local real estate agents for help finding a new house outside the congested center of Riverside's downtown commercial district. More than once Harada had asked his acquaintance, Orange Street resident and real estate broker Jacob Van de Grift to help him find a suitable home in a good neighborhood close to the center of town. By the end of the year and after repeated requests, Mr. Van de Grift, had not replied, so Jukichi decided to pursue the matter himself. On December 8, forty-three-year-old real estate agent Frank Colfax Noble listed a house for sale in a small advertisement in the *Riverside Daily Press*: "Here is your chance. A 6 room house on Lemon Street near Fourth Street, newly painted and papered, fixed for two families if necessary. Price $1600, with $400 cash, balance $100 every 6 months."[1]

Jukichi spotted the newspaper listing and telephoned Frank Noble's real estate office to ask about the house. Noble's office was in the new First National Bank building on the corner of Main and Eighth, just across the street from the Haradas' Washington Restaurant. Named for patriot George Washington, the restaurant was decorated inside with framed portraits of US presidents, some adorned with little American flags. A few blocks to the north, the freshly painted six-room house for sale at 356 Lemon was one of the small wooden cottages built along the outer reaches of Lemon Street during the building boom of the 1880s. Its front door was just a few steps from the street in a row of three nearly identical one-story cottages with open front porches facing west. The house was less than a ten-minute walk from the Washington Restaurant and next door to the quiet and well-kept home of widow Cynthia Robinson. Jukichi and Ken considered the property to be reasonably priced and in a nice neighborhood of respectable people living close to the Japanese Methodist Mission and the town's Lincoln grammar school. Both institutions were near the intersection of Fifth and Mulberry and only a three-block walk from the house on Lemon Street.

The Haradas' five-year-old daughter, Sumi, had just started school at Lincoln in September. The little girl's daily walk in the residential neighborhood between the 300 block of Lemon and her new grammar school would be two blocks shorter and much safer than crossing the wide and busy downtown intersections between the school and the family's rooming house at the corner of Eighth and Orange. Ken and Jukichi were excited by the possibility of owning a clean and affordable home of their own on a quiet, shady street with a nice backyard and located just five blocks from their Washington Restaurant. In a day or two Jukichi told Frank Noble he wanted to take a closer look at the little house on Lemon Street. Seeing the promises of America as worth the risk and believing what they had heard about Christianity from the Reverend So and his kind friends at the Methodist Mission, the Haradas had not considered that some of their neighbors might be extremely upset about them living nearby.[2]

Soon after Jukichi called Frank Noble, Mr. Noble contacted Fulton Gunnerson, the owner of the Lemon Street house. Agent Noble invited Mr. Gunnerson to meet with Mr. Harada to discuss a possible sale. Gunnerson and his wife, Hannah, owned the house on Lemon but they did not live in the neighborhood. Even before he met with Jukichi Harada to discuss the terms of sale, Mr. Gunnerson expressed the first signs of trouble. When he learned the potential buyer for his property on Lemon Street was Japanese, he was not enthused about the pending sale and told Frank Noble so in no uncertain terms. "I won't sell to a Japanese," Gunnerson said. Many others in California would have felt exactly the same way.

When Noble told Jukichi of the complications with Mr. Gunnerson, Harada instructed his real estate agent to stop negotiating and "let it go." Still interested in the sale, or perhaps hearing from Noble that Harada might be willing to offer a cashier's check for full payment of the property, Gunnerson apparently had a change of heart. He soon asked Noble to arrange a meeting with Harada. As the three men talked at the heavy desks in Noble's office at the First National Bank, they discussed a lower selling price for the Lemon Street property and mentioned the house would be a good place for Mr. Harada's children to live.[3]

After a few more minutes, a verbal agreement established that Harada would pay $1,500 for the house, $100 less than the asking price in Noble's newspaper advertisement. With terms of the sale settled, Jukichi must have been relieved his search for a good home in a nice neighborhood was finally over. Harada and his family had already been through more than he had bargained for when he first set out from Japan for a new life in the United States. They had come to a friendly and accepting town known for its large number of Christian churches, so many that some of its earliest Chinese settlers had called the place Yea So Fow, "Jesus City." More recently, Frank Miller of the Mission Inn, owner of the town's biggest hotel, one of Riverside's most influential citizens, and an active member of the First Congregational Church, had also been demonstrating his personal enthusiasm for fostering tolerance and harmony among the races. Famous African American educator and former slave Dr. Booker T. Washington had even spent the night as Frank Miller's guest at the Mission Inn. Mr. Miller's measured acceptance of faces of color and his growing interest in promoting peace among nations suggested that Riverside offered a peaceful and refined setting for demonstrating the principles of Christian brotherhood in ways not practiced elsewhere in less civilized places in the West.

Although the God-fearing citizens of Riverside had over the years been more tolerant than many of their California neighbors, when the Haradas bought their new house on Lemon Street, the Golden State was still the place where some of its grandfathers had comfortably espoused the political campaign slogan "The Chinese Must Go!" Many more men and women in the American West were fretting over the growing number of Japanese immigrants, what had been termed the Japanese Question. And, as Cynthia Robinson's Riverside newspaper had said earlier that year at the preview of motion picture director D. W. Griffith's cinematic triumph *The Birth of a Nation*, the entire country was becoming increasingly occupied with discussions of race and what many still called the "Negro problem." If old Mrs. Robinson or any of her neighbors had been influenced by the disturbing images of director Griffith's controversial motion picture masterpiece, Jukichi Harada's plan to move his family to a nice house on Lemon Street might have made them think their neighborhood was in grave danger. Like the unnerving scene in *The Birth of a Nation* when black soldiers with rifles push a white man and his children off the sidewalk, to Cynthia Robinson and her neighbors living on Lemon Street the idea of a Japanese immigrant moving his family to the center of what the local paper called "one of the most favored residence districts of the city" was simply too much to bear.

Although the Haradas had already suffered one terrible setback when their second son died in 1913, they had made steady advancement over the last few years toward success in sunny California. Yet despite their progress, Ken had already pointed out to Jukichi that they might not succeed in a place that sometimes felt so far away from home to her. If they could just find a house of their own in a good neighborhood among other decent families, a healthier place than living downtown with transient roomers on the second floor of a rented boardinghouse, perhaps they could finally make a better home life for their children. Or so they hoped.

Within hours of Jukichi's first visit with widow Cynthia Robinson, his new neighbor sounded the alarm that a Japanese family was coming there to live. In no time the turmoil bubbling around the Haradas' new house began to spread. Jacob Van de Grift, the property broker who had not answered Jukichi Harada's repeated requests for assistance, lived in a fancy Victorian home just around the block on Orange Street. He soon joined Mrs. Robinson and other concerned neighbors to form a committee to prevent the Haradas from buying the house on Lemon. Other influential people in town, however, sided with the Haradas. Before long, the State of California joined the fray, filing the first lawsuit against a Japanese family under California's Alien Land Law of 1913.

After years of squabbling about the future of the Golden State, a place many had long regarded as White Man's Country, and acting against the wishes of the nation's leaders and others concerned about the emergence of Japan as a powerful player on the international stage, the state legislature had passed its first Alien Land Law in 1913 to halt Japanese advancement in California. When Jukichi Harada, a Japanese immigrant ineligible for American citizenship, bought the cottage next door to the widow Robinson, he landed his family squarely at the center of a social maelstrom that would not subside for another generation. In twenty-five years the battle for acceptance and equality of Japanese Americans as citizens of the United States and equal participants in the American Dream would lead to one of the most challenging and shameful events in all of American history, but in the winter of 1915, long before anyone had ever even heard of a faraway place called Pearl Harbor, the fight was just beginning.

As real estate agent Noble prepared the deed to the house on Lemon Street, he thought it unusual Mr. Harada had asked that ownership of the house be recorded in the names of his three youngest children. All were under ten years of age. The oldest of the three, daughter Mine, was only nine; her sister Sumi would turn six on Christmas Day; and her brother Yoshizo was just three years old. Unlike their oldest brother, Masa Atsu, who had been born in Japan before his parents came to California, the three youngest children were citizens of the United States because they were born on American soil. It was, however, unusual for Noble to record the sale of a house in the names of anyone so young. As soon as the deed to the property was completed and filed at the county courthouse, it took only a few days for Noble to hear that he and Mr. Gunnerson might be in some sort of legal trouble for selling a house to the underage children of a Japanese alien.

Worried about the possible consequences, Noble wrote a brief letter to California attorney general Ulysses S. Webb to find out more. Webb was the state's chief law enforcement officer and one of the authors of the 1913 Alien Land Law, so he should know whether Noble and Gunnerson had violated the law. Noble asked Webb, "Can a Jap boy or girl born here in California acquire and hold real estate?" As Frank Noble awaited Attorney General Webb's reply, others closer to home took far less time to respond. A week after Jukichi Harada purchased the house, regional newspapers reported that a local "storm of protest" was growing quickly into an issue of statewide interest. In a few more months other reports would claim that even the government of Japan and officials in Washington, DC, were closely watching the situation on Lemon Street.[4]

In its disquieting first review of the circumstances brewing in Riverside, "Land Titles to Children; Jap Plan to Evade Law on Aliens," William Randolph Hearst's *Los Angeles Examiner* said one Lemon Street resident planned to isolate himself from his new Japanese neighbors with a "spite fence." Next-door neighbor

Cynthia Robinson, it was claimed, intended to "plow up her driveway which leads to the rear of the Harada home." Other members of the neighborhood committee soon developed more formal plans to oust the Haradas from their new house. Perhaps hearing rumors that hotelier Frank Miller intended to support the Haradas' purchase of a new house, they soon hired Miller's political rival, Riverside attorney and former state senator Miguel Estudillo, to represent them in a lawsuit aimed at evicting the Japanese family. At a meeting in Estudillo's law office, neighborhood committee spokesman Van de Grift and attorney Estudillo tried once more to pressure Jukichi Harada to give up his new house. By then, however, Jukichi's mind was set. He was not about to back down now. Van de Grift told of Harada's refusal to accept their final offer, and the die was cast: "Mr. Estudillo made him an offer of $400 more than he paid, and he said: 'I won't sell. You can murder me, you can throw me into the sea, and I won't sell.' "[5]

TWO

THE SCHOOLTEACHER AND THE SAMURAI'S DAUGHTER

When the delicate *kakitsubata* irises blossomed once again in the shallow marshes of Aichi-ken in spring 1897, new schoolteacher Jukichi Harada caught the eye of fifteen-year-old Ken Indo, and before long the young couple began dreaming of change. Years later, on sunny days in late spring and summer, when temperatures in her prosperous California town at the edge of the great Mojave Desert climbed to 100 degrees or more, this quiet daughter of a samurai, a young woman who would one day be remembered by her children for her bright eyes, beautiful smile, gentle hands, hard work, and forgiving nature, must have thought of the coastal moisture and cool breezes of Aichi-ken. In those quiet moments far from home, she may have also recalled the beauty of the kakitsubata, the rabbit-ear iris, signature flower of her ancestral land.

The fragile purple iris blossoms always returned each spring to the wetlands of Aichi, to Kozutumi-Nishi pond at the northern outskirts of her hometown of Kariya-shi, not far from the old Tokaido Road connecting the ancient cities of Kyoto and Edo. Kariya-shi was a day's walk south of the bustling city of Nagoya on Honshu Island in central Japan. The deeper shades and lighter centers of the kakitsubata flowers nearly matched the slowly fading colors of the indigo-blue kimonos Ken Indo Harada had once packed so carefully, resting them protectively over a small pasteboard box, its dark interior layered with soft white cotton protecting wrapped packets holding remnants of her children's umbilical cords. Each packet included a folded paper note. Written in a solid Japanese hand, the notes recorded her children's births and parentage. By 1920, the kimonos and the packets were hidden from sight, along with other vestiges and receding memories of her Japanese past, beneath lines of laundry drying in the washroom off the kitchen, stored together safely in a big steamer trunk with cracked leather straps curling at their edges like rough tortoise skin baking in the dry desert heat of Southern California. During the forty years of her American journey, she had worked long hours each day with her husband and love of her life to raise their children and realize their dream of owning a home of their own, and the memory of the vibrant kakitsubata iris might have helped the samurai's daughter maintain her own sense of beauty, balance, and inner strength in this new world of reduced expectations, struggle, and confrontation.

Jukichi Harada, like his wife a child of Aichi-ken, was an educated man in his early twenties beginning a secure and honorable career as a public schoolteacher in Japan, and he might also have looked to the kakitsubata irises for inspiration. However, for this independent and ambitious young man, the poetic seasonal image of the rabbit-ear irises might have nourished a different kind of personal strength. Like Ken, Jukichi would certainly have seen the familiar flowers of his childhood as a comfort, as in the old haiku poem, shimmering like the source of rainbows in the morning mist. The young teacher, however, might have also imagined the vivid purple blossoms facing the daily sunrise over the deep blue waters of the Western Pacific as an invitation to try something new. For Jukichi, who saw his homeland grappling with profound changes wrought by contact with the outside world and new ideas from within, the sight of the springtime irises might have even encouraged dreams of escape from the structured restrictions and narrow worldview of his Japanese island past.

Under mounting pressures close to home, young Harada-san was feeling a growing sense of regimentation, prompting him to think his new teaching career would most likely bring him only modest success in what would no doubt be an ordinary life in Japan. Each new season of kakitsubata flowers offered the pensive young man a quiet moment to see his world differently, a chance to break with tradition and perhaps even begin life anew on the other side of the great ocean. Despite the admiration and respect Jukichi enjoyed in his promising first year as a schoolteacher, a nagging "tightening around the shoulders" soon turned his eyes eastward, over the rainbows and toward the sea. Thinking of the future with each new sunrise, Jukichi Harada stepped closer to leaving behind the kakitsubata of Aichi-ken forever.

Today the modern and industrialized Japanese prefecture of Aichi is described on the Internet as "Home of the Samurai Spirit," a place still proud of its rich national heritage of cultural and political influence. The region's most well-known historical figures, Oda Nobunaga, Toyotomi Hideyoshi, and Tokugawa Ieyasu—the "three hegemons," all born there in the 1500s—unified the nation during the late sixteenth and early seventeenth centuries. The youngest of the three, Tokugawa Ieyasu, born in 1543, founded the Tokugawa shogunate, the vast political dynasty that dominated Japan from the great capital city of Edo, later called Tokyo, for nearly 300 years, during the Edo period from 1603 to the restoration of the Emperor Meiji and the beginning of the Meiji Era in 1868. Responding to ideas from the world outside its island borders, Japan in the late 1800s emerged from centuries of isolation to begin a period of dramatic social and cultural change. More than a century later, still celebrating its long-cherished samurai spirit, Aichi prefecture is perhaps now more widely known as the birthplace of the eco-friendly *Prius,* the first mass-produced hybrid automobile, and home to Toyota Motor Corporation, founded there in 1937.

In the last decades of the nineteenth century, fifty years before leaders at the Toyoda Automatic Loom Works began thinking seriously about branching into the automobile business, the people of Meiji Japan were in the midst of a tumultuous journey. A country once isolated by both geography and centuries of feudal custom was entering a swiftly changing world of international contact and influence. Efforts to create a more politically unified, industrialized, and modern nation merged with expansive social experiments abolishing the samurai class and establishing a national education system to create a less stratified, more patriotic, and ultimately more militaristic society able to compete head-to-head with other countries on the international stage. Long-standing traditions of the shogun and samurai ebbed in the face of nearly overwhelming influences from the West and new ideas from within, shaking the very foundations of Japanese life like a Pacific Rim earthquake.

The extended families of the children of Aichi-ken, like others around them in Meiji Japan, faced the growing pressures of changing social rules, beliefs, and practices. Japanese *koseki,* family history registers, tell us that the parents of Jukichi Harada and Ken Indo were among the last generation born in the two decades before the summer of 1853, when Commodore Matthew Perry and his small fleet of American ships steamed into Edo Bay to negotiate the opening of Japan. Of the four parents, Ken Indo's father, Matazo Indo, was born first, in the year Tenpo 4 (1833 on the Western calendar), a son inheriting the social standing and privileges of the samurai family of his father, Mataemon Indo. In his mid-thirties at the beginning of the Meiji Era in 1868, samurai Matazo Indo was one of 157 retainers in the Kariya-han, in what is today eastern Aichi prefecture near Nagoya, the ancient feudal domain established in 1600 by Mizuno Katsunari, cousin of the great shogun Tokugawa Ieyasu.

Upon Matazo Indo's marriage to Tane Okazaki, the newly wedded couple lived near other members of the bride's extended family in Kumamura-shi. They later moved closer to Matazo's ancestral home and the growing settlement of Kariya-shi, still known today in the region south of Nagoya for its beautiful kakitsubata iris marshes. Early in their life together, Matazo and Tane might have assumed they would continue to enjoy the benefits of a traditional life among the samurai, but by the end of the 1870s, the once strong and influential warrior class was in steep decline as the fledgling Japanese government ended its privileges and organized new approaches to the structure of its changing society. As Matazo and Tane Indo faced unprecedented change, they must have wondered how their children would face a future without the status and influence their family had known in previous generations. It was in this changing family and community setting, as the rabbit-ear iris blossoms faded in the summer of Meiji 14, that the couple's second daughter and fourth child, Ken, was born on July 21, 1881. Father Matazo was well past his prime at forty-eight and mother Tane, at forty, very near the end of her childbearing years.

Six summers before Ken Indo's birth near the iris marshes of Kariya-shi, on August 22, 1875, her future husband, Jukichi Harada, was born in Aichi-ken, the second son of father Takanori and mother Tetsu Banno Harada. At the time of Jukichi's birth in the summer of Meiji 8, his father was working as a teacher at the Odaka Gakko, the local district school in Chita-gun. Jukichi's father had been adopted as a boy of eleven and subsequently was recorded in local records as the fourth child of Sakuzaemon Kanie. Young Takanori, supported by the Kanie family, was offered the opportunity to follow earlier Harada generations, joining those before him to become a teacher who would later be remembered for his poetry and fine calligraphy. Takanori and Tetsu Harada's first son, Jukichi's older brother, Naoyoshi, was born in 1873. The boys' two younger sisters, Yoshi and Tama, were born in 1883 and 1888, respectively. Tama would also follow in her family's footsteps and become a teacher.[1]

As children in the 1880s, Jukichi Harada and Ken Indo were required by a new national education law to attend the local grammar school. Some Japanese leaders saw compulsory public education as a key to bringing their country into the modern world. Boys and girls in the families of merchants, artisans, and former samurai were now required to study topics shifting their cultural training from the traditional neo-Confucian ideas of the last 100 years to more modern perspectives emphasizing student individuality and topics in science and technology. In the revamped educational system's earliest years Japanese educators brought scholars from the United States to help establish widespread public education in Japan. Lacking the instructional materials needed to implement many of the nation's new ideas in education, Japan quickly adopted the content of Western textbooks. Some of the newest teaching tools, like the *Marius Wilson Readers* with illustrations depicting everyday life in the United States, were printed in Japanese and sent to impressionable schoolchildren throughout the country.

In addition to this influence from the West, elementary school education in Meiji Japan included a growing emphasis on loyalty to the emperor and filial piety, promoting respect for one's parents and ancestors. In 1890, copies of the new Kyoiku Chokugo (the Imperial Rescript on Education) and portraits of the emperor were sent by the hundreds to Japanese neighborhood schools to be used in local patriotic ceremonies and to reinforce the sweeping educational and social reforms of the Meiji Era. The rescript decreed that all Japanese subjects demonstrate loyalty to their parents, affection to brothers and sisters, and harmony between husbands and wives. It directed citizens to be true to their friends and bear themselves in modesty and moderation, emphasized the pursuit of learning and the arts to develop intellect and morality, and stressed respect for constitutional law and advancement of the public good. Anyone trained as a teacher in Japan in the 1890s would have known of the content of the rescript and would also have been instructed to emphasize loyalty to the emperor, filial piety, and patriotism in their school classes more than ever before.[2]

Because of his family's heritage in education Jukichi Harada was familiar with reading, writing, and learning. His father's graceful calligraphy and poetry compositions might have inspired the boy to spend extra time studying these ancient arts and thinking about how he might someday be respected by his family and his peers for knowing these traditions. As the son of a teacher, however, and even in his early years in elementary school, Jukichi would have been influenced by the recent educational changes from the West. Like others in school at the time, he may have even studied those scenes of everyday American life in the *Marius Wilson Readers*.

As a teenager, young Jukichi appears to have taken his early family and public school experiences to heart. Although these experiences most likely cultivated in him a strong sense of love and respect for his parents and others in his extended Japanese family and community, they may also have prompted unfamiliar thoughts about the world outside Japan. Images from American school books printed in Japanese might have inspired young Harada-san to think about visiting the United States one day. Living in a schoolteacher's family, Jukichi was most certainly inculcated in the manners and habits of his father and the other teachers among his Japanese ancestors. Yet, as a product of his nation's changing school system, he was also learning to think independently. Consequently, Jukichi might have realized that this highly structured society and family heritage limited future possibilities. As the Haradas' second son, Jukichi also knew that by tradition his older brother was entitled to a greater level of family inheritance and responsibility than he. It was this awareness of the limits and family dynamics he would face close to home that helped to motivate the new schoolteacher to seek his fortune elsewhere.

In the early 1890s, having completed the ten-year compulsory segment of his public education, student Jukichi Harada, unlike many of his contemporaries who then ended their public education, attended a course of study for men at the Aichi Jinjo Sihan Gakko, the Aichi Prefectural Lower Normal College. This local post-secondary school offered training for new public schoolteachers. After four years of study, in March 1897, Jukichi completed his courses, graduated from the teachers' college, and just a month later assumed an appointment as a first-year teacher at Kariya Jinjo Shogakko, the elementary school in Ken Indo's town of Kariya-shi. Harada-sensei, the title of honor used by his students to address their new and inexperienced schoolteacher, taught at Kariya Jinjo Shogakko for just one school year, ending his first teaching assignment in March 1898.[3]

Perhaps making new acquaintances during his first teaching appointment in Kariya-shi or happily accepting that assignment because of her presence, Jukichi also found time away from his new teaching job to pursue a non-traditional romance and courtship with the attractive younger sister of his friend Shintaro Indo. When the handsome young schoolteacher met Ken Indo, she was just fifteen. Despite her youth, Jukichi was undoubtedly smitten with Ken's enchanting smile, bright eyes, quiet grace, and radiant beauty. Her samurai family heritage and strict cultural training may have reinforced Ken's attractive qualities, further impressing the smart and ambitious Jukichi Harada.

It was also likely pleasing to Jukichi that Ken was more independent than some of the other young women with whom he was acquainted. Unlike some of her friends, Ken Indo was not living under the watchful eyes of her parents but with the family of her older brother, who as first son had assumed the role as head of the Indo family upon his father's death a few years before. This situation offered opportunities for the young couple to meet and carry on their private courtship with some independence and without the close scrutiny or supervision of the older generation, still common in Japanese culture at the time. Within days, without any help from family matchmakers or others in their parents' generation, the schoolteacher had fallen in love with the samurai's daughter. Ken Indo and Jukichi Harada were married within the year, and by spring 1898 they were expecting the birth of their first child. Jukichi Harada was twenty-two; his new wife, sixteen.[4]

Leaving his post at the school in Kariya after only a year, Jukichi soon received a second teaching assignment at another nearby elementary school, the Jinjo Koto Shogakko in Anjo, just five miles southeast of Kariya. Jukichi's father was working as a teacher in Anjo at the time and he may have helped his son secure his job there, set to begin when the new school year commenced on April 7, 1898. Jukichi Harada's family background, recent educational training, and second teaching assignment suggested to him that he had the potential to command lifelong honor and respect from students, friends, family, and community. Yet, perhaps originally influenced to pursue his teaching career because of the long tradition of teachers in the Harada family, even with his early teaching assignments keeping him close to home, Jukichi was dissatisfied with what he perceived as his limited future in Japan.[5]

Harada's family heritage and fourteen years of public education provided him a foundation for acceptance, stability, and security at home. To a Japanese man coming of age in the late nineteenth century looking out to the world beyond Japan, that same education and national interest may have also turned Jukichi's restless eyes toward the rising sun, away from Asia and to new possibilities in other places. Despite his chances for modest success and respectability at home in Aichi-ken, Jukichi did not want to remain there. Jukichi's oldest daughter, Mine, remembered her father expressing his feelings about leaving the security of Japan for a new life in the United States. "He said it was very—in Japanese they call it 'tightening around the shoulders,'—meaning that things were a little too regimented or that he was restricted too much. He was teaching when he ran away," Mine said. Mine's younger brother Clark said it had not taken his father long to determine that the modest career of a schoolteacher was not what he wanted from life. "He said he would get . . . a small house . . . and he'd get maybe fifteen yen a month to support his family [if he stayed in Japan] . . . He said he didn't like that. So he went out in the world to seek his fortune," his son explained. Ignoring concerns about not honoring his next teaching contract, Jukichi decided to leave Japan and, if things went well, perhaps never return. Facing the increasing responsibilities of his recent marriage and his wife's pregnancy, Jukichi understood that he needed to act quickly if he wanted to reshape the rest of his life.[6]

Around the time Harada gave up his second teaching assignment, he also obtained a Japanese passport for the purpose of conducting academic research overseas. Other young men in Japan had similar interests and a few had already traveled to the United States as students. Shortly after receiving his new passport Jukichi left his wife with family in Aichi, headed east to the busy international seaport of Yokohama, and boarded a ship to pay his first visit to the United States of America. His expectant wife still at home in Japan, Jukichi arrived fascinated and alone in bawdy San Francisco at the end of May 1898.[7]

A month before Harada sailed from Yokohama, US president William McKinley had requested military intervention in Cuba in response to the destruction of the USS *Maine*. The American battleship had exploded under mysterious circumstances in Havana Harbor on February 15. By mid-April, Congress had adopted a joint resolution for war with Spain, and McKinley signed it on April 20. A few days later war was declared and the president called for 125,000 volunteers to join his nation's latest military effort. To end the presence of Spanish forces in the Western Pacific, McKinley had ordered by the middle of May the occupation of the Philippines. At the end of the month American troops were sailing from San Francisco toward Manila.

To protect American shipping during the war, the president also ordered the transfer of the American Revenue Cutter Service, ancestor of the Coast Guard, to military service with the US Navy. Most of the dozen revenue cutters assigned to the navy during the four-month Spanish American War plied waters along the country's eastern shore with the North Atlantic Squadron. Four more vessels patrolled in a second squadron along the Pacific coast between San Francisco and Alaska. One of these four ships, the United States steamer *Grant*, a thirty-year-old vessel outfitted with four mounted guns and commanded by Captain Jefferson A. Slamm, veteran of the Union Navy in the Civil War, was ordered into military service on April 11. *Grant* served the navy in wartime for the next four months, taking on several new crewmen in San Francisco.

On July 3, seeking a job to support his travels, Jukichi Harada joined the forty-seven members of the crew assembling aboard the *Grant* for service in the Spanish American War. Twenty-two years old, Harada signed on as one of eight "boys" working in the galley presided over by the ship's nineteen-year-old cook, Ah Do from San Francisco. Harada and his fellow galley workers were responsible for washing dishes and assisting with meal preparation for the officers and crew, cleaning the mess decks, and keeping the ship's galley in good order. When he joined the kitchen staff, Jukichi was one of only four Japanese crewmen on the coal-fired *Grant*. He signed on for a two-month tour of duty just a few days before the ship steamed out of the Golden Gate as one of the US Navy's four revenue cutters patrolling the coastline to Seattle and protecting valuable shipments from the Klondike goldfields.

Led by Captain Slamm throughout the summer of 1898, the ship's crew comprised sailors from all over the world. About half hailed from several American states and the rest were from Norway, Denmark, Sweden, Germany, England, Australia, China, and Japan. Working alongside the others in its multicultural crew after the war with Spain ended in mid-August, Jukichi extended his time aboard the *Grant* beyond its wartime naval service. Still on the West Coast when Ken gave birth to their first son, Masa Atsu, in Aichi-ken in January 1899, Jukichi soon left the *Grant* and found another job with the crew of the USS *Pensacola*, a Civil War–era ship stationed at Yerba Buena Island in San Francisco Bay.[8]

In October 1900, Harada and several other Japanese crewmen left the *Pensacola* for work aboard a much larger vessel, the USS *Solace*, recorded as the first navy vessel to fly the Geneva Red Cross flag. Converted for use as a hospital ship during the Spanish American War for transporting sick and wounded servicemen back to the United States from Cuba, *Solace* later sailed east around the world to California. The ship was overhauled at the Mare Island shipyards in 1899. *Solace* returned to sea in July with a new assignment: carrying passengers, provisions, and mail between San Francisco and ports of call as far away as China and Japan. Under the watchful eyes of Commander Hubert Winslow, *Solace* left Yerba Buena Island shortly after Jukichi Harada came aboard as its newest civilian crew member on November 1, one of about twenty-five mess attendants assigned to prepare meals and tend to other tasks in the ship's busy galley.

Filled to the brim with new cargo, provisions, and a crew of 200, *Solace* was soon on its first voyage across the Pacific to what Harada's American shipmates would have called the Far East. They arrived in Honolulu on November 9, and at the end of the month the ship stopped in Guam, continued on to the Philippines, and arrived in Hong Kong on December 27. On New Year's Day 1901, *Solace* docked at the mouth of the Yangtze River north of Shanghai at the port of Wusung, China. Six days later, the ship arrived in Yokohama. Jukichi might have had the chance then to see his wife and meet his two-year-old son, Masa Atsu. If so, the family's time together would have been short. Just two days after coming to Yokohama, the *Solace* left Japan for Manila and points east across the Pacific.

Within a few hours of their departure from the Yokohama docks, crewmen in the *Solace* boiler room discovered two Japanese stowaways who claimed they had fallen asleep in the coalbunker after helping load the ship with the fuel needed to fire its massive boilers. On January 10, a week before arriving in Manila, several members of the crew received punishment for being "under the influence of liquor aboard ship." They were sentenced to five days of solitary confinement in the brig and fed only bread and water. *Solace* reached Hawaii a month later. Readying for the last leg of its journey back to California beneath a morning moon in port at Honolulu in mid-February, crewmen loaded 600 pounds of fresh meat, bread, and vegetables aboard and began coaling at 7:00 a.m. Later in the afternoon Corporal Silas Christenberry, wounded the previous July in the China Relief Expedition during the Boxer Rebellion, died aboard the ship after an unsuccessful surgery. The next morning *Solace* flew flags at half-mast in Christenberry's honor as his earthly remains and personal effects were taken ashore. Observing the solemn procession and the half-mast flags in the Hawaiian sky, some of the lonely crewmen working aboard the vessel might have wondered if they would one day suffer a similar fate far from home and family.

Leaving Honolulu under the direction of Commander Winslow and steaming northeast through light sea breezes and drizzling rain, crewmen locked double irons on the ship's several prisoners seven days later as *Solace* passed the Farallones and reached San Francisco Bay on Sunday, February 24. Steaming through the Golden Gate under partly overcast skies, *Solace* made fast to a buoy floating gently in the harbor near the city of Vallejo off the Mare Island Navy Yard just before noon and let its boiler fires die out. After hoisting a quarantine flag signifying review by a Mare Island health officer, the ship's commander ordered his crewmen to throw 150 pounds of condemned fresh mutton overboard. By the end of the day, with hungry gulls and bottom fish devouring great chunks of the odorous mutton floating nearby, thirteen prisoners with their sea bags and hammocks had been transferred from the *Solace* to new quarters ashore at the US Naval Prison at Mare Island.

Finally back in California after their four-month ocean voyage, tired sailors began making new plans. Some crewmen transferred to new assignments on other vessels already docked at Mare Island, but mess attendant Jukichi Harada and some of his Japanese friends still aboard the vessel faced other concerns. Ashore for a brief visit just after their return, Harada and the others were confronted by another *Solace* crewman who refused to let them back aboard their ship. Jukichi explained the encounter himself: "When I working USS *Solace* in Shipyard outside at shore hate us especially our Steward (colored man) said, 'No use Japs' no more for navy. You better go way. I told him I must take care wife + boy, they coming on voyage to US to meet me. He told 'French Leave' OK."

Harada's oldest daughter said that when her father attempted to return to the ship with his Japanese mates, "the Negro boys refused to let them board, threatened them with knives. It seems there was a strike on board ship." Harada-san's "French Leave," an unofficial departure or desertion from military service in other settings, was recorded in the ship's log along with the unscheduled departure of nine other Japanese crewmen, all of them mess attendants, on March 3, 1901. The knives and threats of the African American crewmen were apparently enough to send Jukichi Harada and his friends elsewhere. Harada was owed $17.04 for his last days of work aboard the *Solace*. He began making plans to return to Japan as soon as he could.[9]

By the end of 1902, a year after Jukichi joined his Japanese friends in abandoning their posts aboard the *Solace*, he had once again made his way across the Pacific to Japan. Apparently satisfied that his dreams of a better life for his family might indeed be possible, Harada rejoined his wife and son in Kariya-shi to complete his plan to move his family to the United States of America. To commemorate what would be their last time together as a family in their homeland of Japan, Jukichi and Ken took son Masa Atsu to the Mikawa Kariya Niwa Nisshindou, a local photography studio in Kariya-shi. Father, mother, and son posed before the camera of a Japanese photographer for their first formal family portrait. Staring straight into the camera, Masa Atsu leaned shyly toward his seated mother as his father, a stalwart man the little boy barely knew, stood ramrod straight and tall behind him. Mother and son were dressed in traditional Japanese clothing. Dressed like a Western man, Jukichi wore a dark suit, stiff white collar, leather shoes, and a jaunty derby hat. Anxious to return to California, Jukichi soon began making arrangements to sail back to the United States. He and Ken may have changed their plans when they learned Ken was expecting another baby the next summer. With another child on the way, Jukichi might have felt it would be best if

2.1. Ken, Masa Atsu, and Jukichi Harada, Aichi-ken, Japan, circa 1903 (*left to right*). (Courtesy of the Harada Family Archival Collection, Riverside Metropolitan Museum, Riverside, California)

he went back to California on his own first to find work and a place for his growing family to live before Ken, Masa Atsu, and the new baby followed.

On the ninth day of the fifth month of the thirty-sixth year of Meiji— May 9, 1903—Harada completed his application to travel once again to the United States. Jukichi would never return to Japan and would never see his parents, brother, and sisters again. Within the month he bade farewell to his expectant wife and four-year-old son. On the first day of June his travel documents were stamped at Yokohama, where he boarded the Occidental and Oriental Steamship Company's steamer SS *Gaelic*, set to sail the following day. Earlier in the year the *Gaelic* had taken the first large group of just over 100 emigrants from Korea for new settlement in Hawaii. Now sailing from Japan and again stopping in Hawaii along the way, the *Gaelic* passed through the Golden Gate seventeen days later. Listed in ship records as a student from Japan traveling back to California, Jukichi presented his travel documents to the United States Immigration Service at the Port of San Francisco, where they were stamped and he was allowed entry.[10]

Back home in Japan, less than two weeks after her husband's arrival in the United States, Ken Harada gave birth to her second child, first daughter Mitsuye. The new baby lived just a little more than two months. Her father was 5,000 miles away. Mitsuye's passing in the early morning hours of September 12 was recorded later that day in the family's koseki records in Aichi prefecture. Possibly because of the complications of the child's birth and untimely death, mother Ken and son Masa Atsu did not leave Japan for another year.

Finally ready to depart Yokohama in early October, just a month after the first anniversary of baby Mitsuye's passing, Ken and Masa Atsu boarded the Pacific Mail Steamship Company's SS *Doric*, scheduled for arrival at Angel Island Immigration Station in San Francisco Bay on October 24, 1904. As soon as she arrived in California, Ken reported to immigration officials in San Francisco that she would join husband Jukichi Harada at the Los Angeles address 112 Rose Street, Sanjuro Mizuno's Victorian-era rooming house at the outskirts of the city's growing Japanese neighborhood. Mizuno had established his little two-story hotel in 1898, known as the first Japanese boardinghouse in Los Angeles. It often served as a first stop for Japanese laborers establishing a new life in the United States. Mizuno had been traveling to California from Aichi prefecture as a passenger on the SS *Gaelic* with his wife, Tsume, the same voyage Jukichi Harada had taken when he returned to the United States in 1903. With personal connections to Aichi-ken and a successful business in California, Mizuno may have helped Harada find work at Tasuku Nakamura's New York Kitchen on Center Street in Redlands. Earning $35 a month as a waiter and cook and putting the skills gained working as a galley rat aboard the *Grant* and *Solace* to good use, Harada had finally landed the steady work he needed to support his family. The new restaurant job in Redlands also provided Harada with room and board. With a regular income and a place to stay, he hoped to have his wife and son join him soon in his small rooms above the New York Kitchen.[11]

As Ken and Masa Atsu gathered their things and prepared to come ashore and meet Jukichi on the wharf in San Francisco, the Haradas' hopes for their long-awaited family reunion were dashed when health inspectors at Angel Island diagnosed Ken Harada and four others on the *Doric* with trachoma and told them they could not leave the ship. The infectious eye disease could be contracted during long sea voyages in close quarters with other passengers. Thus, Ken, two other passengers from Japan, and two from China were detained by Inspector D. J. Griffiths.

Worried that Ken might not be able to remain with him in California, Jukichi consulted a physician, who told him Mrs. Harada's eye condition was not threatening. Despite the second opinion, a formal Board of Inquiry convened in San Francisco and decided that the five aliens diagnosed with trachoma would be deported immediately. The board evaluated evidence and concluded that the "aliens in question are suffering from Trachoma, a dangerous contagious disease, which is due to causes existing prior to landing in the United States." After a brief deliberation, the board "denied the aliens a landing." A deportation notice was served to the *Doric*'s steamship company. Ken Harada was ordered to return to Japan, leaving her six-year-old son behind with his father, a near stranger. Mrs. Harada and the others left San Francisco on the *Doric* ten days later for yet another sea voyage across the Pacific to their ports of origin in Japan and China.[12]

Although he had spent all his time with his mother on the trip aboard the *Doric*, son Masa Atsu showed no signs of an eye infection. Therefore, Jukichi and Ken thought it best for the boy to remain with his father in California until Mrs. Harada could return. As Ken went back to Japan alone, Jukichi and Masa Atsu booked passage aboard a lumber schooner sailing down the coast from San Francisco to Los Angeles, where Jukichi went back to his job at Nakamura's New York Kitchen in Redlands. Because Ken's return to the United States would not take place for another nine months and Jukichi's days were occupied with his work as a waiter and cook for Nakamura-san, son Masa Atsu now often spent his days alone.

The boy's father was working at the New York Kitchen from five in the morning to eight at night with a two-hour break between shifts in the late afternoon. Living in a rented room with his six-year-old son and finding, as he said, "no Japanese woman at all in town that time" or anyone else to help him with child care during the day, Jukichi routinely woke his son before daybreak to get him dressed and ready to spend the day alone. For much of those long days throughout the lonely winter of 1904–1905 the only companionship six-year-old Masa Atsu enjoyed was provided by Tom, an English pointer, left with the little boy for most of the day.

One bright spot father and son might have enjoyed together early in the new year was the chance to steal away from Redlands in January to join friends for a trip to nearby Riverside to commemorate the Japanese victory in the Siege of Port Arthur earlier that month. At home or abroad the Japanese were extremely proud of their brave soldiers and sailors who had defeated the Russians so quickly in several key battles in the Russo-Japanese War. For many across the globe, the Japanese victory at the end of the war in 1905 meant Japan now competed on the international stage with other nations.

Like other young Japanese living in California, Jukichi followed the war closely. He held a lifelong interest in the exploits of its Japanese naval fleet commander, Admiral Heihachiro Togo. The local newspaper reported that the Riverside festivities attracted hundreds of Japanese visitors from throughout the inland region. Some traveled from as far away as Los Angeles to take part in a parade of jubilant celebrants riding in carriages and on bicycles and horses with an elaborate float of a Japanese war vessel pulled by an automobile driving slowly down the center of Main Street. If Jukichi did make the trip to Riverside with son Masa Atsu, he might have also made a few new acquaintances in Riverside's growing Japanese community and might have viewed Riverside as a good place to live.[13]

Seeking advice from acquaintances near Nakamura's restaurant in Redlands and hearing from a Southern Pacific Railroad ticket agent that a more circuitous route might improve Ken's chances of gaining entry to the United States, Jukichi soon made new arrangements for her return to North America by way of Canada. Fearful of kidnapping, a threat for Japanese women traveling alone among single men and other nefarious drifters living in rowdy dockside settlements along the waterfront, Jukichi was concerned his young wife might never make it safely back to California. Apparently sharing her husband's worries or perhaps responding to her own recent experiences at sea, Ken Harada took the matter of her self-defense into her own hands. A hundred years later, their granddaughter recalled an old family story recounting Ken Harada's worrisome travels to North America: "I remember Aunty Sumi telling me that when Grandmother came from Japan, she had a small dagger with her. I believe in the old days, daughters of samurai had a small sword and a small dagger. Aunty Sumi said that when Grandfather found out that Grandmother had brought a dagger with her, he lost his temper and broke the dagger and buried it."[14]

Perhaps reassured by the sharp blade of the samurai dagger tucked secretly in the folds of her kimono and nervously holding her Canadian Pacific Railway Company steamship ticket, Ken Harada was hoping for a permanent family reunion in California. Joining the long line of other passengers, she passed uneventfully through the Imperial Disinfection Station at the port of Yokohama on Friday, July 14, 1905. Never to return to her homeland again, she left Japan the next day aboard the Canadian steamer *Tartar*. After nearly twenty days at sea in transit across the Pacific, Ken finally met her son and husband, this time in Vancouver, British Columbia, where Jukichi and Masa Atsu had arrived after traveling by train from California to board the *Princess Victoria* in Seattle for their own brief sea voyage up the coast.

Finally together again in early August, the reunited Harada family went back to Redlands to begin anew in America. Within days of her arrival in the warm desert air of inland Southern California, Ken knew she and Jukichi had conceived another child. If things went well this time, they would be parents again in the spring.[15]

THREE

HERE TO STAY

Now it is two generations walking down
the street—the Japanese subject and his
offspring. It is face to face with you. It
is as much a part of the community as
the well-tilled fields. No longer is the
brown man content to be a field hand.
He wants his home, his family—his wife
and babies waiting on the doorstep.

C. Charles Hodges, "Honorable Gentlemen's Agreement;
And What the Japanese Ladies Are Doing about It—
The Record of a Decade," *Sunset*, June 1917

Faith in the possibility of upward social mobility rests at the heart of the American immigrant experience. The wish to provide one's family with a new house on a nice street among good neighbors is still a cherished American tradition. Like others who came to live in the United States, immigrants from Japan adapted to their new American home by applying and modifying the cultural traditions and behavioral habits of their native land. Their early dedication to moving up the social and economic ladder also shaped the cultural experiences of their American-born citizen children. The compatibility of key aspects of Japanese cultural tradition and American middle-class values played a significant role in the successful adaptation and acculturation of Japanese immigrants. Modest habits on the part of most Nikkei also supported acceptance by a small number of Americans who came to know individual Japanese people as warm acquaintances and loyal friends. However, in the American West during the first half of the twentieth century, long-established anti-Asian racist ideologies often impeded Japanese participation in American middle-class experiences. Members of the growing Nikkei community encountered, both individually and collectively, serious challenges from an American social and legal system that questioned their very right to be here.[1]

Arriving in the wake of fifty years of anti-Chinese agitation and greeted by a robust heritage of anti-Asian legislation in most western states, the Issei, or first-generation immigrants from Japan, were met with hostility and the belief that people of color did not qualify for equal treatment under US law. As with the Chinese, Japanese immigrants were accepted as cheap sources of labor; however, aspiring to anything much more was a different story. For half a century in California as elsewhere in the West, this sentiment was communicated to the Japanese in subtle and overt emotional assaults and, more significantly, through formal legal actions designed to impede their progress toward participating in any form of the American Dream, the idea that one can aspire to happiness and family improvement symbolized and embodied by owning a home. As many people of color already knew, that piece of the American pie was most often reserved for those with much lighter skin. On the West Coast in the several years before World War I, an organized anti-Japanese movement in California developed from the notion that the Golden State should protect the nation's Anglo-Saxon heritage by exercising strict control over Japanese immigrants.[2]

During the last half of the nineteenth century, far-reaching changes in Meiji Japan produced new evaluations of lifestyle and tradition as the remaining traces of Japan's isolated feudal past gave way to an urbanized, industrial, and militaristic nation connected to the wider world as it had never been before. By the mid-1880s, growing socioeconomic pressures combined with more relaxed Japanese emigration policies and American economic opportunities to increase Japanese immigration to the United States. The decrease in Chinese laborers, resulting from the Chinese Exclusion Act of 1882 and other restrictive measures, had prompted a call for new sources of cheap agricultural labor. Then as now, the American economy needed the hard work of efficient foreign laborers. By 1890 about 2,000 Japanese were living in the United States, and most had already found ready work at low wages. The declining number of Chinese workers was soon replaced by thousands of eager and economically competitive Japanese, many of whom reached the US mainland after working as sugar plantation contract laborers in Hawaii.[3]

For the most part, the newly arrived Japanese, primarily young adult males from several economically strained prefectures in southern Japan, were members of the agricultural class. When their country's attention had turned toward industrialization and modernization, small farmers bore the brunt of change in late nineteenth-century Japan. By tradition, ideas of landownership and use were high in the minds of most Japanese immigrants who came to the United States. For the newest arrivals, employment patterns were often established by the few Issei who had immigrated in earlier years. Nikkei labor contractors and proprietors of small businesses developed some of the first job opportunities for Japanese immigrants. Many Issei initially saw American employment as only a stepping-stone to economic security back in Japan, but most soon discovered that their low status in American society did not allow for swift economic progress. Those who accepted reduced expectations, patience, and hard work as keys to advancement gradually became interested in establishing families and residing permanently in the United States. They were here to stay.[4]

At the time of their arrival most Issei men were under thirty years of age, and in 1908 it was recorded that only about one-fourth of them were married. Through the immigration restrictions imposed by the Gentlemen's Agreement, an arrangement of mutual consent negotiated by the governments of Japan and the United States, the influx of Japanese laborers to the states was virtually stopped. In the eight years since the turn of the century, more than 40,000 Japanese had come to the United States. The year before the new agreement went into effect, more than 12,000 Issei arrived. In 1908 the number of Japanese immigrants dropped to 8,340 and in 1909, to only 1,596. Under the terms of the Gentlemen's Agreement, parents, spouses, and children of the Japanese already living in the United States at the time of the agreement could still emigrate from Japan. However, marriages arranged by family members or village associates, a common practice in Japanese culture at the time, soon complicated the intentions of this new immigration policy. An influx of women married by proxy in Japan to Japanese men already living in the United States—called "picture brides" because the only introduction each had to the man she would marry was a photograph sent through the mail—reversed the decline by 1913. This reversal signaled the establishment of new Japanese American families.[5]

Until they could afford a home of their own, many Issei lived with their compatriots in small labor camps or rooming houses operated by other Japanese. This close contact and continued interaction with others from Japan meant that some aspects of the new arrivals' lifestyle mirrored Japanese cultural tradition. Resting on a foundation of principles stressing the family as the essential unit of community development and strength, the new American households were characterized by "strong solidarity, mutual helpfulness, and a patriarchal structure." Because Japanese women arrived later, many Nisei, or second-generation, children were born between 1918 and 1922. Unlike white immigrants from Europe, their first-generation—Issei—parents were ineligible by law to become naturalized citizens of the United States. Through their own hard work and the progress of their American-born children, US citizens by virtue of their birth on American soil, non-citizen Issei fathers and mothers hoped to advance the social and economic position of their families in America.[6]

Japanese immigrants' emphasis on upward mobility and family solidarity had, it seemed, found a sturdy foundation in the American ideals of equality for its citizens. However, the country's new Japanese residents soon learned that influential segments of California's non-Japanese citizenry objected vehemently to their participation in the American Dream. In 1907 former San Francisco mayor and future US senator from California James Duval Phelan explained to *Boston Sunday Herald* readers his reasons for stopping Japanese immigration to California:

> As soon as Japanese coolies are kept out of the country, there will be no danger of irritating these sensitive and aggressive people. They must be excluded because they are non-assimilable [*sic*]; they are a permanently foreign element; they do not bring up families; they do not support churches, schools, nor theatres; in time of trial they will not fight for Uncle Sam, but betray him to the enemy . . . California is white man's country, and the two races cannot live side by side in peace, and inasmuch as we discovered the country first and occupied it, we propose to hold it against either a peaceful or a warlike invasion.[7]

Just three years later, in 1910, an editorial in the *San Francisco Chronicle* expressed the feelings of a steadily growing number of Californians: "Had the Japanese laborer throttled his ambition to progress along the lines of American citizenship and industrial development, he probably would have attracted small attention in the public mind. Japanese ambition is to progress beyond mere servility to the plane of the better class of American workman and to own a home with him. The moment that this position is exercised, the Japanese ceases to be an ideal laborer."[8]

California's anti-Japanese views rested on a well-established heritage of anti-Chinese hostility and racism. Immigration from the Far East was an early topic of conversation during the California Gold Rush and the new American state's earliest decade. During the 1850s the California frontier boomed. Ragtag and often lawless communities composed of men and women with independent minds and sometimes questionable backgrounds sprouted nearly overnight. These communities boasted a strike-it-rich mentality, small businesses outfitting the frantic search for gold, and an extremely diverse mixture of humanity. In 1852 more than 13,000 Chinese entered the United States, prompted in large measure by the unprecedented opportunities, risks, and dreams of the California Gold Rush. Ostensibly to maintain some semblance of community order, although more likely to simply discourage unmarried Chinese men from putting down roots, California officials attempted unsuccessfully to control and tax immigrants from China, acting in direct conflict with the US Supreme Court decision in the Passenger Cases of 1849, which stated that only Congress could regulate immigration.[9]

After the Civil War, times of economic depression fostered more organized anti-Chinese sentiments within San Francisco's labor movement. By the 1870s, California's political campaigns were tied to the issues surrounding Asian immigration. The anti-Chinese precepts of the Workingmen's Party, organized by Irish immigrant and San Francisco drayman Dennis Kearney, set the tone for more strident anti-Asian political activity. Kearney's call to arms was "The Chinese Must Go!" Touring California to promote his cause in 1879, Kearney gave speeches in places like Riverside and San Bernardino, where he was greeted by a torchlight parade and large crowds. Unmoved by Kearney's anti-Chinese crusade, local newspaper editor James H. Roe, founder of the *Riverside Press* and a local druggist and schoolteacher sympathetic to his community's pioneer Latinos, believed Kearney to be little more than a mouthpiece for an angry statewide labor movement.[10]

Through the party's control of California's constitutional convention of 1879, anti-Chinese provisions were soon added to the state's new constitution, declaring that voting privileges would henceforth be denied to "natives of China, idiots, and insane persons." The federal government had enacted its first statute regulating immigration in 1875. Most considered it sensible because it contained provisions aimed at excluding prostitutes and convicts of any nationality. Further action in 1882 prevented the entry of individuals of questionable mental capacities and those who were likely to become public wards. At the same time, with Californians acting as "the most influential instigators," Congress passed the earliest of several exclusionary measures, the Chinese Exclusion Act of 1882. A congressional coalition from the West Coast and the Deep South supported passage of the anti-Chinese legislation, and many believed the new exclusion act would finally settle the question of what to do about Chinese immigration.[11]

Questions concerning the fine points of American citizenship were not determined until after the Civil War. The Civil Rights Act of 1866 declared all persons born in the United States who were not subjects of foreign powers, excluding nontaxed Native American Indians, were, at birth, citizens of the United States. Two years later the new Fourteenth Amendment declared, "[A]ll persons born or naturalized in the United States, and subject to the jurisdiction thereof, are citizens of the United States and the State wherein they reside." It would be thirty more years before issues involving the citizenship of children born to Chinese immigrant parents living in the United States were settled by a Supreme Court ruling, in *United States v. Wong Kim Ark.* Judgment in the 1898 case was rendered under Article I of the Fourteenth Amendment, stating American-born children of Chinese parents were citizens of the United States because of their birth on American soil. However, the constitutional basis for a favorable judgment in the *Wong Kim Ark* case was complicated by an issue not yet addressed by the Supreme Court. In 1790 a naturalization act passed by Congress provided for the American naturalization of "any alien, being a free white person who shall have resided within the limits and under the jurisdiction of the United States for a term of two years." Constitutional amendments of the Civil War era adjusted naturalization privileges to cover not only "free white persons" but also "persons of African nativity or descent." All other non-white, non-African aliens were ineligible to become American citizens until special legislation provided for naturalization. Chinese immigrants would not be granted naturalization privileges until 1943, and the Japanese not until 1952.[12]

Legal foundations for the settlement of landownership issues as they related to the rights of non-white, non-African immigrants and their American-born children were established long before large numbers of Japanese came to the United States, and were based on the early English feudal system. English common law, defining the relationship between landowners and members of the larger community, "left little if any room for the alien; for the alien did not go with the land; he was only a stranger or sojourner, who owed no fealty, no obligation, to any local landowner." In 1850 the Supreme Court linked issues of alien landownership to the states in the case of *Meager v. Grimm*. In 1879, in *Hauenstein v. Lynam*, the justices further addressed states' rights and the regulation of real estate ownership by aliens. The court determined that the treaty-making powers of the federal government allowed an opportunity to establish alien rights, but if a federal treaty governing specific groups of aliens did not exist, state law would serve as the final authority.[13]

After the Civil War, changes in popular opinion reflected a growing national support for racist southern attitudes about African Americans. In the 1880s, additional concern over new tides of immigrants from southern and eastern Europe also fueled growing racial intolerance. Many white Americans feared the new immigrants would destroy the nation's Anglo-Saxon heritage. In 1896 the "separate but equal" pronouncements of the Supreme Court in *Plessy v. Ferguson* reinforced changing popular attitudes. Public concern over the role of non-whites in the future of the United States was raised once more after the Spanish American War, when Hawaii, the Philippines, and Puerto Rico became US territorial possessions. A subsequent judgment by the Supreme Court in the Insular Cases established that "the constitution did not follow the flag," implying to some "that democratic institutions had inherent ethnic limitations."[14]

By the turn of the twentieth century, California's anti-Japanese movement was supported by the legal precepts established in a changing American social climate. Planted in the fertile soil of the Pacific coast's anti-Chinese past, it grew quickly, spreading from Northern California to become a statewide cause touted by far-flung segments of California's populace. Historian Roger Daniels, in *The Politics of Prejudice*, details the evolution of the Golden State's anti-Japanese movement, linking its development to the distinctiveness of the Japanese as an identifiable group, the confrontational nature of early Japanese emphasis on upward mobility, the growing unease over the emergence of Japan as an international power, and, perhaps most significantly, the long-established sensitivity in California to Asian immigration. Although opposing political and social factions in California generally agreed that certain elements of the anti-Japanese movement were steps in the right direction, Daniels explains its primary support came from groups tending, on the whole, to espouse democratic ideals, most notably labor unions and progressives. California's newspapers also played a pivotal role in keeping what soon became known as the "Japanese Question" at the forefront of public consciousness.[15]

The anti-Japanese movement gained steam early in 1905 with a series of articles published in the *San Francisco Chronicle* criticizing the Japanese and prompting the unanimous passage of an anti-Japanese resolution in the California legislature. By mid-year, leaders of the new Asiatic Exclusion League, established in San Francisco as an arm of the city's labor movement, dedicated its membership to the exclusion of Japanese immigrants. A few months later, in 1906, when a new building was under construction at the site of the old Chinese School after April's great earthquake, the Asiatic Exclusion League tried to force the segregation of all Asian schoolchildren. Its members pressured the San Francisco Board of Education to pass a resolution declaring that Japanese and Korean children would henceforth attend school with the Chinese at the reconstructed Oriental Public School.[16]

Protests over the California segregation order arose in Japan, and the Japanese government became increasingly sensitive to anti-Japanese agitation in the United States. Respect for Japan as an emerging international power had grown because of the impressive Japanese victory in the Russo-Japanese War of 1904–1905. Soon after the San Francisco segregation order, President Theodore Roosevelt, mediator in the settlement of the war between the Russians and the Japanese, called San Francisco school board members and other city officials to Washington to discuss compromises that might placate the Japanese government. As soon as the San Franciscans agreed to lessen the school board's original restrictions, Roosevelt and his secretary of state, Elihu Root, resumed their plans for negotiations, producing the Japanese immigration restrictions of the Gentlemen's Agreement in 1908.[17]

In their lawmaking session the following year, however, California's legislators answered the intricate diplomatic arrangements of Roosevelt's Gentlemen's Agreement with a host of discriminatory legislative proposals. From this time forward, according to Daniels, the moving force behind the anti-Japanese movement "became the successive attempts to check the acquisition of agricultural lands by the Issei." The battle over Fresno assemblyman A. M. Drew's Alien Land Bill of 1909 was symptomatic of the growing concern over Japanese landownership in California. California's governor, Republican James N. Gillett, was sympathetic to Roosevelt's desire to limit anti-Japanese legislation. Roosevelt wrote to Assemblyman Drew and telegraphed Governor Gillett to express opposition to the several bills pending in California. Heated public comments from legislators, represented by the remarks of Sacramento Republican assemblyman Grove L. Johnson, former member of the US House of Representatives and father of California's next governor, Hiram Johnson, revealed the substance of the emotional underpinnings of the effort to limit land acquisition by the Japanese immigrants in California. Resentful of Roosevelt's interference, Assemblyman Johnson was fretting over what he saw as an overriding threat to the future stability, health, and security of the Golden State:

> I know more about the Japanese than Governor Gillett and President Roosevelt put together. I am not responsible to either of them . . . I am responsible to the mothers and fathers of Sacramento County who have their little daughters sitting side by side in the school rooms with matured Japs, with their base minds, their lascivious thoughts, multiplied by their race and strengthened by their mode of life.
>
> . . . I am here to protect the children of these parents. To do all that I can to keep any Asiatic man from mingling in the same school with the daughters of our people. You know the results of such a condition; you know how far it will go, and I have seen Japanese 25 years old sitting in the seats next to the pure maids of California. I shuddered then and I shudder now, the same as any other parent will shudder to think of such a condition.[18]

Drew's proposed Assembly Bill 78 required non-citizen property owners in California to become citizens within five years or relinquish the right to own land. Although the Japanese were not specifically mentioned in the bill, their ineligibility for citizenship implied Assemblyman Drew and his supporters had had them in mind when he drafted the measure. After several days of hot debate in Sacramento, Drew's controversial bill was rejected by a vote of 48 to 28. The spreading ideological strength of anti-Japanese sentiment was further revealed, however, in the next statewide election, in which California's three major political parties—Democratic, Republican, and Socialist—all added exclusion planks to their platforms. California's Republicans adopted their platform at the state convention in San Francisco on September 6, 1910, and asserted their position on Asian immigration: "We declare our faith in the unswerving opposition of the people of California to the further admission of Oriental laborers, and we urge on Congress and the President the adoption of all necessary measures to guard against this evil."[19]

With progressive Republican Hiram Johnson's successful gubernatorial bid in 1910, California entered an era of middle-class progressive politics, ending years of legislative dominance by conservative Republicans and the Southern Pacific Railroad. Despite their own campaign statements, and likely to the dismay of Johnson's own father, candidate Johnson and the Republicans paid little attention to the more strident anti-Japanese declarations of the Democrats during the 1910 campaign. However, soon after the election, it would be Johnson's administration that ushered in California's Alien Land Law of 1913, described many years later in a ruling of the US Supreme Court as "the first official act of discrimination aimed at the Japanese."[20]

Based on the earlier judgments of the Supreme Court allowing states the right to regulate alien landownership in the absence of such agreements in federal treaties, numerous states had already enacted statutes governing the ownership of land by non-citizens. Few, if any, however, had been aimed so directly at immigrants from Japan. In 1913, as in preceding years, California legislators introduced a raft of anti-Japanese bills, most proposing regulations for the lease and ownership of agricultural lands. Others went so far as to suggest that aliens ineligible for citizenship should also be prevented from leasing town or city lots for more than five years. It soon became obvious that the legislature intended to stop the spread of Japanese immigrant agriculture in California and perhaps even force the Japanese to leave the state forever.[21]

As the legislators moved to limit landownership rights of "ineligible aliens," the Japanese government, through Japan's ambassador to the United States, Count Chinda Sutemi, expressed concern over the situation in California to the new American president, Woodrow Wilson. Japanese ineligibility for American citizenship meant the government of Japan was still officially responsible for Japanese citizens living in the United States. As a result, authorities of the Japanese government paid close attention to the events affecting its citizens in California. Like Roosevelt, President Wilson was aware of Japanese sensitivities and hoped for moderation to pacify the Japanese government. Of little help to their humble compatriots trying to improve their lives as laborers in faraway California, some factions in Japan protested the pending American legislation as an insulting transgression against Japanese subjects and called for a military invasion of California.[22]

Support in the Golden State for the passage of some sort of alien land bill was on the rise, but it was not universal. Prominent sectors of the state's business community opposed the action. The San Francisco Chamber of Commerce, receiving communications from Japanese acting consul Ujiro Oyama, voted with local business clubs to protest the proposed legislation. The San Franciscans feared that passage of an anti-Japanese bill would negatively affect ongoing negotiations with Japan over the coming Panama-Pacific Exposition. In Southern California, the *Los Angeles Times*, voice of the city's business community and no friend of progressive Republican Hiram Johnson, also opposed the measure. Although the progressives were generally reluctant to support the passage of any anti-Japanese bill, they were apparently unwilling to be held accountable for its failure. Unease in Washington played a part in prompting Governor Johnson to enlist the aid of California attorney general Ulysses S. Webb and progressive Republican state senator Francis J. Heney—who would run unsuccessfully for the US Senate the following year against Democrat James D. Phelan—to draft an alien land bill that might bring some semblance of order to the anti-Japanese legislative chaos.[23]

At the same time, President Wilson arranged for his new secretary of state, famed national orator and former presidential candidate William Jennings Bryan, to travel to California to address the legislature and express the administration's desire to postpone passage of the Heney-Webb Bill. With an eye on the growing discomfort of the Japanese government and some hope his public display might guarantee a positive outcome, Bryan proposed a compromise regarding the bill's restrictions of citizenship requirements for landownership. Undeterred by this pressure from Washington, regarded by some as a hollow gesture intended only to calm officials in Japan, the unruly Sacramento legislators ignored Bryan's call for postponement, passed the bill, and on May 19, 1913, Governor Johnson signed it into law. Aliens "eligible to citizenship" were granted the same property rights as American citizens. All other aliens, most notably the Chinese and Japanese, who by law still could not become naturalized American citizens, were divested of the right to purchase real estate in California unless federal treaties provided otherwise. Individual and corporate leases could be granted for a term of up to three years. Violations of the law would result in escheat or forfeiture to the state of any such property in question.[24]

After the 1913 law went into effect and before the passage of a more stringent law by popular vote in 1920, the Japanese in California were confronted with the choice of accepting the new restrictions or attempting to evade them. Raymond Buell's early analysis of the Japanese response to the California Alien Land Law of 1913 determined that those who decided to buy land in California between 1913 and 1920 used three methods to evade the new law. One way was to establish dummy corporations with American citizens, sometimes infant Nisei children, as majority stockholders. Another way to circumvent this law was to create trusteeships through which Americans purchased property with Japanese funds. And, finally, Japanese parents, acting as guardians, bought land and recorded it in the names of their American-born citizen children. Roger Daniels notes that the last method was used very successfully by the Japanese. He also observes that, despite the new Alien Land Law, Japanese-owned acreage in California increased "more than fourfold" from 1913 to 1919. Buell discovered that during roughly the same period forty-seven city lots in nine Southern California counties were recorded in the names of second-generation Japanese American citizen children.[25]

Although some Issei had obtained small tracts of agricultural land in California prior to 1913, most had not developed their real estate holdings to any extent. It was also extremely difficult for them to purchase residential property in areas matching their dreams for upward mobility and an improved life for their families. Even if Japanese families had the funds to buy a house in a better neighborhood, community objections inspired by racial prejudice often shaped Japanese housing patterns in many communities throughout the West. In California, for example, Kinji Ushijima's story of his pre–Alien Land Law purchase of a Berkeley house reveals the turmoil caused by Issei dreams for rapid social advancement.

Even as Assemblyman Grove Johnson railed in the legislature against mature Japanese aliens sitting in school with the "pure maids of California," Japanese

3.1. California governor Hiram Johnson, circa 1915. (Courtesy of the California State Archives)

native Ushijima already had enough money to buy a new home in one of Berkeley's better residential neighborhoods. Known across the state as "George Shima, the Potato King," he had come in 1889 to California, where he worked to reclaim extensive agricultural acreage originally developed by Chinese laborers in the San Joaquin Delta. By 1909, the *Los Angeles Times* reported that Shima had cornered the California potato market. With thousands of acres under cultivation, he was labeled the "Brown Yankee Potato Boss" by the *Times*, which observed: "All of his money is invested in this State, since he intends that it should always remain his home. As an example of what the Jap can really accomplish, he stands out more than any other in California."[26]

Even though George Shima's hard work and successful agricultural enterprises had made him a millionaire with work habits to match, Roger Daniels explains that when the Potato King bought his big two-story house on College Avenue in Berkeley in 1909, "a cry of protest went up from the citizens of that quiet University town." Shima, who was "obviously embarrassed" by the neighborhood uproar he caused in Berkeley, refused to leave his new home. Living in the stylish residential district just a five-block walk from the state university, George Shima's Caucasian neighbors objected to the presence of a Japanese, millionaire or not,

3.2. California attorney general Ulysses S. Webb, circa 1910. (Courtesy of the California History Room, California State Library, Sacramento, California)

and some of them no doubt made life uncomfortable for him. In 1909, however, they could not legally challenge his purchase of a new house anywhere in the Golden State. But a few years later, with the new California Alien Land Law in effect, Jukichi and Ken Harada's neighbors could invoke the law's restrictions to prevent the less affluent but no less respectable Haradas from moving with their children into a modest home in one of Riverside's better neighborhoods.[27]

Many Californians rationalized the passage of the Alien Land Law of 1913 by pointing to competition for agricultural land. Governor Hiram Johnson epitomized their arguments when he remarked: "The endeavor was made with the alien land law to protect our agricultural lands. We cannot compete in certain occupations with the Japanese, and this we readily concede. The lands devoted to these occupations were readily being acquired by the Japanese."[28]

Like Governor Johnson, other moderate government officials were busily asserting that concern over the stability of their state's agricultural economy was the sole basis for the prohibition of Japanese landownership in California. However, additional comments by Attorney General Webb, proclaimed in an address to the Commonwealth Club of San Francisco, spoke more directly to the rights of the increasing numbers of second-generation Nisei children born in the United States—American citizens of Japanese ancestry—and to the underlying theme of the anti-Japanese movement: "It is unimportant and foreign to the question, whether a particular race is inferior. The simple and single question is, is the race desirable . . . ? [The Alien Land Law] seeks to limit their presence by curtailing their privileges which they enjoy here; for they will not come in large numbers and long abide with us if they may not acquire land."[29]

In light of the subsequent history of Japanese Americans, it is significant and revealing that California's first Japanese court test of the Alien Land Law of 1913 did not result from the purported concern over the future of agricultural lands. The first test came, rather, from the worry and agitation over the purchase of residential property by a Japanese American family trying to live among white neighbors in a place some insisted had been and should always be, as Senator Phelan had said, "White Man's Country."

In Riverside, as in Berkeley to the north, a concern over the expansion of Japanese agricultural activity had little or nothing to do with the neighborhood protests raised over the purchase of California real estate. If the Haradas had not been Japanese, few would have noticed this purchase or questioned their right to own a home in a more fashionable and mostly white neighborhood. This early attempt by disgruntled citizens to use the law to deny the purchase of a six-room cottage by a Japanese family revealed the prejudice and racial intolerance that was to characterize subsequent legal action directed against Japanese immigrants and their American citizen children over the next quarter century.

By the time defendant Jukichi Harada, representatives of the California attorney general's office, and a number of curious townsfolk assembled quietly in Superior Court judge Hugh Craig's courtroom at the Riverside County Courthouse for the trial of *The People of California v. Jukichi Harada*, newspapers up and down the West Coast and even elsewhere in the country had carried the disturbing news of the Harada family's move to a little house on Riverside's Lemon Street. The papers told of the State of California's plans to have them evicted as soon as possible by invoking its Alien Land Law. Folks had also read that the Japanese government and officials in Washington were watching the case closely. Others had heard rumors that the Riverside affair might somehow lead to a war with Japan. After two years' delay by California attorney general Webb and steady pressure from the Haradas' neighbors in Riverside, many believed that the long-awaited trial of this upstart Japanese immigrant would, at last, force him and his family to move out of this nice neighborhood to a place they believed more appropriate for an Issei family.

Settling herself a bit uncomfortably in the sturdy wooden witness chair before Judge Craig, Cora Fletcher, the Haradas' neighbor from the little house across the street at the corner of Lemon and Fourth, was worried about the future of her neighborhood. Like others testifying in the trial that spring, Cora had no misgivings about expressing the feelings shared by many white people living in the United States of America. In her response to a simple question from Jukichi

Harada's attorney, Cora indicated that it might take much more than a single court verdict to change her mind about how to accept, understand, and get along with her new Japanese American neighbors. Attorney Adair asked, "And the tenor of your observation to Mr. Harada was that you did not want a Japanese coming to live in your neighborhood?" Cora Fletcher responded, "Naturally." For Jukichi, Ken, and their children, the attitudes expressed by Cora Fletcher and their other neighbors on Lemon Street were only another obstacle in their long struggle to realize the American Dream.[30]

FOUR

IN THE SHADOW OF
THE MISSION INN

We wish to form a colony of intelligent,
industrious and enterprising people, so that
each one's industry will help to promote
his neighbor's interest as well as his own.

John Wesley North, "A Colony for California,"
March 17, 1870

California has always been a land of possibilities. Its borders have never prevented
dreamers from crossing, challenging, and forever changing the way of life here,
and many a dream has been realized, or at least imagined, in this free land of the
sunset at the edge of the Pacific. The origins of Riverside were no exception. In the
spring of 1870, entrepreneur John Wesley North, an abolitionist who had already
developed new communities in the Minnesota and Nevada territories, proclaimed
from Knoxville, Tennessee, new plans for "A Colony for California." With his
friend Dr. James P. Greves, another anti-slavery advocate, North was promoting
the settlement of a community in Southern California near the lines of the newly
constructed Southern Pacific Railroad. After considering a variety of potential
new townsites scattered throughout the state, North and his colonists finally settled in the south, just across the Rio Santa Ana from the crumbling adobes of the
old Louis Robidoux Ranch. They founded their new community on nearly vacant
livestock grazing lands in what was then San Bernardino County, not far from
San Salvador, the earlier frontier river-bottom settlements of La Placita and Agua
Mansa. San Salvador occupied part of the old Jurupa Rancho at the northwestern
boundary of an arid region inhabited for many generations by the small family
lineages and clans of the First People later called the Cahuilla Indians.[1]

North's small California colony at the river's edge grew with the arrival of additional immigrant settlers, several from Belle Plaine, Iowa. Toward the end of 1870, members of the new Southern California Colony Association agreed to name their square-mile townsite "Riverside." Life in the growing community centered on the development of land surveys, the building of housing, and the construction of irrigation canals supporting agriculture. In the mid-1870s, Samuel Cary Evans Sr., a banker and land developer from Indiana, formed the new Riverside Land and Irrigating Company, buying the land and water rights from John North's troubled Southern California Colony Association. Along with Evans, who was "the town's most powerful individual" until his death at the turn of the century, ambitious young immigrants soon overshadowed the influence of Riverside's earliest pioneer settlers. Other transplants from America's heartland also soon found their way to Riverside, seeking sunshine, a dry climate, and relief from cold winters and wearisome respiratory ailments. Migrants from Canada and England came a little later and established themselves as prominent Riverside investors and landowners in the fresh California air at the edge of the Mojave Desert, adding a modicum of cultural refinement to the city's evolving character.[2]

The town's celebrated first two navel orange trees arrived from Brazil in the early 1870s and were planted in gardens adjacent to the house of eccentric spiritualist medium Eliza Tibbets and her husband, Luther. Flourishing in the California sunshine, the two unusual fruit trees with shiny, dark green leaves and orange fruit were likely tended at times by the couple's attentive Chinese house servant, Lau Ah. Early experiments with irrigation technology, raisin grapes, and more citrus tree plantings established a foundation for Riverside's expanding economic base. In another decade, railroad connections would increase the town's potential as a regional center for agricultural production, processing, and marketing. In the mid-1880s, the newly incorporated city was enjoying steady expansion based on the success of its thriving navel orange industry. As the new town grew, gaining new arrivals nearly every day, acres and acres of neat rows of citrus groves were planted on nearby lands irrigated by ingeniously engineered, creatively financed, and outlandishly expensive water delivery systems.[3]

As the precious water slowly made its way through little hand-dug ditches and to the roots of infant citrus trees, the city grew. Downtown residential streets were surveyed, scraped from the dirt, and named for the abundant fruit now growing so successfully in the dry desert air in small groves within the city limits and in larger tracts of farmland at the outskirts of town. Hundreds of board feet of fragrant new lumber were delivered by horse-drawn wagons to supply busy carpenters as the sounds of young men working with handsaws and hammers measured time each day. Scattered rows of small wooden cottages and a few larger homes, some made of adobe bricks and decorated with Victorian gingerbread trim, went up among the town's citrus groves and along new streets appropriately called Orange, Lemon, and Lime. Paralleling Main Street and crossing the wider numbered thoroughfares, these narrow residential streets became preferred neighborhoods for recent California arrivals in what town founders called the Mile Square, a boundary of pioneer spirit and steadily growing community respectability within which a few brown-skinned people worked but did not live with any great affluence, ease, or comfort.

In Riverside's first years, a few early Chinese pioneers established themselves as downtown laundrymen, cooks, servants, and field hands, dreaming they might make enough money in California—which they called Gumshan, "Gold Mountain"—to send some home to relatives or perhaps even return to China as wealthy men. The first Chinese business downtown, the Hang Wo Laundry, was opened in 1878 along Seventh Street between Main and Market. The town's newest laundry formed the nucleus of what some early settlers would later remember as Old Chinatown. A year later, a much larger concentration of Chinese settlement consisting of a few small businesses, a boardinghouse, and a place for tents housing seasonal Chinese citrus workers in an area soon to be known as the Chinese Quarter took root and began to flourish in the southeast section of the block bounded by Main and Orange Streets between Eighth and Ninth, around the corner from the town's most prominent intersection. Indeed, industrious Chinese laundrymen alarmed some in town when they began washing clothes in an "open ditch along Ninth Street."[4]

In the early 1880s, the number of Chinese truck farmers, some leasing farmlands on the old Louis Robidoux Ranch from landowners along the Santa Ana River, began to exceed the number of the town's Chinese laundrymen. Reliable Chinese peddlers selling fresh vegetables door to door from the back of horse-drawn wagons soon became an essential fixture of the steadily growing community. In October 1882 the Riverside Cannery Company made what seemed at the time a smart business decision, ordering the employment of some 150 Chinese cannery workers "because only a limited number of whites showed up." Two years later, one of the town's first Chinese businessmen, Charles Wong, former proprietor of a San Francisco washhouse who had just come to town as the new manager of the Hang Wo Laundry, purchased what may be the earliest paid advertisement placed by a Chinese merchant in the local newspaper, Luther M. Holt's *Riverside Press and Horticulturist*. To curry favor from the many churchgoers among his new town's non-Chinese population, Mr. Wong mentioned smartly in his August newspaper listing that he had already converted to Christianity, listing as a reference his San Francisco pastor.[5]

Ever since Congress passed the Chinese Exclusion Act of 1882 suspending Chinese immigration, Luther Holt, the new crusading editor of the *Press and Horticulturist* and an active Southern California real estate promoter, had become Riverside's most strident public voice against the Chinese remaining downtown.

A former journeyman printer and schoolteacher from Michigan and Iowa who walked with a bit of a limp, Holt had come to Riverside from Los Angeles in 1880 as a man of forty to take over the town's struggling newspaper. Holt soon changed the paper's name, expanded operations, and moved to new headquarters on the corner of Orange and Eighth Streets, just steps away from the strange sights, smells, and sounds of the town's new Chinese Quarter. In summer 1885, six months after the Quong Mow Lung Company's general store around the corner on Ninth Street earnestly promoted itself in his newspaper as a source for "Chinese and Japanese Nick Nacks for the Holidays," Holt urged his fellow townsfolk to "drive the Chinamen out and tear down their filthy quarters."[6]

One month later, the town board of trustees enacted a series of restrictive city health ordinances. Chinese merchants were arrested by the city marshal, who charged them with a variety of minor public nuisance violations. As in other communities pressuring Chinese settlers throughout the West in the 1880s, the local police soon evicted the Chinese, mostly single men originally from Guandong Province, "out of crowded shacks and tents they had been occupying in the downtown block." Two dozen commercial laundries and ironing shops, small businesses operated primarily by the Chinese, were eliminated swiftly from the Mile Square. In early 1886, Luther Holt's newspaper reported the demolition of Sam Gee's laundry, directly across the street from Hayt's Livery Stable on Main Street. Gee's laundry was among the last Chinese business establishments downtown. It was removed just in time for the construction of the Castleman Building, the new home of the First National Bank. The majestic three-story bank building was built in the same square block and adjacent to the now mostly vacant Chinese Quarter. With the four round faces of its great clock tower, each nearly as big around as a man was tall, the First National Bank would soon become "the biggest and most impressive financial institution in town, both in quarters and in assets."[7]

After the Chinese residents were evicted from the downtown commercial district, some people hoped they might leave town forever and be replaced by "more tolerable" white workers from the East. Newspaper editor Holt was much more pragmatic. "The Chinese are bad enough," he asserted, "but what would become of the raisin crop and the coming orange crop were it not for the Chinese to save it?" Holt did not want the Chinese to leave the community permanently. He and other prominent businesspersons just wanted them out of the way of growth in the center of town. In one of his sermons earlier in the year, the Reverend George H. Deere, founding minister of the All Souls Universalist Church, made the same observation, saying if the expulsion of "John Chinaman" came to pass, "we shall be sure to miss his ready service when he is gone, and find ourselves surely pressed by want of it."[8]

At the end of the decade, Riverside's Chinese, still valuable to many locally as merchants, labor contractors, produce vendors, house servants for the wealthy, and agricultural workers known for their reliability and willingness to work hard in the citrus groves and packing sheds at low wages, moved to a separate site outside the Mile Square. At the city's edge in the dusty arroyo just below Tequesquite Avenue, finally removed from what was considered the more respectable center of town, they soon built their own small but prosperous Chinatown. Its new main street was lined on each side with two fine red-brick buildings, wooden plank sidewalks, a house of worship, a village shrine, and a string of less permanent Western-style false-front structures where the noise of holiday firecrackers and smell of sandalwood incense could fill the air without disturbing the peace downtown.[9]

In just thirty years, advancing from primitive sketches of early life in the new pioneer town above the Santa Ana, Riverside had steadily painted its own verdant landscape of a prosperous California community. Mirroring the rich and colorful views of orange and palm trees framed by distant snow-capped mountains on penny postcards fanning out across the nation from the small post offices of Southern California to those less fortunate souls living in colder climates in the Midwest and along the East Coast, Riverside was well on its way to a new and visionary century of progress. The city's growing economy, infrastructure, population, and political influence had already resulted in its selection as the seat of government for California's new Riverside County, carved from portions of the adjacent counties of San Bernardino and San Diego in 1893. Some of its earliest wooden and brick pioneer buildings had been torn down and replaced by much larger and more impressive structures, like the Castleman Building.[10]

The move to separate from the influence of the older rough-and-tumble county seat of San Bernardino was, in part, founded on the desire of Riverside's citizens to distinguish themselves from the frontiersmen and prostitutes of their somewhat less civilized community neighbor. Longtime Riverside newspaperman and historian Thomas W. Patterson suggested that the new county's founding fathers and mothers had a strong interest in having their infant community stand apart from the earlier and, to some, much more colorful frontier traditions of their nearest political rival. "Riverside kept its moral corset more tightly laced than San Bernardino, and its more righteous citizens often complained of the celebrated D Street redlight district and of the greater prevalence of saloons in San Bernardino," Patterson observed.

In an effort to assert some control over how life would be lived at home and to ensure an abundance of Christian fellowship on Riverside's sunny streets, town fathers generously offered churches city land at no charge. Many of Riverside's earnest pioneers worked diligently to be sure that, in marked contrast to San Bernardino, the religious institutions in their new town just might, God willing, outnumber its saloons. One child of the 1880s, Jean Aldrich, whose rather prim Victorian family had arrived in town in 1883 to become local citrus growers, remembered that "Sunday School class parties, ice cream socials in summer,

4.1. Intersection of Eighth and Main Streets showing the Evans Building (*left*) and Castleman Building (*right*), Riverside, California, circa 1900. (Courtesy of the Riverside Metropolitan Museum, Riverside, California)

oyster suppers in winter, a picnic now and then, and sometimes a play at the Loring Theater were about the extent of our amusements." "Many young people danced," Aldrich added, "but church people were pretty strict and we were never allowed that amusement."

The town's earliest Chinese migrant workers found work in the raisin packing sheds. It is perhaps because of the presence of so many churches compared to other communities that some dubbed their new town Yea So Fow, "Jesus City." One early county historian, Luther Ingersoll, observed other distinguishing qualities shaping the developing character of the new Riverside community: "Riverside grew more rapidly than San Bernardino. Her citizens were largely young men from the East, whose ideas and methods were different from the conservative movements of San Bernardino's solid citizens who had been trained in the school of circumstances rather than in the colleges and the rushing business life of eastern cities."[11]

One of the members of the Riverside lobby supporting the creation of the new county in the early 1890s was Frank Augustus Miller, proprietor of the Glenwood, a modest New England–style tourist hotel established by his father in the 1870s on a full city block in the Mile Square commercial district. Now in his mid-thirties, Miller had come to town by stagecoach as a teenager with his mother, brother, and two sisters in fall 1874. Frank's aptly named father, Christopher Columbus Miller, a native New Yorker educated as a civil engineer in Ohio, had already discovered Riverside earlier that year, arriving in the spring without his family and finding work there "as an engineer at the Temescal Tin Mines south of town." Seeing the new community in the California sunshine as a safe and attractive place to raise a family, C. C. Miller arranged for his wife, Mary, and their four children—Emma, Frank, Alice, and Edward—to leave their Wisconsin home and join him to settle permanently in California at the end of the year.

Finding his skills as a civil engineer useful in the growing settlement, the elder Miller became involved with mapping the new community, developing irrigation canals, and building the twelve small rooms of his new Glenwood Cottage, a two-story, adobe-brick lodging house finished smartly with wooden clapboard siding, nice porches, and a high-pitched gabled roof. The new hotel faced Seventh Street on Miller's big city block right in the heart of town. Five years later, oldest son Frank, then in his early twenties, bought the new hotel from his father with money saved from his own fledgling local enterprises of growing oranges and seed potatoes and managing Main Street's Blue Front Store. For the next fifty years, Frank Augustus Miller, in his later years a benevolent gentleman with snow-white hair and spectacles who was accustomed to dining al fresco on shady hotel patios with a blue and gold macaw clinging to his arm, built many local enterprises and his personal legacy on the economic success and widening popular appeal of his city's citrus industry and its relationship to the burgeoning growth of Southern California. Often sounding more like an unassuming small-town minister than an aggressive urban business promoter, and always more diplomat than potentate, as Tom Patterson observed, "by 1900, Miller's was probably the most influential voice in Riverside in matters of city planning and design as well as in politics."[12]

Long before movie producers like Cecil B. DeMille or Sam Goldwyn built the sound stages and back lots from which Hollywood created its more famous land of fantasy, Frank Miller established his own early Southern California magic kingdom by expanding his hotel, changing its name and architecture, and forging Riverside's cultural identity through his unique community centerpiece, the Mission Inn. Centered on a flat, unremarkable square city block occupied by fragments of the old Glenwood Cottage, rough frontier lumber and adobe bricks at its heart, the new Glenwood Mission Inn boasted magnificent towers, soaring arches, and sweeping carriage entrances reviving and celebrating the Golden State's Spanish mission heritage, a feature never really part of the city's past. Unabashedly manifesting one of his favorite expressions, "Dramatize what you do," Miller boldly remodeled his family's old Glenwood Cottage, dismantling its original wooden gabled roof and replacing it with neat horizontal rows of rounded dark orange Spanish roof tiles installed atop a low overhang along a flat one-story roofline. Renamed "The Old Adobe," the original Glenwood, or what was left of it, was now just a small curiosity dwarfed and surrounded by the much larger Mission Inn.[13]

Shortly after his fanciful new Mission Revival hotel opened to great regional acclaim at dusk on the evening of May 7, 1903, hotelman Miller reached the early zenith of his community boosterism when the president of the United States arrived by horse-drawn carriage at the Mission Inn to spend the night. Earlier in the day, the cornerstone of the new county courthouse had been lowered into place as the town's temple of justice was symbolically anointed with corn, wine, and oil in festivities commemorating the tenth anniversary of the founding of Riverside County. The local newspaper said the new courthouse was "as stately and beautiful in its lines and proportions as an old Greek temple." A time capsule buried within its big cornerstone was stocked with photographs, business cards, and a sprig of one of the town's original navel orange trees. For the president's arrival by train at 6:00 p.m. sharp, downtown streets were lined with American flags and decorated lavishly with bunting, palm fronds, flowers, and displays of twinkling red, white, and blue electric lights. Here and there around the Mission Inn courtyard, an enthusiastic *Los Angeles Times* said that the soft orange glow of "scores of Japanese lanterns added to the effect."[14]

A surprise power failure of the overloaded electrical system at the bustling hotel on Thursday evening interrupted the pleasant California night as government bodyguards threw themselves over President Theodore Roosevelt in anticipation of a possible attack. Still, President Roosevelt arose early the next morning, and at 7:30 a.m., wearing a dark suit, his trademark spectacles, and a presidential top hat, he personally took part in Frank Miller's unabashed rearrangement of California's landscape and history. Posing before a photographer's camera with Miller and his wife, Isabella; local dignitaries; and forty eager onlookers, the president turned the first shovel of dirt, transplanting one of the late Eliza Tibbets's two parent Washington navel orange trees into a gaping hole excavated for the grand occasion right in front of Miller's ersatz Old Adobe.

Frank Miller's personal perceptions and dreams for his glorious Mission Inn and its role in local cultural, civic, and political affairs dominated community history for fifty years and lasted well beyond Miller's death in 1935. His program for community identity and civic improvement revolved around four themes that viewed the Mission Inn, its surrounding commercial and civic center district, and nearby Mount Rubidoux as the focus for the promotion of Riverside's national and international identity. Frank explained the themes himself: "As the mountain commemorates, so does the Mission Inn; first, the California Missions, second, Mexican and Spanish art, third, the meeting on the Pacific Coast of the Americas of the art of Europe and the Orient, fourth, world friendship and international appreciation."[15]

Not surprisingly, Miller's first two commemorative themes addressed the Hispanic cultural heritage and popular romance of the Golden State. His view of California as a place where the art

4.2. President Theodore Roosevelt replants parent navel orange tree at the Mission Inn with Frank and Isabella Miller, 1903. (Courtesy of the Riverside Metropolitan Museum, Riverside, California)

of Europe and Asia converged in international harmony was somewhat less predictable, although it provided him a lasting and expansive vision of Riverside's future. Never one to miss an opportunity to boost his city's image as a center for cultural enlightenment and international goodwill and fond of sending boxes of oranges freshly picked at his hotel from Eliza Tibbets's orange tree to prominent people whenever he could, Riverside's "most influential backstage political man" directed a variety of community activities emphasizing his four multicultural themes. Frank Miller regularly entertained international celebrities, a few US presidents, national and international thinkers, government officials, educators, Civil War veterans, and local dignitaries at lavish banquets and formal discussions of world affairs. The ever-changing architecture and interior design of Miller's landmark hotel complemented his far-flung cultural interests.[16]

Frank Miller's early attachment to his city's community of Japanese immigrants and their American children reflected his enthusiasm for cross-cultural cooperation and allowed him to support the Nikkei by playing the role of what scholar Harry Kitano called the "influential Japanophile": "Although it may have seemed to the Japanese that most everybody in the United States was always against them ... , this was not so. There were regional differences; there were social class differences and there were always a number of influential 'Japanophiles'— those who 'loved' Japan and the Japanese."

Several community studies surveying the town's attitudes and practices toward its Japanese community suggest that Riverside, although not immune to the hostility so commonly expressed against the Japanese and others from Asia in many other places throughout the West, provided a relatively favorable environment for them when compared to most other California communities. Riverside's regional hospitality was an upper-class expression facilitated by the many civic activities and personal influences of Frank Augustus Miller.[17]

During the early twentieth century, the Japanese served Riverside as its primary agricultural labor force. By the time the first Japanese immigrants arrived in town, the number of the region's Chinese workers had already been reduced by the Chinese Exclusion Act of 1882. Its extension, the Geary Act of 1892, banned the immigration of Chinese laborers and led to the deportation of many others already living in California. Since their departure, much of the success of Riverside's famous citrus industry was now based on the backbreaking work of immigrants from Japan. Replacing the once ubiquitous Chinese, young Japanese men were soon hard at work harvesting the bulk of the brightly colored citrus fruit now bursting forth from the city's outskirts each harvest season. Riverside had become their new golden land of opportunity.

Most Japanese arrived in Riverside after 1900 but a few had established themselves with small businesses in the 1890s, a time when the prosperous "Riverside citrus growers had made their community the richest city per capita in the United States." In 1895, the *Riverside Daily Press* reported, Japanese orange pickers were working for good pay at $3.50 to $4.00 per day, the same as their white counterparts. At the same time, the *Pacific Rural Press* mentioned the arrival of large numbers of Japanese agricultural workers on the West Coast, adding that "several thousands will find employment in this year's fruit handling."[18]

In Riverside, the Kumaru brothers from Japan opened a grocery store in 1890. The first American-style restaurant operated by a Japanese proprietor was founded in 1895 by Isokichi Ezawa. At the turn of the century some local Japanese businessmen were also acting as labor contractors, middlemen between laborers and citrus grove managers, arranging agricultural labor contracts for Japanese immigrants who worked in the citrus groves and made up the bulk of the city's growing Japanese population. Increasing each year, Riverside County's recorded Japanese population jumped from 97 to 765 individuals in the decade from 1900 to 1910. During the annual citrus harvest, however, estimates suggest that as many as 3,000 Japanese would arrive in the area to work as migrant workers, following the crops throughout Southern California. Thinking of the earlier Chinese, some folks in town and many others across the state saw the large numbers of Japanese migrant workers as a threat to the character of their communities and even the future of the nation.[19]

The *Riverside Daily Press* responded to such concerns on Christmas Eve in 1906, reporting on its front page just eight months after the Great Earthquake that San Francisco's mayor Eugene Schmitz was ready to "lay down his life . . . in fighting the Japanese hordes." The newspaper explained that Schmitz believed "the Japanese were more of a menace than the Chinese." On page four of the same paper, echoing earlier concerns about Riverside's Chinese settlement patterns, the *Press* sounded Mayor Schmitz's alarm over more recent Japanese arrivals now living much closer to home, reporting that Riverside's "Japanese village is growing in rapid strides, and on Sunday when the Japs are not working, presents a lively though slovenly scene. About 40 or 50 live in one big shack, and other less reputable shacks are going up around the main one. It is a wonder that the city allows such haphazard building on one of the main thoroughfares."[20]

By 1910, 75 percent of the Japanese in the county were living within the Riverside city limits. A year later 700 Japanese were reported to be working as laborers in Riverside's booming citrus industry, by far the largest concentration of Japanese citrus workers counted in the state. Early city directories suggest that at about the same time, other Japanese were also establishing themselves as workers and owners in a small selection of local service businesses, including rooming houses, pool halls, grocery stores, and restaurants. A few were also developing outlying chicken ranches and produce farms. Some, both men and women, found seasonal jobs in Riverside's fruit-packing houses. Others worked inside the downtown Mile Square for Frank Miller as domestics and gardeners at the Mission Inn. One Nikkei businessman with the patriotic name of Ulysses S. Kaneko, born in Japan in 1860, operated his Golden State Restaurant in the heart of the city's commercial district on Eighth Street in the same block once occupied by the crude shanties, tents, and alarming laundry ditch of the city's earliest Chinese settlers.

Ulysses Shinsei Kaneko had come to California from Niigata prefecture in the late 1880s and was first employed in San Francisco doing housework. His wife, Chiyo, and the couple's first son, Arthur, later came to California from Japan, and the family moved south with Kaneko's San Francisco employer, George Meet, to live in Redlands, just fifteen miles from Riverside. In Redlands the ambitious Kaneko soon acquired his own small orange grove. In 1896 he became one of the only Japanese immigrants to attain American citizenship before the law was changed to prevent naturalization for the Japanese. A year later the Kaneko family moved to nearby Riverside, where Ulysses opened his Eighth Street restaurant and a small downtown hotel. He soon developed a poultry ranch in nearby Moreno, and within another decade, Kaneko was widely accepted by the larger Riverside community, serving as a member of the county grand jury, court translator, and a city auditor.

Citizen Kaneko's prosperity in his new American home and his early conversion to Christianity in Japan, influenced by a Methodist missionary working in Tokyo in the 1880s, helped to advance his acceptance by others in the town's white business community. Moreover, Kaneko offered more recent immigrants from Japan a solid model for success in Riverside and beyond. From the back room of his Golden State Restaurant downtown, Kaneko catered to prominent white businessmen, developing positive business and social relationships with them over the years, bolstered by his successful community business activities, Christian faith, and unusual status as an American citizen.

Ulysses Kaneko was reportedly the earliest Japanese immigrant to purchase land in Riverside, shortly after his arrival in 1897. He was later chosen by other Issei as the first president of the city's new Japanese Association. Building on his Methodist religious faith, Kaneko was also one of the founders of Riverside's Japanese Methodist Church in 1901. He quickly became the most visible and widely accepted Nikkei businessman downtown, an active member of the Riverside Chamber of Commerce's board of directors, brokering contracts among his community's prominent white citrus growers and groups of immigrant Japanese laborers. Before his passing in 1918, Kaneko also fostered positive relationships between the Nikkei and his contacts in the white business community. He offered social connections and employment for some of the Japanese immigrants who settled permanently in Riverside, advancing his own business interests while helping them get established in their new California home.[21]

Unlike Riverside's permanent Chinese settlers living in the concentrated Chinatown community among the fragrant eucalyptus trees at the edge of town in Tequesquite Arroyo, Riverside's Japanese were scattered throughout the city. By 1910, though, two small clusters of Japanese settlement had developed in town. One was centered in the Mile Square, in the downtown commercial district around Kaneko's Golden State Restaurant, the other in a less fashionable neighborhood across the railroad tracks to the east around Fourteenth Street. During the next five years, additional Japanese settlement spread southwest to the area between Magnolia and Victoria Avenues, near today's Van Buren Boulevard and the location of the village of Japanese citrus workers described with such alarm in the *Daily Press* in 1906. With their sights set on more promising opportunities, Riverside's pioneer Issei immigrants soon descended their tall fruit-pickers' ladders, abandoned the city's citrus industry, and, as in the rest of the Golden State, were eventually replaced by migrant agricultural workers from Mexico. In the few years around the Great War, many Japanese gradually drifted away from Riverside to settle elsewhere in California. The number of the city's Japanese residents dropped from about 750 in 1910 to only 340 by 1920. Those who remained succeeded modestly in small city businesses and outlying produce farms. They also became the nexus of an upper-class interest in the cultural traditions of Japan.[22]

Riverside's Chinese population had peaked at about 500 permanent residents in the 1890s. A decade earlier, some of the town's church parishioners had become interested in learning more about the steadily increasing numbers of Chinese residents living among them. Supporting a strong missionary heritage, church leaders hoped they could persuade at least a few local Chinese to shed their traditional religious practices and replace them with the Christian faith. As early as 1886 a minister at the Methodist Church had presented a warmly received lecture about Chinese culture, prompting Luther Holt's *Press and Horticulturist* to say the anti-Chinese sentiments commonly held by the town's downtown business leaders and in other places in California at the time had, at least among Riverside's apparently kind-hearted Methodists, "not a very strong foothold among them." Seven years later, in September 1893, as renewed agitation in California over the Geary Act led to the deportation of droves of Chinese laborers and reduced the population of many California Chinatowns, the *Daily Enterprise* reported a tolerant Riverside had become a refuge for Chinese fleeing Los Angeles and other less sympathetic communities. The paper said five to ten new Chinese residents were now arriving in town each day. Riverside was described as a "safe asylum for terrified Mongolians from other places." But some of its citizens did not subscribe to this tolerant attitude. On the evening of September 7, local labor unions scheduled a meeting to strategize how "to get rid of some of the surplus heathens." A month later, once again at the apparently welcoming Methodist Church, native of China Wang Foo Shun presented another lecture of interest, "Customs of the Chinese," to a polite and attentive audience.

The annual harvest of the Washington navel orange crop was already under way in 1896 when the town's Congregational Church offered a presentation about the need for new Christian missionaries in China. The following spring the Methodists hosted the Reverend Morizo Yoshida from the new Japanese Methodist Mission in Los Angeles. Yoshida had come to town to help the Reverend Mary Bowen establish another Christian outpost in Riverside, which was said to have sixteen eager Japanese ready to enroll. In February 1899, building on this apparent wave of Christian religious fervor among the Japanese, a housewarming was held at the Sixth Street cottage of longtime resident the Reverend George Deere of the All Souls Universalist Church. Reverend Deere's church was the stout Gothic Revival house of worship built of dark red blocks of Arizona sandstone at the corner of Lemon and Seventh Streets. The housewarming was held to celebrate the opening of yet one more fledgling Japanese Christian mission in Jesus City.[23]

The renewed emphasis on developing Christian missions for Asian immigrants in Riverside had taken a new twist among the Japanese because, unlike the town's earlier Chinese residents, who were mostly unmarried males, some of the young Issei men working in Riverside were accompanied by their wives and a few young children. Years before, Reverend Deere had believed Riverside's Chinese bachelors and the town would benefit if the men were permitted to go back to China and return to California with wives. In his Sunday sermon delivered on March 7, 1886, Reverend Deere had declared, "If we could but have John back, never to return as John Chinaman, but as Mr. Somebody able to introduce a Mrs. Somebody, bone of his bone and flesh of his flesh, we should have no more swarms of degenerating Chinamen, but a self-limited quantity of the Chinese, adding harmoniously to the variety in the progressive unity of American life."

As Reverend Deere worked to establish a new Japanese mission in Riverside fifteen years later, he might have easily transferred his earlier ideas of Christian brotherly and sisterly love to his city's immigrant Japanese families, for, as he had believed in 1886, "[t]he family, husband, wife, and child, is the unit in every normally constituted community of human beings. No number of men by themselves, no number of women by themselves, but a man, woman, and child are the elements necessary to the completion of the social unit." If they remained on a fairly straight and narrow path, the few families of Japanese ancestry making their way to Riverside were well suited to be accepted by at least some of the town's most influential Christian leaders.[24]

"Adding harmoniously to the variety in the progressive unity of American life," in 1901, Riverside's First Congregational Church, founded in 1872 as the First Church of Christ, reported eight Chinese members. Among its trustees and parishioners was Frank Miller, who regularly made substantial financial contributions to the church. Miller also influenced its reconstruction in Spanish Renaissance Revival style on a big corner lot steps away from his downtown hotel in 1912. Two years later, under the leadership of Eva Purington, wife of prominent Riverside attorney and church trustee William A. Purington, the Women's Union of the church was also actively involved in supporting its Japanese Mission on Fourteenth Street.[25]

As the number of local Japanese declined in coming years, the city's two Japanese missions of the First Congregational and Methodist Churches merged to form the Japanese Union Church with a single Nikkei congregation. Within Riverside's Japanese community, especially for families living on isolated produce farms and poultry ranches outside town, church functions often provided the sole basis for intra-community support and social interaction. Longtime Riverside resident Mabel Sumiko Fugimoto recalled: "For a long time, these churches . . . prospered and became the focal point for the lives of the Japanese people here in town because they had no other way to get together. Church became a big thing in their lives."[26]

The early involvement of local Japanese in Riverside's Christian religious activities fostered acceptance by influential non-Japanese church members, but the upper-class interest in Japanese religious practices was also perceived as somewhat patronizing by at least one younger member of the Riverside Nikkei community, Edwin C. Hiroto. "Reflecting upon my attitudes as a member of the church, it seemed to me that it was a somewhat self-righteous activity . . . I get the suspicion that that's why the Riverside . . . community was tolerant. It's like the missionary going to save the heathen approach," Hiroto surmised. Insight into the religious motivations of one non-Japanese community member supporting early Japanese church activities corroborates Hiroto's view. In 1921, five years before Edwin's birth, Mrs. H. J. Craft wrote of her friend Sue Caldwell and her recent preparation of Christmas goodies for the children at the Japanese church Sunday school in Riverside, "She made and filled seven 1 lb. Boxes for her Jap S. S. boys & says she would not make another lb. to keep them from being Buddists [sic]."[27]

In addition to the progressive social functions organized by these hometown missionaries, Mission Inn proprietor Frank Miller's keen interest in Japanese culture, Asian art, and devotion to the promotion of international harmony provided frequent and open public displays of support for Riverside's Japanese community. Miller's curiosity about Japan and his interest in world affairs is reportedly traced to the influence of Wilson Crewdson, a wealthy British investor and art collector who first came to town to enjoy Riverside's warm climate in the winter of 1884–1885, staying at the Glenwood Hotel while convalescing from a respiratory illness. Crewdson's early and repeated visits to Riverside and his ongoing involvement with the city's irrigation canal promoter, Matthew Gage, eventually led to substantial British investment in the Riverside Trust Company, composed of Crewdson's relatives and business associates headquartered in London. He helped finance important water projects in Riverside and hosted Gage on a trip to London to meet trust investors, negotiating a $280,000 personal loan for him from British financial sources. Before long, according to Patterson, Crewdson was involved in "a considerable English investment in Riverside and an influx of English people who would flavor its social scene as well."[28]

Wilson Crewdson's maternal uncles, the three Waterhouse brothers—architect Alfred, accountant Edwin, and solicitor Theodore—were all active and well-known in British social and financial circles. Uncle Alfred had designed many of the Victorian era's most substantial Gothic Revival civic buildings, colleges, and country houses. Edwin was cofounder of the Price Waterhouse investment partnership. With his new connections in Riverside, Wilson Crewdson introduced his uncle Theodore to Matthew Gage in the late 1880s and accompanied Waterhouse on a return trip to California in the winter of 1889–1890 to explore investment opportunities in Gage's irrigation projects. As Waterhouse observed from

Riverside, writing enthusiastically to his sister back home in England, "It is such a delightful thing to have a hand, however small, in developing what Mr. Gage has begun, the fertilization of one of the most beautiful tracts of country on the face of the earth."

During their visit to the wilds of California in 1890, on an outing with Gage near Riverside in February, Wilson and Theodore were stranded midstream and their buggy was nearly swept away by the swift current of the Santa Ana while crossing the river at sundown near a washed-out bridge. The pair abandoned the buggy in the middle of the river, turned their horses loose, removed most of their clothing, and waded awkwardly through deep water and shifting sands to the safety of the riverbank. Soaked and cold, the two men were soon reunited with Gage, who had raced back to town for help. Dressing again onshore and leaving the buggy awash in the river, a grateful but undaunted Crewdson and Waterhouse returned to the warmth of Gage's home for a much more civilized evening of religious hymns and, as Waterhouse recalled, "some violin playing from one of . . . Gage's friends—about as good as I ever heard anywhere."

Before he sailed back to England in March, Waterhouse paid visits to San Francisco, Los Angeles, and Pasadena, becoming ever more confident of the progress and opportunities he saw throughout the Golden State. He returned home to convince his brothers and other affluent business associates that further investment in Riverside was well worth the risk. Traveling in Greece a year later, Uncle Theodore remembered fondly the positive impressions of his visit to the West with his nephew and the attractive new community taking shape along the Santa Ana, telling a friend, "California spoils one a little for other countries . . . I am continuously saying to myself how miserable are these olive trees, these orange groves, these lemons: while even in Greece, if a landscape is more than usually beautiful, it seems the natural thing to say 'how like Riverside.' "[29]

His legacy known even today to the staff of the Victoria and Albert Museum in London, Wilson Crewdson was born in Manchester of Quaker family roots in 1856, attending King's College at Cambridge from 1877 until his graduation in 1880. He was awarded a bachelor's degree from the college the following year and a master's degree half a decade later. A student and lifelong acquaintance of celebrated Cambridge educator Oscar Browning, Crewdson was also an active man of the world, a fellow of the Geographical Society and the Society of Antiquaries and a member of the Council of the Japan Society.

Crewdson, a twenty-three-year-old student in the summer of 1879, bicycled through the French countryside with two other college friends from Cambridge. In July he outlined a few details of their cycling adventure to Professor Browning, the controversial gay lecturer and historian at King's. Young Crewdson wrote to Browning of memorable conversations with "country people" about their "love for the Bonaparts" and visits to "damp cathedrals." Expanding his interests in cultures far beyond Britain and France, Crewdson became well-known among his influential uncles and others in London some years later as "a keen collector of Japanese objects of art." In England in the 1890s, Wilson Crewdson explored wide-ranging topics in Japanese culture and history, later arranging museum gifts and exhibition loans from his personal collection of Japanese textiles, prints, and drawings.[30]

Crewdson had also been involved in the earliest activities of the Japan Society of London. Founded in the early 1890s, the society was known for its explorations of Japanese customs, lectures by visiting dignitaries from Japan, and work to promote positive Anglo-Japanese relations. After the turn of the century, Crewdson authored books and papers about Japanese art and history, speaking at Japan Society dinners presided over by the Japanese ambassador to England. Crewdson served as chairperson when the society's 1,300 members supported the Japan-British Exhibition of 1910 and, like others in the Japan Society, maintained "a lifelong interest in things Japanese." Wilson Crewdson wrote *The Dawn of Western Influence in Japan*, published by the Japan Society in 1903; *The Textiles of Old Japan*, published in 1914; and *Japan Our Ally*, his cordial portrait of Japanese history and observations about the strategic value of Japan's friendship and military alliance with Great Britain in the Great War, published in London in 1915. Among his personal art collections was a diary of the esteemed Japanese *ukiyo-e* wood-block print artist Ando Hiroshige, known for his masterful depictions of life along the old Tokaido Road between Edo and Kyoto.[31]

Crewdson was a young man with time on his hands during his convalescence at the Glenwood Hotel in the 1880s, and during his later stays in Riverside in the 1890s, he may have been entertained by Frank Miller's stories of early California and the American West. Miller's biographer, Wisconsin writer and novelist Zona Gale, asserted, for example, that Standard Oil industrialist John D. Rockefeller had once been driven in a carriage to the Glenwood from the Southern Pacific railway station in nearby Colton by Frank himself and "was manifestly entertained by his driver's talk and by his stories of the west." Indeed, when Rockefeller returned to the area some years later, he "wired for carriages and demanded 'the same driver I had before.'" Like the visits by Rockefeller and other influential visitors from more refined places to the east who found themselves inspired by the possibilities of California, Wilson Crewdson's brush with the Wild West in the rushing waters of the Rio Santa Ana and his warm evenings spent on the peaceful veranda of the old Glenwood might have encouraged his ongoing enthusiasm for a sense of adventure and romance in the promising Golden State.[32]

Perhaps enchanted by Frank Miller's tales, but certainly seeing potential in the young American businessman and his pleasant lodging house in sunny Riverside, Wilson Crewdson may have encouraged Miller to expand his view of how the Golden State and his growing hotel could benefit from greater connections to the rest of the world. Miller's formal education consisted only of his early school days in rural Wisconsin, and he did not visit Europe until 1907. Much more widely traveled and highly educated than his new California friend, Crewdson was a sophisticated Cambridge graduate who arranged complicated international financial deals, but he was also a gentleman with enough leisure time for bird-watching and art collecting. His educational background and interest in travel and international affairs, as well as his important social connections in Great Britain and elsewhere, provided him with the foundation to offer Miller a vision of the world the provincial hotelman had simply never known. In addition, Crewdson's early interest in Japanese culture and his ongoing involvement with the cross-cultural activities of the Japan Society would have helped the worldly hotel guest from England turn Frank Miller's inquisitive eyes toward his Pacific Rim neighbors from Japan.

Much closer to home, in his early years as the owner of the Glenwood, Miller most certainly relied on the talents, manners, and education of his first wife, the former Isabella Hardenbergh, to help cultivate his growing interest in cultural affairs. One of Riverside's first schoolteachers, Isabella was described by local historians as having "a background of education and culture" that helped "to educate her husband." As his closest confidante, Isabella could have joined Frank and prominent wintering guests like Crewdson in discussions of current events and other topics during relaxed moments while sitting in the high-backed wooden rocking chairs gathered outdoors near small potted palm trees at the Glenwood Tavern. All three could have also spent time talking about how the Miller family hotel might play a larger part in shaping cultural life in California.

Along with Crewdson's influence, Isabella's gentle encouragement of more social interaction and a broader outlook on the world might have gradually nudged her small-town husband ever closer to the role of the worldly raconteur he would play quite comfortably over the next several decades in California as Master of the Inn. Zona Gale credits Crewdson with introducing Frank Miller to the benefits of cross-cultural understanding, but little is known about the details of their relationship. Nevertheless, whatever the influence of Wilson Crewdson on Frank Miller, it is clear that by the time Crewdson died at the age of sixty-two, "pushing his bicycle along" at the East Sussex summer resort of Bexhill-on-Sea—on May 28, 1918, the very same day the trial of Jukichi Harada commenced at the Riverside County Courthouse—Miller was infatuated with the Japanese.[33]

Frank Miller's involvement with the activities of the First Congregational Church and his employment of Japanese domestic help at his hotel introduced him to members of the local Japanese community. Among his many hardworking hotel employees was Masao Nakabayashi, a native of Kyushu in southern Japan. She came to Riverside at the age of sixteen and found work at the Mission Inn as the Miller family's personal waitress, serving Miller "milk toast and a baked apple for breakfast." As close to Frank Miller as nearly any other Issei in Riverside at the time, Nakabayashi remembered that Miller was kind to those in the local Japanese community. In 1920, Nakabayashi, later known to most in Riverside by her American name, Martha, married Gyosuke Iseda, who worked at the Mission Inn as a busboy and gardener. The young Nikkei couple helped Miller to maintain his relationship with other Japanese in Riverside as he steadily added features of Japanese architecture and design to the Mission Inn.[34]

The year following Masao Nakabayashi's arrival in Riverside, Frank Miller created a basis for further cooperation with local Japanese when he invited "some 60 Japanese residents of the city" to a banquet "on occasion of the birthday of the emperor of Japan." Annual springtime celebrations honoring local Japanese boys and girls saw Miller's grand hotel decorated with Japanese paper lanterns strung festively across the courtyard. Hotel guests could also see *koi nobori* windsock banners flying high above the inn, tied to the ends of long bamboo poles bending slowly in the warm California breeze. Special exhibits of Japanese objets d'art and lavish banquets thrown for local Japanese and visiting dignitaries from Japan provided opportunities for cultural interaction between Riverside's social aristocrats and the far more humble members of the city's Japanese community. Mabel Fujimoto recalled of Miller: "He was one of the exceptionally kind men to the Japanese people. These old Issei farmers had no idea of the order of silverware. Every year he'd have them over to the Mission Inn for a big dinner. They'd have finger bowls and all this . . . silver and these poor men didn't know one thing from another."

Despite their lack of sophistication and likely uncomfortable moments for the hardworking Issei farmers with their suntanned faces and callused hands, dressed in their nicest clothes and seated awkwardly together while staring at the silverware glistening on Frank Miller's long tables, Miller's Japanese guests were welcomed with open arms. His banquets were regularly attended by both Japanese and prominent white Riverside residents. Subsequent community connections between local Japanese and the other Riverside citizens who attended Miller's banquets at the Mission Inn helped to develop cultural understanding among the two groups and strengthened Riverside's acceptance of its well-behaved Japanese minority.[35]

In 1925, still deeply interested in Asian culture, Miller and his second wife, Marion, accompanied by his younger sister, Alice Richardson, toured Japan and China. It was reported that the Miller party was welcomed to Japan in Yokohama by the former Japanese consul of Los Angeles, and they enjoyed free transportation throughout the country during their trip, compliments of the government railroad. In Miller's absence, friends back home in Riverside built the Mount Rubidoux Peace Tower, commemorating his interest in improving international relations. Designed by Mission Inn architect Arthur Benton, the imposing dark stone tower was decorated with international insignias. Beneath its arched bridge and terraced walls, the tower's hillside landscaping soon also featured a small garden

4.3. The Mission Inn with Japanese decoration, circa 1920. (Courtesy of the Harada Family Archival Collection, Riverside Metropolitan Museum, Riverside, California)

planted and maintained by members of Riverside's Japanese community.

Shortly after returning from his trip to Asia, Miller created the Mission Inn's Fuji Kan, Pagoda, and Silk Rooms, furnished with recently acquired Asian artifacts, including Chinese carvings, "Buddhist priest's robes, rare wall hangings, and embroidered fabrics." Riverside author Esther Klotz described the enchanting new Fuji Kan Room as a magical place furnished with "beautiful brasses, old Buddhas, and silken fabrics lit by many tinted lanterns." The Fuji Kan Room also provided a formal entrance to the inn's new Japanese Tea Garden, "through which a little stream flowed between stone lanterns and temple dogs." A few steps from the tea garden, the nearby Lodge of the Samurai was decorated with "suits of armor and paintings of various Japanese Emperors." In the more impressive Temple of Buddha, a huge gilded representation of the Buddha obtained by Miller from a demolished temple during his trip to Japan in 1925 rested serenely inside the broad golden petals of a giant lotus flower, overseeing the many other objets d'art from Japan in the Mission Inn's engaging Asian fantasyland. Like his late art collector friend, British Japanophile Wilson Crewdson, by the end of the 1920s, Miller was quite comfortable displaying and celebrating his own abiding interest in all things Japanese.[36]

4.4. Frank Miller receives Small Order of the Rising Sun from Japan, Mission Inn, 1929. (From the Jane Clark Cullen Collection, Mission Inn Foundation and Museum)

In 1929 new Japanese emperor Hirohito and the government of Japan officially recognized Frank Miller as a longtime friend of the Japanese people. Miller was "decorated by the Emperor" in appreciation for his sustained gestures of goodwill and for his promotion of international understanding between Japan and the United States. Dressed for the occasion in formal Japanese clothing, Miller stood beneath the crossed flags of Japan's rising sun and the American stars and stripes as he accepted the award from the Japanese consul acting on behalf of Emperor Hirohito. The ceremony in the Carrie Jacobs Bond Room at the Mission Inn bestowed "upon Frank Augustus Miller, a citizen of the United States of America, the Fourth Degree of Merit of Meiji" and decorated him "with the small order of the Rising Sun as His Majesty's mark of appreciation."

Four years later, in the depths of the Great Depression, his dream hotel wanting for guests, Miller was again honored by the Japanese government with the presentation of a commemorative emblem exhibited by Japan at the Century of Progress Exposition in Chicago. In "Frank Miller Hails Japan Gift; Decorated Battledore Sent to Peace Worker," the *Los Angeles Times* reported, "Miller has long been regarded by Southern California Japanese as one of their staunchest friends." The *Times* said Miller had received one of only two emblems presented to American citizens, the other going to President Franklin Roosevelt as "the highest mark of friendship possible for the Japanese government to make from its Chicago exhibit."[37]

After Miller's death at the age of seventy-eight in 1935, his actions on behalf of the Japanese were regarded as a major part of his career. Accompanying a photograph of the Japanese Tea Garden in the Mission Inn brochure, his accomplishments with regard to the Japanese were commemorated: "From early pioneer days Mr. Miller enjoyed the friendship of the Japanese people, the Inn is noted for its work in international understanding, and especially in expressing friendship and appreciation of this oriental neighbor." Two decades before the influential Master of the Inn passed forever from the California scene, Frank Augustus Miller, acting characteristically through a third party, firmly established his pro-Japanese reputation in the mind of at least one of his Japanese neighbors when he discreetly offered to assist Jukichi Harada in his purchase of a new house on a nice shaded street not far from the Mission Inn.[38]

PILGRIM'S PROGRESS

Despite Frank Miller's promotion of world peace, international goodwill, and cultural understanding, and despite Riverside's relative tolerance and refinement, most of the Mission Inn's beds and banquet tables catered to the pleasures and comforts of white folks. Although men and women of varied ethnic origins worked together day and night at Miller's welcoming hotel as chambermaids, waiters, cooks, liverymen, and gardeners, the greatest number of the community's people of color lived some distance from the famous Mission Inn. Some of Riverside's wealthier neighborhoods were clearly reserved for the families of upstanding, fairly well-to-do, and mostly white citizens. Other less affluent areas nearby were home to people with strong hands and weary faces of darker colors whose descendants would come to believe that they also could share in the American Dream.

Four miles north were the smoky, wood-fired hearths of the whitewashed adobes of the old settlement of La Placita de los Trujillos, founded in the 1840s along the busy pioneer trade route between Santa Fe and Los Angeles. Romantically called Spanish Town by the white residents of the much newer community of Riverside, this area was home to dozens of self-reliant Spanish-speaking families, whose cultural history was linked to frontier New Mexico and other strains of a rich Latino past. Just to the south lay the sturdy brick walls of Tequesquite

Arroyo's Chinatown, where lonely single men remembered the hard days of their childhoods along the Pearl River's banks in Guangdong's provincial village of Gom-Benn. These two settlements existed on the city's dusty margins.

At Sherman Institute, another four miles southwest past Chinatown, homesick American Indian children stood in rows by the hundreds at the government boarding school, where they were steered away from the venerable traditions of their parents and other tribal elders and forbidden to speak their native languages in class. Told to follow the rules and learn a trade, these children were forced to abandon their culture and become assimilated far from home. Closer to the center of Riverside, to the east beyond the railroad line, lived hardworking African American families, the children and grandchildren of former slaves doing their best to live their faith and worship each Sunday at the Second Missionary Baptist Church at the corner of Twelfth and Howard Streets. That same eastside neighborhood was also home to families of Mexican and Indian heritage, as well as a few Japanese immigrants and less affluent European Americans who, like their African American and Mexican neighbors, made a modest but honorable living for their growing families on the other side of the tracks.

The little hotels and boardinghouses scattered throughout the city's business district around the Mission Inn provided affordable shelter for many of Riverside's more recent arrivals, people of diverse cultural backgrounds and ethnicities from overseas or less promising places in America. Some rented inexpensive lodgings and lived in crowded rooms with little furniture and a shared bathroom until they could set aside enough money for a better place. In these tight quarters, German, Danish, Greek, Hungarian, Spanish, Japanese, and English could be heard in animated conversation, hushed arguments, or little bursts of laughter, along with the restrained sounds of men and women making love behind thin walls in the dim evening lamplight. In those cramped rented rooms, immigrant families tried to learn enough English to find steady work in the citrus groves and packing sheds, or elsewhere, as soon as they could. People from all over the world were coming to California to make something of themselves, and at the end of the first decade of the twentieth century some were doing better than others.[1]

For the better part of a day in April 1910, Riverside census taker Arthur Erickson methodically worked his way along the western end of Eighth Street within sight of Mount Rubidoux. On that day Erickson carefully recorded the names, ages, origins, and occupations of fifty of his town's working-class residents living in the several rooming houses near the two big banks housed beneath the stately corner towers of the Evans and Castleman Buildings at the imposing intersection of Main and Eighth Streets. This had been the center of town since the pioneer brick buildings had joined the earlier wooden and adobe storefronts along Main Street in the 1870s.

Erickson completed his section of Main Street on Thursday and reached the rooming house at 746 Eighth on Friday. Writing in clear cursive hand-writing, the census taker carefully completed the next few lines of his second precinct enumeration form, doing his part to gather information about the people living in the central downtown area of Riverside for the thirteenth census of the US population. The 148th family in his notes was that of thirty-four-year-old restaurant proprietor Jukichi Harada and his twenty-eight-year-old wife, recorded by Arthur Erickson in the census as "Land Lady" Ken Harada. Following the lines listing the young husband and wife from Japan, Erickson's careful notes next listed, in birth order, the couple's four children: Masa Atsu, Mine, Tadao, and Sumi.

5.1. Eighth Street and Mount Rubidoux, Riverside, circa 1905–1910. (Courtesy of the Riverside Metropolitan Museum, Riverside, California)

When census taker Erickson knocked on the Haradas' rooming-house door in 1910, daughter Mine was a month shy of four years of age; second son Tadao, born in the spring of 1908, had just turned two. Baby daughter Sumi, who had arrived the previous Christmas Day in 1909, was only four months old. Like his parents, bright-eyed twelve-year-old Masa Atsu, the family's oldest son and one of the few Japanese boys close to his age at the public school, was noted as having been born in Japan. The three younger children were listed as native Californians.

Along with the other fourteen people living at the rooming house, most of them reported as "Roomers" seemingly renting their simple lodgings for a couple of dollars a week from landlady Harada, Erickson noted that Jukichi, Ken, and son Masa Atsu were all "able to speak English."

Like Jukichi, four of the other young Japanese men living in the rooming house, along with the six members of the Harada family, were employed in the restaurant business. "Motoo Matsuda" and "Somatseo Minai" (as Erickson spelled their names), both unmarried men from Japan in their late twenties, were working as waiters. Seiichiro Odate, renting rooms with his wife and daughter, and Chozi Sato, also married and living in the Harada rooming house with his wife, Maoto, were both employed in town as cooks. The other workingmen at the address—three more from Japan, two from California, and two from Europe—were laborers or worked in small businesses nearby. The younger of the two California bachelors did odd jobs. The older man was a laborer for the telephone company. S. Sakamoto was a janitor at a drugstore and Morrii Fujimatsu had his own barbershop. Mr. Adachi had a job at a flower store; another single chap worked outside town at the cement plant.

Most of the thirty other neighbors living close to the Harada family were single men, many young but some quite old, ranging from late teens to sixty years of age. Twenty-nine-year-old California-born Frank Philipa, his mother and father both from Portugal, cared for the horses at the nearby livery barn. Also twenty-nine and a bachelor, James Savage from Pennsylvania, his mother from Wales and father also a native Pennsylvanian, had a job as a machinist at the automobile shop. A native Ohioan, forty-three-year-old Edward McBride, told Erickson he was working in Riverside as an "Orange Picker," and several younger men reported they had jobs out at the cement plant.

Around the corner at 875 Main Street was Iowan Ribba Pierce, who at thirty-six years old was, like Ken Harada, a landlady in the neighborhood and one of the few women living in the area. Landlady Pierce was listed as the head of her family of three daughters and a son, two born in Nebraska and two in Oklahoma. Pierce's mother had been born in Ireland; her father was English. Some of the Pierce family's closest Main Street neighbors, all of them men, included a blacksmith from Hungary, a butcher from Indiana, a laborer from Denmark, a machinist from Greece, a carpenter from Scotland, and a young Texan working in a tailor's shop. As in other places around California, the population of Riverside County had nearly doubled since 1900 and, when Arthur Erickson's downtown numbers were added to the total, reached just a few souls short of 35,000 in the national census of 1910. Within the city limits, 15,212 people, nearly half of everyone in the county, called Riverside home.[2]

It had been nearly five years since the three pioneer immigrants of the Harada family moved to Riverside from Redlands. In their first half decade in the United

States, the Haradas had begun to see some modest success. Their prosperous California town was finally feeling more like home. When they set foot in Riverside in 1905, the Haradas rented rooms in a small house not far from the corner of Orange and Seventh Streets, the future site of Riverside's City Hall, just across from the Mission Inn. As new residents of the town's culturally mixed downtown neighborhood, both Jukichi and Ken found jobs working for the most well-established Japanese couple in town, Ulysses and Chiyo Kaneko. The Haradas' new workplace, the Kanekos' Golden State Restaurant on Eighth Street, was just a minute's walk south from the rented rooms in the house on Orange Street.

With few, if any, Japanese women living close to her in Redlands, Ken must have been pleased to become acquainted with Chiyo Kaneko and now live close to other young Issei women in Riverside's larger Japanese community. These women spoke her language and knew about helping with childbirth. They could talk together about adapting the customs and traditions of Japan to their new lives in California. With an immigration story of family separation, reunion, and struggle for a new life in the Golden State similar to that of the younger Haradas, the Kanekos had also established their first home in Redlands. Kaneko-san's old acquaintances there might have even helped newcomer Harada make his introduction to Riverside's most prominent Japanese businessman before Jukichi decided to give up his job at Nakamura's New York Kitchen in Redlands, accept work with the Kanekos, and move his family the fifteen miles to Riverside in 1905.[3]

Daughter Mine, the baby conceived shortly after Mrs. Harada's return to the United States, had been born in the rented house on Orange Street on May 10, 1906. Mine was the first American citizen in the Harada family by virtue of her birth in California. A few days after she was born in Riverside, her father reported Mine's arrival to the Japanese Consulate in San Francisco. Following the traditions of her ancestors, Mine's birthday was also soon listed in the Harada family history registers in Japan. With the birth of her citizen daughter, more work to do caring for the new baby at home, and the memory of losing first daughter Mitsuye still in mind, Ken Harada thought it best to stop working at the Kanekos' Golden State Restaurant. Father Jukichi continued working for the Kanekos for a short while longer. He also attempted to advance himself, trying his hand as a gardener, but did not enjoy immediate success. Many years later, daughter Mine remembered her mother joking pointedly with her father, the former schoolteacher, about his first days trying to find work as a gardener to support his wife and two children: "My mother used to kid him—said he'd never had a hoe or a rake in his hands in all his life and he was trying to make a living on that. He hardly knew how to scrape the soil, she said."

Just about the time of Mine's first birthday, Jukichi had seemingly abandoned any idea of a career in horticulture. Instead, hoping for more stability, he opened his own small rooming house in a rented building at 746 Eighth Street.

5.2. Masa Atsu, Mine, and Jukichi Harada, Riverside, circa 1907 (*left to right*). (Courtesy of the Harada Family Archival Collection, Riverside Metropolitan Museum, Riverside, California)

Father, mother, son Masa Atsu, and baby daughter Mine soon moved from their rented rooms on Orange Street around the corner and a block west to the rooming house on Eighth, where they were one of only a few families with children in this part of town. Although they did not own the building, a place later known as the Ohio Hotel, it is easy to imagine that the Haradas' rooming-house business might provide them with more independence and opportunity. "My mother did the housekeeping," Mine recalled. The residents were "mostly laborers, usually people that couldn't find places elsewhere to live, Mexicans and Japanese," she said.[4]

Surrounded by single men, the Haradas hoped to find a better place for their children to live. A boardinghouse full of laborers was certainly not the best place to raise a family. Once in a while the local police might even run across what some in town would characterize as immoral activities taking place in such locales. As when the town's law enforcement officers scrutinized the Mile Square's Chinese laundries in the 1880s, the police chief launched in 1913 what the *Riverside Daily Press* called a "Clean-up Crusade," inspecting some of the boardinghouses in the downtown district. Chief Corrington, the paper said, "declared that he was positive that unmarried men and women were being entertained in these places right along." In spite of this questionable behavior from its humble clientele from time to time, for the most part the Haradas' rooming house was uneventfully inhabited by transient laborers, salesmen, visiting cattle ranchers, California desert travelers, perhaps a furtive scoundrel or two, and others of modest means. These unmarried workingmen, who rented rooms by the day, week, or month, provided steady income but little companionship and certainly not much sense of a stable home and family life for the Haradas.

Jukichi and Ken were soon expecting another baby. Although their rooming-house business was successful enough to pay the bills and put food on the table, they dreamed of finding some other way of making a living and owning a home of their own. Their son Masa Atsu was able to help with chores, washing out the rooming-house bathtub and helping with other unpleasant chores around the place after school. Nevertheless, even with his assistance, the Haradas knew they would have to do still more to advance themselves.[5]

In Meiji 41, on April 10, 1908, second son Tadao was born at the Eighth Street rooming house. As with sister Mine, his birth was reported to the Japanese Ministry of Foreign Affairs and his name was likewise added to the Harada family history registers back in Aichi prefecture. Like father Jukichi, baby Tadao was the family's second son. As the first male American citizen in the family, the little boy was the apple of his father's eye. In a year or two, little Tadao would be big enough to fit into a new sailor's suit, reminding his father of the brave men of Admiral Togo's naval fleet in the Russo-Japanese War.

In their earliest family portrait in California, the weary but proud parents posed with their three healthy children. Father Jukichi held daughter Mine, a squirming two-year-old. After living in the United States for just three years, mother Ken was dressed in modern Western clothing, no longer wearing her traditional kimono or hairstyle from Japan. She smiled happily at the camera with a twinkle in her eye and baby son Tadao held tightly on her lap. Her ten-year-old son, Masa Atsu, wore a stylish dark cap and bow tie and stood straight and tall between his parents.

With two new mouths to feed, father Jukichi had recently taken small profits from his family's rooming-house business to assume the ownership and management of the city's Washington Restaurant at 641 Eighth Street. The two-story brick structure was just a block south and straight down the alley from the Mission Inn, behind the bigger Evans Building at the corner of Eighth and Main. The building housing Harada's new restaurant, already called the Washington and named for the first US president, was built during the economic boom of the 1880s on one of the later parcels to be developed in the central downtown district. It had been completed just about the time the Chinese were forced to leave the south side of the block occupied by the old Chinese Quarter. Beginning in the 1890s, various investors in succession had owned the property, which in its early

5.3. Washington Restaurant, Eighth Street, Riverside, 1912. (Courtesy of the Harada Family Archival Collection, Riverside Metropolitan Museum, Riverside, California)

years had been used as a hardware and agricultural warehouse. By 1895 or so, with small rooms for rent upstairs and fine new granite curbstones along the concrete sidewalk and graveled street in front, the ground floor had been divided into two commercial storefronts featuring carriage harnesses and poultry for sale. Other buildings in the block housed a real estate office, sausage factory, print shop, and cabinetmaker.

In 1905, just about the time Jukichi and Ken Harada started working for Ulysses and Chiyo Kaneko across the street, Issei immigrant Tsurumatsu Ohashi was operating his own small restaurant in the solid brick building at 641 Eighth, most likely in friendly competition with Kaneko's more prominent eatery, the Golden State. When Arthur Erickson added Jukichi Harada's name to his 1910 census records, saying Jukichi was the proprietor of his own restaurant, it is likely that Harada had just taken over the Washington Restaurant from Ohashi or his struggling successor, Y. Ekeo, another interim operator of the Washington, who lived in the building and ran the restaurant for only a year or so in 1909.

As soon as Jukichi opened his new restaurant, displaying a large framed portrait of its namesake, George Washington, and the enticing sidewalk message offering meals for as little as fifteen cents, he had a local sign painter add "J. Harada Proprietor" to the big glass window at the building's entrance. A cook and a couple of waiters in long white aprons, perhaps some of the several Japanese men

WASHINGTON RESTAURANT

J. HARADA, Proprietor

Open from 5 a.m. to 8 p.m.   Prompt and Courteous Service

DINNER, 15c, and Up

Dinner includes bowl of Soup, and one cup of Coffee, Tea, Milk, or Orange Kola
and one order of Dessert. Chocolate, 5c extra. Side Dish of Meat or Fish,
10c extra and Up. Extra orders of Dessert or Milk, 5c extra.

living with the Haradas in their rooming house down the street, joined Jukichi as the restaurant's small but able
staff. Mrs. Mary Fowler shared part of

5.4. Washington Restaurant menu heading, circa 1910–1919. (Courtesy of the Harada Family Archival Collection, Riverside Metropolitan Museum, Riverside, California)

the building, running the Lynn Hotel with furnished rooms on the second floor.
Harada's most immediate business neighbor was the Asami Barber Shop, housed
in the adjacent storefront facing Eighth Street, its three-chair shoeshine stand in
the open air near a red, white, and blue barber pole.[6]

Joining Jukichi and his family, nearly 500 other Japanese residents, the some
25 children and 70 women far outnumbered by the 400 men, were all now living
surrounded by orange groves year-round in the clean, fragrant air of the warm
California city above the Santa Ana River. The more industrious among them supported themselves and provided their Japanese friends and a few others in town
with a variety of services and products offered by their small businesses, including "two grocery stores, four pool halls, two barbershops, two rooming houses,
one hotel, two bicycle shops, three restaurants, one tobacco shop, one confection-
ary, two labor contractors, three employment agencies, one fish market, and one
tailor." By contrast, as new Nikkei families grew and the Japanese population of
Riverside County continued to climb, reaching just over 750 in 1910, the census
also reported the county's Chinese population had dropped from 316 in 1900 to
just 187. Half a mile from town, Riverside's once vibrant Chinatown had already
begun its slow decline, its village shrine—a small stone tablet and low wall at the
foot of a healthy willow tree along Tequesquite Avenue—often baking untended
in the sun.[7]

Before long Jukichi Harada would proudly decorate the interior of his new
restaurant with framed portraits of other US presidents, adorning them with small
American flags. His oldest daughter, Mine, who would soon begin helping out at
the restaurant after school, remembered her father's plan to add a new presidential

portrait every time he had the chance. "He had Washington and Grant and Lincoln . . . He had Taft and Roosevelt, Theodore Roosevelt. I guess every time there was a new president, I think he put another one up," Mine said. Harada's decision to add patriotic American images to his restaurant's walls might also have helped him counter the lack of acceptance from some white customers that he and his family had begun to notice. A mix of ethnicities was usually found at the tables, behind the cash register, and over the kitchen stove inside the Washington Restaurant, but daughter Mine remembered that some white customers did not like the idea of dining under the same roof with minorities. She explained that the Washington served all ethnicities, including Mexican patrons: "We had Negroes and . . . we used to have Indians . . . We had quite a few white people even though white people shunned us, you know. I mean the people who came in and looked around and saw the clientele, and then they'd walk out . . . We had a lot a' that. And they were all white who would do that, because they saw the different colors in there . . . and they'd walk out."[8]

To make a go of it and to attract as many customers of as many ethnicities as possible, the restaurant needed to be open seven days a week from five in the morning to eight at night. Its printed café menu featured George Washington's likeness from the dollar bill, familiar to all regardless of the color of their skin. A restaurant bill of fare boasted an American-style "Breakfast and Short Orders" and that "All Meat Orders Include Bread, Butter, Potatoes, Cup of Coffee, Tea, Orange Kola, or Milk," with "Chocolate 5 Cents Extra." It also advertised "Mush and Hot Cakes Free with Breakfast" and "Prompt and Courteous Service." A plain beefsteak could be had at the Washington for fifteen cents; an "extra thick" rib steak for thirty. Fried potatoes were extra but a fragrant hot plate of liver and onions was a sensible bargain at fifteen cents. Sweet pie and cake were five cents each and customers could buy a ticket for twenty-one hearty meals for a total of $3.00 paid in advance. At the bottom of the menu, Jukichi also advertised his boardinghouse rooms for rent, starting at twenty-five cents per day or $1.50 per week. Interested roomers were directed to "Inquire of Cashier or Waiter."[9]

Having already worked there nearly every day for two years, Jukichi was slowly becoming more confident of his steady progress at the Washington Restaurant. To supplement his family's income, Harada also expanded his rooming-house business, and by 1912 he was advertising rooms for rent from two more addresses along Eighth Street. Third son Yoshizo was born at the rooming house on June 6, and everyone in the family was again busy helping Ken look after the new baby. After all these years in California, the Harada family had finally begun to prosper. Living at 746 Eighth Street for the last five years and now finding success with the Washington Restaurant, long hours and hard work notwithstanding, Jukichi felt good about his upward social progress from ship's galley attendant to immigrant to proud patriarch and restaurateur.[10]

SIX

LITTLE LAMB GONE TO JESUS

All in all, life in this California town had been hard but good for the Haradas. Standing at the great front window of his Washington Restaurant on some slow afternoons, Jukichi could watch the steady progress of his adopted hometown. After hearing stories of less civilized places from his Issei friends and other acquaintances—stories that suggested the United States still had a long way to go to realize its ideals of freedom and equality for all—the growing city of Riverside was a good place to live and raise a family.

When Jukichi, Ken, and Masa Atsu had come to town, the rough gravel of Eighth Street had been paved with concrete asphalt for only a couple of years. Its palm-lined route through the heart of the city, remembered by old-timers as muddy in winter and dusty in summer, was still most often occupied by horse traffic. However, with each passing day it seemed that automobiles, or "horseless carriages" as some of Jukichi's older customers called them, were slowly outnumbering those passing by on horseback, in fancy painted rigs, or in worn-out farm wagons pulled by tired draft horses. Forward-thinking Frank Miller had added his own small fleet of ten Stearns automobiles to a new garage at the Mission Inn in 1906, hiring younger brother Edward and his sons to drive hotel guests out to the orange groves and all over Riverside. Now, less than a decade later, some people watching the noisy machines rattle by wondered how their restless horses would

6.1. Harada family (*back, left to right*: Jukichi, Masa Atsu, Ken; *front, left to right*: Mine, Sumi, Tadao), Riverside, circa 1911. (Courtesy of the Harada Family Archival Collection, Riverside Metropolitan Museum, Riverside, California)

ever get used to the smoky and unreliable contraptions that were taking over every major downtown street, at times making walking a hazard.[1]

Another remarkable innovation that came to town was the new moving pictures. Some of the younger people in Riverside began to believe that traveling performers like Sarah Bernhardt, Isadora Duncan, and John Drew, who had appeared in person for so many years onstage at the Loring Opera House, might soon be replaced by the novel black-and-white images just beginning to flicker onto the silver screen. Most young businessmen in Riverside supported these changes enthusiastically. And some of the more established town leaders joined in supporting these innovations, trying their utmost to uphold Riverside's reputation as a land of wealth, opportunity, and progress.

Across the street from Harada's Washington Restaurant, the old Victorian-era Castleman Building and its tall clock tower, constructed during the building boom of the 1880s, had recently been demolished and replaced by the modern business offices of the new First National Bank. Just a block away, Frank Miller and his architect were busily completing impressive new hotel rooms and other major additions to the Mission Inn. Miller and some of the more affluent investors in Riverside's business community were also actively maintaining the cultural development and high-minded character of their town by adding new architectural monuments to the downtown area and vying to establish their town as the peer of other well-regarded Southern California cities like Pasadena and Santa Barbara.

The Japanese Christian missions of two of the most important churches in town also helped to demonstrate, at least on Sundays and sometimes even during the week, that some of Riverside's most influential citizens practiced what they preached about tolerance and the equality of the human spirit before God. Others in the community were not so sure. As the Haradas had begun to observe in their Washington Restaurant, the town's progressive Christian beliefs of acceptance and inclusion were not held by all Riversiders. Many still reserved their full acceptance only for white folks. The recent passage of the state's Alien Land Law and national concerns about new waves of foreign immigrants and the advancement of those whom the more polite called "colored people" reflected fundamental divisions in US society over race and national origins. This atmosphere set the stage for an unexpected confrontation in Riverside, where many of its residents had been proud that conflicts among its neighbors, regardless of ethnicity, had been few and far between.

In the eight years since their move to Riverside, Jukichi and Ken Harada had made great progress, but life had not been easy in the Golden State. A disapproving glance or comment from a man or woman on the street could make even the warmest day in sunny California feel quite cold and remind the Haradas how far from home they were. Still, they continued to make modest but encouraging gains over the years. But just six months after the state legislature in Sacramento passed the Alien Land Law in spring 1913, Jukichi and Ken faced a devastating loss.

Most Sunday evenings offered an opportunity for the exhausted young couple to steal a moment together, breathing in the sweet perfume of orange blossoms wafting up the narrow stairwell of their crowded rooming house. With the long workweek at the restaurant at a close and all the chores for their many tenants completed, Sunday evenings offered time for family, normally a rather quiet and restful interlude in the Haradas' upstairs rooms at 746 Eighth Street. On this Sunday in November, however, Jukichi and Ken spent the night awake with worry as, without any warning, a little boy's normal precocious vigor faded and disappeared in just a few hours as the swiftly moving symptoms of diphtheria enveloped him.

Before a vaccine was developed in the 1920s to combat the dangerous bacterial infection, diphtheria was a leading cause of death among children. Living in a rooming house with transient strangers who could have easily spread the communicable disease, five-year-old Tadao Harada was now in grave danger. Without immediate detection and treatment, invasive bacteria can quickly inflame the cells lining the upper respiratory tract, causing severe breathing difficulties. Breaking the silence of the darkened rooming house just after midnight, Tadao was fitfully choking and gasping for breath as his lungs were paralyzed and his airway

6.2. Funeral of Tadao Harada, Olivewood Cemetery, Riverside, 1913. (Courtesy of the Harada Family Archival Collection, Riverside Metropolitan Museum, Riverside, California)

blocked. Jukichi tried desperately to help his son but in just a few minutes the breathless little boy lost consciousness and died in his father's arms. At that tragic moment in the darkness at one o'clock in the morning of November 17, 1913, Jukichi and Ken Harada were overcome with sorrow over a loss too much to bear. Losing a child at birth or soon thereafter was sad but not that uncommon at the time. The couple had already lost one daughter in infancy, but the sudden death of their recently healthy five-year-old was different. The passing of son Tadao, Ken and Jukichi's third surviving child and the first Harada male born in the United States, seemed to shatter their dreams of a new and prosperous life in the United States, leaving them with the horror of their worst nightmare.[2]

During a solemn funeral just a day or two later, Tadao's small wooden coffin was taken in sad procession to the shady cemetery south of town and carefully covered with flowers. A hired driver and white horse waited patiently with a fringe-topped surrey nearby. After a brief graveside service offered with kindness by Christian minister Otoe So, the new spiritual leader of Riverside's Japanese Methodist Mission, the little casket was lowered slowly into a grave beneath tall palm trees not far from the cemetery gates. With father Jukichi and mother Ken, sisters Mine and Sumi, and brothers Masa Atsu and baby Yoshizo together at the grave, Tadao's casket was also surrounded by thirty-five well-dressed members of Riverside's small Japanese community. Along with them, a few other friends gathered at the cemetery to pay their final respects and offer some measure of comfort to the dead boy's grieving parents.

Within weeks the death of Tadao Harada was dutifully recorded in the prefectural records of his ancestors in Aichi-ken, a world away from the cramped and weathered California boardinghouse in which he had died. Sometime later at Olivewood Cemetery, workmen installed a heavy black granite tombstone over his grave bearing the inscription "Tadao Harada, A Little Lamb Gone to Jesus," as his parents turned more frequently to the reassuring comfort they found with Reverend So and his Christian faith, which was offered with great compassion at the Japanese Methodist Mission. Back in town at the rooming house, in solitary moments of sadness and reflection, Tadao's young parents committed themselves to giving meaning to his passing by meeting the next episode of their California lives with resilience and determination. Nearly ninety years later, their youngest son explained how Tadao's untimely death in the crowded rooming house changed his father forever:

> My dad told me many times how he had held Tadao in his arms . . . He cradled him and tried to help him with his breathing. He was choking to death—and did eventually die in my dad's arms . . . I think that really changed his whole life because he wanted to get his family out of there and into a better environment. And I don't think Heaven or Hell could stop him . . . from purchasing a home that he thought would be . . . in the best interests of his family and his children.[3]

Ken must have known at Tadao's funeral that she was expecting another baby. Toward the end of the annual orange harvest in spring 1914, she was about seven months pregnant, due in late May or early June. But any sense of promise from anticipating the new baby had been overshadowed by the recent torment of Tadao's passing just four months before. Ever since his death in the rooming house, Ken and Jukichi had not been comfortable living there. Awful memories of their son's tragic struggle in the night would not go away. As they grieved for Tadao, they worried about the health of their four surviving children and the baby on the way. They knew the crowded living conditions at the stuffy downtown rooming house and Tadao's exposure to its many transient residents might have caused his sudden illness and death. Shortly after his funeral, Jukichi and Ken turned their thoughts to moving their family to a safer and healthier environment as soon as they could. Before long, leaving sad memories behind, they moved away from 745 Eighth Street to another upstairs rooming house at the southwest corner of Orange and Eighth. The brick building just across the street and a few doors east of the Washington Restaurant was the former home of the *Riverside Press and Horticulturist,* the same newspaper in which editor Luther Holt had railed against the Chinese in the 1880s. Settled here temporarily, the Haradas hoped to stay only long enough to find a better and more permanent place to live.

Some of the more sophisticated and successful people in Riverside might have viewed their town's history as a rich tapestry woven of prosperity and refinement, but others of more humble means might have seen it more as a rough and simple patchwork quilt of many different colors. In either case, the unfinished weave of Riverside's cultural development was still a work in progress. And, on the eve of the Great War in Europe, a few more colorful threads were about to be stitched into its sturdy fabric over the top of Mount Rubidoux and right through the middle of town. Just as Jukichi and Ken were worrying about finding a better place to live within walking distance of their restaurant, important things were happening just a block away at the Mission Inn. Once again, neighbor Frank Miller was hard at work making arrangements for his next big event celebrating his community as a place of diversity, tolerance, and acceptance.

Proud to host former slave and famous African American educator Dr. Booker T. Washington, founder of Alabama's Tuskegee Institute and the most widely known national spokesman for the country's black community at the time, Miller was busy helping to organize three speaking engagements for Washington in Riverside, set for a single day at the end of March. When Dr. Washington had dined at the White House as a guest of President Theodore Roosevelt and family in 1901, just a month into Roosevelt's presidency, newspapers around the country reported the event as front-page news. In Tennessee, one newspaper editor railed against Washington's visit with the Roosevelts: "The most damnable outrage which has ever been perpetrated by any citizen of the United States was committed yesterday by the President, when he invited a nigger to dine with him at the White House." Angry southern segregationist politicians were boiling over. Mincing no words, South Carolina's senator "Pitchfork" Ben Tillman seethed, "The action of President Roosevelt in entertaining that nigger will necessitate our killing a thousand niggers in the South before they will learn their place again."[4]

Theodore Roosevelt personally shared the same beliefs as most other white Americans did forty years after the Civil War, confiding to a friend, "Now as to Negroes, I entirely agree with you that as a race and as a mass, they are altogether inferior to whites." This was a time of continuing conflict about racial issues, when the lynching of blacks was on the rise and Jim Crow laws legally denied them equal access to the voting booth and most other promises of American life. Still, the president was willing to acknowledge Washington's status, offering the well-deserved if backhanded praise when he described him as "the most useful, as well as the most distinguished, member of his race in the world." Criticized by more radical thinkers in the changing black community as subservient and accommodating to whites, Washington was supported by influential white donors like wealthy industrialists Andrew Carnegie and former Mission Inn guest John

D. Rockefeller. While others were founding the National Association for the Advancement of Colored People and working across racial lines to stem the rising national tide against the idea of African American equality, Washington was seen by many outside his own community as the only public spokesperson for Americans of African descent.[5]

Washington was so acceptable to many of means and influence within the white community that Thomas Dixon Jr., a popular North Carolina Baptist minister turned author and lecturer, sought Washington's review of his most recent novel, *The Leopard's Spots: A Romance of the White Man's Burden, 1865–1900*. Dixon's new book was the first of three seminal race-baiting—and best-selling—works critical of the Reconstruction speaking to those terrified of miscegenation and wary of blacks' future role in the United States and serving as a hate-mongering fount for renewed interest in the Ku Klux Klan. Booker T. Washington apparently paid little attention to the author's request for a book review. Nonetheless, Thomas Dixon's latest publication soon became popular throughout the nation, along with his next two sensational novels: *The Clansman: An Historical Romance of the Ku Klux Klan*, published in 1905, followed by *The Traitor* two years later.[6]

Before long, in a country seemingly hungry for the story of how the Civil War and its aftermath might have led the nation away from its efforts to remain a "White Man's Country," Thomas Dixon's *The Clansman* became the basis for the screenplay of one of the most notorious American motion pictures of all time, D. W. Griffith's controversial cinematic masterpiece *The Birth of a Nation*. By this time, some US citizens had genuinely sought to improve race relations since the Civil War and Reconstruction. Many more were now supporting women's right to vote, although plenty of others still considered this notion outlandish. Despite these advancements, most of the country's citizens were not ready to accept that people of color should be dining with the president at the White House or making any progress toward the American Dream.

Booker T. Washington's three presentations in Riverside began in the morning in the sanctuary of Frank Miller's own place of worship, architect Myron Hunt's recently completed First Congregational Church. Shortly after finishing his remarks, spoken to a mostly white audience in the heart of town, Dr. Washington was taken to the other side of the railroad tracks to appear before the African American congregation of the Second Missionary Baptist Church. Like the white population, the number of Riverside County's African Americans had doubled since 1900, totaling just over 500 in the 1910 census. For Booker T. Washington's 1914 appearance, crowds from the smaller African American communities of nearby San Bernardino and Redlands reportedly flocked to town, joining most of the 400 others then living within the city limits to hear his speech at the overflowing Second Baptist Church. In his talk to the eastside brethren, enhanced by the Baptist Church choir singing "Old Time Religion" and "Old Black Joe," songs reportedly performed at his request, Dr. Washington spoke with measured eloquence of the fight against illiteracy. He also stressed his belief in the importance of education, telling his listeners he viewed himself and those stirring in their pews before him as members of "a new race" with a great future before them.

Sometime before Washington's evening capstone speech to a third large crowd filling every chair at the Cloister Music Room back at the Mission Inn, Frank Miller took his famous guest to the top of nearby Mount Rubidoux, site of the first Easter sunrise service in 1909. The pair was photographed standing together atop the mount, hats in hand in the California sunshine. Wearing dark glasses, white-haired Master of the Inn Frank Miller rested in the shadow of the former Virginia slave. Dr. Washington, the right side of his face bathed in sunlight, stood prominently in a place of honor a step or two above his host on the rocky mountaintop overlooking the well-irrigated Garden of Eden of Frank Miller's promised land. Rooftops, church steeples, and healthy green citrus trees dotted the landscape below. At the end of Washington's evening presentation at the Mission Inn, those assembled in the large music room just off the hotel lobby rose to sing a patriotic rendition of the "Star Spangled Banner." After the national anthem Washington urged attendees to contribute to his Tuskegee Institute before thanking his admirers and retiring for a night of comfort at the Mission Inn.

Although nothing more controversial than the topic of African American education was mentioned in his Riverside speeches and Dr. Washington's public remarks remained well within the bounds of civilized discourse, Frank Miller's warm welcome of Booker T. Washington likely signaled a level of acceptance of African Americans that many white folks in other American communities, and also probably quite a few in Riverside, did not support. Washington's visit to Riverside had lasted only a day or two. It was reported in respectful tones in the local newspaper and did not seem to fundamentally change how the town looked at people of color. It might have even been seen by some as just one more attempt by Frank Miller and his sympathetic Republican church friends to promote their odd personal interest in cross-cultural goodwill among the races. To others, however, Washington's visit to Riverside, with his night at the Mission Inn, was a disturbing event. Among some of the less tolerant white citizens of Riverside, whispers could be heard revealing the prevailing national ambivalence about allowing non-white citizens to have a status equal to that of whites.[7]

This is not to say that Riverside was seething with racial tension. Among the many parishioners of the Reverend Horace Porter's First Congregational Church in early spring 1914, the recent acceptance of African Americans practiced by the reverend and church member Frank Miller in their welcome of Dr. Washington to Riverside supported ongoing intercultural activity of interest to all. Just a month after Washington's departure, the more attentive of Reverend Porter's flock read

6.3. Dr. Booker T. Washington and Frank Miller, Mount Rubidoux, Riverside, 1914. (Courtesy of Mission Inn Foundation and Museum)

a First Congregational Church handbill announcing a smaller but still interesting upcoming community event promoting cross-cultural interaction: "At the Woman's Club next Friday evening the Japanese Mission of this church will give a concert. There will be music by the Nagahara family of Los Angeles, and some rare magic work by Shigeta, the Japanese magician."[8]

Living nearby and new members of the Japanese Mission, expectant parents Jukichi and Ken Harada might have taken their four inquisitive children to see the musical performance and magic show, joining the mission's pastor, the Reverend Hata, and a few others from the First Congregational Church. And just a few weeks later, at the end of the month as expected, another daughter, Yone, was born to the Haradas. Once again, sadly for Jukichi and Ken, serious complications arose and their new baby did not survive. On June 1 she was buried near brother Tadao beneath the shady trees at Olivewood Cemetery. With the loss of another child, the young couple grew more anxious to move their family from the crowded second-floor quarters of the rented boardinghouse.[9]

An immediate move, however, was impossible. Ken's most recent pregnancy had delayed their plans to leave 606 Eighth Street. The rooming house was certainly not suitable for their growing family, but it was close enough to the Washington Restaurant for easy trips back and forth across the street if necessary. Riverside's little white cottages, where other young mothers and fathers often spent peaceful warm evenings on open front porches and happy children played safely in the fresh outdoor air, must have seemed the perfect place for Ken and Jukichi to raise their family, but they knew they would have to set aside the funds needed to purchase a house. They had to be patient, because even once they had the money in hand, it might still take a few months to find a promising and affordable location. In the meantime, however, other events in town were influencing the Haradas' Riverside neighbors to look differently at themselves and the faces of color among them.

Just across Main Street from the Mission Inn, shortly before two o'clock on New Year's Day 1915, the projectionist at Riverside's Loring Opera House, the elegant 1,000-seat theater known across the region since the 1890s for its impressive stage productions, carefully organized the dozen reels of a new motion picture. The film had just arrived from Los Angeles and was finally ready for its first public preview at a Riverside matinee that afternoon. As the first reel was threaded carefully into the motion picture projecting machine, curious townsfolk living nearby began taking their seats in the big opera house. Seven members of a small orchestra settled into place with their instruments tuned and ready to provide musical accompaniment to the silent black-and-white picture for the next three hours. Anxious for his story to begin, the film's confident forty-year-old executive producer and director anticipated the reaction of the audience. Earlier in the day, Friday's edition of the *Riverside Daily Press* had announced one of the new year's biggest events:

> Today at the Loring theatre, what is said to be the greatest achievement of the motion picture art will be thrown on the screen for the first time. The drama from which the scenario was arranged is Thomas Dixon's famous story, "The Clansman." D. W. Griffith, one of the best-known producers and directors of the motion picture world, directed the work of producing the masterpiece, and he will be here to see the initial showing. With him will be from 20 to 40 of the principals of the drama. The picture will be shown this afternoon, tonight, Saturday afternoon and Saturday night . . . The admission is 20 and 30 cents.

A paid advertisement of an "Announcement Extraordinary" for *The Clansman* in the *Daily Press* told everyone in town that they could come to the Loring to see some "25,000 Soldiers in Action on battlefield, including troops of cavalry and 30 batteries of artillery [and] Artillery duels with explosive shells used for first time in history of motion pictures." Billed as "the most powerful plea for universal peace that could possibly be devised," the picture promised:

> Battle Scenes at Night.
> Burning of the Entire City of Atlanta, Ga.
> Sherman's historical march to the sea.
> Assassination of President Lincoln, by Wilkes Booth.
> Famous raids of the Ku Klux Klan.

Kentucky native David Wark Griffith had come back to Hollywood from New York the previous year, ending his long association with the American Mutoscope and Biograph Company, where he had already directed hundreds of short films, some with American Civil War settings. Moving quickly to reestablish himself on the West Coast, D. W. Griffith directed two more pictures in California before filming began for *The Clansman*, based on Thomas Dixon's popular novels of the day and a Dixon play of the same name. Griffith's new motion picture play had begun production the previous summer, filming in the vacant hills of Whittier and several other rural Southern California locations before its completion at the end of October. By the end of the year, the cinematic story was completed and printed, and Griffith had his new film ready for its preview, taking its twelve reels to Riverside for four presentations to its first public audiences.

When *The Clansman* came to town, most of the working-class families in Riverside still did not own automobiles. People living in the Mile Square close to the center of town, within walking distance of the Loring, were quite comfortable conducting their daily business on foot or by streetcar. With up to 1,000 people at each showing over the next two days, the theater was the perfect venue for D. W. Griffith's motion picture, offering the cross section of average Americans that he sought for the preview of what his Riverside newspaper advertisement had immodestly characterized as the "Most Wonderful Motion Picture Ever Produced."[10]

Like Frank Miller and his second wife, Marion, his much younger former secretary he had married in 1911, three years after the death of his first wife, many of the town's well-known and respected citizens lived in the downtown neighborhoods near the stylish Miller family rooms at the Mission Inn. Back just a block or two from the busiest roadways downtown, narrower cross streets were lined with pepper trees shading nice houses in a prosperous and well-maintained residential area the newspaper later described as "one of the most favored residence districts of the city." To the amazement of friends and relations back east, some of the houses even had new little orange trees planted in the front yard.

Prominent citizens—like Riverside attorney and California native son Miguel Estudillo, a former state assemblyman and senator, and his wife, Minerva, a *Mayflower* descendant from New Hampshire—lived among the families of other well-to-do professionals and businessmen just a few blocks from the banks and real estate offices at Main and Eighth. Senator Estudillo did not always see eye-to-eye with the more conservative Frank Miller of the Mission Inn and was politically active with the state's progressive Republicans. He was well-known in town as the grandson of early Jurupa Rancho settler Don Louis Robidoux. Members of Mr. Estudillo's distinguished California family had been important officials in San Diego long before statehood, and Estudillo personified Frank Miller's dream of a modern-day Riverside linked to California's Mission-era past. Like her husband, who was instrumental in guiding the state legislation for the University of California Citrus Experiment Station in Riverside and an active member of local fraternal organizations and country clubs, Minerva Estudillo was also involved socially in town, no doubt supportive of her progressive husband's opinion that women should have the right to vote, and busy working with neighbor Frank Miller and others to establish beneficial community organizations like the county's Hispanic Art Society.[11]

George and Clara Parker lived a few blocks northeast of the center of town. Mr. Parker was the successful inventor and owner of the Parker Machine Works, maker of box-nailing machines and other practical devices used to improve the manufacture of orange crates and streamline other fruit-packing processes. The Parkers lived in a nice house at the corner of Fifth and Mulberry. Their home was close to the Lincoln grammar school and the First Congregational Church's Japanese Mission. George Parker's most prominent business competitor and future partner, Fred Stebler, a "tinkering genius" with citrus machine inventions after an isolated pioneer childhood in Iowa and South Dakota, had come west to Riverside in 1899. Mr. Stebler lived with his wife, Eva, and their four children in a large, two-story chalet-style bungalow built for the well-to-do family in 1911 along the upper end of Sixth Street, several blocks west of the Parkers toward Mount Rubidoux.

Between Main Street and the railroad, Mission Inn builder and architect G. Stanley Wilson and his wife, Florence, lived on Orange Street, an easy stroll just two blocks north of Frank Miller's downtown hotel. The family of Gaylor Rouse lived a few doors north of the Wilsons on the same side of Orange toward Fourth. Mr. Rouse was president of the town's favorite department store. A block north on the other side of Orange, Jacob and Clara Van de Grift occupied a big Victorian house on the west side of the street. Indiana natives, the Van de Grifts had lived in Riverside since the early 1880s. They moved to a single-story house at 351 Orange Street in the 1890s. At the turn of the century, Jacob and Clara expanded their home, adding a second story and an "elegant front porch with eleven pillars." Living comfortably in their big house on Orange Street, the Van de Grifts and their two daughters, thirteen-year-old Clara Josephine and twenty-five-year-old Nellie Frances, did well enough from Jacob's property investments in 1910 to have a live-in Japanese house servant, a young man in his mid-twenties they all knew as Richard. A member of the First Congregational Church like Frank Miller, Mr. Van de Grift had once served as the town's postmaster. By 1915 he was known in Riverside as a successful real estate investor and considered one of the town's "leading citizens."[12]

Within sight of the big Van de Grift home on Orange Street, half a block to the north, attorney William Ansel Purington and his wife, Eva, president of the Women's Union of the First Congregational Church and a supporter of its Japanese Mission, resided in another big house at the corner of Orange and Third. Just a block east of the Puringtons, in a corner house at Lemon and Third, the biggest and most ornate in that stretch of Lemon Street, lived the family of William and Lucy Farr. The Farr home was a two-story Craftsman with a wide front porch and an elegant Palladian window in the high roof gable facing the street. Neat rows of fish-scale shingles covered the outside walls upstairs. A palm tree graced the front yard not far from a heavy curbside carriage block inscribed with the family's last name. In his late fifties when D. W. Griffith's new motion picture came to Riverside, livestock dealer William Farr had lived in the big house on Lemon Street with Lucy and their five children, four daughters and a son, for the last eight years. Their attractive home suggested to passersby that they were among the most afflu-ent people on Lemon Street. William Farr's parents were from Germany; Lucy's were born in Virginia. Mr. and Mrs. Farr both hailed from Missouri but, before coming to California, had lived for a time in New Mexico, where all of their chil-dren were born.[13]

Among the large houses of the Van de Grifts, Puringtons, and Farrs, on smaller lots scattered on the same side of town, neat little painted cottages and more rustic shingle-covered California redwood bungalows surrounded by lush gardens and rows of flowers, some with front porches graced with pink and red geraniums planted in old green ceramic ginger jars from Chinatown, housed the families of somewhat less affluent homeowners. In these small houses lived men and women not as wealthy as some of their more prominent neighbors but just as interested in living a respectable and productive life in the warm California sunshine. Hardworking storekeepers and physicians, a stenographer, bookkeeper, barber, automobile mechanic, wallpaper hanger, sign painter, insurance superin-tendent, produce salesman, nurse, jeweler, practitioner of Christian Science, and even a fortune-telling medium lived close together on the narrow, tree-lined resi-dential streets near the Mission Inn and between the railroad tracks and the Santa Ana River. These respectable families formed the working middle-class backbone of Riverside's Mile Square community.[14]

On nearby avenues on the same side of town, other families of well-to-do ranchers and citrus growers also made their homes alongside the tidy houses of steadfast tradesmen, including an electrician, mason, carpenter, millwright, house painter, plumber, paper hanger, brick maker, contractor, and house mover. Liv-ing just a block from the Farrs on Lemon a little closer to the town center were three schoolteachers, two students, the pastor of the United Presbyterian Church, a city constable, a cashier for the town's electric light and water company, a dress-maker, the proprietor of a shop selling ladies' furnishings, and the caretaker of the Odd Fellows Hall. Even though they all lived only a short walk from the little ho-tels and boardinghouses downtown—noticeably farther away from Chinatown, Spanish Town, or the Indian boarding school—these white homeowners gener-ally thought of themselves as superior to the many single men and few immigrant parents living with their American-born children in cheap rented rooms within the town's business district.

Unlike Miguel Estudillo, whose family had been in California for generations, most of the adults living in the nicer houses downtown were not native sons and daughters of the Golden State. On Lemon Street, Michigan native John Hansler and his wife, Minnie, born in Illinois, lived with their California-born children in a simple house with a high-pitched roof one lot north of the Fletchers, at the intersection of Lemon and Fourth. John Hansler's mother and father were both from Germany, like Mr. Farr's parents. Mr. Hansler was apparently doing well in California, supporting his family as vice president of the Ark Housefurnishing Company. Three doors north of the Hanslers on the same side of the street, naturalized American citizens from Canada, George and Annie Urquhart, lived in a fine two-story house next door to William and Lucy Farr. George Urquhart, his father from Scotland and mother from Canada, was a horticulturalist with his own orange grove. George later supplemented his citrus grove income by working as an insurance agent. Except for the many Native Americans at Sherman Institute and a few others like Miguel Estudillo or the grandchildren of American slaves living on the other side of the railroad tracks, almost everyone living in Riverside had ancestors from another country and a family story of immigration and struggle not unlike that of the Harada family.

Similar to the rooming-house managers downtown, some of the two dozen widows living in the neighborhood and a few less well-to-do residents often rented furnished rooms to boarders to help make ends meet. One older widow, Mrs. Cynthia Robinson, was now living alone on a government pension in a small cottage at 342 Lemon Street. She was the widow of Civil War veteran and former Riverside County Courthouse janitor the late Alvin W. Robinson. Cynthia was Alvin's second wife and fifteen years his junior. She and her husband had lived in their little house on the same block as the wealthier Farr family for nearly twenty years. Before Alvin died at the age of eighty-five on the day after Christmas in 1913, he and Cynthia had been among Lemon Street's oldest residents. Both native New Yorkers, the Robinsons had moved to Riverside in the 1890s, and already in his sixties by then, Alvin found janitorial work at the courthouse, employed by the Riverside Bar Association.

Along with most other Civil War veterans of the Union Army also living in Riverside, honored old men who had joined the local Grand Army of the Republic Post 118, an active veterans' group known in town for planting trees and engaging in other worthwhile civic improvements, Alvin Robinson might have gathered with the other old soldiers taking part in Frank Miller's annual Decoration Day celebrations held a few blocks away at the Mission Inn. If old Mr. Robinson attended the 1913 reunion with the other fifty graying Civil War veterans, lining up for the commemorative photograph beneath the tall pepper trees outside the

inn's flag-draped sidewalk arcade along Seventh Street, it would have been his last, for by the end of the year Alvin was gone and Cynthia was filing for her Civil War widow's pension.

6.4. Cynthia and Alvin Robinson, circa 1900? (Courtesy of the Harada Family Archival Collection, Riverside Metropolitan Museum, Riverside, California)

In her later years, Mrs. Robinson identified herself to wide-eyed neighbor children as a widow of a Civil War veteran. And now, with *The Clansman* just a few minutes' walk away, if she had the time, inclination, and 20 cents, Cynthia Robinson could have been seated at the Loring among many of her Riverside neighbors to witness the thrilling Civil War revival that film director D. W. Griffith described as the "picturisation of history." The grown children and families of Civil War veterans from both the Union and Confederate Armies were among the ordinary folks D. W. Griffith had in mind when he sent his new picture to Riverside to see how mainstream America would respond to the story he would soon retitle *The Birth of a Nation*.[15]

As the lights dimmed and the music began at the Loring Opera House, Griffith's latest motion picture came to life for the first time on the silver screen. The new film not only startled its viewers with pioneering cinematic techniques, changing moviemaking forever, but also opened old wounds to expose a nation still profoundly troubled and divided by racism half a century after the end of the Civil War.

Scene 7

Fade in. TITLE:

"The bringing of the African to America planted the first seed of disunion."

Scene 8

Tableau of a minister praying over manacled slaves to be auctioned in a town square. Fade out.

The picture's dramatic scenes of bloody Civil War battles between Yankees and Rebels, and later confrontations between blacks and whites in the tumultuous aftermath of Reconstruction, might have made the Loring Opera House audience think uneasily about the future of their diverse communities of citizens living together and trying to get along as residents of a modern nation.

Scene 723

In a crowded meeting hall, white men explain the rally signs to blacks: One sign reads:

EQUALITY
Equal rights
Equal politics
Equal marriage

Another sign reads:

40 ACRES AND A MULE for every colored citizen.

Scene 724

A black speaker is delivering an impassioned speech to the crowd, while a few feet from him a white man is making a point vigorously with his clenched fist to another white man.

Scene 813

TITLE:

"The case was tried before a negro magistrate and the verdict rendered against the whites by the negro jury."

Scene 819

A white family sit listening. The father pulls his small daughter close to him.

Scene 822

Four black men in military uniform push a white man and his two small children off the sidewalk into the street.

Scene 823

A white family is being dispossessed, and as they walk forward and out left, a black officer violently pushes the lame old man as one of the black soldiers looking on laughs.

In its perceptive early review on January 2, the *Riverside Daily Enterprise* recognized immediately that Griffith's cinematic triumph might sell plenty of tickets but it might also arouse wide and heated public discussion:

> Whatever may be the attitude of the audience toward the pro-southern ideas of the play, there is no denying that it grips the attention from the start and that it works up into a tremendous climax in the scenes that show the activities of the Ku Klux Klan . . . The play is certain to be well advertised over the country, as it will arouse discussion of the negro problem both south and north. The resulting arguments will surely mean increased patronage of the motion picture houses showing it.[16]

D. W. Griffith's disturbing motion picture spawned heated public discussion and arguments far beyond the neighborhood around the Mission Inn, revealing that the concerns about the protection of American home and hearth depicted in the film were just as much a mirror of the present as a window to the past. In crowded theaters across the country, the flickering bright white light of the motion picture projecting machine did not simply bring Griffith's complicated tale to life for thousands, it also exposed the dark reaches of the national psyche. *The Birth of a Nation* struck like a red-hot poker thrust at the round bellies of the country's respectable middle-class white neighbors in all regions to rekindle national fear and prejudice never far from the surface. Griffith's well-timed epic offered a popular history of the defeated South, a gripping narrative showing how the sentimental Garden of Eden that was southern society before the Civil War and Reconstruction, a symbol of modern American society itself, could be resurrected from the ashes of the country's greatest national trauma and defended forever by the kinds of beliefs promulgated by the white-hooded vigilantes of the Ku Klux Klan.

Like the upstanding, hardworking citizens who first saw *The Clansman* in Riverside in 1915, most of their white contemporaries in other places across the nation saw the simple themes and stereotypes of D. W. Griffith's stirring melodrama as central to maintaining the stability and social order of their communities. These were the places they believed they had built and had come to know as home, just as other hardworking people of other colors were working to make their own American

Dreams come true. Ensuring white supremacy, maintaining states' rights, protecting the American family, and keeping colored men far away from white women were the picture's key messages and were shown with innovative color tinting in chilling close-ups, sweeping panoramas, and spectacular moving images the California townsfolk at the Loring Opera House would not soon forget.

Within three months of the New York premiere of *The Birth of a Nation* in March, Dr. Booker T. Washington was asked to provide photographs of educational activities at his Tuskegee Institute for an exhibition connected with showings of D. W. Griffith's new motion picture play. Washington refused, seeing such support as an endorsement of the controversial film. By June he had joined the rising chorus across the country in condemning the picture, calling it "a thoroughly harmful and vicious play" and adding that he wanted "to do everything possible to prevent its being exhibited." The National Association for the Advancement of Colored People joined other civil rights groups to organize educational campaigns against the picture. Some communities refused to allow its presentation, fearing the inflammatory film could lead to race riots.[17]

Later in the year, some five months after Dr. Washington expressed his disapproval of Griffith's film, suffering from hypertension and exhaustion, Washington collapsed in New York City and was taken home to Alabama, where he died at the age of fifty-nine on Sunday, November 14. Three days after Washington's passing, at the Mission Inn in Riverside, Frank Miller honored the memory of the former slave and his former hotel guest with a devotional religious service led by Miller's pastor and Washington's acquaintance, First Congregational Church minister Horace Porter. Reportedly chaired by the city's mayor and attended by "both blacks and whites," the Reverend Porter's memorial service was held in the Mission Inn's Cloister Music Room, the same place Dr. Washington had addressed his appreciative Riverside audience the year before.[18]

As Thanksgiving approached, *The Birth of a Nation* continued making its controversial way to motion picture houses across the country. From the impressionable crowds in the audience to those in the streets who refused to set foot in any theater showing what they believed was a bigoted story, just about everyone in the United States was thinking about conflict among the races. Back in California, as some of the more tolerant churchgoers in Riverside had completed their public demonstration of Christian brotherhood by paying respects to the memory of Dr. Washington at the Mission Inn, Jukichi and Ken Harada turned their attention to finding a permanent home for their children and expected new baby, due to arrive sometime in April, still banking on a future beneath the American flag, like the ones hanging on the walls of their Washington Restaurant.

SEVEN

THE PEOPLE OF CALIFORNIA
VERSUS HARADA

Jacob and Clara Van de Grift's big Victorian house on Orange Street stood in marked contrast to the little six-room cottage for sale around the corner on Lemon. Reflecting the wealth and social status of its prominent owners, the much more expensive and elegant Van de Grift home featured "a spacious entrance hall with leaded glass windows and a beautiful staircase. The parlor and large dining room had almost floor-to-ceiling windows with curved tops and fine woodwork. In the front yard a round fountain had two cupids holding up the water spout." Just inside their big front door, the approach to the Van de Grifts' sweeping front staircase looked remarkably like the entrance hall to the Cameron family's colonnaded southern mansion in D. W. Griffith's *The Birth of a Nation*.[1]

Mr. Van de Grift's family had lived in America since the seventeenth century. Some of his paternal ancestors fought in the Revolutionary War with General Washington. Others helped develop early settlements in Pennsylvania. Compared to some long-established American families, many of whom had little or no acknowledged contact with people of color, some in the extended Van de Grift clan seemed quite comfortable living happily among them. Although Jake had become a successful but rather straitlaced businessman and real estate investor in Riverside, others in his immediate family had been known for their unconventional habits and associations. As a young man, Jake's lumberman father once defended a group of pacifist Quakers in a Philadelphia fistfight. Jake's sister described their father as having a "hasty temper but a generous heart, and while his hand was always open to the poor and unhappy, it was a closed fist ready to strike straight from the shoulder to resent an insult or defend the oppressed."

In frontier Indiana in the early 1840s, Jake's mother had been baptized a Presbyterian in the waters of the White River by abolitionist social reformer and clergyman Henry Ward Beecher. Beecher's church stood next door to the Van de Grift home in Indianapolis, and Jake's father and Beecher were described as "great friends." Years later, two of Jacob Van de Grift's five sisters became well-known as relatively freethinking women in the West. Youngest sister Nellie Van de Grift Sanchez, an accomplished California historian and writer, spoke Spanish and married into an old Latino family in Monterey. Oldest sister Frances, nicknamed Fanny, had divorced her first husband after falling in love with a man ten years younger when studying art in France. Sister Fanny smoked cigarettes, wore "exotic clothes," went without shoes at times, and learned to shoot a pistol with some accuracy. As younger brother Jake was establishing himself and settling down in Riverside in the 1880s, sister Fanny left the conventions of the United States far behind, sailing off to the South Pacific with her new younger love, Scottish adventurer and novelist Robert Louis Stevenson, who had by then become her second husband.[2]

Perhaps inspired by their independent accomplishments as modern women, Jake and his wife, Clara, had named their first daughter Nellie Frances in honor of Jake's two adventurous sisters. Despite the fact that Mr. Van de Grift's sisters had spent some of their happiest days among California Latinos and Pacific Islanders and brother Jake had once employed a Japanese house servant in his own home, after living in the big house on Orange Street for nearly twenty years Jake's concern for the value of his property investments far outweighed his compassion for people of color. As the years went by, Mr. Van de Grift's business enterprises and responsibilities with the Riverside Real Estate Board had apparently led him to approach his own life much more conservatively than Fanny and Nellie did.

Like many white Americans of their day, many of Riverside's residents held the notion that people with faces of color had no place in their neighborhoods unless they were delivering furniture, scrubbing floors, or providing other menial services for the people who could afford to hire them. And as long as the little cottages and bungalows scattered among the more stately homes of the Van de Grifts and the Farrs were owned or occupied only by white people, there would likely be no trouble on their side of town.

Several times Jukichi Harada had asked property broker Van de Grift for help finding a new home in a good neighborhood but Mr. Van de Grift never replied. Perhaps he knew Mr. Harada was looking for a house where few would want him to live. Giving up on Mr. Van de Grift but still anxious to find a home for his children near their church and school, Jukichi began checking real estate listings in the daily newspaper by late 1915. When he noticed property agent Frank C. Noble's advertisement for the freshly painted six-room house for sale on Lemon Street, Harada made owner Fulton Gunnerson what he believed was a reasonable offer. Although Mr. Gunnerson was at first unwilling to sell his investment property on Lemon Street to Mr. Harada because he was Japanese, after a discussion with agent Noble, seller Gunnerson and buyer Harada finally agreed on a price of $1,500. Fulton and Hannah Gunnerson had owned the house on Lemon for just two or three months and a quick sale to Harada at the agreed-upon price would mean a healthy profit over the $1,150 they had recently paid for the property.

With the price settled and their casual discussion completed, the trio formalized the deal. They met at the First National Bank, where Harada provided the funds for purchase. He asked bank cashier Myron Millice to issue a cashier's check for $1,500 to Gunnerson. The three men then walked back to Noble's office to prepare the deed. Noble described the transaction: "Mr. Gunnerson asked me if I would make the deed and I said yes, and I turned to Mr. Harada and says, 'whom do you want the deed made to,' and he told me these three children's names [Mine, Sumi, and Yoshizo]." Noble asked Harada about his children's citizenship but did not mention the Alien Land Law. Jukichi was aware of the restrictions imposed by the law and, knowing his three children born in Riverside were American citizens, did not ask to have the name of his first son, Japanese-born Masa Atsu, added to the deed.[3]

Mr. Harada also knew that, as a non-citizen immigrant from Japan, he could not legally own real estate in California because of the Alien Land Law. Perhaps thinking ahead, Jukichi had already quietly tested the restrictions of the new law when just a few months before the purchase of the house on Lemon Street, he bought a small lot on the east side of town from Kikugiru Watari and recorded it in the name of his American-born daughter Mine. It is not known whether Harada was intentionally testing the Alien Land Law by recording the eastside lot in the name of his oldest citizen child, but an absence of any objection from local authorities at the time of the sale must have suggested to him that this method of purchasing property was acceptable. As daughter Mine later recalled, when her father bought the lot from Watari, objections were never raised, likely because Harada was buying real estate on Fourteenth Street beyond the railroad and among African Americans, Mexicans, and other Japanese in a less affluent section of the city: "Papa bought it from another Japanese family that was moving away. Papa's friend was an alien, but had to sell to citizen. No one bothered or hollered because it was across the tracks," Mine said.[4]

Whether or not he was intentionally testing California's new law, Jukichi did know the only real chance for him to provide a safe and permanent home for his children rested in the rights of the three American citizens in the Harada family.

As he later said, "I buy it for the children. I can't buy it. It against the Alien Land Law, everybody know that. My children is already sick in the rooming house. I lost a good boy." When Jukichi was asked if he ever intended to regain ownership of the house from his children, thinking once more of son Tadao's untimely death, he answered emphatically: "Never; if one die two take it; another one die, give it to the other one. I never mind to get anything back." Pressed to answer whether he knew at that time his children were American citizens because they were born in the United States, Harada simply answered, "Yes."[5]

When the deed to his family's new home was completed, Harada took it in hand, walking two blocks south to the Riverside County Courthouse, where he gave it to the office of Isaac S. Logan, the county recorder. The deed was filed by Logan's office on December 15, but uncertainty in the recorder's office over the apparent purchase of property by a Japanese alien caused the deed to be withdrawn on the same day, when Jules Covey, Logan's courthouse deputy, wrote "withdrawn by consent of filer" in red ink on the line of original entry. Unsure about the sale, County Recorder Logan later said that he called naturalization agent W. T. Jones, a US immigration officer in Los Angeles, asking for an opinion about the propriety of recording a real estate deed filed by a non-citizen. Logan said Jones told him to record the deed. So on Wednesday, December 22, 1915, the newly painted and papered six-room cottage at 356 Lemon Street next door to Mrs. Cynthia Robinson was officially recorded at the courthouse as belonging to nine-year-old Mine, five-year-old Sumi, and three-year-old Yoshizo Harada.[6]

Soon after the children's father left Isaac Logan's office, an acquaintance told real estate agent Frank Noble that "this business was liable to get [Noble and Gunnerson] into trouble." With this warning, Noble wisely composed a brief letter to California attorney general Ulysses S. Webb in which he asked, "Can a Jap boy or girl born here in California acquire and hold real estate?" In his reply to Noble, Webb apparently put to rest the questions raised by those concerned with the restrictions of the Alien Land Law: "In reply Section 1 of the 14th Amendment of the Federal Constitution provides, 'all persons born or naturalized in the United States and subject to the jurisdiction thereof are citizens of the United States and of the state wherein they reside.' And any citizen of the United States and of this State may acquire and hold real estate in California. Very Truly yours, U. S. Webb, Attorney General." With Webb's prompt and straightforward reply, both Noble and Harada must have believed they had not violated the Alien Land Law and were not in trouble with the authorities. But some of Harada's new neighbors had other ideas in mind.[7]

A few days before the real estate purchase was completed, Frank Noble and Jukichi Harada had paid a visit to the small cottage at 342 Lemon Street, chatting with its sole occupant, widow Cynthia Robinson. When the property sale went through, Mrs. Robinson would become the Haradas' next-door neighbor. In her early seventies and living alone in her Lemon Street cottage since her husband's death the previous year, Mrs. Robinson was later remembered by the impressionable Harada girls as somewhat frightening because she normally wore her gray hair pulled back tightly in a bun in a way that reminded them of a storybook witch. Mrs. Robinson said Frank Noble asked "if I had any objections to a Japanese buying the place next to me and living there." During their earliest conversation Mrs. Robinson offered no strong reply to Noble and Harada; however, within moments of their departure she quickly spread the alarming news that a Japanese family was coming to live on Lemon Street. One of the first people to hear the story was neighbor Jacob Van de Grift, the real estate investor who had ignored Harada's inquiries. Stepping off the wide front porch of his stylish Victorian home just around the block, Mr. Van de Grift soon joined Mrs. Robinson and a few other nearby neighbors to see what they could do to stop the sale.

For Jacob Van de Grift, it was acceptable to have a Japanese man living in his home as a servant, but he did not want the Japanese man from the Washington Restaurant, or probably any other, buying a house just around the block. If people like Mr. Harada wanted to buy a house, Mr. Van de Grift and others on the real estate board believed, it would be better for them to live in places like the neighborhood on the east side of town beyond the railroad tracks.[8]

In just a day or two more, Mrs. Robinson, Van de Grift, and several other concerned neighbors agreed to form a citizens' committee to stop the Lemon Street sale. Two days before Christmas, the local paper explained the motivations of the group: "[T]he presence of a Japanese family in the neighborhood will lower property values there. It is said they fear if one sale is made to a Japanese family in the neighborhood, similar sales will follow until the whole east side of Lemon Street between Third and Fourth will come into the possession of the Japanese." It, however, did not matter to anyone that the other side of Lemon Street was already inhabited by naturalized Canadians and a sprinkling of children and grandchildren of Germans.[9]

When Jacob Van de Grift and some of his worried neighbors were finally ready to approach Mr. Harada a few days later, seven families were represented by the citizens' committee. At age sixty-seven, committee spokesman Van de Grift was the oldest male in the group. He was joined by Lemon Street widow Cynthia Robinson, age seventy-one; livestock dealer William Farr, sixty and owner of the fancy two-story house with the palm tree and carriage block on the corner of Lemon and Third; Farr's next-door neighbor, orchardist A. George Urquhart, sixty-one, himself a naturalized US citizen born in Canada with family roots in Scotland; and John G. Hansler, vice president of the Ark Housefurnishing Company, whose house with the high-pitched roof was across the street and down a few doors toward town from Mrs. Robinson. At age fifty, Mr. Hansler was the youngest man in the group but still a decade older than Jukichi Harada. Cora Fletcher, Hansler's forty-five-year-old neighbor living next door to him in an older and rather small house with a central brick chimney poking out of a wood-shingled roof on the corner of Lemon and Fourth, and a Mr. Fritz, perhaps carpenter Israel Fritz, age sixty-four, who lived around the corner on Fourth Street, completed the committee's membership.

Headed by Van de Grift, the only member of the group acquainted with Harada, the committee went downtown to the Washington Restaurant. Not finding Harada there, they walked across the street to the Haradas' rooming house. In the hallway at the head of the stairs the neighbors confronted Jukichi, asking him about his intention to buy the house on Lemon Street. They made it clear that they did not want his family to move five blocks north into the heart of Riverside's downtown residential district. The group complained that if Harada moved into the area, property values would drop. "We told him that we did not care to have him on that street, it would depreciate our property," Cora Fletcher explained. They also urged Harada to delay recording the deed and, as Fletcher added, asked if he would accept "a bonus for what he had spent on the place." The committee then proposed a plan to stop Harada from completing the sale. Neighbor William Farr explained:

> Our purpose in going there . . . was to talk to Mr. Harada and see if we could not make some deal with him to get him to give up that property there which he had bought, and to move to some other part of town.
> We offered to buy back the property of him and give him a little profit on it, and get him a lot over on the east side, and he said he didn't care to go over in that part of town, because he had bought this property because it was in a good neighborhood and he wanted his family to live there among good neighbors, and said if he wanted to live on the east side he had a lot already that he could move onto, but he could not do any business with us.[10]

Hearing the confrontation, Ken Harada, her next baby due in four months, joined her husband and the neighborhood group standing in the crowded hallway. Committee members understood that Mrs. Harada was concerned about moving her children into a hostile neighborhood and did not want her family to live where it was not welcomed. Cynthia Robinson recalled: "Mrs. Harada came and she said, 'I don't want to go where I ain't wanted. My money paid for this.'" Jukichi insisted he bought the house to provide better living conditions for the couple's children, telling his neighbors he had no intention of giving up the property. He directed the committee to contact real estate agent Noble or Myron Millice, the cashier at the First National Bank. Avoiding Noble, some in the anxious group soon met with bank cashier Millice. They urged him to call Harada to ask for a delay in recording the deed. After meeting with Millice at the bank, Jacob Van de Grift and George Urquhart went back once more to see Harada. They offered Jukichi $1,800 for the house on Lemon Street, $300 more than the price Harada had negotiated with Noble and Gunnerson. Van de Grift said Harada accepted their offer and gave the citizens' committee several days to raise the money. Harada, however, insisted he never agreed to sell.[11]

Shortly after Urquhart and Van de Grift thought that Harada had accepted their offer, Mr. Urquhart visited Harada once again, urging him for a second time to delay recording the deed. Urquhart also asked Harada to join him in his automobile for the short ride to the recorder's office at the Main Street courthouse, but Harada walked. According to Harada, Urquhart and Van de Grift told him they were going to the courthouse to "fix the recorder." Recalling his activities with the two men, Harada said, "I didn't know what the idea was, but I went there." The courthouse was just a short walk south down the alley from the Washington Restaurant. With Harada standing nearby, Urquhart and Van de Grift asked County Recorder Logan to postpone recording the deed. Confronted at the courthouse office with their latest tactic to delay the sale, an increasingly recalcitrant Harada opposed the delay, telling Logan, "Go ahead and record, rush." With pressure mounting from the neighborhood committee, Mr. Harada became more committed to moving his family into the well-to-do white neighborhood, and even with continuing opposition, he was not about to give up his family's new house on Lemon Street. Upping the ante, Van de Grift increased his offer to $2,000, but Harada still refused to sell.[12]

As word of Harada's refusal spread through Riverside, reaction was mixed. Mr. Sawahata, a Japanese gardener at the Mission Inn, told him to "give up" and not pursue the purchase of the Lemon Street house. Because membership in Issei community organizations was based primarily on Japanese prefectural origins, Jukichi felt isolated from his countrymen in Riverside because most Japanese in the Golden State were not from his home prefecture of Aichi-ken. Most in Riverside's Japanese community had come to the United States from Wakayama and Fukuoka prefectures. As Jukichi's daughter Mine observed, "Very few Aichi people are in California. That's why . . . he said he had a hard time getting people to support him because he was from a different prefecture."[13]

In marked contrast to the protests voiced by the members of the neighborhood committee and growing numbers of their supporters in town, another non-Japanese faction began to take an active, albeit relatively quiet interest in assisting the Harada family. In the ten years that Jukichi Harada had lived and worked in Riverside's central commercial district, like his mentor, Ulysses S. Kaneko, he had become acquainted with influential members of the city's white community, many of whom had their businesses or offices close to the Washington Restaurant. As Mine explained, Harada soon received moral support and a rather astonishing offer from one of the town's most prominent and influential white citizens:

> Were it not for his staunch Caucasian American friends, who gave him moral encouragement, my father would have been afraid to go it alone. My father met

with Frank Miller, who referred him to his brother Ed Miller. He went to see him and Mr. Miller . . . said, "If you have any trouble, I'll get my brother to help you." And then Ed Miller told my father, "Well, if they try and take the land away from you, I'll buy it and then you can always stay there."[14]

It was at this time, as historian Tom Patterson observed, that Riverside reached "the peak of its image as a city of grace and high average wealth." Its political leadership, dominated by influential citrus growers, was fairly evenly divided between conservative and progressive Republican factions. Patterson also explained that "discontent was expressed in politics, although it appears that political changes did not run deep enough to alter the conditions of any large group in a basic way." At times, though, the division among the Republicans was strong enough to elicit varying degrees of support or opposition to selected political issues. Perhaps because of Frank Miller's interest and the growing support from a few other prominent people in town, opinions within the Riverside community about what some viewed as Harada's bold and unacceptable decision to move his family to Lemon Street soon began to crystallize. Frank Miller, for years affiliated with the Southern Pacific Railroad and the conservative wing of the Republican Party, was the town's acknowledged social and political leader. Gaining on Miller's strength since the election of liberal Republican governor Hiram Johnson, in 1910 were Riverside's progressives, who included former state assemblyman and senator attorney Miguel Estudillo, an ardent supporter of Hiram Johnson, and Dr. E. P. Clarke, editor of the *Riverside Daily Press* and "one of the leaders of the reform movement in California Republicanism."[15]

At the time Jukichi Harada spotted Frank Noble's advertisement for the Lemon Street house in Dr. Clarke's newspaper, Riverside's two Republican factions were vying for position in the upcoming elections of 1916. Representing the interests of the progressives, Miguel Estudillo had been chosen as the Riverside delegate to the Republican National Convention, which would meet in June in Chicago. Earlier in the year, he mentioned to a political ally that Frank Miller's more conservative group was, predictably, solidly opposed to progressive governor Johnson in his ultimately successful bid for a seat in the United States Senate. In most statewide political matters little love was lost between Frank Miller and Miguel Estudillo. Miguel complained to a friend at the end of February: "Frank Miller and the rest of that gang of course have no use for any man who feels friendly towards Governor Johnson. The whole gang was ready this year to do politics with me, if only I would agree to throw down Governor Johnson and his friends here."[16]

Frank Miller might have been fairly open about his disdain for Hiram Johnson and the progressives. On the other hand, like other men of prominence and strong convictions that live in one community for a lifetime, the Master of the Inn often exercised his influence less obviously through a third party. Miller was

7.1. Edward Miller, circa 1920. (Courtesy of the Harada Family Archival Collection, Riverside Metropolitan Museum, Riverside, California)

his city's most visible dreamer and civic booster, comfortably heading the table at Mission Inn banquets and frequently involved in key community events, hosting some of the most well-known personalities of the day. Despite such public visibility, however, Miller was also quite used to the idea of influencing some local affairs behind the scenes. As Henry Coil, onetime president of the Riverside Planning Commission and a civil acquaintance of Miller, recalled, "You would see his hand, but you didn't see him."[17]

By the 1920s, Miller was routinely assisted by his political aide-de-camp, Mike Westerfield, "a Riverside printer whose wife was a sister of Mrs. Ed Miller." Seven years younger than his more successful brother, Edward Miller "worked all his life" at the Mission Inn, starting out by driving the Glenwood's horse-drawn passenger coach and meeting hotel guests at the closest train station in nearby Colton. Remembered by many as "good-looking and jovial," in the early days Ed also commanded Riverside's hearse in slow trips over to San Bernardino before Riverside had a mortuary. Perhaps developing his youthful sense of humor and perspective on life during his otherwise somber journeys with the hearse and its silent passengers, Ed proposed marriage on one of his trips to San Bernardino to his future wife, Emma Havens, a lively young Riverside woman who sometimes joined her beau in the driver's seat of the hearse, sitting close to him high above the horses.

While working as proprietor of the horse stables at his brother's Glenwood Hotel, Ed Miller had lived in the 300 block of Lemon Street in the late 1890s, the same neighborhood as the Haradas' new house. He later managed the automobile fleet at the Mission Inn's garage and supported his older brother in other ways, sometimes acting as a third-party aide on brother Frank's behalf instead of brother-in-law Mike Westerfield. When Ed Miller discreetly offered to help the Haradas buy their new house on Lemon Street, he was quite likely supported behind the scenes, both financially and politically, by his more affluent brother. Frank Miller believed in demonstrating cross-cultural harmony and may have even seen some parallels between the Haradas' situation and his own family's early struggles to run a small lodging house in the center of town. In 1915, Frank had money in his pockets. He was in the position to offer financial assistance to the Haradas. Not only was he the town's most influential citizen, but his Mission Inn had enjoyed substantial financial success when the Panama-Pacific International Exposition in San Francisco and the Panama-California Exposition in San Diego flooded the state and Miller's Riverside hotel with well-to-do tourists. Frank even told the town's newspaper publisher that "the Inn made so much money that year that it easily rode through some lean years which followed."[18]

On January 5, 1916, William Randolph Hearst's *Los Angeles Examiner* outlined Riverside's developing Harada case. In "Wholesale Purchase of California Farm Property by Nipponese for Children Predicted," Hearst's newspaper warned that if actions such as Jukichi Harada's were not dealt with swiftly, a wave of similar purchases would soon allow the Japanese to control vast portions of California's agricultural lands. A photograph of the Haradas' new house "Among White Neighbors," the paper said, and another of Harada children Sumi, Yoshizo, and Mine were published on the *Examiner*'s front page. The Los Angeles paper also claimed that Attorney General Webb had answered one inquiry about the case by saying, "Natives of Japan, parents of . . . children born in the United States, have the right to buy property in the names of their minor children born here, such property to be held until their American-born children reach the age of 21 years."[19]

At about the same time, solid in his convictions and undaunted by those who wanted his family evicted from their neighborhood as soon as possible, Jukichi Harada was busy making arrangements to adapt the small Lemon Street cottage to the needs of his growing family. Expecting the birth of their next child in just three more months, Jukichi and Ken decided to repair and enlarge their new house before the family moved in. Harada explained his reasons for improving the thirty-year-old residence: "The foundation not be good. The water go through under the floor, all moisture, no good for living there yet. Must improve." Fulton Gunnerson might have been lucky to find a willing buyer for his house with the sagging foundation and water going "through under the floor," but an optimistic Jukichi was undeterred and signed a contract on January 8 with Riverside builders Herman and Raymond Harp to add a second story to the Haradas' new home.[20]

From his office in San Francisco, Attorney General Webb again wrote to real estate agent Frank Noble and Lemon Street neighbor John Hansler separate letters refuting the claims of the Southern California press reports. Webb insisted that the office of the attorney general had *not* expressed views regarding Japanese aliens purchasing real estate in the names of their citizen children. He also sent copies of his letters to the deputy attorney general in Los Angeles, Robert M. Clarke, a former Superior Court judge from Ventura. The following day in Washington, DC, California's Democratic senator James D. Phelan addressed the National Civic Federation. Phelan claimed the Japanese were "an enemy within our gates," adding that California faced imminent trouble with its Alien Land Law. Back on the West Coast, Hearst's *San Francisco Examiner* was busy beating the anti-Japanese drum and sounding Phelan's alarm over the yellow peril by publishing "Preparedness Essential to U.S. Says Phelan; Japanese Ever-Present Menace to This Coast" on January 10, "Jap Foe Is Now Here Says Phelan" on January 19, and "Phelan Reveals Pacific Peril" three days later. Apparently aware of the growing controversy in Riverside, Senator Phelan wrote to Governor Johnson the following month, asking about the news reports of the purported evasion of the Alien Land Law by the Japanese. Phelan also requested that Johnson determine both the scope and legality of Japanese aliens' placement of the ownership of land in the names of their minor children.[21]

The governor assured Senator Phelan he would have the offices of the labor commissioner and attorney general keep him informed of further developments. Governor Johnson also added that until the arrival of Phelan's letter he was unaware of the rising complications over the Alien Land Law. Later correspondence suggested to Phelan that one Alien Land Law case, filed by the state against Chinese native Gin Fook Bin early in February, had already begun in Santa Barbara County. Phelan responded by expressing his concern over the "evasion of the spirit of the law," adding, "I trust the action brought in Santa Barbara County will put an end to the attempt to acquire land which certainly is against public policy and may also lead to serious domestic trouble, as well as possible war-like action on the part of our bellicose neighbor. The inner circles regard the Japanese question very seriously, and we must be alert to meet the dangers as they arise—diplomatically, yet firmly."[22]

With pressure mounting over his earlier statements, Attorney General Webb composed a ten-page letter to attorneys in Santa Barbara in answer to a question about guardianships for California-born children of Japanese nationals. He said that although it was not generally the responsibility of the attorney general to provide legal advice beyond the offices of certain state officials and district attorneys, he would comment unofficially on the widely discussed issue of Japanese landownership in California. Webb outlined the law as it applied to the rights of American citizens by quoting passages from the federal and state constitutions and applicable legal judgments. He discussed the rights of states to control landownership by non-citizens, saying alien landownership in the United States could be regulated by federal treaties. Section 5 of California's 1913 Alien Land Law was introduced to explain that violations of the law would result in forfeiture of the property to the state.

7.2. Miguel Estudillo, circa 1912. Elmer Wallace Holmes, *History of Riverside County, California with Biographical Sketches,* 1912. (Courtesy of the Riverside Metropolitan Museum, Riverside, California)

The attorney general said if an adult alien provided funds for the purchase of real property in the name of a citizen child and if it could be shown the purchase was not in good faith—that is, the purchase was intended specifically to violate the restrictions of the Alien Land Law—the property would escheat and the state would become its lawful owner. He concluded by saying, however, that land could be purchased and owned legally by children born in California to Japanese aliens so long as neither parent was an employee of the Japanese government at the time of the child's birth. The attorney general qualified his remarks by explaining any such purchase must be made in good faith, with the child's own funds, and not as a circumvention of the Alien Land Law.[23]

Webb's unofficial, although accurate, interpretation of California law revealed the giant loophole in the Alien Land Law of 1913. Until a more stringent measure could be passed, if challenged in court the 1913 law would most likely prove ineffective in preventing the purchase of California real estate by ineligible aliens acting in good faith on behalf of citizen children. In spite of Webb's explanation, it did not take long for lawsuits claiming violations of the 1913 law to be filed against Japanese aliens and their citizen children as some people in California expressed their growing displeasure with Americans of Japanese ancestry who had enjoyed some measure of success.

In Riverside, Frank Noble was "roasted . . . to a deep brown" by the city's real estate association for his involvement in the Harada purchase. Less than a month after Jukichi Harada bought the house on Lemon Street, the Riverside Re-

alty Board adopted "strong resolutions" expressing displeasure with the sale to "emphatically denounce not only this particular transaction, but the practices

7.3. James D. Phelan, circa 1910. (Courtesy of the California History Room, California State Library, Sacramento, California)

generally of certain real estate dealers in placing members of other races in localities heretofore devoted exclusively to members of the Caucasian race." Emphasizing the belief that such practices would lead to the depreciation of property values, the board asserted they were also "unpatriotic" for "arousing unnecessary and deplorable race antagonisms."

When Miguel Estudillo failed in his final attempt to persuade Jukichi Harada to give in to his neighbors' demands to sell his new house for a higher price, he wrote to Attorney General Webb in San Francisco, saying the citizens' committee wanted him to work with the office of the attorney general to file an escheat case against a Japanese who had purchased a house and lot for his children. Miguel suggested that Mr. Harada wanted a test case and asked whether the attorney general would be interested in help from a local attorney. Estudillo waited more than a month for Webb to reply and, hearing nothing from the attorney general, wrote once again, asking if he was interested in pursuing the matter.[24]

On Tuesday, April 11, 1916, two weeks after Estudillo's second letter to Webb, in the family's downtown rooming house Ken Harada gave birth to the Haradas' fourth son, Clark Kohei Harada. Following Japanese custom, Ken carefully preserved a portion of Kohei's umbilical cord, wrapping it in cotton and placing it in a small box, along with those of her other children, stored carefully in a big brown steamer trunk strapped and buckled closed, now ready for the short trip to the family's new home on Lemon Street. The baby's birthday was reported by his father to the office of Japanese consul Ujiro Oyama in Los Angeles on April 21. A listing of his birth in the Japanese calendar year Taisho 5 was later added to the family's prefectural records in Aichi, Japan. With Clark's safe arrival and the family's commitment to live in the secure surroundings of a new home in a nice neighborhood, the Haradas excitedly began packing their belongings for their move to Lemon Street.

Most of the family's possessions consisted of secondhand furniture accumulated a piece or two at a time in the years Jukichi and Ken rented rooms for "25 Cents per Day and Up" to their Eighth Street rooming-house tenants. But daughter Mine remembered her parents taking some of their hard-earned money to purchase a brand new Arts and Crafts mission oak living room set just before the family moved in. "They bought . . . the living room . . . furniture new . . . before we moved. I remember that. Because we were told to be very careful with it. But . . . the rest of the furniture, . . . I think, was all stuff that we had when we were living in the rooming houses," Mine said.

Wooden dressers with large mirrors, ornate iron bed frames with open springs, cotton mattresses and bedding, boxes of kitchen utensils and pots and pans, wooden tables both large and small, a Victorian sideboard for the dining room, chairs, books, toys, clothing, and other personal household effects, including a few carefully guarded things like the hand-dyed indigo blue kimonos bearing memories of home in Japan, were soon organized, packed, and carried down the narrow staircase. After ten years of struggling in California, the Haradas were finally on their way to a home of their own, a place the *Los Angeles Times* later described as "a fashionable home in Riverside."[25]

In addition to the purchase price, Jukichi and Ken Harada spent just over $1,000 to improve their new house. With its new brick and concrete foundation and a second story with electric lights, sturdy oak floor, new bedrooms, and a second bathroom, the new upstairs walls all hand-finished with smooth Victor Patent plaster, their freshly painted gray house with the white trim and the little barn and yard in the back must have made the Haradas proud. Second daughter Sumi recalled: "We thought it was wonderful . . . You've never lived in a rooming house . . . It's just a bedroom and a little kitchen where you ate. And not many places to play except if we'd gone to the park or gone outside and walked around. But here, we had that whole back yard to play in."[26]

Compared to the stuffy downtown rooming houses where they had lived for more than a decade, the remodeled house with its simple Craftsman elements, warm breezes of fresh air, and open front porches upstairs and down provided a very different setting for the Haradas' family life. The house on Lemon Street offered a safe place for baby Kohei and welcoming outdoor spaces for the rest of the family to enjoy. Things they never had in the rooming house—a fenced yard for the kids and a family dog; a big front porch with wooden *shoyu* tubs planted with green asparagus ferns, ti plants, and even a small palm tree; and other plants in flowerpots arranged more randomly on old red bricks in shady corners of the garden—were soon added to the Haradas' new house. With any luck, a bountiful peach tree in back, an electric radio for the parlor, and a used Model T Ford touring sedan in the driveway might also come in time.

Behind the house was room for a small chicken coop and flowers like irises, roses, violets, cannas, geraniums, deep blue morning glories climbing the fence, along with a few edible Japanese plants in small beds beneath the sheltering branches of an abundant backyard apricot tree, all contributing to fond childhood memories that would last forever. As Sumi told me, "We never knew what it was to see fruit on a tree. And there was an apricot tree in the back, and I remember we ate so much that . . . we suffered from diarrhea the next two or three days and my mother said not to eat so much fruit at one time. No, I still remember . . . But, you know, you wouldn't call us real citified people, but we never knew what a tree was, to have fruit on it."[27]

With still no word from the attorney general, Miguel Estudillo and the neighborhood committee began to question Webb's interest in pursuing their proposed lawsuit against the Haradas. By midsummer, further pressure from members of the Riverside community led Estudillo to reestablish communication with Attorney General Webb. Estudillo told Webb that the members of the neighborhood committee were still very interested in the escheat action. He also asked the attorney general to confirm the earlier offer to associate Estudillo with the case. The Riverside attorney agreed to handle the suit for only $300 to cover his personal expenses.

By September, Webb had authorized his deputy in Los Angeles, Robert M. Clarke, and Riverside's Miguel Estudillo to "commence the action" against the Haradas. Clarke told Estudillo no legal precedents had been set regarding the Alien Land Law and the pair would be, in his view, "blazing a new trail." The state's first information and complaint was filed in Riverside Superior Court on October 5, 1916. Local papers carried news of the lawsuit and predicted the case would have "far-reaching" importance and possible "international complications." Once the State of California filed its papers at the Riverside County Courthouse, it did not take long for interest in the Haradas' new house on Lemon Street to expand well beyond the city limits.[28]

EIGHT

WORLD WAR AND
A BASKET OF APPLES

Word of the coming court test of California's Alien Land Law soon spread throughout the state. On the East Coast, details of the case were published in a brief front-page article in the *New York Times* on Friday, October 6. Other similar reports of the lawsuit were appearing in hometown papers across the country. In the nation's capital *The Washington Post* also published an article about the anti-Japanese litigation pending against the Harada family in California. Surrounded by nosy reporters seeking information about his character and background by speaking with his new neighbors and others in town who knew little about him and photographers taking pictures of his new house and his citizen children, Ju-kichi Harada was bothered that most of the newspaper stories and even some official court documents frequently misspelled his name. Before long the prideful former schoolteacher telephoned attorney Estudillo to set the record straight. "By the way, Harada called me up," Estudillo told Deputy Attorney General Clarke, "he claims that we have not spelled his name right, and wants it corrected."[1]

The following Saturday, in "Jap Government Stirred over Harada Case," the *Riverside Enterprise* claimed the government of Japan planned to hire a lawyer for Harada. Even Miguel Estudillo had predicted that, although Harada had been dealing with the local law firm of McFarland and Irving, "the Japanese Counsel [*sic*] of Los Angeles will get 'bigger guns' to really fight the case." Harada's attorney,

Chauncey McFarland, told Estudillo that Japanese consul Oyama was asking for a thirty-day extension to prepare for an appearance in the case. "They claim that a copy of our complaint has been forwarded to the Japanese government, and also to the Japanese Ambassador at Washington," Estudillo said.[2]

At the end of the month, Harry Carr of the *Los Angeles Times*, a popular newspaperman, sometime motion picture actor, Hollywood screenwriter, and sympathetic acquaintance of Miguel Estudillo, recapped the early developments of the *Harada* case. In his Sunday *Times* article "Japan vs. America in a Riverside Suit," Carr described Jukichi Harada as "a bashful, quiet little Jap who has lived in Riverside ten or twelve years and has raised his family there." Explaining that Harada "bought a house so his children would have a healthful place to live," Carr included comments from Jukichi explaining his motivations for buying the house on Lemon Street. Carr quoted Harada: "I have lived in America now a long time. My heart is American. All my sympathies are American. I think American, but the law will not let me become an American . . . We do not mean to do harm to anyone, but I think we have the right to place our children in the proper surroundings, where they will not be sick." Carr also observed that if Harada were to win his case, "the whole force and effect of the alien land law will have been destroyed." Some readers of the *Times* were no doubt even more alarmed to read Carr's claim intimating a connection between this case and war with Japan:

> With a new and warlike premier in the saddle in Japan; with the Japanese freely admitting their touchiness concerning the American discriminations against them, it goes without saying that the decision in this suit will be watched anxiously not only in the State departments of the two nations, but by the diplomats of other countries who are alarmed over the ruffled state of the Orient. It will perhaps be watched with special interest in Canada, where a regiment was recently sent to the front with this toast. "Here's to the two yellow races—Japan and the United States! May they soon be at war."

Besides his incendiary suggestion that the Riverside case could somehow lead to war, Carr also implied Jukichi Harada had not understood the ramifications of his actions in relation to the aspirations of other Nikkei families in the Golden State. He said that a Los Angeles Japanese newspaper claimed Harada "would have served the Japanese residents of California to much better advantage if he had . . . purchased property in some other locality." The day before his article was published in Los Angeles, Carr expressed his confidence in the abilities of Riverside attorney Miguel Estudillo, telling him, "I always enjoy the little visits in your office. It seems to me that this Harada suit is likely to develop into a very famous case and I am glad it is in such good hands."[3]

As the attention paid to the *Harada* case continued to grow, the prestigious Riverside law firm of William A. Purington and A. Aird Adair replaced McFarland and Irving as Harada's representation. New Hampshire native and Yale-educated William Ansel Purington, his father a Universalist minister who had served as a chaplain in the Union army during the Civil War, came to Riverside in the late 1880s as a lawyer from Chicago. Purington had an earlier career working as a schoolteacher and high school principal in Illinois and Minnesota. Purington's wife, Eva, a member of the Daughters of the American Revolution and, like her husband, from an old established family in the East, was active with the First Congregational Church and its Japanese Mission. The prominent Riverside couple lived in the big corner house facing Orange Street just a block west on Third, right around the corner from the Haradas' new house on Lemon. Joined by Frank Miller, another well-known member of their church, the Puringtons now played a more public role supporting Jukichi Harada in his move to Lemon Street. Miller's and the Puringtons' open support demonstrated that important people in town were not only interested in helping their Japanese neighbors stay in their new house but were also willing to live next door to them.[4]

A year had passed since Frank Noble had listed the little Lemon Street house for sale in the local newspaper. On Monday, December 4, 1916, despite repeated requests from attorney Estudillo to delay the court proceedings, Harada's new lawyers succeeded in having Superior Court judge Hugh H. Craig hold the first hearing in the case. The following day, stirring an unsettling memory from those dramatic images in *The Birth of a Nation*, the *Los Angeles Times* described the curious mixture of anxious onlookers attending the hearing in Judge Craig's Riverside courtroom: "More than half the spectators was composed of a quiet company of little brown men, whose eyes never left the judge and the lawyers arguing the case. The remainder of the audience was plentifully sprinkled with white women, residing in the district where Harada . . . purchased a house for his three minor children." Deputy Attorney General Clarke was traveling back east on business in Washington, DC, and was unable to appear on behalf of the state. Soon after the hearing, Miguel Estudillo expressed his concern about the speed with which the case was beginning to move. He told the office of the attorney general that, on short notice, he decided to argue the case alone because he was unwilling to let it drop by default.

The issue at hand was the 1911 treaty between Japan and the United States. Purington and Adair noted the authority of federal treaties over state laws, charging that the Alien Land Law was in conflict with the 1911 treaty. They also claimed the treaty allowed residential landownership by Japanese citizens living in the United States. According to Estudillo, Harada's attorneys argued that if the treaty allowed Japanese nationals to own and lease *houses* in the United States, the opportunity for them also to own land was, therefore, implied. They claimed the Alien Land Law was written to accommodate the content of the treaty of 1911 and it had thus acknowledged the landownership rights of the Japanese residents of California.[5]

During the hearing, Estudillo was annoyed that attorney for the Los Angeles Japanese Association Louis B. Stanton, a former resident of Riverside attending the hearing with Japanese consul Ujiro Oyama from Los Angeles, had taken pains to spread the assertion that Attorney General Webb was not interested in pressing the *Harada* case. Stanton claimed it was only Clarke and Estudillo who were "kicking up a muss." Estudillo "branded . . . the report as false." When Clarke returned from Washington, the deputy attorney general telephoned Stanton, confronting him with Estudillo's complaint and challenging the veracity of his comments about Webb's lack of interest in the case. Stanton told Clarke his remarks at the hearing were "based entirely on rumor." If Louis Stanton and the Japanese Association were trying to coax some sort of commitment from the office of the attorney general regarding the *Harada* case, they succeeded. Clarke informed Stanton, "General Webb is very much interested in all of this litigation and will be personally present, as I understand it, at the time the matter is finally tried."[6]

As plaintiff and defendant awaited Judge Craig's decision about the treaty of 1911, another article, published in the Holiday Number of *Sunset*, the West's popular monthly magazine, raised new questions about the impact of the *Harada* case on the Japanese in California. Like many other printed stories about him, the new *Sunset* article misspelled Harada's name. Its picturesque introduction of immigrant "Yukihi" Harada and his Horatio Alger–style rise to success in the Golden State was overshadowed by the ominous title "The Japanese Cloud." The *Harada* case was viewed as a possible catalyst for further anti-Japanese legislation: "Thus the anti-alien land legislation of California will be reopened in all its phases, and it is not improbable that bills will be introduced in the Sacramento legislature to extend the scope of the law."[7]

Three months later Judge Craig returned his initial opinion in the case. Craig reviewed the amended information and complaint and noted two major points made by the counsel for the state. First, the treaty of 1911 did *not* provide for Japanese landownership in the United States; second, Jukichi Harada, an alien ineligible for citizenship, had "acquired an interest in fee" in the property on Lemon Street. By alleging Harada's interest in fee, the state was charging that he was, in fact, the owner of the property even though his name did not appear on the deed. As a result, the state claimed that when Harada bought 356 Lemon Street in the names of his citizen children, the provisions of its Alien Land Law automatically applied and, at the moment Harada accepted the property, the house and land had escheated to the state and did not ever belong to the three Harada children.[8]

Judge Craig upheld the validity of the Alien Land Law, noting it intentionally acknowledged the legal superiority of federal treaties over state statutes. He also added that its provisions did not conflict with federal treaties and stressed that the carefully composed language of a treaty is most often intended to be "free from ambiguity." Addressing the first point made by the plaintiff, that the 1911 treaty did not provide for Japanese landownership, Judge Craig based his decision on the interpretation of a passage in the first section of the treaty, explaining it allowed Japanese subjects the right to reside and carry on business in the United States. He added, however, this did not necessarily include a right of residential ownership. Although the treaty did allow the Japanese the right to "own or lease and occupy houses, manufactories, warehouses and shops," Craig argued it was "not uncommon" to own a structure without owning the land it occupied and stressed further that, in his opinion, the diplomatic language of the treaty did not provide for landownership by citizens of Japan living in the United States.

Regarding the second point in the complaint, that Jukichi Harada had acquired an interest in fee, Craig was quick to emphasize that although the original complaint said Harada had acquired such an interest, the amended information and complaint failed to allege Harada held title to the property at the time the complaint was filed. It also did not claim that Harada's holding title to the Lemon Street house was in violation of the law. As a result, Craig deemed the amended information and complaint deficient and sustained the defendant's demurrer. Thus, the initial confrontation produced a positive judgment for the state. Judge Craig neatly disposed of the concerns over the treaty of 1911 and did not challenge the constitutionality of the Alien Land Law. However, because of his ruling about the amended complaint's deficiencies, Judge Craig left the door wide open for further conclusions in the case.[9]

With this initial victory, it might have been expected that Attorney General Webb would pursue the *Harada* case to a swift conclusion. Only five days after the judge's opinion was issued, Webb expressed his initial satisfaction to his deputy in Los Angeles, but he also ordered that further action against the Haradas be suspended immediately because of dramatic international developments: "I . . . note with pleasure the result of the hearing in that case. For reasons which you and the Court will readily appreciate, I think after you have filed your amended complaint and issue has been enjoined thereon that it would be advisable to drop this case from the calendar . . . There is at present no reason for pressing this suit."[10]

Three days before Webb instructed Clarke to drop the *Harada* case, President Woodrow Wilson had signed a joint congressional resolution declaring war on Germany. The United States had entered the Great War, World War I. In April, Allied shipping losses to the Germans reached an all-time high and a US victory in Europe seemed a distant goal. Even before the United States entered the war as an ally of Japan against Germany, pressure was applied on Californians to minimize all anti-Japanese activity. As early as 1914, former president Theodore Roosevelt helped to convince California governor Hiram Johnson that "our great object should be to avoid anything that may cause serious trouble with Japan, until the

European world-war has come to an end." Roger Daniels observed, "[T]hrough-out the war years, and beyond, responsible leaders in California either exercised restraint or had it thrust upon them." And, as another California attorney general would explain many years later, the lack of emphasis on enforcing the Alien Land Law was a "reflection of the National policy to refrain from acts which might be regarded as unfriendly to the Japanese race and the Japanese empire."[11]

To defer further action in the case against Jukichi Harada was, for California attorney general Ulysses S. Webb in the spring of 1917, the only prudent course of action. Deputy Attorney General Clarke echoed Webb when he expressed to Miguel Estudillo his own concern over "international complications," adding "that following our initial victory our case should not be pressed on for trial at this time." From Los Angeles, Japanese consul Oyama wired Judge Craig in River-side, asking for a copy of the amended information and complaint. Deputy Clarke wrote to Estudillo, stressing it would now be the policy of the attorney general to refrain from urging anti-Japanese legal actions. As Clarke and Estudillo worked to delay the proceedings by moving for an extension of the deadline for the state's complaint amendment, Harada's attorneys seized the opportunity to press the case. Conscious of the attorney general's reluctance, Purington and Adair refused an extension of the state's time for an amendment.[12]

Both sides jockeyed for position as Harada's attorneys tried to place Clarke and Estudillo at a disadvantage. When Judge Craig questioned the plaintiff's complaint regarding the status of the three Harada children listed on the deed, Deputy Attorney General Clarke strategized a course of action to resolve the con-flict caused by their US citizenship. Estudillo was especially concerned that the state would not be able to provide a precedent on which to base the escheat of the Harada property. He began pondering the constitutionality of the approach the state was taking against American citizens. On June 25, 1917, he wrote to Clarke, saying, "I sincerely hope that you have some cases that will help us out . . . for, to be frank with you, the more I study the complaint and the law, the more I am convinced that we are wrong."[13]

Delayed by international developments, the *Harada* case languished in legal maneuverings for the next several months. In the fall, Frank Miller hosted his ban-quet at the Mission Inn for his Japanese neighbors in celebration of the Japanese emperor's birthday. Miller's banquet was held "to give expression of the appre-ciation of the community for the good work done in subscribing for the Liberty loan." Riverside's patriotic Japanese Association reportedly had raised "nearly $5000" to help support the country's war effort. At the banquet's conclusion at-torney Purington discussed the details of the *Harada* court case and predicted en-thusiastically the Haradas' ultimate legal success in the Supreme Court. The *Riv-erside Daily Press* said Purington also made positive comments about "the change in sentiment regarding the Japanese which has taken place in California since the war broke out." For the several weeks prior to Miller's banquet, Secretary of State Robert Lansing was conducting negotiations in Washington with Japanese viscount Kikujiro Ishii. The negotiators were working toward a series of foreign policy statements regarding the future interests of Japan and the United States in the Far East. In its final form the Lansing-Ishii Agreement provided for an American recognition of Japan's interests in China and a Japanese acknowledgment of the integrity of the US Open Door Policy. The *Daily Press* published reports of the growing cordial relationship between the two governments.[14]

Meanwhile, back on Lemon Street, some local residents had made friendly gestures toward the Harada children. The earlier expressions of the neighborhood committee and a few threatening acts against their family had, however, led Jukichi and Ken to interpret overtures toward their children as potentially dangerous. Living among the 300 white folks in the attractive residential area around Orange, Lemon, and Lime, daughter Sumi remembered her parents offering careful instructions about how to behave in their family's new neighborhood. "My father said: 'Don't go beyond the confines of the fence. Stay within your yard.' My mother and father kept saying: 'Don't accept food. If it's given, bring it into the house,' and they would dispose of it. They told us not to screech and yell," Sumi said. Her older sister, Mine, also recalled her earliest challenging days on Lemon Street:

> It was not very pleasant at the beginning to walk [through] the neighborhood. I remember very vividly a kind neighbor who came out and offered me a basket of lovely red apples, which I had to refuse very politely, as we had been warned by our parents that people might try to harm us . . . My mother . . . was fearful of the neighbors because . . . they had tried to keep us from that neighborhood, and she didn't know what they might do to us. And so she was always afraid of . . . us being poisoned by anyone.
>
> So she told me, "Be careful and whatever anybody offers, why just thank them and not take it." And we refused to take it. I remember that vividly because this lady was so kind, you know, and she was very nice. And, afterward, I always felt that she was trying to be friendly. That she wanted to show that there were neighbors that weren't . . . thinking the same way as the others. But . . . even though the apples were so beautiful, I wasn't to take them.[15]

Indeed, other neighbors expressed their opposition to the presence of the Harada family in ways the Harada children would never forget. Mine recalled: "[T]here was a . . . German boy who lived across the street . . . [He] was the one that used to throw rocks at me." Sumi explained that for the family of livestock dealer William Farr, the neighborhood committee member living in the largest and most stately house on the block, a new line in the sand had been drawn straight down the middle of Lemon Street: "I remember one woman came—she lived at the corner house . . . She stood on the curb and she [said]: 'You Japs stay on your side of the street. Don't you ever walk over here.' Even after I grew up, I used to be scared if I walked by that corner."[16]

Although some of the less tolerant residents of Riverside openly challenged the Haradas, others expressed their regard for the family. The *Riverside Enterprise* reported that Jukichi and his family exemplified American middle-class values, observing, "He and his family are members of the Methodist mission of this city and it is a matter of common repute that they are quiet, clean, respectable people. Harada himself, it is admitted, is an honest, thoroughly reliable business man and his rooming house has never been under suspicion."

Supported by a record of solid personal habits, his family's newly adopted Western religious practices, and, to some perhaps, even his own controversial interest in openly demonstrating the benefits of American citizenship, Jukichi Harada was well positioned to win community favor in a relatively tolerant place like Riverside. His use of President George Washington's likeness on his restaurant's sidewalk sign and menus and his decoration of the restaurant's interior walls with portraits of presidents adorned with American flags reinforced his position as a patriot. Jukichi's simple displays of support for the United States celebrated the national symbols of his adopted country, but they were also reminiscent of the former schoolteacher's Japanese heritage, as seen in his Aichi-ken classroom, and classrooms throughout Japan, all of which displayed portraits of the revered emperor. But for those unaware of how closely some of Harada's behaviors reflected his Japanese upbringing and educational training, his fervid Americanism suggested that Mr. Harada was fully embracing the American way of life and should not be considered a threat to his adopted country.[17]

After living in the United States for nearly fifteen years, Jukichi Harada had transformed himself into a Westernized Issei reflection of his most visible downtown neighbor and behind-the-scenes supporter, Japanophile Frank Miller of the Mission Inn. But whereas Harada dressed in a suit and tie for family portraits and attended Christian religious services, Miller sometimes wore fancy Japanese clothing to entertain hotel guests. Miller's efforts to promote world peace and international harmony set the tone for respectable community life, making Riverside more hospitable for the Japanese than many other California communities. The Haradas' solid reputation as "quiet, clean, respectable people," their conversion to Christianity and ongoing involvement in the Japanese Methodist Mission, the prayer meetings at their home on Lemon Street, and social involvement in church activities also helped them foster acceptance by many in the community. Over time, encounters between the Haradas and their less hostile neighbors slowly began to smooth over some of the problems caused by their controversial move to Lemon Street. Delays in court proceedings generated by international events also provided time for the neighbors and the Haradas to adjust to their proximity. Unlike the masked posse of the Ku Klux Klan in *The Birth of a Nation*, vigilantes who might have taken the law into their own hands, the fretful citizens of the neighborhood committee were apparently willing to limit their protest to legal proceedings and let their lawsuit run its course within the California legal system.[18]

Attorney General Webb's concern about pursuing the Harada case had increased proportionately with the cooperation between the United States and Japan during World War I. In December he sent an anxious wire to Estudillo, saying the *Harada* case should be deferred for "reasons of very grave import." Webb advised that the reasons for the deferral, already explained to Estudillo in earlier private communications, should be discussed directly with Judge Craig. Ulysses S. Webb had no desire to jeopardize his political future by pursuing the *Harada* case at such an inopportune time. His latest recommendations were based on his deepening concern over the international situation during the war. The attorney general also assumed Judge Craig would accommodate the state's interest in delaying the case but did not want to go on record with a formal communication to Craig. Webb told Clarke to call Craig and Estudillo on the telephone, saying, "I did not feel at liberty to send a direct wire to Judge Craig; [I] suggest, however, that you call Estudillo and the Judge by phone and more fully cover the situation." Perhaps remembering the gist of Deputy Clarke's telephone call, Miguel Estudillo explained the sensitivities surrounding the *Harada* case many years later: "There was a great tension in political circles at the time the case was filed and before it was tried. It was an open secret that Washington had communicated with Riverside in reference to the danger of the case and possibility that [a] decision in the case might lead to war with Japan."[19]

In early 1918, a year and a half after the Haradas moved to Lemon Street, Robert Clarke entered private practice and resigned his post as deputy attorney general in Los Angeles. Joseph L. Lewinsohn soon assumed the deputy's duties with regard to the *Harada* case. Deputy Attorney General Lewinsohn continued to follow Webb's instructions to delay the proceedings, but Estudillo informed him the case was set for trial at the end of March. Earlier in the year Estudillo attempted to arrange a further continuance with Harada's attorneys but Purington and Adair would not relent. Estudillo was angered by the opposition's refusal to delay the case, declaring that "their desire for a fee quenches the little spark of patriotism that one would expect to find in them. They will not consent to a continuance."[20]

In a private conversation, Estudillo carefully communicated to Judge Craig that Attorney General Webb preferred a continuance. Craig said that he would grant a continuance only if the State Department requested it, suggesting that Washington should be more openly involved in the case. Following the chain of command, Estudillo told Lewinsohn of Craig's conditional acceptance of Webb's desire to delay the trial. The new deputy attorney general contacted Webb to explain Craig's thoughts about how to make the delay happen. Lewinsohn also reported what appeared to be a more sinister twist in the case. He told Webb that Estudillo was claiming Harada was being financed secretly by the Japanese Association and was saying that he had purchased the Lemon Street house with the specific intent of challenging the Alien Land Law. The money for the sale was presumed to have come from a Japanese bank in San Francisco. Estudillo said the information linking Harada to the Yokohama Specie Bank came from an employee of Riverside's First National Bank "whose identity [Estudillo] promised not to disclose." Webb responded quickly that it would be inadvisable to discuss a continuance with the State Department because, he said, "If the department desires a continuance, the reason for such desire is one that with propriety could scarcely be disclosed." Webb's direction to avoid contact with the State Department meant the trial could no longer be postponed.[21]

As the office of the attorney general in San Francisco perhaps considered tracing the suggested connection between Harada and wider Japanese financial interests—although these monies might simply have been wired to Ken Harada as an inheritance from her brother in Japan and not provided secretly by the Japanese Association—an unexpected two-month continuance was granted. According to Estudillo, it was Riverside's long-standing battles over water rights that forced another delay in the case when it was crowded from the court calendar by an upcoming water trial. The *Harada* trial was reset for May 28, 1918. Estudillo warned that they would be unlikely to receive another continuance, adding, "I think the best thing we can do is go to the bat." His eagerness to take the case to trial was overshadowed once again by U. S. Webb's ongoing efforts to drop the case. Despite months of involvement by the attorney general's office and great anticipation in Riverside of the trial, Webb told Lewinsohn if another continuance could not be granted, the *Harada* case should be dismissed. In his most straightforward comments about the impact of the *Harada* case, Webb explained what he saw as a no-win situation in the upcoming trial, telling Lewinsohn,

> A renewed agitation relative to the California Alien Land Law . . . can produce
> no good results—possibly quite the contrary. I am unwilling that the trial of
> this case should be made the vehicle through which the government at this
> time is embarrassed in the slightest degree. The feeling engendered by the pass-
> ing of this statute, and renewed, in part, at the commencement of this action,
> would be most unfortunate if reawakened, and I very much fear that the trial of
> this case would now have that result.[22]

Webb sent an accompanying letter, asking that it be used by Lewinsohn to explain the dismissal to the press. He suggested that the state's original complaint, besides claiming Harada had a deeded interest in the property, should have also stated specifically that he had violated the Alien Land Law and his property had, therefore, escheated to the state. Webb added that the complaint could eventually be changed and refiled later even if a dismissal was granted. In the letter to be used by his deputy in interviews about the status of the Harada case, Webb made no mention of his concerns over the earlier agitation surrounding the enactment of the Alien Land Law or the current international situation. He told Lewinsohn to imply the suit against the Haradas would be dismissed simply because of the inefficiency in "labor and expense" of trying it at the same time as the state's ultimately successful Alien Land Law case against Gin Fook Bin, the Chinese immigrant who had purchased half-interest in a small lot and two-story building in Santa Barbara's Chinatown in 1915.[23]

As lawyers for the state were weighing Webb's new orders for dismissal, back in Riverside Jukichi Harada's well-known attorney, William Purington, died suddenly of heart trouble at his home on Orange Street. Purington's law partner, A. Aird Adair, and Riverside city attorney A. Heber Winder were at Purington's home at the time of his death. On April 19, Purington's obituary in the *Daily Press*, "Death of W. A. Purington Casts Gloom over Entire Community," described him as the "most revered, beloved and brilliant personality in the bar of this county." A review of Purington's many contributions to Riverside emphasized his skillful handling of water rights cases but did not mention his current involvement with the *Harada* case. At the funeral a short time later, Purington's pallbearers included Frank Miller of the Mission Inn. Back on Lemon Street, Jukichi and Ken Harada must have wondered if the loss of their most public advocate would now jeopardize their family's future in California.[24]

With attorney Purington's untimely death, responsibility for the *Harada* case dropped unexpectedly into the lap of his able law-firm associate, Alexander Aird Adair. Aged sixty at the time of his partner's passing, born and educated in Canada, and a Presbyterian "since boyhood," attorney Adair had a personal understanding of some of the issues and feelings involving American citizenship and the rights of aliens because he had once been one himself. Forming a new law practice with City Attorney Winder, Adair assumed Purington's responsibilities with the *Harada* case, and he was soon busy planning his strategy to defend the Haradas in Riverside's Superior Court. Despite the potential for a delay because of Purington's death, the ongoing efforts of Miguel Estudillo and his Riverside clients to pursue the case did not subside. Less than two weeks after Purington died, Deputy Attorney General Lewinsohn wrote a cautiously worded letter to Webb, outlining Estudillo's disagreement with Webb's plan for a dismissal. Lewinsohn said Estudillo was evaluating the situation from a relatively narrow vantage point.[25]

Miguel Estudillo soon traveled to Los Angeles, visiting with the deputy attorney general to discuss the pair's next cautious steps in pursuing the *Harada* case. Lewinsohn showed Estudillo "in confidence" Webb's two letters asking for a dismissal of the case. The following day Estudillo wrote to Webb, claiming that

Riverside rumors were reporting that the attorney general had contacted Harada's attorneys and Louis Stanton of the Los Angeles Japanese Association to say the case would be dismissed. In a last-ditch effort to change Webb's mind, Estudillo pointed out that local interest in the case had not diminished.

A few days later, only a little more than a month after Webb's call for a dismissal, he responded to Estudillo's objections, saying the reasons for his earlier call for a dismissal were no longer sufficient because they were "of much less force than at that time." The attorney general thanked Estudillo for denying the claims he had contacted Harada's attorneys and the Japanese Association, adding, "your denial . . . was absolutely correct." Webb concluded by saying that Harada's attorneys might have pressed the case to force a dismissal and if he had known of such a motive he "would not have contemplated dismissing the action at all." He also said if further postponement could not be negotiated with Judge Craig and Harada's attorneys, Lewinsohn and Estudillo should prepare to take the case to trial as scheduled.[26]

NINE

FACE-TO-FACE

Sitting inside his farmhouse on Chase Road at the northeastern outskirts of River-side, writing in Japanese in a small notebook as he did nearly every day, Issei immi-grant farmer Toranosuke Fujimoto added a brief note to his personal diary. Trans-lated into English, it said: "Harada closed his business today. I went to the court." Fujimoto had purchased his own land in Riverside shortly before the Alien Land Law was passed in 1913. Joining several of his Issei friends heading downtown to the courthouse to await the outcome of the state's lawsuit against Jukichi Harada, like many other young Japanese fathers in California at the time, Fujimoto-san was now deeply concerned about his own future as a landowner and farmer in the Golden State.[1]

By the time Mr. Fujimoto reached Main Street on Tuesday morning, May 28, 1918, now more than two years after Jukichi Harada bought his new house not far from the center of town, the trial of *The People of the State of California v. Jukichi Harada* was finally getting under way at the Riverside County Court-house. As the witnesses for the plaintiff and defendant ascended the wide steps beneath the soaring columns of the town's impressive Beaux Arts Classical-style courthouse, such a stately contrast to Riverside's more parochial Mission Revival civic monuments, the two sides assembled there for a showdown beneath the stained-glass dome of Judge Hugh H. Craig's imposing courtroom. Arranging

9.1. Riverside County Courthouse, Riverside, circa 1920–1925. (Courtesy of the Riverside Metropolitan Museum, Riverside, California)

his papers on the heavy wooden table before Judge Craig, California deputy attorney general Joseph Lewinsohn prepared to question Jukichi Harada, the first to testify. Although some were anticipating a jury to quickly rule against Harada, the jury box sat empty on Tuesday morning. In an earlier action, Judge Craig had denied the state's last-minute request for a jury trial. Craig based his decision on the fact the plaintiff did not request a jury when the trial date was set a few months earlier. With this action Judge Craig shifted the verdict to only one voice, giving himself the final say in the outcome of the case.

As its lone judge, appointed to the bench in 1916 by Governor Hiram Johnson to succeed the late Judge F. E. Densmore, Hugh Henderson Craig had the last word in Riverside Superior Court. A stout and balding, moon-faced but still youthful man, Judge Craig was a former city newspaper reporter and editor from Keokuk, Iowa, who had come to California to practice law in 1908. At forty-three, he was just a year older than defendant Jukichi Harada but shy of Harada's own residency in the Golden State by five years. Without a jury for the Harada trial, making Judge Craig, in effect, the sole juror in the case, he would pay close attention to the courtroom strategies and testimony of all who gathered before him.[2]

The trial began with Jukichi Harada seated in the witness chair. All eyes were on the defendant as morning sunlight highlighted the muted green shades of the leaded-glass dome high above the courtroom. Deputy Attorney General Lewinsohn first asked Harada to recall his purchase of the Lemon Street house

9.2. Judge Hugh H. Craig on the courthouse steps, Riverside, circa 1918. (Courtesy of the Riverside Metropolitan Museum, Riverside, California)

in the winter of 1915. He then presented the state's major contention in the case: "The sole issue of fact here is whether this deed taken in the form that it was taken was simply a cloak or scheme to give semblance of versimilitude [*sic*] to a bold and unconvincing narrative . . . We will show . . . that the property has been treated by the witness as his own," asserted Lewinsohn. Assisted in the courtroom by Riverside attorney Miguel Estudillo, Lewinsohn moved to show that through Harada's financial support, a "resulting trust" or overriding interest in the Lemon Street property had been slyly crafted for his own benefit.[3]

In California, previous cases involving escheat procedures established that it was the state's duty to show cause for an escheat action. Other precedents had been set regarding the purchase of real estate by parents for their children. In the case of *Russ v. Meibus,* judicial findings established the right of a parent to buy land for his or her children. In *Hamilton v. Hubbard* it was decided that if funds were provided by one person for the purchase of real property by another, a resulting trust in the property could be considered "only in transactions between strangers." In other words, if a provider bought real property for a spouse or offspring, it was considered part of a "natural, moral or legal obligation to provide" and would not necessarily lead to a resulting trust in the property. The relatively limited scope of the 1913 law left the state with but one course to follow in the Riverside trial. California's attorneys had to show how Jukichi Harada could be considered the actual owner of 356 Lemon Street or the property could not be regarded as eligible for escheat and confiscation by the state.[4]

Without ever mentioning Harada's purported violation of the Alien Land Law, Lewinsohn moved to show he had acquired ownership even though his name did not appear on the deed. Harada's courtroom attorney, A. Aird Adair, objected to Lewinsohn's claims and tried to find fault with the state's allegations. Judge Craig stressed that he would give the plaintiff a chance to show how Harada could be considered the owner of the property. Craig said the state was making "the bare, naked allegation, that the defendant took the property in fee. That is denied [by the defendant], and that is the issue here."[5]

Deputy Lewinsohn methodically explained the details of Jukichi Harada's interest in the house at 356 Lemon Street, introducing as evidence several checks provided by Dwight Velzy of the Securities Savings Bank. The checks showed that funds for the recent improvements to the house came from a bank account started by Harada for his three citizen children. Additional exhibits included the building contracts between Jukichi and the Harp brothers, the building contractors who added the second-story addition in 1916. As Lewinsohn added a few more examples of Harada's financial involvement with the improvements to the house on Lemon Street, Judge Craig began to question the state's approach. When Lewinsohn presented evidence to show Harada had paid the gas bill, Adair objected and Craig interrupted, commenting, "I would be very much surprised if he had not paid it. I suppose he paid the grocery bills there too." Lewinsohn replied, "I think that is an entirely different matter." Judge Craig retorted, "I don't think so." Estudillo argued the payment of a gas bill meant relatively little standing alone. He said it was only "a link in the chain of circumstances" connected to a larger and more meaningful pattern of proof against defendant Jukichi Harada. Growing weary of Lewinsohn's remarks, somewhat impatiently Craig declared, "It seems to me it goes to prove this man was supporting his family." Ignoring Judge Craig's hints, Lewinsohn asked one more question. "Mr. Harada, during this period you have also been paying the electric light bills, have you not?" Watching Craig closely, Adair objected quickly to Lewinsohn's line of questioning. Craig sustained Adair's objection and set aside the attempt to prove Harada's interest through the payment of gas and electric bills.[6]

Although claims had been made that Harada was being financed by Japanese interests for the purpose of testing the Alien Land Law, potentially a more controversial aspect of the case, no evidence of such a relationship was introduced during the trial. It was, however, probable that Harada or his attorneys received some legal advice from representatives of the Los Angeles Japanese Association and perhaps the Japanese Consulate as the case progressed. Adair later explained that former law partner William Purington's original fee for taking the case to final judgment in superior court was set at $300, the same amount that the neighborhood committee paid Estudillo. Adair said Harada would pay the bill but also mentioned that if the case reached a higher court, it was his understanding that the Japanese Association would contribute money to help meet added costs. Mine Harada Kido remembered: "Our father . . . was . . . very proud of the fact that he had been able to finance it all himself. [Although] the Japanese vernaculars carried the news in detail and the Japanese communities were all concerned, none made any effort to ease the financial burden."[7]

As the Haradas' Lemon Street neighbors appeared one at a time as witnesses for the People of California, Lewinsohn pressed them to remember the details of the original transaction and the subsequent activities of their neighborhood committee. Adair responded by stressing Harada's personal motivations for buying the house so his children could live in a healthier neighborhood close to their church and school. When the witnesses recounted their activities as committee members, some corroborated Harada's claims that he wanted to improve his family's housing situation. Committee member Cora Fletcher added, however, that she was "naturally" opposed to having Japanese neighbors.[8]

Tempers escalated as morning turned to afternoon. When Adair asked witness Cynthia Robinson to express her personal feelings about the Harada family, Miguel Estudillo objected.

> **ADAIR:** He is a very good neighbor?
> **ROBINSON:** They are nice people.
> **ADAIR:** Kindly people?
> **ROBINSON:** Yes.
> **ESTUDILLO:** We object to that as not proper cross-examination.
> **ADAIR:** I don't suppose Mr. Estudillo would like to hear anything good about anybody.
> **ESTUDILLO:** I would like to hear something good about you.

Before Adair and Estudillo could elaborate, Deputy Attorney General Lewinsohn told Judge Craig that the state would rest its case.[9]

Witnesses for the defense were then called to fill in a few details. County recorder Isaac Logan reconstructed his actions, explaining how the deed was filed. Jukichi Harada returned to the stand to review his activities with real estate agent Frank Noble. Harada reiterated his interest in providing a better home for his children. "I buy it for the children . . . To keep the children, play outside on the ground. Get fresh air . . . I give them a present, a Christmas present," Harada insisted. When Adair asked his client if he had purchased the Lemon Street house for himself, Harada explained he paid for the property but he could not own it because of the Alien Land Law. "I can't buy it. It against the Alien Land Law, everybody know that," Harada explained. Jukichi was the first person to raise the issue of the restrictions of the Alien Land Law during the trial. The concern over his implied violation of the law was never introduced directly by the state. Deputy Lewinsohn did not intend to evaluate the applicability of the law. He was simply moving to show how Harada should be viewed as the true owner of the house on Lemon Street. The law would be applied after Harada's ownership was established. With the opening day of the trial completed, an overnight recess was called and court was adjourned late Tuesday afternoon.[10]

Jukichi spent what must have been a restless night back at the house on Lemon Street, wondering what more he could possibly say to defend himself and his family in their efforts to keep their new home. Could Harada have asked himself if he was being too ambitious? Should he have given up as Mission Inn gardener Sawahata had advised? If he lost the case, would his family be forced to move away from Riverside? Would they all have to go back to Japan? If he won, would the neighbors continue to threaten his children? When he left the courthouse Tuesday afternoon, looking west across Main Street from the top of the courthouse steps, Jukichi could plainly see the big wooden cross in the distance high atop Mount Rubidoux. What would his Christian friends at the Methodist Mission want him to do? Perhaps he should just leave it all up to God.

When court reconvened Wednesday morning, Deputy Attorney General Lewinsohn reiterated the state's contention, saying that although "the court . . . may find that the strict, bare, dry legal title was in the children['s names] . . . the substantial interest, the use, the trust . . . is in the father." Lewinsohn urged Judge Craig to consider the facts of the case and ignore what he viewed as legal technicalities. One of the last witnesses called to the stand for the defense was real estate agent Frank Noble. He recalled his role in the events surrounding the sale of 356 Lemon Street, noting Harada's claims that he was interested in providing improved living conditions for his family. Noble also testified about his early correspondence with Attorney General Webb. Using the earliest written reply received by Noble from the attorney general, Harada's attorney smartly added to the record Webb's own quote of the Constitution's Fourteenth Amendment. By noon the defense rested.[11]

After lunch, Judge Craig allowed the case to be submitted for final judgment. The Haradas' future was now in the hands of a white man. Jukichi might have worried silently to himself, wondering if the kind-looking Riverside jurist was like those angry people of the neighborhood committee or some of those other haughty, pink-faced *hakujins* downtown, the white men and women who sometimes came into his restaurant only to walk out abruptly as soon as they observed the color of the faces of its staff and some of the customers. It was true that most of the newspapers and even some of his Issei acquaintances seemed to think he had pushed things too far. Could Judge Craig be of the same mind? During the trial, however, the judge had said that some of the evidence offered by the state had shown Harada was a good man. "It seems to me it goes to prove this man was supporting his family," Judge Craig had said at the trial. That really was all Jukichi was trying to do when he bought the house on Lemon Street; he just wanted to support his family the best way he knew how. He hoped Judge Craig might be more sympathetic, as Mr. Miller or his attorney and Mrs. Purington had already been. Only time would tell.

Throughout the summer of 1918 those involved with the Harada case anxiously awaited the judge's opinion. Finally, in mid-September, to the great relief of the Japanese American family living in the boxy two-story house on Lemon Street, Judge Craig reached a decision in favor of the Haradas. The family could stay. Craig's straightforward opinion evaluated the applicability of the Alien Land Law, reiterating that aliens ineligible to become American citizens could not own land in California. He added, however, that, like anyone else born on American soil, their citizen children were entitled to the constitutional guarantees and privileges of American citizenship. Craig also claimed that although the money for the Lemon Street house purchase was provided by Jukichi Harada, the evidence presented by the state did not prove its contention that Harada held a resulting trust in the property. Judge Craig emphasized the simple fact that the deed to the house was not written to include Jukichi Harada, and as a result, Harada could never claim a legal interest in the property, "even if there were no anti-alien land law."[12]

Craig directed additional criticism to the state for disregarding the fundamental issue in the case—the rights of the American citizens in the Harada family. He pointed to US constitutional guarantees as they pertained to the Harada children, saying, "They are American citizens, of somewhat humble station, it may be, but still entitled to equal protection of the laws of our land . . . The political rights of American citizens are the same, no matter what their parentage." Craig also mentioned Jukichi's interest in providing his family with "a home near a good school and the church which they attended, and one that had open spaces about it, instead of the rooming house, where one child had died." He restated Attorney General Webb's quote of the Fourteenth Amendment, adding, it "correctly sets forth the law." The judge also reprimanded the state for using what he described as "suspicions and inferences" against Harada. He went on to discuss the conflicts in the witnesses' testimony and discounted the contradiction between the statements of Van de Grift and Harada, pointing out Harada's disagreement with Van de Grift's claim that Harada had agreed to give up the property for the higher price offered by Van de Grift. Craig believed the contradiction was, most likely, a result of Harada's difficulty with English.[13]

Lemon Street neighbor Cora Fletcher's testimony as a witness for the state corroborated the testimony of defense witnesses Jukichi Harada and real estate agent Frank Noble. All three testified that Harada said he purchased the house for the benefit of his children. Judge Craig also pointed out that this claim was not denied by other members of the neighborhood committee. In his concluding remarks, the judge implied that if the state moved to impose a tougher Alien Land Law, it would have a difficult time adapting it to the authority of the United States Constitution.[14]

In Los Angeles, Deputy Attorney General Lewinsohn read Judge Craig's decision with what he said was "great disappointment." Miguel Estudillo, recently returned from a Wyoming hunting trip, also expressed his regrets. Both Lewinsohn and Estudillo asserted that Craig misunderstood the state's contentions. They continued to stress the notion that the Harada children did not have title to the property and, therefore, the state was not trying to take the house away from them. Estudillo lost no time in pursuing local interest in further legal action against the Haradas. He told Lewinsohn he hoped the attorney general would soon appeal the case. Lewinsohn responded by telling Attorney General Webb that the conflict in the testimony of Harada, Fletcher, and Van de Grift was resolved in favor of the Haradas. As a result, Judge Craig's decision would most likely survive intact if an appeal were made.

Some California newspapers reported that the state would continue to press the case, but Webb knew that even though a decision of the Riverside Superior Court would not set a legally binding precedent throughout the state, an appeal was inadvisable because the resolution of the conflict of evidence in favor of the defendant would most certainly affect a later decision of the appellate court. As Webb correctly understood, judgment of the facts in the Riverside trial would not be ignored in any future action against the Haradas.[15]

After Judge Craig's decision was handed down, further moves were made by the state regarding the possibility of a new trial. Ujiro Oyama, the Japanese consul in Los Angeles, represented the Japanese government's ongoing interest in the *Harada* case when he wrote to the deputy attorney general, asking about its possible continuance. Joe Lewinsohn responded, saying the state had already filed a notice of intention to move for a new trial. In Riverside on January 18, 1919, Lewinsohn and Estudillo appeared once again before Judge Craig, arguing for a new trial, but Craig reiterated his earlier position, saying Harada had not specifically intended to evade the Alien Land Law, and he denied the state's motion. Several months earlier, Lewinsohn had predicted Judge Craig's denial, saying it would be unlikely for Craig to reverse his own judgment to grant another trial.[16]

On January 21, the *Riverside Daily Press* printed the judge's latest decision and called it the "second chapter" in an "internationally famous Japanese land case." In another article on the paper's front page, the *Press* reported that, as predicted, California's Japanese were beginning to purchase large tracts of real estate in the names of their American citizen children. Dispatches from Tulare County claimed parcels as large as 10,000 acres were now being sold to Japanese children because of the *Harada* decision. The *Riverside Enterprise* said it was not yet known if the state would appeal to the Supreme Court, but it soon became apparent that the attorney general would not press the case. Webb explained that the resolution of the conflict of evidence in favor of Harada indicated to him there was "no hope for reversal."[17]

Despite his stated reason for not pressing the *Harada* case, Attorney General Webb may have realized that a more detailed examination of the facts in the Riverside case could negate the Alien Land Law altogether. Webb might have surmised that it was better to avoid having a higher court examine more closely Judge Craig's ruling that the Fourteenth Amendment "correctly sets forth the law." Despite the sense that a reversal of the verdict in the *Harada* case should not be pursued in a new trial, Webb and others might now have also believed that new steps should be taken to strengthen the 1913 law. A more stringent, narrowly focused version of the Alien Land Law might counter any possible advances the outcome in the Riverside case might have encouraged for other Japanese immigrants and their American citizen children.

Even if the *Harada* case never went before a higher court to overturn the Alien Land Law, Webb must have understood that the 1913 measure could not effectively control landownership by US citizens of Japanese ancestry now living in California. He had already said as much when Jukichi Harada bought the house on Lemon Street in 1915 and real estate agent Noble first sought Webb's comments about the rights of US citizens of Japanese ancestry. When Webb had replied to Noble, more than two years before the *Harada* case went to trial, he confirmed the rights of children of Japanese ancestry born in California, citing the Fourteenth Amendment and concluding that "any citizen of the United States and of this State may acquire and hold real estate in California." If the 1913 law had been more restrictive from the beginning, perhaps Japanese landownership could have been curtailed. Had it been more closely aimed at limiting ownership of agricultural lands and not used as a vehicle for discouraging all Japanese from remaining in California, it might have been more effective in preventing an expansion of real estate ownership by the Japanese and their US citizen offspring.[18]

Miguel Estudillo, speaking on behalf of some of his disappointed fellow citizens in Riverside, expressed dissatisfaction with Craig's decision. "Ever since the people decided not to appeal the Harada case, I have been hearing all kinds of lamentations, and believe that if Judge Craig were to run for office tomorrow, the decision would hurt him seriously," Estudillo said. In some ways, the attorney general might have been relieved the case was finally over. Although there was really no other decision possible under US law in 1918, surveying his long career as a Riverside attorney many years later, Miguel Estudillo proposed his own final analysis of the outcome of the *Harada* case. "It may be that after all, at that time, the decision rendered by the Court was a wise and happy solution to a very ticklish case," implying it was best for Riverside and the State of California to have avoided any hint of a confrontation with Japan during the Great War.[19]

Back at the house on Lemon Street, although still concerned about the immediate safety of their five children, Jukichi and Ken Harada slowly began to feel at home. Successful in his challenge to the Alien Land Law, grateful to Judge Craig for his verdict in the court case, and appreciative of the support offered by several of the city's most prominent white neighbors, Jukichi routinely reminded his sons and daughters of his solid belief in the integrity and promise of the US legal system. As a confident father at the head of the table, Jukichi urged his children to always stand up for what they believed. His oldest daughter, Mine, remembered the family joking with her father about his patriotic enthusiasm for life in the United States of America. "We used to kid him because he was such a patriot even though he wasn't a citizen," Mine told me some seventy years after the Haradas moved to Lemon Street. As the weeks passed, Jukichi and Ken became more assured that their children were safe and their family was, indeed, home at last. With what they believed their biggest challenge now behind them, they had no plans to ever live anywhere else.[20]

Keep California White

International developments and pressure from Washington contributed to Attorney General Webb's handling of the *Harada* case and to a marked decrease in anti-Japanese agitation in California during the Great War. Even though it was already obvious to some California officials that the 1913 Alien Land Law was ineffective in limiting Japanese landownership and that new legislation would be required to check further acquisition of land by the Japanese, widespread anti-Japanese sentiment in California did not resurface until after the armistice between the Allies and the Germans was signed on November 11, 1918. Seeking reelection in 1920, Senator James Duval Phelan, by now California's perennial foe of the West Coast Nikkei, took advantage of growing anti-Japanese hostility fostered during the war primarily by "the Hearst press and the German propaganda machine within the United States." Anxious for votes, Senator Phelan jumped at the chance to re-kindle the old Japanese Question, launching a strident anti-Japanese campaign. Its slogan, "Keep California White," quickly spread across the state in support of Phelan's efforts to retain his seat in the US Senate.[1]

The senator's chilling election poster, tacked to wooden fences and handed to prospective voters, featured the image of a dark Oriental hand with long, sharp fingernails clawing its way into the heart of the Golden State. Restraining the dark hand in the nick of time, a white wrist clad in stars and stripes halted its sly advance as the poster's message asked voters to reelect Phelan to "let him finish the work he now has under way to stop the SILENT INVASION." The campaign's bold "Keep California White" proclamation stated clearly that the angry supporters of the renewed anti-Japanese movement were not simply concerned with Japanese ownership and use of California's agricultural lands; most now wanted the Japanese out of California forever.

Support for an anti-Japanese program was garnered within the new California Oriental Exclusion League and other similar groups comprising primarily members from the Native Sons of the Golden West, Native Daughters of the Golden West, American Legion, California State Federation of Labor, and the California State Grange. Their policies called for the cancellation of the Gentlemen's Agreement, the exclusion of Japanese immigrants, the denial of permanent US citizenship eligibility for all Asians, and the addition of an amendment to the federal Constitution, "that no child born in the United States shall be given the rights of an American citizen unless both parents are of a race eligible to citizenship."[2]

By the end of 1919, interest had also been expressed in drafting a more stringent Alien Land Law to permanently stop Japanese real estate purchases in California. Unlike the earlier anti-Japanese bills developed within the California legislature, with signatures supporting the measure gathered across the state by the anti-Japanese coalition, the new proposal was offered for popular vote as an initiative on the 1920 ballot. The people of California now had the chance to cast their own votes for a new and more restrictive Alien Land Law. The fourteen sections of the new law were aimed at closing the gaps in the Alien Land Law of 1913. Besides shifting authority for escheat actions to county officials and preventing Japanese aliens from leasing land, Section 9(a) stated that if aliens ineligible for citizenship financed any purchase of real estate and subsequently placed ownership of property in a name or names other than their own, they would have violated the Alien Land Law and would be subject to prosecution.[3]

As the anti-Japanese forces organized their campaign in favor of the measure, members of the Riverside community gathered to discuss their state's renewed interest in the Japanese Question. The *Riverside Daily Press* reported that local sentiment regarding the Japanese was "evenly balanced." It also said the issues of what to do about Japanese landownership were discussed in a "calm and friendly manner." Citrus grower Burdette K. Marvin claimed that the Japanese "do not really displace the whites, but are doing certain productive work in berrying, fishing, gardening, etc., that Americans will not do." Ethan Allen Chase, a city land developer and citrus producer, also supported the Japanese and mentioned the dignity of Japan as a respectable international power.

The *Press* failed to mention whether the citrus growers acknowledged their own reliance on early Japanese immigrant contributions to the success of their Riverside citrus industry and did not point out that the city's Japanese population had declined by more than half since 1910. The paper did, however, report D. E. Bennett's observation that the people of Riverside did not really understand the seriousness of Japanese advancement in the Golden State, "because it is not a live question here as it is in the San Joaquin." Other local residents expressed fear over predictions that the Japanese, if left unchecked, would one day dominate the economy of California and make up the bulk of the state's population by the end of the twentieth century. Lyman Evans expressed further opposition: "We don't want the Japs or chinks here. They don't regard women as we do."[4]

Later in the year, the House Committee on Immigration and Naturalization held a series of summer hearings on the West Coast to examine the current topic of Japanese immigration. Just over 150 witnesses from both sides of the fence were heard in public meetings in California and Washington. Potato King George Shima from Berkeley and California senator James D. Phelan represented opposing views at the committee's opening session at the St. Francis Hotel in San Francisco on July 12. Testimony came from statewide farming and business interests, Japanese immigrants, and a few young American citizens of Japanese ancestry. Reports of Japanese laborers sneaking north across the Mexican border, questions about Buddhism and the high birthrate of the Japanese living on the West Coast, and comments about California Japanese purchasing property in the names of their infant citizen children were all added to the record. In one line of questioning involving a proposal to remove Japanese settlers from scattered rural areas in California for possible concentration in a single settlement in the Imperial Valley, Senator Phelan remarked, a bit ahead of his time: "If we have the Japanese here and cannot get rid of them, we can prevent others from coming. I do not know how we can get rid of those who are here. It might be better to segregate them."[5]

When the president of the Japanese Association of America, millionaire businessman George Shima, was asked by California representative John Raker whether he supported the idea of intermarriage between Japanese and Americans, Shima came up with what he believed was a practical comparison from his experiences growing potatoes in the Golden State:

> **MR. RAKER** Is it your belief that it would be a bad thing for your people to intermarry with our people?
> **MR. SHIMA** I think it a very good thing.
> **THE CHAIRMAN** Very good?
> **MR. SHIMA** Yes. I will tell you why: I was a potato grower. Any time you leave the potato seed in the same soil the seeds will rot and become weak—very bad color. Then we have to buy Oregon seed, and the trouble was the first year it was very small yield, because it did not acclimate. We have to leave it acclimate first. That is why we plant in sandy soil in California and get a small crop and dug early . . . and the second year got a beautiful crop . . .

THE CHAIRMAN   Then you think that intermarriage between the white people and the Japanese would bring a beautiful crop of men and women?
MR. SHIMA   Yes.[6]

Additional testimony, written statements, and exhibits were added to the record in fifteen days of hearings. In Exhibit A, investigator Albert Chapelle of Los Angeles offered a detailed brief about alien landholdings in California, comments about the motivations and character of Japanese picture brides, and other wide-ranging observations about what Chapelle described as the "increasing Japanese menace." Chapelle's review claimed, "The presence of the Japs in other States will convince the real American citizens of those States that the protests of Californians are well founded." After weighing in on various legal matters, Chapelle complained that picture brides were part of "an organized scheme of Japanese colonization, plus Japanese greed for California land," adding, "Under our laws as they are now written, their offspring, born in this Golden State, with the inherent reek and taint of the orient upon them, are American citizens, entitled by their birth upon our free soil all the rights and privileges under the laws of real Americans." A few lines later, Chapelle's exhibit also included passing mention of the results of a recent court verdict in Southern California: "By decision of an honorable judge of the superior court of Riverside County, Calif., in the Jukichi Harada case," Chapelle asserted, Japanese American infants could now acquire title "to as many acres of California land as the combined funds of the Jap colony of the vicinage may procure and hold for the benefit of his race."[7]

Back in Riverside, a confident Jukichi Harada joined his community's dialogue about the Japanese Question and the proposal for a new Alien Land Law. Harada displayed a large poster in the big front window of his Washington Restaurant for all to see. Opposing the 1920 initiative and supporting Issei farmers by mocking Senator Phelan's "Keep California White" with its own "Keep California Green," Harada's window poster registered his opposition to the Golden State's coming ballot initiative. As his oldest daughter, Mine, then age fifteen, recalled, her father's most recent public expression was short-lived. "The American Legion was up-in-arms about it," Mine said, "and they told him, 'Harada, take that sign down' . . . He refused but I told him to take it down just for the sake of peace. The police were . . . afraid he'd get attacked. So he very reluctantly had to take it down."[8]

On Election Day in November, Senator Phelan lost his bid for a new term, along with six other incumbent Democratic senators in a Republican sweep across the nation. The lopsided vote rejected the policies of the outgoing president, Democrat Woodrow Wilson, and repudiated his support of the new League of Nations. Republican candidate Warren G. Harding was elected president, garnering a hefty 60 percent of the popular vote to the Democrats' 34 percent. Despite

Phelan's loss, California voters overwhelmingly approved the state's revised Alien Land Law of 1920. However, the new law was as ineffective as its 1913 counterpart. In the words of historian Roger Daniels, "The 1920 measure was an attempt to lock the door after the horse had been stolen. Had it been enacted in 1913, when native-born Japanese were less numerous, it would have seriously inhibited Japanese acquisition of agricultural land. By 1920 its enactment was an empty gesture, an ineffective irritant; it caused much litigation, but it in no wise significantly affected land tenure in the state." In his later review of the 1913 Alien Land Law's impact, attorney Frank Chuman observed:

> When the California Alien Land Law of 1913 was enacted, the number
> of Japanese who actually owned agricultural lands was insignificant. In 1912,
> according to county assessors' reports, Japanese owned only 12,726 acres of
> farms as compared with more than 11,000,000 acres of improved farmlands in
> the state of California at that time. Even as late as 1920 . . . the Japanese owned
> only 74,767 acres and leased 383,287 more for a total of 458,054 acres . . . of
> the 27,981,444 acres of farmlands then reported in operation by the California
> Board of Control.[9]

The revised Alien Land Law approved in 1920 had shifted authority for the prosecution of escheat cases to county superior courts. In 1922 a case from the court in Sutter County, *The Estate and Guardianship of Tetsubumi Yano*, reached the California Supreme Court. Perhaps encouraged by the outcome in Riverside's *Harada* case, Hayayo Yano placed the ownership of fourteen acres of agricultural land north of Sacramento in the name of his infant citizen daughter, Tetsubumi, in 1920. In marked contrast to his first comments about the *Harada* case, when he quoted the Fourteenth Amendment and said US citizens could purchase real estate in California, Attorney General Webb said during *Yano*, "If it were not for the Alien Land Acts of 1913 and 1920 it might be conceded that the Fourteenth Amendment . . . would be applicable." By the time the *Yano* case came to trial, Webb was likely changing his position about the Fourteenth Amendment because of the outcome in the *Harada* case. A year earlier, in a letter explaining the Riverside case, Webb said the Office of the Attorney General had not issued a formal opinion regarding the constitutionality of the 1913 law. He added, however, that as one of its original authors in 1913, he had "dealt with it continually since its adoption on the faith of its constitutionality."[10]

In his arguments against Hayayo Yano, Webb based his contentions on states' rights and stressed that, through its Alien Land Laws, California had exercised proper jurisdiction over the property rights of its residents. Webb must have assumed that, unlike *Harada*, his case against the Yanos had a much better chance of being decided in favor of the state. By the time the *Yano* case went to trial, the Alien Land Law had been strengthened by popular vote. Furthermore, *Yano* involved not an urban residential lot and house but several acres of agricultural land. The case defending the Harada family's right to seek a better home environment was relatively easy to establish. The defendants in the *Yano* case, reportedly using *Harada* as support during the trial, argued that the income produced by the ownership and use of farmland was vital to the well-being of the Yano family. Unlike Jukichi Harada in Riverside, Hayayo Yano had lost an earlier decision in Sutter County Superior Court. Despite Attorney General Webb's "faith of its constitutionality," the 1920 Alien Land Law did not fare well in Yano's appeal to the California Supreme Court; the lower court was reversed and Section 4 of the 1920 Alien Land Law prohibiting guardianships by Japanese parents for minor children was declared unconstitutional as a violation of the Fourteenth Amendment.[11]

Additional cases involving the California Alien Land Law reached the United States Supreme Court in 1923. In *Porterfield v. Webb* and *Webb v. O'Brien*, separate cases decided in November, the court upheld the constitutionality of the land law. Six months later the new Immigration Act of 1924, aimed primarily at reducing the number of immigrants from southern and eastern Europe and maintaining the current ethnic composition of the nation, also included the Asian Exclusion Act, ending Asian immigration to the United States. Subsequent major legal challenges to the California land law were slow in coming. It was not until 1948 that the Supreme Court of the United States finally echoed some of the original findings of Riverside's judge Hugh Craig, issued so many years before, ruling against the California Supreme Court in *Oyama v. California* to declare Section 9(a) of the Alien Land Law unconstitutional and a violation of the equal protection clause of Section 1 of the US Constitution's Fourteenth Amendment.

When the Supreme Court ruled against the California law in the *Oyama* case, Associate Justice William Francis Murphy, a former US attorney general nominated to the high court by President Franklin Roosevelt, offered perceptive remarks to explain his concurring opinion in favor of the petitioners, son Fred and father Kajiro Oyama:

> The California Alien Land Law was spawned of the great anti-Oriental virus which, at an early date, infected many persons in that state. The history of this anti-Oriental agitation is not one that does credit to a nation that prides itself, at least historically, on being the friendly haven of the tired and the oppressed of other lands.
>
> . . . The more basic purpose of the statute was to irritate the Japanese, to make economic life in California as uncomfortable and unprofitable for them as legally possible. It was thus but a step in the long campaign to discourage the Japanese from entering California and to drive out those who were already there.

Moreover, there is nothing to indicate that the proponents of the California law were at any time concerned with the use or ownership of farm land by ineligible aliens other than those of Japanese origin.

... That fact has been further demonstrated by the subsequent enforcement of the Alien Land Law. At least 79 escheat actions have been instituted by the state since the statute became effective. Of these 79 proceedings, 4 involved Hindus, 2 involved Chinese, and the remaining 73 involved Japanese. Curiously enough, 59 of the 73 Japanese cases were begun by the state subsequent to Pearl Harbor, during the period when the hysteria generated by World War II magnified the opportunities for effective anti-Japanese propaganda.[12]

Within another few years two more California cases would move the judiciary to rulings that eventually led to the extinction of the Alien Land Law. In 1952 the California Supreme Court reached similar conclusions in *Sei Fujii v. State of California* and *Haruye Masaoka v. State of California*. Prompted by the outcome of the *Oyama* case in 1948, Japanese native and non-citizen Sei Fujii, crusading publisher of a bilingual newspaper in Los Angeles, challenged the 1920 Alien Land Law by purchasing a small city lot and recording it in his own name. The state soon filed an escheat action against Fujii and he lost his case in superior court. Two years later, when the case was finally heard on appeal before the California Supreme Court, the lower court's decision was reversed and Fujii's position upheld. The court found that the sections of the Alien Land Law barring ineligible aliens from landownership were unconstitutional. It also challenged the conclusions of the US Supreme Court in the 1923 case of *Porterfield v. Webb*.

Like the escheat case filed by the State of California years earlier against Jukichi Harada, the case filed in superior court against Issei immigrant widow Haryue Masaoka in 1950 was also decided in favor of the defendant. The Masaoka family had been accused of violating the section of the Alien Land Law prohibiting the gift of real estate from the American citizen children in the family to their non-citizen mother. However, unlike its retreat after Judge Craig's early decision in favor of Jukichi Harada, when Attorney General Webb decided to take no further action against the Haradas after they won their case in superior court, the state filed an appeal to the state supreme court in the *Masaoka* case. When the case finally ended shortly after the Fujii verdict was issued in 1952, the court based its findings on the recent outcome of *Fujii* and affirmed Masaoka's earlier victory in superior court.

At the time Haruye Masaoka's case had first been decided in Los Angeles Superior Court in 1950, Judge Thurmond Clarke ruled that what remained of the Alien Land Law was, in its entirety, unconstitutional. Clarke concluded: "[T]he Alien Land Law is directed at persons of Japanese ancestry solely because of their race. It is clear that the State legislation which seeks to impair the constitutionally protected civil rights to acquire, own and enjoy real property violates the due process and equal protection clause of the Fourteenth Amendment. Accordingly, I hold that the Alien Land Law of California under the facts of this case is unconstitutional."

When Judge Thurmond Clarke gave these concluding remarks in 1950, it had been nearly thirty-five years since his own father, Deputy Attorney General Robert M. Clarke, had filed suit in Riverside in 1916 for Attorney General Webb and the people of California against Jukichi Harada to test the Alien Land Law of 1913.[13] After the victories in the *Fujii* and *Masaoka* cases in the early 1950s, a few more years would pass before the people of California finally put an end to the original intentions of the Alien Land Law of 1913. It was not until 1956, more than a generation after the 1913 law was first enacted and a dozen years after the Harada family and the Japanese American community had experienced their greatest losses, that a new statewide initiative passed two-to-one by popular vote to formally repeal California's Alien Land Law. Soon after the vote, *Pacific Citizen*, voice of the Japanese American Citizens League, finally offered its own conclusion to half a century of racial discrimination and legal harassment directed against Japanese Americans, observing that the repeal of the Alien Land Law "was a tribute to the Issei whose love for the land kept them steadfast through years of discrimination. America's Issei and Nisei, so recently removed from the harsh and discriminatory years of the war, today enjoy a freedom from statutory prejudice which persons of Japanese descent have not known since the first Alien Land Law was passed in 1913."[14]

Long before the coming challenges of World War II, in the years immediately following the Alien Land Law court case, the Harada family continued to grow and diversify. Finally settled at home on Lemon Street and enjoying the national prosperity of the 1920s, milestones of family life were observed with great pride but little fanfare as each year passed. Between the Harada house and the Washington Restaurant, Frank Miller continued to expand his beloved Mission Inn, adding features of Japanese design and launching his Institute of World Affairs in an effort to maintain his lifelong hope for cultural understanding, international harmony, and peace among all. Jukichi and Ken Harada joined their town's Nikkei neighbors, Frank Miller, and other friends from time to time to attend Miller's banquets and community events at the Mission Inn. Annual celebrations of Japanese boys' and girls' days welcomed local Nikkei children to Frank Miller's big hotel, flavoring the Mission Inn's inclusive cultural atmosphere.

However, just as Frank Miller was founding his Institute of World Affairs, in other less tolerant quarters of town, by invitation only at closed meetings over at the Odd Fellows Hall at the corner of Ninth and Main, some other local men were also busy organizing their own chapter of the Ku Klux Klan. The white supremacist group witnessed a revival in communities across the country in the early 1920s, and Riverside was no exception. In 1923, local Klansmen announced a plan to recruit 500 new members by the Fourth of July. The *Riverside Enterprise* said, "The membership list here is being kept secret, and just what Riversiders belong to the white-robed Klan is a matter of surmise as yet."[15]

A year later, touted in its local recruiting announcement as "the most selective organization in the world," the Klan was even trying to persuade the town's mayor to join their plan "to organize 100 per cent American men and women, all owing their first allegiance to the United States of America, believing in Protestant Christianity, having ever before them the living Christ as their criterion of character, and sworn to uphold the laws of our country both in mind and conduct, and to safeguard the constitutional rights awarded us by our forefathers."[16]

Their unsigned questionnaire to Mayor Samuel Cary Evans Jr. from the Imperial Palace, Invisible Empire, the Knights of the Ku Klux Klan, was sent to the mayor on stationery adorned with a white-hooded klansman on horseback, the same image as the one used for D. W. Griffith's advertising posters for *The Birth of a Nation*. The new group sought Evans's reply to a long list of questions about his religion, ancestry, and whether he was "of the white race or of a colored race." A few years before, when Mayor Evans was serving as Republican state senator in Sacramento, he had worked to prevent the return of *The Birth of a Nation* to hometown Riverside. Senator Evans declared that the picture "unnecessarily affronts the negro who is a citizen and voter and proved his loyalty in the great war." Evans and most other decent people in town apparently ignored the Klan's recruitment materials, but the undercurrent of intolerance represented by those supporting the secret organization would continue to simmer in the nation's shadows for many more years.[17]

In this time of prosperity and increasing anti-Japanese sentiment after the Great War, one member of the old neighborhood committee, widow Cynthia Robinson, finally accepted the Haradas as "kindly people." In the years before her death in 1922, old Mrs. Robinson gradually became one of the Harada family's closest Lemon Street friends. At Robinson's request, Sumi said her father removed a corner of the Haradas' backyard fence to provide their neighbor a shortcut to another friend's yard. Sumi's older sister, Mine, fondly recalled visiting her elderly neighbor and speaking with her at some length about her travels to Egypt and the Holy Land, remembering numerous friendly interactions with old Mrs. Robinson. "On holidays Mama always fixed a special tray for her," Mine said, "and whenever we had something special and unusual we always took her some. We never saw any of the neighbors visit her or do anything for her."[18]

Other members of the old neighborhood committee, however, were much less friendly. Of the Urquharts and the Farrs, Mine said, "Neither family ever spoke to us." Former committee member and trial witness Cora Fletcher continued to live in her small house on the northwest corner of Fourth and Lemon, caring each day for an invalid brother whose "cries of pain could be heard [throughout] the neighborhood," Mine said. "As I recall, Cora Fletcher never spoke to us . . . Perhaps because of the illness of her brother she was unable to keep up her home and yard. We wondered how she could have thought Japanese neighbors would depreciate property," Mine observed pointedly.

The Harada sisters both said their family was often so busy with work and school they had little time to develop deep relationships with friends or neighbors. Knowing well the discomfort a person of color might face in the wrong circumstances, however, with Mine's clear memories of the neighbor boy throwing rocks or Sumi's of the woman in the Farr family telling her in no uncertain terms to stay on her own side of the street, the two Harada girls might also have been reluctant to open themselves to possible rejection. "We didn't pay too much attention to the neighbors," Sumi observed. Mine recalled her later years in Riverside's public schools, saying it was sometimes difficult to be seen with her white school friends.

> During my . . . school years, . . . I could feel the . . . discrimination all the time. And . . . it was hard to overlook, you know? I had a very good friend . . . and . . . I used to take the family Ford . . . to junior college. And there's a friend of mine that . . . I always picked up . . . Lots of times on the way home, I'd have to stop at the restaurant . . . to leave my books or something, and I'd let her wait in the car. You know, she'd scoot under. She didn't want to be seen in front of my father's place . . . My American friend, my white friend.
>
> But I had another friend that never thought anything like that. And I often wondered, "Gee, maybe I should invite her in," you know. But . . . I never knew . . . when I'd be rebuffed. So no, none, none, none of my friends ever found out how good my mother's fried chicken was.[19]

Still making her popular Sunday chicken dinners at the Washington Restaurant, just after the New Year in 1923, forty-one-year-old Ken Harada was perhaps shocked to realize that she was pregnant again, expecting another baby the following summer. She and her husband had now lived nearly twenty years in California, and already as old as some grandparents among their white Riverside friends and neighbors, just a week before Jukichi's forty-eighth birthday, the Haradas became new parents again when Ken Harada gave birth to the couple's last child. Fifth son Harold Shigetaka Harada was born in the front downstairs bedroom of the Lemon Street house on Wednesday, August 15, 1923. The boy's American name was intended to honor a family friend named Harlow. However, as the family story goes, someone completing the baby's birth certificate confused his father's pronunciation of the name "Harlow," which Jukichi pronounced as "Harodo." Misunderstood by straining Caucasian ears as the name "Harold," the new name stuck.[20]

Not long after Harold's summer arrival, Jukichi moved the family's Washington Restaurant from its original location on Eighth Street to a much larger space at 638 West Ninth, where the business would remain for a few more years. Although they were normally busy seven days a week at their Washington Restaurant, both Jukichi and Ken Harada were also active with Riverside's Japanese Association and the Japanese Union Church, consolidated from the earlier Methodist and First Congregational Japanese Missions as the city's Japanese population declined. Jukichi served as president of the local Japanese Association for a time, helping to coordinate community activities and promote positive relations among the Issei in Riverside and beyond.

Just a couple of weeks after Harold's birth in the summer of 1923, California's Japanese Associations and the Japanese Red Cross Society in Japan responded to the devastating Great Kanto Earthquake, tsunami, and subsequent fires striking the cities of Tokyo, Yokohama, and the hinterlands of the Haradas' origins near Nagoya on September 1. Like other California Japanese, Jukichi contributed his own hard-earned money to the earthquake relief fund. As a token of appreciation he received a small enamel pin from the Japanese Red Cross commemorating his donation. In other small but no less significant ways, former schoolteacher Harada also gained respect among local Issei for his skill in providing Japanese calligraphy for many of his small community's tombstone inscriptions. Sumi recalled her father with his brush and ink, preparing each inscription carefully on large sheets of paper for later engraving on the stones by professional tombstone makers. Many of Riverside's Japanese grave markers from the 1920s, it is believed, hold inscriptions first crafted with brush and ink by Jukichi at his home on Lemon Street.[21]

With his family's restaurant close to the city police department downtown, Jukichi was also asked to provide meals from the Washington to prisoners at the nearby city jail. Even before the State of California accused him of violating the Alien Land Law, Jukichi had already had a brush with local police authorities. During one of Chief Corrington's well-publicized cleanup crusades involving several downtown rooming houses in 1913, the *Daily Press* reported Mr. Harada might be facing a "stiff fine." Examining the names in rooming-house guest registers, Chief Corrington had determined that during recent overnight activities at Harada's rooming house, an "Indian boy and girl from Sherman were allowed to occupy the same room in the place . . . It is said the two registered under different names, yet they occupied the same room in the rooming house."[22]

Jukichi's later experiences at the county courthouse and his relationship with some prominent citizens in Riverside's legal community and staff at the jail provided a basis for Mr. Harada to become familiar with some of his city's leading law enforcement authorities. Future chief of police Nestor Brule lived next door to the Haradas on Lemon Street before and after World War I and came to know the family fairly well. Like his original employer and mentor in Riverside, Ulysses Shinsei Kaneko, Jukichi had a fair command of the English language, which sometimes allowed him to serve as a courtroom interpreter for local Japanese. Harada also helped some members of the fading Chinese community faced with minor legal issues. Jukichi's youngest son, Harold, recalled one notable incident when his father apparently prevented one local Japanese man from going to jail.

> One old . . . Issei man was . . . apprehended in an orange grove and was allegedly said to be stealing oranges. Well, my dad went to court for the man, and when the judge asked my dad, "What was he doing in the dark in the orange grove if he weren't stealing oranges?" And my dad's English was really great. He said, . . . "Oh, he pee pee in the orange grove." And that was his . . . great command of English, and I'm sure it impressed the judge because I think the man . . . was exonerated.

Because of this kind of ongoing community involvement and visibility, Riverside's police chief awarded Jukichi with what he regarded as an official distinction, Special Police Badge Number 13. Although some in the police department and elsewhere may have smirked at Jukichi's unlucky badge number, alerting most in Riverside that Harada was, perhaps, not so official after all, he was proud to have it, noting that for him the badge's number thirteen was meaningful because it was the same as first son Masa Atsu's birthday, January 13.[23]

With their former schoolteacher father emphasizing his family's heritage of educators, the younger children in the Harada family continued their grammar school education in Riverside public schools. The older siblings moved out of the house and on to college, starting careers and families of their own. Masa Atsu and Mine, the Haradas' oldest son and daughter, both migrated north to the San Francisco Bay Area. Masa Atsu, the son born in Japan, left home first. In his late teens, when the Alien Land Law court case was still pending, Masa graduated from high school in 1917 and moved away from Riverside to attend the University of California at Berkeley. Despite Jukichi's emphasis on the importance of education—daughter Sumi recalled her father often reminding his children, "Education can't be taken away from you"—Mine held mixed emotions about her own educational opportunities. "My parents believed in education . . . except for the women," she observed curtly. Mine also explained that the Riverside Nikkei community helped to support brother Masa Atsu's university education, providing donations to an educational loan fund to help pay his tuition.

> Neighbors and friends would get together . . . and they would . . . put in, 'bout twenty-five or fifty dollars a month, everybody would, and then, whoever needed it, got to bid for it. And that's how they used to . . . help each other out . . . I remember one time . . . he was quite worried because he wasn't able to . . . get the money for his . . . tuition. And so, . . . we had to go make the rounds. I had to go with him one night . . . to . . . get the consent of all the others, . . . that he would get the next loan.[24]

10.1. Harada family (*standing, left to right*: Mine, Mary [Mrs. Masa Atsu Harada], Masa Atsu with son Calvin, Sumi, Clark; *seated, left to right*: Yoshizo, Ken, Jukichi with son Harold), Riverside, 1928. (Courtesy of the Harada Family Archival Collection, Riverside Metropolitan Museum, Riverside, California)

Masa Atsu completed his first degree at University of California at Berkeley in 1921, later graduating from the university's medical school across the bay in San Francisco. He met Mary Yoshiko Eimoto one evening at a student dance at the university and the pair married in Napa in 1924. Little more than a year after baby brother Shigetaka's birth on Lemon Street in Riverside, Masa Atsu and Mary presented Ken and Jukichi with their first grandchild, baby Shig's nephew, Calvin Kenichi Harada, named after President Calvin Coolidge. Calvin's Japanese name, Kenichi, was bestowed to honor his grandmother, Ken Harada, indicating he was her first grandchild. After graduation from medical school in 1925, new physician Dr. Masa Atsu Harada began his medical practice in San Francisco and was also associated with the university's Department of Surgery, at times teaching classes there in the late 1920s and early 1930s. Masa Atsu and Mary's second child, daughter Lily Ann Yuriko Harada, given two first names like her father Masa Atsu and a Japanese name, Yuriko, for the lily flower matching her American name, was born in spring 1929 in San Francisco. In the early 1930s the family moved to Sacramento, where Dr. Harada would continue his medical practice for another decade.[25]

Oldest daughter Mine finished high school in Riverside in 1923 and went on to attend the local junior college until leaving home three years later. That summer, in 1926, Mine moved north to Pacific Grove near Monterey, working as a cook's helper at Asilomar, architect Julia Morgan's Arts and Crafts Young Women's Christian Association camp and conference center. While working at Asilomar, Mine earned $26 a month plus room and board. Leaving Monterey at summer's end, Mine moved north to San Francisco, where her older brother was already working as a physician and surgeon in his first medical office. Within the month, Mine found work as a sales and office clerk at Hada Retail Art Goods, a souvenir and art shop on Chinatown's main street, Grant Avenue, earning $100 a month. Living in a rented room on Laguna Street in the city's Nihonmachi, later called "Japantown," Mine learned to string pearls at the art goods store while waiting on customers seeking exotic souvenirs from the Orient. At age twenty-one and on her own, Mine had a steady monthly income that made her much more independent than some of the other young single women she knew.[26]

One of brother Masa Atsu's best friends from the University of California was a diligent young law student from Hilo, Hawaii, and a 1926 graduate of the university's Hastings College of Law. Three years younger than Dr. Harada, Saburo Kido, whom Masa Atsu called "my protégé," had just passed the California State Bar Exam and was thinking about starting his first law practice in San Francisco. One day in Dr. Harada's medical office, believing the two might make a good match, Masa Atsu introduced his eligible college friend to his younger sister Mine. Reminiscent of the moment thirty years earlier in Japan when Ken Harada's older brother introduced her to the attractive young fellow with a new job as a schoolteacher, Masa Atsu's introduction of the slight young man from Hawaii would soon change Mine's life. Kido's father had been a sake brewer and bookkeeper in the Hilo area on the Big Island but had lost his business when Prohibition was passed in 1919. Leaving the territory of Hawaii and returning to Japan when their third son, Saburo, left Hilo for California to attend college in Berkeley, the elder Kidos never returned to the United States, and Saburo would never see his father and mother again.[27]

After a courtship lasting just over a year, Miss Harada and Mr. Kido were anxiously making plans for a springtime wedding in Riverside by the early months of 1928, but they did not proceed without first honoring their Japanese family traditions. As Mine explained,

> When I was getting ready to get married, my parents wanted to find out all about my husband's . . . family lineage. And, if it didn't pass, . . . I would be going against my parents if I went through . . . with the marriage. So we had to . . . find somebody that knew his family. And [we] were very fortunate that . . . the . . . Buddhist priest in Pasadena was an old family friend of . . . my husband's family, and so he supplied all the family history to my parents.

10.2. Mine Harada and Saburo Kido, wedding portrait, Riverside, 1928. (Courtesy of the Harada Family Archival Collection, Riverside Metropolitan Museum, Riverside, California)

... My mother was very particular because ... samurai, you know, were very, very particular about family lineage. And, so, ... when ... the family heard about Kido's family, why, it was OK. But ... I have friends where ... they weren't allowed to marry because the family lineage was not what the family wanted.[28]

At the end of May 1928, as Jukichi and Ken prepared for the Riverside wedding of their oldest daughter, they arranged for the Harada family to gather at Brinkmann's Photography Studio for what would be their last formal family portrait. Standing at the rear of the group, Masa Atsu, his wife Mary, and their three-year-old son Calvin join aunties Mine and Sumi standing close to Uncle Clark. Seated in the front with son Yoshizo to her right, Ken Harada sits with Jukichi holding Harold on his lap, his youngest son at age four dressed in shorts. On Sunday, May 20, Mine and Saburo were married in a ceremony performed by the minister of the local Japanese church, who was joined by the Reverend Otoe So, the former leader of Riverside's Japanese Methodist Mission and an old family friend who had once helped Ken and Jukichi Harada through their grief when son Tadao died in 1913. Reverend So had returned to Riverside at the family's request to take part in Mine's wedding ceremony. Not long after the wedding, one of the last times the Harada family would all be together at the same time at the family home, Jukichi and Ken proudly added Mine and Saburo's new wedding portrait to the walls of an upstairs bedroom of the house on Lemon Street.

As soon as the newlyweds returned to San Francisco, Saburo went back to work in the small law office he had already opened at 1621 Webster Street in the city's growing Nihonmachi district. Able to read and speak Japanese with some fluency, Kido soon had established himself within the city's Nikkei community as a general practice attorney handling routine legal matters for individual clients seeking help with real estate transactions, interpreting, and divorce proceedings. He would also represent Nikkei businesses, farmers, poultry ranchers, and flower growers and help to organize small-business cooperatives and assist local community organizations, including the San Francisco Japanese Chamber of Commerce and Japanese Labor Association. Kido sometimes branched out to handle transactions for Japanese religious institutions and write pro bono legal opinions on civil rights matters for local civic organizations, such as the San Francisco Wholesale Grocers Association and the Nippon Trade Agency.

Like his college friend Dr. Harada and other recent US university graduates of Japanese ancestry, Saburo soon came to understand that few outside the Nikkei community were interested in securing his professional services. Mine's early anticipation about the opportunity to establish her own home and family with her new San Francisco attorney husband was soon tempered by Saburo's growing interest in community improvement. Despite his education at the university and new law career, Kido was struggling to support his family from fees from a small client base that had little money to spare for paying for the legal services offered by the young, mild-mannered, and often kind-hearted lawyer who would never lose the sensibilities, inflections, and preferences of his Hawaiian island childhood. At its beginning, Saburo's fledgling law practice was only "bringing in about forty dollars a month," so Mine soon went back to her job at the art goods store on Grant Avenue, selling Asian souvenirs, stringing pearls, and surpassing her new husband's monthly earnings with her $100 monthly salary from Hada's.

In the early years of their marriage, Saburo and Mine began to develop their mutual interests in community service, joining other young Bay Area citizen Nisei in establishing what would soon become the first national Asian American civil rights organization in the country, the Japanese American Citizens League. Among the earliest second-generation Nisei in California and the first US citizen in her own family, Mine would always maintain a strong sense of personal and community justice inspired by her parents' early efforts to provide a good home for their family and secure the rights of their citizen children.

Just five months after their wedding in Riverside, in San Francisco on October 19, 1928, Saburo Kido was chosen as president of the New American Citizens League. Fifty Bay Area Nisei soon held the group's inaugural banquet at San Francisco's Clift Hotel. As its earliest leader, Kido agreed to house the new group's headquarters in his modest Webster Street law office. Within weeks, the organizers of the Bay Area citizens' league began working closely with other West Coast Nisei federations to found the national Japanese American Citizens League (JACL) at a convention in Seattle in 1930. Saburo Kido chaired the convention committee that drafted the league's first constitution. Jimmie Sakamoto's *Japanese American Courier* newspaper covered the meetings and said Kido was the "root of unity" at the Seattle convention.

Through the activities of the Japanese American Citizens League, Saburo Kido and other young, assertive American-educated Nisei began to shift some of the power within the Nikkei community away from the older Issei-dominated Japanese Associations and toward the Nisei-dominated JACL. Mine remembered taking part in the organization's earliest local meetings in San Francisco and suggested that the fledgling JACL, comprising primarily new American voters, provided a small forum for Japanese American participation in the US political process. Unlike their immigrant parents who, because of their ineligibility for citizenship, were not allowed to vote, the American-born Nisei were soon regarded by at least a few local politicians as a potentially valuable voting constituency. Mine recalled:

> As soon as JACL was formed, we got interested in politics and during campaign time we tried to get the candidates to come to our meetings. We didn't realize that they'd all come and outnumber the members. I remember once we had so few members at an announced meeting for candidates I had to slip back home to phone friends to please show up. Most of them had worked hard all day—beginning of the Great Depression and people who had jobs did their best to hold onto them—very tired, and in bed, but they'd dress and rush over just because we had called them.[29]

Saburo Kido was one of the founders of the Japanese American Citizens League. In his central role of building unity at the league's Seattle convention in 1930, Kido had been seated proudly with other delegates in the middle of the front row in the organization's convention photograph. Urged by West Coast friends and associates several times to consider serving as its president, Mr. Kido thought it best to postpone that distinction for some time longer. Like their hardworking and dedicated friends in San Francisco and most other Americans at the time—not to mention Mine's mother and father, who were still hard at work each day at Riverside's Washington Restaurant—the Kidos would now turn most of their attention just to making ends meet during the Great Depression.

ELEVEN

THE ONLY TIME I SEE THE SUN

Perhaps Jukichi was thinking of his own father, Takanori Harada, who had been adopted by another family in Japan more than half a century before, when he unexpectedly adopted a Japanese American boy who had recently lost both parents. When he brought the boy home to Lemon Street, he was responding to a family tragedy in the Southern California Nikkei community in the summer of 1928. On August 11, busy residents of the City of Angels read details of the sensational story on page three of their Saturday morning paper:

Japanese Kills Wife and Self

Obsessed by an insane fury, Yoshitaro Hashimura, Japanese gardener of Torrance, yesterday morning shot and killed his wife Itoyo, and when his 11-year-old daughter Kiyoko refused to execute him with the shotgun that killed her mother the Nipponese turned the weapon upon himself and ended his own life, according to reports at the Sheriff's office.

Within days, the only boy in the devastated family, orphan Roy Yoshiharu Hashimura, born in Long Beach in 1919 and just nine years old, was taken from Los Angeles to Riverside to live at the Harada house as the last permanent addition to the Harada family. Even though the little boy was accepted warmly into the family as another son, behind the scenes Ken Harada was surprised and even somewhat upset that her husband had not consulted her about this important decision. Her son Harold recalled,

> My mother was quite upset, bewildered and all, to learn that she had another son to raise. Roy was nine and I was five. And we became the closest, I believe, of all of us brothers . . . And Roy was as much . . . a brother to me as my real brothers.
>
> . . . This tells the spirit of my dad, I think, and reflects his philosophy of being generous. Dad was not wealthy. He had a business but we were living hand to mouth, and for him to bring in an orphan to our family, our big family, pretty tough.[1]

Besides coming to the aid of an orphaned child in need and meeting his responsibilities as an older leader in the Nikkei community, Jukichi, at age fifty-four with his oldest boy already gone from home, no doubt also felt another pair of young hands would be of some help both at home and at work at the new location of his Washington Restaurant in the larger rented building on Ninth Street. Roy's four orphaned sisters—Kiyoko, Miyoko, Toshiye, and Sumiko—were each sent to live elsewhere. Sumiko, the youngest at just two years of age, was initially sent to the Shonien, the Japanese Children's Home in Los Angeles, but was later taken in by relatives. Toshiye went to live with her grandmother in Japan. The two older girls soon joined family in other parts of California. Roy believed Jukichi Harada had been acquainted with his father sometime in the past, and Sumi mentioned her father had known Roy's father in Riverside many years earlier. Whatever the circumstances, young Roy had never met the Haradas before he came to Lemon Street. "Nobody else wanted me," Roy observed. "I never saw the Haradas before that. I didn't know them. I had no choice," he said. Closest in age to stepbrother Shig, Harold Harada's shortened nickname for his Japanese middle name Shigetaka, Roy remembered his early challenging days in Riverside, playing with his new brother in the Haradas' big Ninth Street restaurant.[2]

With Wall Street's stock market crash in October 1929 and the beginning of the Great Depression, Jukichi soon moved his business again to a smaller rented space at 541 Eighth, just a block east on the same side of the street as the first Washington Restaurant. The new location would be the Washington's last stop downtown. As the Depression deepened and restaurant customers dwindled, Jukichi must have regarded his shift to the smaller and less expensive rented storefront a wise move. The small-business economy and the interconnectedness of the West Coast's Nikkei community proved an advantage in hard times, preventing widespread economic failure among the Japanese in California. Like most Americans of average means at the time, the Haradas scaled back as the remaining Harada children, now joined by new brother Roy Hashimura, assumed increasing domestic responsibilities. Sumi remembered that her mother learned sewing from a local seamstress and made some of the family's clothing during those years, including shirts for the Harada boys, on her foot-powered Singer sewing machine. Harold described one of his jobs at home, remembering the hard work it took to wash the family's laundry in the big claw-foot bathtub in the downstairs bathroom using a handheld metal plunger with a long wooden handle. "Since we didn't have a washing machine or any of the modern conveniences, the bathtub was . . . where we washed the clothes," Harold said. Each child pitched in to help maintain the family business, routinely working after school at the Washington Restaurant.[3]

The decline in family prosperity prompted some regrets. Although the Haradas now owned their own home, the restaurant business, and a couple of small rental properties on the east side of town, Ken Harada was remembered by her oldest daughter for joking with husband Jukichi about his grand choice to abandon what would most certainly have been a stable and possibly more prosperous career as a schoolteacher in Japan to seek his fortune in the United States: "My mother always used to kid him . . . when they were having a hard time running the restaurant . . . 'Why, if he'd been a good boy and stayed in Japan, he'd a' been a principal by this time.'"[4]

Among the family, mother Ken Harada, comfortable speaking mostly Japanese throughout her life, and sometimes more competent with her limited California Spanish than with English, was remembered primarily for her long days of isolation and hard work from sunrise to sunset at their downtown restaurant. As Sumi recalled: "She used to say, 'The only time I see the sun is through the kitchen window' . . . I guess she could look through the top pane . . . and see the sun through there . . . That always stuck with me because . . . I thought, in a way, it was a very sad thing to say . . . But, . . . she didn't say it in a sad way."[5]

Adopted son Roy Hashimura also recalled his mother's solid work ethic. Despite her many years of toiling over the kitchen stove in the back room at the Washington Restaurant, he observed that Ken Harada "was the most beautiful Japanese lady in Riverside among the Issei . . . She was beautiful. Beautiful smile. She was sweet. The sweetest person you could ask for. Never showed anger . . . But I always felt sorry for her because she never got to go anyplace. She was always working in the kitchen. She always stayed in the kitchen. She seldom came out to the front. It was all work at the restaurant."[6]

As with Roy, annual progress through the grades in school, chores at the house on Lemon Street, and afternoon work at the family restaurant were recalled by the other Harada children still at home as core experiences of the 1930s. For most of its years, the Washington Restaurant was open seven days a week, serving three meals a day from five in the morning to eight at night and making a small profit of about $250 a month after paying for rent, supplies, and, in good years, as many as four or five extra helpers. Offering an American menu influenced by onetime galley attendant Jukichi's observations of the appetites of his hungry shipmates aboard the *Grant* and *Solace*, the Washington offered hearty fare with mother Ken's special chicken dinners "served every Sunday." The only Washington Restaurant menu item even remotely Japanese was boiled rice offered at five cents a serving. The star ingredient for Mrs. Harada's Sunday chicken dinners was often supplied by the Inaba family poultry ranch on Jurupa Road, across the Santa Ana River beyond the small community of Rubidoux. Two generations of Harada children would sometimes escape life in the city to play on the Inaba ranch. Some remember climbing on tractors or catching crayfish in the irrigation ditches with other youngsters in the Inaba family or bathing in the relaxing steaming waters of the Inabas' wooden *ofuro* soaking tub, heated with firewood to what some of the Harada grandchildren still recall as nearly scalding temperatures.

Roy Hashimura remembered preparing the Inabas' farmyard chickens for the Washington Restaurant's Sunday dinner patrons: "They used to bring them in a little box with wire covering it and they'd have six or seven chickens in there. They were alive. I killed a few. I'd get the legs and wings together and we'd have a wooden block . . . and I'd get the hatchet and chop off their neck. Then I'd put them in a can and cover it and they'd make all kinds of noise in there, hopping around . . . We'd put the chickens in a great big tub of hot water, take the feathers off."[7]

Jukichi and Ken, their two oldest children married and gone from home, still spent most of their waking hours working together at the Washington Restaurant on Eighth Street, urging their boys to do well in school and hoping for more help each year, both at the restaurant and at home, from Sumi, their only daughter still at home. Her youngest brother, Shig, remembered that the Harada children went through a gradual process of assuming increasing responsibility in the jobs each was given by their father at the family restaurant:

> Our first . . . job was to . . . announce to my dad that a customer had arrived . . . We would say, "Oh ki yaku san," which would mean . . . a customer or a visitor . . . So, that was . . . the beginning . . . [Another] was when the . . . customer had finished his meal, he would arise from the table and, at the moment he rose . . . it was our duty to say . . . "Tata yo," which means . . . he stood up. And . . . that indicated to my dad [to] move to the register to . . . receive the . . . meal . . . costs from the customer.
>
> . . . Our other chores . . . were to clean up and maybe sweep up, and, if . . . we were old enough, we could . . . perhaps . . . dish the tables, . . . and . . . wipe up the tables and clean around the area . . . as we became older.
>
> And then . . . after that . . . by the time we were in junior high school, we could take orders. Perhaps repeat the menu to the customer, and . . . take orders . . . and maybe even serve the customer, if we could carry the dishes.[8]

As in its earlier years, the modest restaurant's small tables and lunch counter were still presided over by framed portraits of Presidents George Washington and

Abraham Lincoln, and later joined by successor Woodrow Wilson at the time of the Great War. By the 1930s, the dour pictures of the few US presidents still hanging honorably on the Washington Restaurant's otherwise drab walls were accompanied by the much happier and more vibrant faces of several young and attractive Japanese women with rosy cheeks, images likely saved by Jukichi or his teenaged sons from the monthly pages of outdated advertising calendars. For the most part, though, the Depression's long workdays at the restaurant passed uneventfully. Supplies were ordered, meals cooked, customers served, and bills paid. Riverside still relied on the produce of its surrounding citrus groves but it was also exploring new ideas for economic growth and community stability, over many years gradually transforming the army's old Alessandro Flying School into March Air Force Base, and the state's Citrus Experiment Station into the Riverside campus of the University of California.[9]

Having abandoned his rooming-house business in the town center soon after his family moved to Lemon Street, Jukichi replaced his family's modest room-rental income with equally modest proceeds from the two small residential properties the Haradas owned on the east side of town. One, near the Teshima family over on Fourteenth Street between Howard and Park, was rented for many years by the Yonemuras; the other, around the corner on Howard Street with upstairs living quarters rented by the Amamoto family, included a small community hall on the ground floor. Local Japanese would sometimes gather in the downstairs community center for cultural events and perhaps a short American movie or two. As Harold recalled,

> The Japanese community would . . . gather there for . . . different kinds of
> events . . . such as showing a movie, or . . . a travelling . . . magician's show, . . . a
> magician from Japan . . . travelling through . . . various cities in California . . .
> would perform . . . there—musicians, dancers, whatever . . . It was sort of a com-
> munity center . . . but very modest . . . Most of [the performances featured] Japa-
> nese themes . . . They might have shown an American movie or something, or
> a little comedy kinda' thing, perhaps, but I think . . . mainly Japanese cultural
> kinds a' things.[10]

At their home on Lemon Street not far from the old apricot tree, Harold remembered his mother growing a few Japanese vegetables and "long green chili peppers" in small plots here and there around the house. In later years, the Haradas also planted a new backyard peach tree and added a small concrete fishpond nearby, landscaped in miniature with attractive water plants. Received by the Haradas as a gift from Masaichi Ohka, who made the concrete ponds in his spare time after work at his chop suey restaurant downtown, the small pond was dug into the ground at the end of a narrow wooden plank pathway leading from the back patio behind the house. The little pond, stocked with a few struggling goldfish from the five-and-dime store, offered the family a hint of a restful Japanese garden oasis on hot Riverside evenings.[11]

On Saturday, June 15, 1935, Riverside's small Japanese community lost its strongest advocate and greatest friend when the Mission Inn's Frank Miller died of cancer at age seventy-eight. For the afternoon funeral two days later, city offices and stores in town were closed in honor of the Master of the Inn. Shortly before a private memorial service at the inn's St. Francis Chapel, many of Miller's longtime hotel employees filed past his flower-covered bier illuminated by "the soft light of flickering candles." Miller was eulogized by his friend of fifty years, Harry Chandler, publisher of the *Los Angeles Times*, and the Reverend T. C. Hunt, former pastor of Miller's First Congregational Church. Chandler commemorated Miller's long-standing interest in promoting international goodwill, remarking, "So long as the Easter sun rises over the rocky peak of Rubidoux, so long as this city of his heart remains, so long as peace and international brotherhood endure as an ideal of humankind, so long will his spirit live."

The day following Miller's funeral, publisher Chandler's *Los Angeles Times* described the services at the Mission Inn, reporting "the nave of the chapel and the adjoining patio were piled high with blooms from a hundred gardens." Condolences from several foreign countries included a cable from Koki Hirota, Japanese minister of foreign affairs, and a telegram from Hiroshi Saito, Japanese ambassador to the United States. Hirota's cable read, in part, "Mr. Miller's active leadership and the tremendous influence he had in establishing friendliness among nations, besides his own personal loyalty to Japanese friends, have made him a revered person in Japan whose memory will live forever."

Ambassador Saito's message said Miller's "memory will forever be a monument to the strong bond of friendship between America and Japan." At the conclusion of the service, Miller's son-in-law, De Witt Hutchings, husband of Miller's daughter, Allis, read the last verse of "A Perfect Day," Carrie Jacobs Bond's popular parlor song of 1910. Bond had written the song at the Mission Inn as a hotel guest in 1909. Pallbearers for Miller's burial in the family plot at Evergreen Cemetery near old Chinatown included his former third-party aide, Mike Westerfield, and Ken Nakazawa, professor of Oriental art and literature at the University of Southern California.[12]

In the fall, a more elaborate memorial service attended by hundreds more was held near the great cross at the summit of Mount Rubidoux. The September service concluded with the placement of two wreaths on the mountain's Peace Tower just across the arched stone bridge and stairway leading upward from the monument's hillside Japanese garden. Within a few years of Miller's passing, the Mission Inn's operations were adapted in response to the financial pressures of the settlement of his estate and the economic impact of the Great Depression. The remaining members of Miller's family sought to make their aging hotel more attractive to the ever-changing tastes of the California public, and sold some of the family's landholdings on Mount Rubidoux to help pay the bills. Elements of Frank's lifelong dream of providing a setting for international harmony and friendship were soon replaced by more modern spaces built to attract new and younger hotel visitors.

Two years after Miller's death, his once impressive but rather sedate Fuji Kan Room, with its elaborate displays of Japanese and Chinese objets d'art, was unceremoniously converted into the hotel's swanky El Mundo Cocktail Lounge, the Mission Inn's first bar. The new cocktail lounge offered a much livelier setting, with air conditioning and room for 100 patrons. In another two years, as Japan became ever more aggressive on the international stage and some began worrying war might become inevitable, the lower level of the inn's Court of the Orient was replaced by the new Lea Lea Room. Featuring a tropical South Pacific theme, the hotel's latest addition was enhanced by "ten tall artificial palm trees, . . . bamboo side chairs, cane and teakwood tables, thatched walls, soft lights, and a splashing waterfall." The softly lit Lea Lea Room, a hip—at the time—South Seas mid-century descendant of the old hotel's much earlier California Mission Revival patios and courtyards, soon became a popular fantasy hot spot with dance bands playing past sundown for local girls and some of the 4,000 boys in uniform taking part in anti-aircraft training at nearby March Field and Camp Haan.[13]

In contrast to some of the quickly fading Japanese elements at the Mission Inn, and like so many other hardworking Issei of their day who often felt they were slowly losing parental influence over their American-born and less restrained Nisei offspring, Jukichi and Ken tried to instill in their children a connection to Japan. They prepared Japanese food for rare special occasions at home and offered their children thoughtful guidance about the relationship of Japanese tradition and family values to the larger lessons of life. Harold recalled the small selection of Japanese food his mother fixed for the family dinner table:

> In the evenings, usually Mother fixed a Japanese dish or two . . . Boiled or steamed rice, and . . . *tsukemono*, the Japanese pickles, and those kinds a' things . . .
>
> And on . . . holidays or Sundays, . . . most times . . . it would be Japanese food . . . She used to make *okazu*, . . . a mixture of . . . beef and . . . vegetables, maybe eggplants, or . . . carrots, maybe . . . the long white radish, daikon, . . . cooked together . . .
>
> Oftentimes . . . we would have *sashimi*, if the fish were fresh. Ah, *sukiyaki* . . . or *teriyaki* chicken, or teriyaki beef, or teriyaki pork . . . An assortment of . . . Japanese dishes as Mom would concoct them and . . . maybe she . . . dreamed up a few, maybe, but . . . typically Japanese . . . Soy sauce and . . . a little sugar.

Both Harold and Roy also remembered quiet moments at home on Lemon Street with old father Jukichi offering his boys bedtime reminders about what it took to be a good citizen and responsible man in the world. Harold explained his father's influence:

> He was a very gentle person . . . and he had . . . a very generous and kind heart. I think that he demanded a lot of us. I think he really wanted us to be loyal citizens, and he wanted us to be honest . . . He wanted us to be . . . as full of integrity as we could be.
>
> . . . At bedtime, . . . he would relate to me stories about his Japanese learnings . . . And he almost nightly told me about . . . Admiral Heihachiro Togo who was the fleet commander of the . . . Japanese war ships that got into an engagement with the Russians. And my dad kept telling me that story over and over again . . . But it seemed that every time he told me it was . . . another new adventure.
>
> I . . . recall that he made me memorize . . . the battle flag that Admiral Togo had put up for his sailors, and I've committed that to memory and I can still recall it . . . It was, "Ko koku no kohai kono issen ni ari, nanjira funrei doroku sei yo." And as I understand it, and I'm no student of Japanese, but . . . the way my dad described it, was that Admiral Togo said to his seamen that this was the hour, this was going to be the . . . major battle and that they needed to really excel in all of . . . their duties, and that they must commit themselves to this battle.
>
> . . . As a child . . . it really moved me or caused me to believe . . . that we had to be warriors . . . And I think that he kept repeating this to me to make certain that I would become an upstanding citizen.

Reflecting Jukichi's paternal advice about family values and the importance of loyalty, commitment, patriotism, and military service, ideas espoused by Harada's family in Japan some fifty years before, the three remaining Harada boys—Yoshizo, Clark, and Harold—along with adopted brother Roy, all served in the Reserve Officers' Training Corps (ROTC) at the local high school. Dressed in their dashing military uniforms and posing earnestly for school and family photographs in the 1930s, the four boys shared the same ROTC sword, passing it down from one brother to the next over the years while learning about the responsibilities of US citizenship and military values at school, and sometimes dreaming of samurai ancestors at home. As Harold explained,

> My brother Yoshizo . . . participated in ROTC at high school, and he . . . worked up the ranks and became a lieutenant, . . . carried a saber, wore a Sam Brown belt and all that . . . My brother Clark . . . became a commissioned officer in the ROTC, too . . . My adopted brother, Roy, . . . became an officer . . . in ROTC, and I, too, . . . became a commissioned officer in the ROTC at the high school . . . We all carried the same saber, I believe, from Yoshizo all the way down.[14]

American and Japanese themes were reinforced in pictures scattered on walls throughout the Harada house, with several framed photographs and prints hanging in dimly lit rooms both upstairs and down. One bedroom featured a small lithograph of George and Martha Washington, depicting the brave patriot restaurant icon's spouse and home life. Jukichi Harada's father and mother, Takanori and Tetsu Harada, looked down from another century in a large gold-framed charcoal rendering hanging over the double bed in the room where their California grandson Harold Shigetaka was born in 1923. The portrait connected the family's Japanese ancestors to the new American lives taking shape within the house on Lemon Street. A blue-tinted tableau of the Japanese imperial family, depicting the emperor with his wife and children, honored the emperor of Japan while supporting family pride in Japanese cultural origins. In the parlor facing the front porch, hanging on the wall just above the family's dark Mission-style oak furniture set, the small portrait photograph of a white man, the Haradas' late Riverside attorney William A. Purington, served as a daily reminder of his personal contribution to the family in their fight to own a home of their own, a modest shrine to their triumph over Attorney General Webb.

Upstairs, Mine and Saburo's framed wedding picture and another nearby family portrait held visions of family progress, solidarity, and strength. A few scattered prints of flowers, colorful pastoral scenes of cows and milkmaids, and a gold-framed painting of a white calla lily brought hints of nature indoors to otherwise plain interior walls, perhaps reminding Ken Harada of the kakitsubata iris of Aichi, left behind so many years before. Elsewhere in the house, photograph albums with wide black pages and thick leather covers preserved less formal images of everyday family life. Black-and-white snapshots of a smiling Jukichi near his backyard chicken coop, the Harada children posing in the family Ford, friends standing together at the base of the big wooden cross high atop nearby Mount Rubidoux, community gatherings at the Mission Inn, and pictures of well-dressed grandchildren from Northern California captured the sense that life was still good, even in difficult times.

Arousing fears and sad memories of the death in 1913 of brother Tadao, Clark Kohei Harada, the boy born in the rooming house shortly before the family moved to Lemon Street, contracted rheumatic fever in the early 1930s and had to convalesce at home. Ko missed school for two years while his brothers were engaged in happier pursuits, playing baseball and tennis when they could find the time. In 1934, now two years older than his classmates because of his illness, Ko finally returned to his studies at Riverside's Polytechnic High School, where he enjoyed wide acceptance. Most local Nikkei children in high school did well in public school. For some in Riverside's fairly hospitable social environment, extracurricular activities included membership, with non-Japanese high school students, in the Booklovers' Club, Tennis Club, Latin Club, Nursing Club, Press Club, Bible Club, and Future Farmers of America. Like his brothers, Clark was involved in ROTC at the high school, receiving straight A's in his senior-year military-training class. His Japanese name, Kohei, could be translated as "veteran" or "old soldier," and dressed proudly in his high school ROTC uniform, Clark took its significance to heart.[15]

In the eyes of senior-class prophet Betty Finley, writing for the high school yearbook *The 1938 Orange and Green*, Clark's involvement in ROTC, the high school Rifle Club, and the Junior Institute of World Affairs, offspring of its parent organization at the Mission Inn, had prepared him for future success in the US military. Finley's humorous essay about life in far-off 1955 predicted the escapades of notable Polytechnic High School seniors twenty years into the future. In her imagined encounters with former classmates, Betty finds them in various illustrious and sometimes nefarious occupations. A highlight of her journey finds her in Washington, DC, where she meets old friends Shirley Johnson and Clark Harada: "At a ball given for the president's birthday I met none other than Shirley Johnson, now the chief bouncer at the Palace de Raz. And over there, in that corner, under a burden of medals is Clark Harada, Japanese Military Attache," Finley wrote.

Most of the other half-dozen Japanese Americans in Riverside's graduating class of 1938 went largely unnoticed in the high school yearbook, so the mention of Clark Harada in the senior-class prophecy shows that he had made a positive impression among his classmates and developed meaningful friendships at school. Unlike Shirley Johnson, however, whose future career as a bouncer at the Palace de Raz was not contingent upon her ethnicity, Clark would soon learn in a much less humorous context that his Japanese ancestry would once again define his future.[16]

Mine recalled, like many other elder children, that her parents slowly relaxed their child-rearing standards with her younger siblings:

> Our parents were very strict with us, but as they grew older they became more lenient, and I think the younger ones benefited. At least, I felt quite deprived. The younger ones could go to the movies at least once a week—I never could, unless some friends invited me which was seldom. One time after much discussion I got permission to see a play—Shakespeare.
>
> I did a great deal of work for the Church, which my parents approved. They were both Christians and went to Church as often as they could. Our parents had prayer meetings at home. They were deeply religious and there was no smoking or drinking in our home.[17]

Within their rather straitlaced Christian home and family, Jukichi and Ken also did their best to help their Nisei children live safely and responsibly by maintaining some of the manners, habits, and customs of their Japanese homeland. Mine recalled her mother telling stories about her own father, samurai Matazo Indo, and his observance of strict family rituals. Mine said, "[W]e never talked of these family matters to anyone." She explained one distant family practice recounted by her mother: "When the father was alive, he was very fussy about . . . family traditions, especially the samurai traditions . . . He used to have a festival and only family members could be greeted at that time. And, she said . . . it would last about two weeks and they had to prepare food that would last for about two weeks . . . I think it was . . . some kind of a sword festival, because they displayed the family swords."[18]

Adding to Mine's stories of a long-vanished samurai past, Harold also remembered several important Japanese folkways imparted to him by his parents in the 1920s and 1930s:

> One of them was that you had to eat every kernel of rice in your bowl or you would go blind. And, goodness, who wants to go blind when you're five or six years old, you know? So you eat every grain of rice in the bowl.
>
> . . . If you attended a funeral, you had to cleanse yourself with two or three throws of salt over your left shoulder before you entered your house, otherwise someone in your family was going to soon depart this good world if you didn't do that. Well, you don't want any family member to die so you threw salt over your shoulder before you came in the house. And Sumi insisted on that with me . . . even in our older years . . . I think it makes you aware of life and death . . .
>
> Another one was . . . you shouldn't cut your fingernails at night . . . So we had to do that during the daytime . . . That's what we were told.
>
> We were told not to burn hair because you'll go crazy if you burn hair . . . Certainly we didn't want to go crazy.
>
> . . . If you didn't put your clothes on in a certain way, it was not good luck . . . You had to put your clothes on in a certain manner or otherwise it was bad luck.
>
> A lot of things . . . pointed to bad luck if you didn't do those things. But it was a good way to make one adhere to the rules of the house.[19]

The Harada children also remembered interactions with a few neighbors, friends at school, and the mix of customers at the Washington Restaurant. Many whites, a few African Americans, Mexican laborers, workers from nearby March Field, Japanese friends, and Native Americans who came to town on the weekend ate at the family's restaurant and contributed to the Haradas' limited social lives. Of all the Washington's many patrons, bachelor Jess Stebler, a Riverside blacksmith, was remembered as the family's favorite. Born in Minden, Iowa, in 1876 and forced to wear a cumbersome hearing aid in later years after going nearly deaf from years of work as a blacksmith, Jess Stebler was the younger brother of Riverside's more affluent citrus machine inventor and businessman, Fred Stebler.

Brother Fred founded the California Iron Works in Riverside in 1903 and was the wealthy and successful businessman who lived with his family in the nice chalet-style bungalow across from the Estudillos at the western end of Sixth Street.

Beginning his friendship with the Haradas in the 1920s, Jess Stebler, a solid man with a strong jaw, dark moustache, and rumpled clothing, worked during the week as a blacksmith at his brother's citrus packing machine company. With his strong hands and solid work ethic, Jess helped to craft the inventions and machinery that built the Southern California citrus industry. Living alone, Mr. Stebler took his meals at the Washington Restaurant nearly every day. As Harold recalled,

> I think that Jess was more or less a black sheep because he did not attend any of the functions that his wealthy brother participated in or anything like that. Jess was a loner. He was a bachelor. And he lived in this hotel about a block away from where our restaurant was, and he was a customer of my folks for twenty or thirty years. And he lived the very simple life. His breakfast was the same. He took a brown-bag lunch every day that my mother prepared for him at the restaurant and he took [it] with him to work every day. He came home to his hotel room and then came to the restaurant to have dinner, and that was his routine almost seven days a week.[20]

During the Depression, Sumi remembered, business at the Washington Restaurant was often "slow and hard-going." The eatery's few steady customers, like solitary bachelor Jess Stebler, took on great prominence within the Harada family. Besides his presence at the restaurant each day, Harold and Roy remembered Mr. Stebler taking some of the Harada children on extended auto trips from time to time. The old blacksmith with the dark, wide-brimmed fedora must have been a sight driving along California highways in his stylish but aging 1927 Cadillac coupe, stopping briefly at gasoline filling stations and small roadside produce stands or grocery stores, accompanied only by three or four Japanese American children looking curiously out the thick glass windows of what might have been a hand-me-down automobile from his wealthy brother. As Harold explained, "[Mr. Stebler] took us children on vacations in his 1927 Cadillac coupe to different places; to San Diego or San Francisco . . . just for a couple of days. And he was like a part of the family. Birthdays, Christmas, New Year's, whatever the celebration, Mother would fix him a . . . special dinner just as we might have . . . and he ate with us . . . He was part of the family."[21]

Roy Hashimura told of one memorable trip riding with Mr. Stebler in his car from Riverside all the way to Los Angeles, where Roy bought his first camera from tip money saved from a weekend job waiting tables during the evening at a chop suey restaurant on Main Street. "That's when I started taking pictures," Roy said, and many of the last Harada family photographs taken in the late 1930s, only a year or two before the coming war, were snapped by adopted son Roy with the camera

11.1. Jess Stebler, Riverside, circa 1935–1940. (Courtesy of the Harada Family Archival Collection, Riverside Metropolitan Museum, Riverside, California)

he purchased on Mr. Stebler's trip to Los Angeles. With their images captured in Roy's black-and-white photographs, standing alone or side by side in the bright afternoon sunshine while taking a break from work to gather briefly on the sidewalk outside the Washington Restaurant with their adult children and some of their young grandchildren, Jukichi and Ken remained knowing and vibrant in their eyes and smiles. However, their aging bodies, once so vigorous, strong, and upright in earlier Harada family photographs, now looked weary, old, and fragile.[22]

As her parents began facing the limitations of old age and mounting health problems, and with her younger brothers growing up and spending little time helping out at the restaurant, second daughter Sumi, by now in her late twenties, gradually accepted more responsibility managing the family business. Sumi's work at the restaurant also helped her parents support the education of her younger brother, Yoshizo. No longer living in Riverside, Yosh was busy with his dental school studies at the College of Physicians and Surgeons in San Francisco. Between school terms, he found work crating carrots at a farm in Santa Maria, but with farmwork providing little more than bus fare back to San Francisco, he later took a more promising summer job on an Alaskan salmon fishing boat and cannery to help support his studies.[23]

Day by day, new demands within her family began to make Sumi think she might not ever enjoy the personal freedom experienced by her older sister, Mine.

In some ways, by the late 1930s, Sumi was slowly losing her grasp on a life of her own. The last few years had not been easy. Little by little, Jukichi's and Ken's health continued to decline. The old couple spent more and more of their time at home, no longer physically able to work full days at their downtown restaurant. Along with these slow transformations at the Washington Restaurant, the area around the house on Lemon Street also began to change from a place with settled and reasonably prosperous middle-class residents to a much more transient and less affluent neighborhood. "The families were always moving . . . They weren't the same people all the time . . . It was so many families I can't remember their names," Sumi would say of the years before Pearl Harbor.

Like other former small towns in California, Riverside was changing from a fairly close-knit community relying on local jobs supporting a lively downtown shopping district and cultural center to a more widely dispersed and less cohesive suburban city where lonesome commuters and big-box outlets would one day become the norm. To accommodate this steady growth, before the war, city officials changed its downtown street address numbering system, and the Haradas' fifty-year-old house at 356 Lemon Street became 3356. Some folks living in the less affluent sections of town simply painted or tacked up a new number in front of their former short address. Other property owners became absentee landlords, breaking up some of the area's older single-family homes into smaller rental apartments as Riverside began to lose some of its former grace and prominence in an ever-changing California.[24]

At the close of the era between the two world wars, memories of some of the Haradas' old friends and adversaries had dimmed. Former superior court judge Hugh Craig had collapsed and died at the age of forty-seven in 1922. The local paper called Craig's passing an "irreparable loss." A resolution from the county bar association signed by several local attorneys, including Harada trial opponents A. Aird Adair and Miguel Estudillo, proclaimed Judge Craig had been widely respected for "an intuitive sense of justice." Courts were adjourned for his funeral and Riverside's Japanese Mission sent tributes in his memory. A few months after Judge Craig's passing, former neighborhood committee spokesman Jacob Van de Grift and his wife, Clara, were both struck by a car and mortally injured crossing the street at the corner of Sixth and Main. Mrs. Van de Grift suffered a fractured skull. The old couple succumbed to their injuries within a few days of one another. A decade later, next-door neighbor and friend Cynthia Robinson was gone, and by 1939, members of only three of the original seven families in the old citizens' committee still lived near the Haradas in the Lemon Street neighborhood. The others had all died or moved away.[25]

During this time, in Sacramento Dr. Masa Atsu Harada ended his twelve-year marriage to Mary after a romance with Martha Matsuye Nakagawa, the young widow of dentist Dr. Takeo Chiba. Harada's medical office associate in Sacra-

mento, Dr. Chiba had recently died of tuberculosis. This affair led to a stormy divorce and emotional battles over child custody and alimony payments. Dr. Harada shocked some in Sacramento's close-knit Nikkei community by marrying Martha in 1937, not long after his divorce was final. Mary and her two children, Calvin and Lily Ann, soon moved back to San Francisco to live near relatives in a small flat near other Japanese families on Sutter Street at the western edge of the city's Nihonmachi. Even with her degree from Heald's Business College, Mary faced limited employment opportunities because of the Great Depression. Daughter Lily Ann remembered that her now-single mother was finally able to land a modest job in San Francisco, where she found work "at a Japanese gift shop as a sales girl during the day and beaded evening gowns and dresses at night." Masa Atsu and Mary's son and daughter, just eleven and seven when their parents separated, would experience lifelong personal distress in their attempts to maintain a relationship with their estranged father and reconcile their feelings about the dissolution of their family.[26]

Perhaps admiring some aspects of her older siblings' personal freedom and more sophisticated adult lives in bigger cities far from Riverside, sister Sumi once tried to establish herself away from home, working for several months in Sacramento as a hospital receptionist. She returned home to Lemon Street at the end of May 1939, offering help to her ailing father in his recovery from an abdominal surgery to repair the hernia he had had since an injury suffered as a young man working aboard the USS *Grant* at the turn of the century. Once again back at work in the familiar setting of the Washington Restaurant just a short walk from home, before long Sumi would bid farewell to brother Clark, who, along with adopted brother Roy, also left home to find work in the Bay Area. With lingering resentment over his older brothers' college educations and professional careers, Clark left Riverside soon after graduating from high school. Roy moved away after a couple of years of attending classes at Riverside Junior College. Like brother Masa Atsu and sister Mine, who had already migrated north, Clark and Roy moved to Berkeley, living with Mine and her family while seeking scarce jobs toward the end of the Great Depression. The two young men both eventually found employment with an East Bay optometrist.[27]

Back home in Riverside, the elder Haradas' daily presence at the Washington Restaurant was now curtailed because of their physical limitations. Sunday automobile rides with Shig and Sumi around nearby Fairmount Park were often their only form of recreation outside their house on Lemon Street. Despite mounting ailments, both parents remained interested in and dedicated to the progress of their immediate family. Jukichi and Ken no doubt worried about son Yoshizo's marriage to Sumiye Kusunoki in 1938, because with only "$25 to his name," he had not yet become well established as a new dentist. Still, Yosh's parents were proud of his recent graduation from dental school, the start of his new dental practice in Sacramento near brother Masa Atsu, and his commission as a first lieutenant in the United States Army Dental Reserves.

Because of their frailty, Jukichi and Ken were unable to travel alone to visit their children in Northern California but they continued to take part in the few family activities they could manage close to home. Their second granddaughter, Mine and Saburo's daughter Rosalind, recalled a surprise springtime gift sent to the Bay Area from her grandparents in Riverside. "I do remember one Mother's Day when we were living in Berkeley," Rosalind said. "My mother received a box from Grandmother and Grandfather . . . It had fried chicken in it and a dress for me."[28]

His strength waning, grandfather Jukichi spent time gathering information about his life in anticipation of one day becoming an American citizen. He hoped a record of his service on the USS *Grant* during the Spanish American War in 1898 would support his efforts. Even though it was still not possible for most natives of Japan to become naturalized American citizens—that chance would not come for Japanese immigrants until 1952—a few had been promised the opportunity if they could prove their World War I military service to the United States. With help from son-in-law Saburo Kido and others active in the Japanese American Citizens League, a new law passed in 1935 had reestablished the chance for alien veterans to become American citizens.

Jukichi believed his time aboard the *Grant* in wartime might also qualify him for citizenship. To support his longtime desire to become an American citizen, Harada composed several pages of notes about his service aboard the *Grant* and *Solace* at the turn of the century. Recording the details of his personal history in English in his own hand, Jukichi listed fragments of information about his early life in California, the immigration of his wife and son in 1905, and his success with the Alien Land Law court case. He also included a list of the funds he contributed toward the college educations of his first and second sons, Masa Atsu and Yoshizo.[29]

As required by law at the time of the Great War, even for aliens, both Jukichi and son Masa Atsu had registered for the American military draft in the fall of 1918. Jukichi explained in his personal history notes that he was qualified to serve during World War I but was exempted from service because he had "too many children." He now hoped his earlier service in 1898 could support his citizenship application. Jukichi also mentioned his interest in supporting the activities of his Japanese Union Church in Riverside and the Japanese American Citizens League. Despite his service and efforts, he was soon disappointed when his request for citizenship was denied.[30]

One day at the house on Lemon Street, high school senior Harold Harada was going through the daily routine of chores and homework. A few steps away, her aged but still beautiful face reflected, perhaps, in the large mirror of the dresser in what the family called the *kamitoku*, the "hair-dressing room" at the center of the house downstairs, Harold's mother slowly arranged her straight white hair. Since the days of her youth, influenced by memories of samurai grooming traditions of long ago, Ken Harada had always been careful with her hair. On this ordinary day, feeling numbness and a sudden loss of function in her right hand, Mrs. Harada suffered a mild stroke. As the months passed, Mrs. Harada's physical condition declined. She developed further weakness in her arms and legs, spending more time at home, sometimes unable to leave her bed. Sumi, Harold, and Jukichi all did their best to assist her, but Ken's decline did not subside.[31]

So much of what was once a house full of life was now gone and slowly fading from within, but springtime was still a time to recognize renewal at the house on Lemon Street. Replacing the happy sounds of noisy misbehaving children laughing at the radio, whispering late into the evening on the upstairs sleeping porch, or running in and out of slamming doors and into the yard, the quiet sights of spring now brought a different kind of joy to Ken and Jukichi Harada. In April, blossoms from the family's peach tree filled the yard behind the house with delicate pink petals floating gently in the wind. A raggedy bed of purple violets near the front door flourished safely in the shade beneath the mock orange hedge near the mailbox on the porch. Dark blue iris, red geraniums, roses in full bloom, morning glories on the fence, and other flowers were often seen outside the kitchen door and in other sunny garden spots in May, and sometimes there were peaches on the backyard tree by the Fourth of July. On hot summer days, when the temperature inside their old house soared to well above 100 degrees and it seemed thermometers would burst, the family spent time outside on the open sleeping porch upstairs at the front of the house, trying to catch an evening breeze and cool off in the shade of the two big pepper trees at the curb out front, their red, round peppercorns crunching fragrantly underfoot amid slim green leaves carpeting the sidewalk.

In their warm Southern California town, some plants along the south fence near the Haradas' driveway could still be in bloom as late as December, but by the end of 1941 another season of colorful garden flowers and backyard fruit had largely come and gone at the house on Lemon Street. On hazy mornings, listening to the plaintive call of nearby mourning doves cooing softly, the plump birds perched heavily on sagging black electric wires strung high above the sidewalk, Ken and Jukichi welcomed the cooler weather of December, the beginning of what would be their last winter at home.[32]

Far from Riverside, halfway across the Pacific, at the first hour of this Sunday morning in Hawaii some of the young American military officers and crewmen stationed on the island of Oahu were ashore for the weekend. Others were already sound asleep in their narrow bunks aboard rows of ships moored closely together in the harbor. Earlier in the evening a young couple drove down from the low hills above Honolulu to Waikiki for dinner and dancing at the Royal Hawaiian Hotel. Beneath tall palm trees and a background of pink stucco, stepping onto one of the best dance floors on the white sandy beach near Diamond Head, the dancers paused for a moment as the hotel band played the national anthem at the stroke of midnight on December 6: "Saturday night . . . Joe and I dined and danced at the Royal Hawaiian until midnight when, as customary, the . . . orchestra struck up the Star Spangled Banner and we all stood at attention on the dance floor under the stars, with the surf rolling in and the palms waving in the breeze. It was a solemn but happy ending to an evening and a time which now seems to belong to another world."[33]

Along the beach at Waikiki, as the strains of the national anthem floated across the gently rolling surf and into the darkness over the Pacific, the dance floor under the stars at the Royal Hawaiian Hotel emptied slowly. A few remaining couples lingered close together under tropical skies in the balmy night. Two hundred miles north of the island, on huge carriers at sea, hundreds of youthful warriors, their hearts pounding in wild anticipation, pilots and support crews for more than 400 aircraft of the Kido Butai Task Force of the Imperial Japanese Navy under the command of Vice Admiral Chuichi Nagumo, waited anxiously for takeoff.

TWELVE

FAREWELL TO RIVERSIDE

By mid-morning on this winter Sunday, December 7, 1941, Saburo Kido had already left his family's home at 1804 Stuart Street in the East Bay community of Berkeley, where he had been living for the last four years with his wife, Mine, and their three young children, daughter Rosalind and sons Laurence and Wally. Shuttling over to meet friends across the bay in San Francisco, once again Saburo was away from his family while taking care of community business on the weekend. In a few minutes, perhaps riding on a ferry or hitching a ride in a friend's car, Saburo, representing the Japanese American Citizens League as its president, crossed the chilly waters of San Francisco Bay to attend a morning unity meeting of Nikkei community leaders. The meeting had no sooner begun when, arriving a little late, Dr. George Baba made the surprising claim that he had just heard brief radio reports of Japanese planes bombing American military targets at Pearl Harbor in Hawaii. "That's too fantastic to believe," Kido said. "The report must be wrong, probably just another rumor."[1]

Like others along the West Coast that Sunday morning, eighteen-year-old Harold Harada was at home in Riverside with others in his family, getting ready for the day. "I remember listening to the radio here in the house just before I left for the restaurant, [hearing] . . . that the Japanese had bombed Pearl Harbor. And it shocked me. I didn't know what the consequences would be . . . And when I told my dad . . . he was shocked . . . He was really taken aback," Harold said.[2]

Back in San Francisco, Harold's brother-in-law and the other community leaders abruptly recessed their morning meeting just after noon to catch the midday radio report of National Broadcasting Company newscaster H. V. Kaltenborn. In "stunned silence" the anxious group heard Kaltenborn confirming that targets in both Hawaii and the Philippines were, indeed, under surprise attack by Japanese military forces. Saburo quickly left the group, rushing to the newspaper office of the *New World Sun*, one of the city's Japanese-language papers and where he published his own daily newspaper column, "Timely Topics," and also sometimes served as legal counsel. As journalist and historian Bill Hosokawa explained in *JACL: In Quest of Justice*, when Kido reached the newspaper's office, "The telephone was ringing. Reporters for the San Francisco newspapers and the local correspondent for the *New York Times* were asking for comment. Kido could still not believe war had come, but he composed himself quickly and issued a statement condemning the attack, pledging the loyalty of the Nisei and offering full support of the war effort."[3]

Later in the day, when the initial commotion had briefly subsided, Kido took a few moments to regain his composure. Organizing his thoughts, he began drafting an urgent telegram to President Franklin Delano Roosevelt. In his carefully worded message, wired hurriedly to the White House before the end of the day, Kido included references he felt would help the Japanese American community distinguish itself from the sweeping public anger and false claims he feared were now sure to follow:

> The Japanese Americans are stunned and horrified by this morning's unwarranted attack by Japan upon American soil, our country. We want to convey to you that we unequivocally condemn Japan for this unprecedented breach of good faith. In behalf of our 15,000 members in the 56 chapters of our Japanese American Citizens League, we unreservedly volunteer the facilities of our office to the defense of our land.
>
> . . . In this solemn hour we pledge our fullest cooperation to you, Mr. President, and to our country . . . Now that Japan has instituted this attack upon our land, we are ready and prepared to expend every effort to repel this invasion together with our fellow Americans.[4]

Just a few hours after Kido's telegram reached the White House, President Roosevelt was greeted by warm applause from those gathered for a hastily called joint session of Congress the next day. Cords of radio microphones crossed each other like a big spiderweb draped over the front edge of the podium in front of the president. As the applause subsided, Roosevelt began to address the anxious Senate and House members, justices of the Supreme Court, his cabinet, and the nation, opening his somber remarks with "Yesterday, December 7, 1941—a date which will live in infamy—the United States of America was suddenly and deliberately attacked by naval and air forces of the Empire of Japan." Initially, the congressional chamber in Washington was stone silent as the president referred to recent diplomatic negotiations with Japan and ongoing discussion "with its government and its emperor looking toward the maintenance of peace in the Pacific." He then quickly shifted his remarks to reveal what most saw as the heartlessness and deceit of Japanese government officials, noting, "Indeed, one hour after Japanese air squadrons had commenced bombing in the American island of Oahu, the Japanese ambassador to the United States and his colleague delivered to our Secretary of State a formal reply to a recent American message. And while this reply stated that it seemed useless to continue the existing diplomatic negotiations, it contained no threat or hint of war or of armed attack." The president reported, "[V]ery many American lives have been lost." He said severe damage had been done to American naval and military facilities in Hawaii, adding ominously for those listening intently to their radios on the Pacific Coast, "American ships have been reported torpedoed on the high seas between San Francisco and Honolulu." Roosevelt then outlined sweeping Japanese attacks at several other locations across the Pacific, describing them as "a surprise offensive extending throughout the Pacific area."

Hearing the president's startling remarks on the radio, citizens on the West Coast, including some of the more than 70,000 American citizens of Japanese ancestry and about 50,000 of their non-citizen Issei parents still prohibited from becoming US citizens because of their birth in Japan, were shocked. Voicing the fears of those in Riverside and elsewhere on the coast, teenager Harold Harada believed it was now possible that Japan might soon attack California. "I know some of us thought that maybe . . . Japanese bombers might be coming over, but that was sort of a highly speculative guess, but then it wasn't too speculative; it was almost fact," Harold said.[5]

The respectful silence sustained during the first half of the president's address was finally broken by moderate applause as he continued: "The facts of yesterday and today speak for themselves. The people of the United States have already formed their opinions and well understand the implications to the very life and safety of our nation. As Commander in Chief of the Army and Navy, I have directed that all measures be taken for our defense. But always will our whole nation remember the character of the onslaught against us."

When the president resolved, "No matter how long it may take us to overcome this premeditated invasion, the American people in their righteous might will win through to absolute victory," he was interrupted by stronger applause and a few hearty cheers. At the end of his remarks, an extended round of scattered whistles, whoops, and hollers from congressmen of both political parties and audience members in the packed gallery above supported the president after he summarized his country's determination to respond in triumph to Japan's surprise attack:

> I believe that I interpret the will of the Congress and of the people when I assert that we will not only defend ourselves to the uttermost, but will make it very certain that this form of treachery shall never again endanger us. Hostilities exist. There is no blinking at the fact that our people, our territory and our interests are in grave danger. With confidence in our armed forces, with the un-bounding determination of our people, we will gain the inevitable triumph, so help us God. I ask that the Congress declare that since the unprovoked and dastardly attack by Japan on Sunday, December 7, a state of war has existed between the United States and the Japanese Empire.[6]

After the president's address, toward the end of December 8, Roosevelt's attorney general, Francis Biddle, announced the FBI had already apprehended several alien Japanese as threats to national security. Even though Biddle explained that only a small number of suspected aliens would likely be detained, before the end of the week about 1,200 Japanese had been arrested. Four days after the attack on Pearl Harbor, with concerns about possible further Japanese attacks mounting, the United States Army activated the Western Defense Command at the old Presidio in San Francisco. Headed by Lieutenant General John L. DeWitt, the command was charged with the defense of the Pacific coast.

At the end of the month in Washington, Attorney General Biddle authorized raids without search warrants in Japanese American homes inhabited by at least one non-citizen resident. In the earliest weeks of the new year, Biddle also announced the formation of more than 100 "restricted zones from which all enemy aliens must move" by February 24. The attorney general declared that wartime curfew zones in California would be established "where all remaining aliens must be in their houses from 9 p.m. to 6 a.m. [and] must never travel more than five miles from home."[7]

In small towns and cities throughout the West, frightened local citizens began preparing for war. In Riverside, Harold Harada and some of his friends from the city college "went down to the Santa Ana River bottom and filled sandbags to protect campus buildings." Servicemen at nearby March Air Field were put on alert. Growing war hysteria and the confusing public announcements about the requirement for non-citizens to leave the coast by the end of February soon alarmed Sumi and Harold Harada. With their non-citizen parents now both living as invalids at home in Riverside, their mother frequently bedridden, they began worrying about how to handle their care if the forced departure actually came to pass. In the first few hectic days after the attack on Pearl Harbor, some assumed the non-citizen Issei might indeed be separated from their families for a time. It was also believed their children, the second-generation Nisei, would not be forced to leave because they were US citizens. In a meeting in San Francisco on January 4, less than a month after the surprise attack, the Western Defense Command's General DeWitt made a chilling claim about the citizen Nisei, asserting, "I have no confidence in their loyalty whatsoever." By mid-month, Santa Monica congressman Leland Ford joined DeWitt and a growing chorus of others insisting that "all Japanese, whether citizens or not, be placed in inland concentration camps."[8]

Bill Hosokawa said: "Congressman Clarence Lea, unofficial chairman of the California congressional delegation, mustered his forces in support of Ford. Senator Hiram Johnson, who as governor had helped pass California's anti-alien land law, stirred things up in the Senate in the name of national security." Hosokawa's observation linking some of those involved with the passage of the Golden State's Alien Land Laws earlier in the century to the growing fury now demanding immediate removal of all Japanese Americans from the Pacific coast in 1942 points to the solid relationship between the original intent of the Alien Land Laws and what most Americans believed at the time was a new idea prompted only by military necessity—the forced removal and incarceration the government called "Relocation." In fact, the one grew from the other.

Mine Harada Kido, thinking about her family's early battle to keep their home in opposition to California's Alien Land Law, was keenly aware of the years of legal conflicts and confrontations faced by humble people like her father and mother. As an adult, Mine also observed and supported sustained efforts to counter ongoing challenges to the very existence of the Nikkei community. In her view, Mine said, the forced removal during World War II was a "culmination." Historian Milton R. Konvitz explained the origins of the Alien Land Laws, observing that "the real intention of these laws was to drive persons of Japanese ancestry out of California altogether. The opportunity to effect the mass expulsion came with Pearl Harbor." More recently, scholar Keith Aoki has asserted that the Alien Land Laws "provided a bridge that sustained the virulent anti-Asian animus that linked the Chinese Exclusion Act of 1882 with the internment of Japanese American citizens pursuant to Executive Order 9066."[9]

In winter 1942, with support from the president of the United States, secretary of war, military commanders, West Coast congressmen, governors, attorneys general, city and town officials, nationally known figures in print and broadcast media, and less august citizens on most American street corners, the long-established prejudice, hatred, and mistrust of Asians among many in the West steadily reinforced the consensus for General DeWitt's urgent call to remove all Japanese Americans from the Pacific coast. A nation of others, most knowing little or nothing about Japanese Americans except for what they had been hearing recently on the radio or reading in their local newspapers, did not question these events. Even longtime friends of those in the Nikkei community were, for the most part, subdued or under pressure to avoid expressing public opposition to the proposed expulsion. With war against the Empire of Japan already declared by the president, many believed there was simply no room for the sympathetic protests or suggestions from those now openly called "Jap lovers." Members of the Japanese American community were on their own.[10]

Early one morning in Riverside, only days after Attorney General Biddle's authorization of raids without search warrants, the Harada house on Lemon Street was quickly approached without notice and searched throughout by two men identifying themselves as agents of the Federal Bureau of Investigation. Both Sumi and Harold were working downtown at the Washington Restaurant. After cooking pancakes, bacon, and eggs for the breakfast rush, Sumi fixed lunch for her parents, packing it for Harold to take home from the restaurant at noon, as usual. When Harold arrived at the house on Lemon Street, he found his parents distressed, alone, and agitated. "When I got home, Mother looked absolutely shocked. She was pale, mortified, practically. Dad was a little more active, but was upset," Harold said. "The FBI came during the day while my sister and I were at the restaurant and Mother and Dad were alone here in the house. And they presented themselves, evidently, and Dad allowed them in. And they searched every room. They went and emptied every dresser on the beds . . . They searched for everything high and low. Even went through my sister's box of sanitary napkins, tore them apart looking for contraband."[11]

Calming his worried parents as best he could, Harold hurried back down to the restaurant, telling his older sister the disturbing news. Sumi explained:

> He came back about . . . one o'clock and he said, . . . "Do you know what's happening?" I said, "No, I, I don't know what's happening." He said the FBI . . . had been at the house . . . He said . . . "They . . . had a four-hour search of the house. And the folks had to sit in the kitchen . . . while the search was being made." He said they went from top to bottom . . . They'd gone through the rooms and everything was all . . . topsy-turvy.
> . . . He thought that they made a fairly thorough search because there wasn't a thing that wasn't touched. He said, "And then they went into your room, and they, they threw your sanitary pads all over the bed. You're gonna be mad when you get home" . . . But, this search was done in every Japanese home, so, ah, . . . we couldn't get too . . . upset about it. I mean, we had to accept it.

During the search, the agents rummaged clumsily through every room in the Harada house, looking for what the government was describing as "contraband." In other Japanese American homes, things like cameras and short-wave radios were being confiscated as potential tools for sabotage and espionage. "That's what they called it—contraband," Sumi explained. "Anyone had short wave . . . radio,

12.1. Ken Harada Alien Registration, February 1942. (Courtesy of the Harada Family Archival Collection, Riverside Metropolitan Museum, Riverside, California)

that was considered contraband. Well, we weren't that modern. We didn't have any short wave . . . radios in our house."[12]

After combing through crowded drawers and dumping piles of materials onto beds upstairs and down at the house on Lemon Street, the FBI men discovered and confiscated Shig's Eastman Kodak camera and the tiny box holding father Jukichi's Japanese Red Cross pin, received for his donation to the relief fund of the Great Kanto Earthquake of 1923. After the FBI search, although apparently no record exists to prove it, the Harada boys' ROTC sword was gone and never seen by the family again. At the time, Sumi resigned herself to the situation, applying the Japanese cultural phrase *shi kata ganai*, "it can't be helped." Her more vocal teenaged brother thought otherwise about the invasion of their privacy in his family home and the embarrassment of his aged parents. Harold observed more than half a century later: "It was, I think, something that was very, very unnecessary; something that was highly insulting, I think, as I look back on it now . . . To me, it was a disgrace to have the FBI come in and . . . search our household, but war is war."[13]

Perhaps only hours after the FBI search of his house, apparently alone and unnoticed by his wife or others, Jukichi took down the blue-tinted portrait of the Japanese imperial family that had been hanging on the wall inside his house on Lemon Street for so many years. Wondering what else he could do to demonstrate his loyalty to the United States, Harada took one last look at the longtime cultural leaders of Japan, turned the image facedown, and removed the portrait from its frame. Likely feeling great personal anguish, Jukichi then destroyed one of the few remaining tangible links to his Japanese homeland. As daughter Sumi explained, "He must have destroyed 'em because the only thing we found . . . were the frames . . . He was afraid that the FBI would say, 'Well, you possess these so you're considered an . . . enemy.' Because that was . . . the standard that they went by, that, if you had anything . . . that pertained to . . . the Japanese government, . . . you were considered . . . an enemy, so you were supposed to be . . . taken to these . . . internment camps."[14]

California governor Culbert Olson, a New Deal Democrat supported by President Roosevelt in his gubernatorial election in 1938, soon called Saburo Kido and several other Nikkei community leaders to Sacramento. Bill Hosokawa said Kido knew only a few of the two dozen Japanese Americans attending the February 6 meeting and was "outraged" when Olson proposed that "all Japanese males," citizen and non-citizen alike, leave their homes and families voluntarily, move to inland concentration camps, and work as agricultural laborers supporting the California food-production industry as part of the war effort. According to Hosokawa, attorney Kido told the governor that Nisei citizens "were entitled to equal protection under the law and demanded to know why the state could not safeguard the lives and rights of law-abiding Japanese Americans." The *Los Angeles Times* reported that Kido "told the Governor he for one is willing to co-operate in the defeat of Japan, but said members of his race will 'lose face' if, after trying to be loyal American citizens, they are denied constitutional rights." Governor Olson was unmoved. Ignoring Kido's questions about the rights assured to American citizens by the Constitution, Olson turned away from him and told the rest of the group he was interested only in hearing "attitudes and willingness to cooperate."

Characterized by Hosokawa as "usually mild-mannered," Saburo Kido was described as "truculent" in other news reports of the meeting with the governor, which ended without results. Hearing Olson's words firsthand, Saburo Kido's heart must have sunk. With no support from the governor in Sacramento, Kido, a lawyer educated at his adopted state's well-regarded public university and a professional man who believed that those who played by the rules would be heard and respected, now surely began to realize the Japanese American community was in grave danger from people he normally would have trusted to uphold the rights of American citizens. Nevertheless, at this point Kido still apparently retained some optimism, thinking the growing animosity toward his community could somehow still be defused. When Oakland friend Fred Nomura told him that the city's police chief said removal of both non-citizens and citizens was under serious consideration, Kido replied: "You're crazy. We have constitutional rights as citizens! So they can't do that." To the dismay of anyone who had hoped to avoid such an outcome, however, just a few days after Governor Olson's meeting in California,

Secretary of War Henry Stimson recommended to President Roosevelt in Washington that all people of Japanese ancestry be removed from the West Coast. Roosevelt reportedly gave Stimson the approval to proceed as he felt necessary.[15]

On February 16, *Time*'s "Scare on the Coast" claimed: "No one could say how many thousands would have to pack up and go. Nor did anyone know where they would go to." The magazine said non-citizen Japanese, Italian fishermen, and Japanese farmers were all now under suspicion: "All along the West Coast the presence of enemy aliens became a suddenly, sinisterly glaring fact: Japanese and Italian fishermen along the water front, Japanese who worked all day on hands & knees in geometrically perfect truck gardens which sometimes overlay oil pipelines, Japanese settlements near big airplane plants and military posts."

Time also explained that many of the West Coast's agricultural produce gardens were tended by Japanese and Italian farmers, adding that the crops of string beans, spinach, beets, and celery in the Los Angeles area took "infinite work and patience" to produce. The magazine included comments about California's reaction to Attorney General Biddle's orders, revealing that prominent members of the state's law enforcement community believed Roosevelt's chief law enforcement officer had not gone far enough with his plans and adding they had no intention of taking the matter lightly:

> But the West Coast valued safety more than vegetables, more than the comfort or livelihood of foreigners who might be innocent but were still foreigners. Francis Biddle's measures struck most West Coast citizens, indeed, as wishy-washy, especially in giving aliens one to three weeks of grace to move from restricted zones. From California's Attorney General Earl Warren, from 100 sheriffs and district attorneys and from Los Angeles' Mayor Fletcher Bowron came a demand that all enemy aliens be removed at least 200 miles inland. The Los Angeles County Defense Council wanted them all interned.[16]

As government officials began circling the Nikkei community and average citizens were stirred up by print and broadcast media, every Japanese American on the West Coast now faced new prejudices and suspicions, sometimes from strangers and sometimes even from longtime friends and acquaintances. They coped with the challenges they faced as best they could. In close-knit urban Nikkei neighborhoods, Japanese American children experienced overt discrimination for the first time. Shortly after Pearl Harbor, Lily Ann Harada, Jukichi and Ken's twelve-year-old granddaughter, who was then in the seventh grade and living with her mother and brother in San Francisco near relatives, described a ride home from school on the bus:

> One day when I was riding on a bus on my way home from school, I heard people say derogatory things against me: "Look at that Jap girl. She's our enemy."

Until then, I never realized I was different from anyone else. I ran home to tell my mother about what happened, and she wisely told me that I am Japanese with slanted eyes, but I should be proud of my heritage.

She told me about the samurais that my grandmother's family represented, the beauty of the people and the language, the culture, and she made me feel happy about myself. She also emphasized my American citizenship and what it represents. Being Japanese American was a great combination.[17]

On Valentine's Day, General DeWitt called for immediate action:

On February 14, 1942, I recommended to the War Department that the military security of the Pacific Coast required the establishment of broad civil control, anti-sabotage and counter-espionage measures, including the evacuation, therefrom of all persons of Japanese ancestry. In recognition of this situation, the President issued Executive Order No. 9066 on February 19, 1942, authorizing the accomplishment of these and any other necessary security measures.[18]

Roosevelt's Executive Order 9066 never mentioned Japanese Americans. It did, however, authorize the secretary of war to establish military areas "from which any or all persons may be excluded, and with respect to which, the right of any person to enter, remain in, or leave shall be subject to whatever restrictions the Secretary of War or the appropriate Military Commander may impose in his discretion." The order further declared, "The Secretary of War is hereby authorized to provide for residents of any such area who are excluded therefrom, such transportation, food, shelter, and other accommodations as may be necessary." Of no help to California's Japanese American citizens and their parents was the incident at the end of the month when a Japanese submarine lobbed a few shells at an oil refinery on the beach near Santa Barbara. The following night, a massive false alarm response of helmeted air-raid wardens and an alarmed citizenry, with searchlights focused on mysterious objects flying overhead in the California sky and blazing anti-aircraft guns dropping jagged chunks of shrapnel across a jittery Los Angeles, made nearly everyone on the coast believe that a Japanese invasion was imminent. Within hours, under the headline, "Coast Alert for New Raids," the *Los Angeles Times* issued another front-page story: "Immediate Evacuation of Japanese Demanded." The *Times* reported that Congressman Alfred J. Elliott, a Democrat from Tulare, told the House of Representatives in Washington, "We must move the Japanese in this country into a concentration camp somewhere, some place, and do it damn quickly." The next day's paper informed thousands of frightened Angelenos that, despite doubt from some officials, the US Army had confirmed the authenticity of the previous evening's air-raid alarm. On February 27 the front page of the *San Francisco Examiner*'s Friday morning extra edition blasted the big headline, "OUSTER OF ALL JAPS IN CALIFORNIA NEAR!"[19]

12.2. 14th and Broadway, Oakland, California, February 27, 1942. (Dorothea Lange photograph, War Relocation Authority photographs of Japanese American Evacuation and Resettlement, Series 14, Volume 56, Section G, WRA no. A-36; courtesy of the Bancroft Library, University of California, Berkeley)

Distressed by the earlier national call to force aliens from restricted zones by the end of February, and now by the new executive order from the president, the Harada children discussed how to plan for their aged parents' care and possible move from home. Making early efforts to have Ken and Jukichi exempted from removal because of their poor health, Harold said one advisor told the family to leave Mrs. Harada, age sixty and unable to walk normally because of her stroke, as a patient in the county hospital. Harold replied: "No. Absolutely not. I'd tote her on my shoulders to where we were going if I had to." Mine said the family also made inquiries of Nestor Brule, their old acquaintance and former next-door neighbor on Lemon Street, now the city's chief of police. They asked Brule if their parents' removal could somehow be averted. "Mr. Brule was very good to my father and he did everything possible . . . to see if he could remain at home . . . instead of being evacuated. But he couldn't do anything about it . . . I heard that he came in tears to my father to tell him that he wasn't able to," Mine said.[20]

In anxious discussion and consultation, the children, including those no longer living in Riverside, decided that even if taken to some unknown location far from home, their ailing parents would be best supported by the care and medical attention that could be provided if they first moved in with their oldest son, Dr. Masa Atsu Harada. Referred to as "Doc" by the family and now in his early forties, Masa Atsu was still working as a physician in Sacramento and living there with his second family, wife Martha, thirty-four, and their two-year-old daughter, Kimiko. Japanese tradition held that the family's oldest son should take responsibility for his parents in times of need, and Doc's medical training and professional experience also supported the decision to move Jukichi and Ken to Sacramento as soon as possible.

Harold and Sumi carefully explained the situation to their parents as they hurriedly prepared them to leave their Lemon Street home for a temporary stay with Doc's family up north. As Sumi explained,

> My mother, . . . since her mind was, you know, that way, . . . she was almost childlike, my father would explain to her . . . that they would have to move, and join my brother, and she accepted it . . . But . . . then my father knew that he didn't know when the family'd be together again.
>
> . . . He didn't say too much, but I could understand . . . the feeling . . . He just methodically . . . gathered his things up . . . But . . . they accepted it . . . My father being very religious, he said that he would leave it to God.[21]

Jukichi and Ken Harada, who for so many years had their lives linked intimately to their family and home in Riverside, were soon to leave on a tiring road trip north, bound for an unknown future. Perhaps wanting to balance their worries about the unknown future, on March 2 someone in the family, probably Jukichi, prepared a handwritten inventory of the family's modest possessions. Addressed "To Government of United States of America," the record was intended to help if the family ever needed to explain what was left behind at the Lemon Street house. Composing the list must have brought memories of the lives of his wife and children to mind. He might have also thought about his battle to keep his new house when his family first moved to Lemon Street some twenty-five years before as he contemplated the rights of American citizenship that had once validated his family's quest to own a home of their own.

Notes written down the right side of each page of the list included the estimated value of each piece of furniture in the house. Most items were worth only a few dollars. Down the left side, careful notations of beds, tables, and chairs also included the names of the soon-to-be former occupants of every bedroom in the house. Jukichi might have wondered how soon they would be coming back home and perhaps hoped that it would not be too long. For whoever made the record, each family name on the list would have served as a reminder that something much more than a simple inventory of household goods was being left behind inside the house on Lemon Street.[22]

Sumi and Harold worked together, helping their mother and father prepare to leave their family's longtime home. They packed some of their parents' clothing and a few personal effects into parcels small enough for one person to carry. Not knowing where the old couple's journey would lead, the children included a small selection of clothing that could be worn in both cold and warm weather. On the morning of their departure, Harold and Sumi helped Ken and Jukichi into Shig's Pontiac sedan, the car the Harada boys called the Green Bomber. Shig soon left Riverside, driving his mother and father far away from Southern California, their few belongings stacked in the back of the Pontiac. The three Haradas followed the route of earlier Dust Bowl migrant refugees, over the Tehachapi Mountains and into the great San Joaquin Valley. In ten hours or so, after driving some 400 miles north through the vast, flat agricultural lands in the center of the state, Shig and his parents finally reached the outskirts of Sacramento, the high Sierras rising abruptly to the east.

Three miles southeast of the state capitol, Shig pulled up to his oldest brother's painted Craftsman-style wooden bungalow at 1567 Santa Ynez Way, unloading his parents' suitcases and other baggage onto the curb. Helping them carefully out of the car, perhaps even carrying his invalid mother up the few steps past the dark stonework supporting the home's low-pitched, overhanging front porch roof, Harold took his mother and father into their temporary home. Jukichi and Ken welcomed the chance to see their oldest son, daughter-in-law Martha, and their newest granddaughter, Kimi. Within a day or two, Harold bade his parents farewell and drove back to Riverside to attend to pressing family matters. Their parents now homeless but, for the moment, safely with Doc and Martha in Sacramento, Harold and Sumi turned their attention to the uncertain future of the Washington Restaurant and the family house on Lemon Street.[23]

THIRTEEN

LEAVING LEMON STREET BEHIND

The Washington Restaurant was the first to go. Because the family did not own the Eighth Street building in which their small business was housed, a real estate listing and sale were unnecessary. Letting only a few know the restaurant was for sale, they quickly sold its contents and fixtures. However, like most Nikkei families at the time, they were forced to make hasty decisions and lost money on the deal. Harold recalled: "We sold it for $150 and, . . . as I recall, it was to a Latino couple . . . The restaurant had a large . . . stove, . . . two large grills, . . . perhaps eight or ten burners, two ovens . . . It was a well-built stove. We had . . . silverware, chinaware, . . . and pots and pans, and refrigerator. It was just the business . . . inventory of our restaurant. And that was it."[1]

Without a livelihood after selling their restaurant, its few remaining American flags and patriots' faces left hanging on the walls, Sumi and Harold next turned their attention to saving the family home on Lemon Street. Worrying about their possessions and the safety of the house if left empty or unattended for some unknown time, they really had no idea how to keep the old place. They considered renting it to strangers with everything inside, boarding it up, or just locking the doors and hoping for the best. In preparation for departure, many Japanese American families in communities along the coast were quickly selling long-held family properties, homes, businesses, and farms, all at a substantial monetary loss.

Others were hurriedly throwing books, papers, and family photographs into fireplaces and farmyard burn piles. Nikkei memories went up in smoke. To Sumi and Harold, a quick sale and further personal and financial losses seemed out of the question, as they searched desperately for another alternative.

Just as things looked darkest for the future of the family home, the tangible centerpiece of the family's American Dream that their parents had worked so hard to hold on to so many years before, their old friend, bachelor blacksmith Jess Stebler, stepped forward. As Harold explained,

> He asked us if there was anything that he could do for us . . . So we asked him if he wouldn't mind living in our house free of rent, collect the rents from two of the houses that my dad had, and if he would just water the lawn, take care of the garden the best he could, and he agreed to it . . . He was a simple man so . . . it didn't take much for him to have a bedroom, and maybe a place to cook or whatever, and this was adequate for him.
> . . . That man had a lot of guts. A lot of courage. But I guess, a friend is a friend and I think that's the mark of a good friend . . . I don't know whether I would do that today if we were to go to war with whomever, and I knew that that family was going to be imprisoned in a camp.[2]

Meanwhile in Northern California some involved with the Japanese American Citizens League wanted Sumi and Harold's brother-in-law, JACL president Saburo Kido, serving the organization in an unpaid honorary role as national president since 1940, to move inland to Utah, away from what the military was describing as the coastal "evacuation" zone. Other JACL officials expected Kido to help the organization establish a new national headquarters in Salt Lake City. Mr. Kido had other plans. Insisting he and his family should now join the Japanese Americans coping with the removal process in California, Saburo remained in the Bay Area for the next several weeks, preparing for his family's departure.[3]

Kido had been elected JACL president at its most trying time in history. He would later say that when chosen president at the group's Portland convention in 1940, he had "welcomed the responsibility of guiding the destiny of the organization which [he] had helped to found." He also was well aware of the potential consequences of serving as president for what he thought might only be a single term, from 1940 to 1942. "I would not be able to blame anyone else for whatever might happen to JACL during the next two years. But I was hoping against hope that there would be no war between the United States and Japan, and I could turn over JACL to my successor in a time of peace," Kido said. Since December 7, however, Kido had been mistaken on two counts: he would serve as JACL president until after the war, and a time of peace would be long in coming.[4]

At the beginning of March, his wife and children about to leave Berkeley for a temporary home outside the restricted coastal military zone, Kido wired every JACL chapter, asking for representatives to come to San Francisco on March 8 for an emergency meeting. The forced removal was set to begin before the end of the month. Despite unrelenting pressure and confusion in their homes, about 200 delegates from sixty-six JACL chapters in ten states made it to San Francisco for the three-day meeting. As Bill Hosokawa described the gathering, Saburo Kido once again "established the keynote for the meeting with a sober summary of the problems" confronting the organization of Japanese American citizens. Without significant leadership from other quarters in the Nikkei community, whose Issei ranks had been decimated by business closures, arrests, home searches, and other confrontations, the JACL now attempted to respond to the federal government's consideration of "Japanese Americans as a group rather than as individuals."[5]

In his opening address to the delegates in San Francisco, Saburo outlined the international and national circumstances bringing the Nikkei community to the brink of disaster. He also acknowledged recent activities of the group's national secretary, Mike Masaoka. Working as the JACL's only paid staff member, Masa-oka was primarily responsible for most of the organization's day-to-day decision making. Kido said that through the efforts of Masaoka and local JACL chapter leaders, "our organization has come to be recognized as the representative body of the Nisei in this country."

Kido then remarked on larger issues: "When the first ominous signs pointed to possible Japanese-American hostilities, we began to make preparations to miti-gate the blows which may be directed against us because of our Japanese extrac-tion." He explained that the many JACL chapters represented at the meeting had attempted to educate the American public about the Japanese American commu-nity in recent weeks to help distinguish it from the current aggressors from Japan, a place most Nisei had never been. "It is a fact that everyone worked hard to meet the emergency, although many of us were lulled into overconfidence because of the friendly expressions extended us by our American friends," Kido said. No doubt realizing the likely collapse of his current effort to put the matter in its proper constitutional perspective, Kido added: "It has been our constant fear that race prejudice would be fanned by the various elements which have been constantly watching for an opening to destroy us. They included many of our economic com-petitors and those who believe this country belongs to the 'whites.' Many of them wanted to indulge in the unpatriotic pastime of using us as a political football in this hour of America's greatest peril."

Saburo was breathing carefully to maintain his composure. Recalling his dead-end meeting with California's governor Olson only a few weeks before and other recent unfriendly encounters with representatives of the US military and Federal Bureau of Investigation, he continued his remarks. "We all had expected that the public officials, at least, would serve as a buffer against possible mass hysteria. We never dreamed that such a large number of them would ride the band wagon, to reap the political benefit out of this abnormal condition," Kido asserted. Few outside the JACL's hastily called meeting in San Francisco were listening.

Shortly before the emergency meeting, Kido and others in the California Nikkei community had been told by military officials that the decision for a mass expulsion was simply not a matter for discussion. Twenty years after the war's end, Kido remembered an informal meeting he had attended at the Fairmont Hotel in San Francisco with Colonel W. F. Magill Jr., provost marshal and director of the Western Defense Command. Magill told a small group that if anyone intended to oppose the military order, there was "no sense in talking." Kido explained: "The military intelligence people and the army people said, 'We're not here to discuss . . . the pros and cons of evacuation. If you people are going to take that kind of a position, there's no use talking about it.' The military was not receptive to . . . stop the mass evacuation or anything like that. They were going to carry [out] the orders."

Colonel Magill said the only role Nikkei leaders could play was to make the removal process as smooth as possible for those who would now be ordered to leave the coast. "As far as we were concerned, . . . the matter was, we felt, inevitable at that stage," Kido said. Other recent confrontations solidified Kido's impression that there was now virtually no hope of reversing the tide turned solidly against his community, and he believed some level of cooperation might now be the only viable option. One afternoon, after a more formal encounter at the Whitcomb Hotel on Market Street with several government representatives from Washington, Kido was called to the San Francisco office of the FBI. "That afternoon we went there and were balled out by the FBI . . . that we were worse than the rats who attacked Pearl Harbor . . . I didn't know what the hell he was talking about," Kido said.[6]

Proceeding with his speech at the emergency meeting, President Kido questioned the motivations of those bent on ousting American citizens from their homes, as he described them, "the homes in which we were born and raised, or which we have purchased through the small income we have saved. The very foundations which have taken years to build up are being torn from under us." He continued,

> When we hear our erstwhile friends of peaceful days, those who praised us to the skies as model citizens, brand us more dangerous than the so-called "enemy aliens," we cannot help but wonder if this is all but a bad dream. The past few weeks have been a regular field day for those who have awaited for the day to "clean up the Japs." When many of our friends of long years standing begin to entertain doubts about us, it is a bitter pill to swallow. One cannot help but realize how lonesome we are today.

Kido went on to raise important constitutional issues: "I am confident that the day is coming when those who are responsible for these outrageous violations of our rights will be ashamed of their conduct." He then outlined fears, suggesting the expulsion was being ordered by the military "to prevent mob violence from running rampant, thereby interfering with the successful operation of the war." Because the nation was already involved in a war declared by the president against Japan, some believed it possible that attacks against individual Japanese Americans might take place if they did not comply with the military order to leave the coast.

Kido, along with others in the JACL, would soon be roundly criticized for urging compliance with the removal order and for claiming in his address that "as patriotic citizens and law-abiding residents, we should be willing to place our future into the hands of the Federal government." However, despite the potential for criticism, at the time of his remarks in March 1942, Saburo Kido most certainly believed he was doing the best he could to respond to challenges from those at the highest levels of authority who had already confirmed that they had absolutely no interest in protecting the rights of American citizens of Japanese ancestry.

As the dutiful organization president, Kido then spoke of the future of the JACL and its newspaper, *Pacific Citizen*. He said he expected the league to continue, in a reduced fashion, to promote its causes by communicating with its members on a national level, wherever they might be. With his next remark Kido perhaps unknowingly set the stage for another future controversy—when he announced his decision to advocate for US military service by Japanese American citizens, many of whom would soon be locked up behind barbed wire by their own government. He believed that Japanese Americans' service in the military would prove their loyalty to the United States. "If nothing is done to counteract the impression which is being created by many of these public officials who are enjoying the grand picnic of trampling upon the weak and defenseless, we shall remain forever a despised group," Kido feared.

Although some had hoped that a more aggressive opposition to the expulsion by JACL leaders or others in the Nikkei community would have an effect, Hosokawa asserts that by this time both "Kido and Masaoka knew that the Evacuation decision was a *fait accompli*, that, right or wrong, the Army was poised to carry out its orders." Others close to the situation agreed. Some even placed blame on the older generation of Issei community leaders, who in their view had not done enough to connect with the American mainstream. Few, if any, ever mentioned that the Issei had been forced to maintain ties to Japan because they were regarded as permanent aliens ineligible for American citizenship. Because of their birthplace and ancestry, the United States would not allow them to become naturalized citizens and full partners in the American Dream for another decade.

Hosokawa said that Kido never doubted "the wisdom of the decision [to cooperate] although there was a time when he thought seriously of violating the Evacuation order as an individual to symbolize Nisei outrage." Ultimately, Saburo

Kido and the JACL set aside any idea of violating the order and turned the group's attention toward compliance, leaving challenges to the government's removal process to other members of the West Coast's Nikkei community—Mitsuye Endo, Gordon Hirabayashi, Fred Korematsu, and Minoru Yasui. Many later found fault with the JACL's decision to cooperate, and some never forgave its leaders for doing so. Years later, an embattled Kido tried to explain the situation they faced in the early months of 1942: "I am sure that if we (as a group) had uttered defiance to the evacuation orders we might have been popular with some, but most foolish under the circumstances . . . We may not have had the orderly evacuation. Any interference with the military when it was decided to be a military necessity may have been construed as sabotage and a treasonable act on our part."[7]

Kido ended his San Francisco address with the direction to "leave with a smiling face and courageous mien." Speaking as a Nisei, Saburo acknowledged the contributions of the pioneer Issei, trying to inspire the conference attendees: "Let us conquer whatever frontiers may await us with the same fortitude and patience as did our fathers and mothers who contributed more to the development of the west than most of us realize. Let us serve our country in the hardest way possible for us to serve, keeping in mind that we have the same objective in mind as a hundred and thirty million other Americans, the ultimate and complete victory of democracy's forces."

At the end of the three-day conference, Kido spoke once again to close the proceedings but was unable to finish his remarks. Bill Hosokawa explained: "Kido began to speak, thanking his friends for their loyal support, wishing them good luck, admonishing them to keep the faith until they could meet again, but he was unable to finish. The tears flowed down his cheeks and many of the delegates wept with him. Then they scattered for home, knowing difficult tasks lay ahead."[8]

The day following the JACL conference in San Francisco, across town on March 11, General DeWitt established the Wartime Civil Control Administration (WCCA) "to implement army-issued civilian exclusion orders" and begin the removal process. At the same time, the WCCA's Manzanar Relocation Center was already under construction in central California on the eastern side of the Sierras near the tiny isolated settlement of Lone Pine.

Back on Lemon Street in Riverside, Sumi Harada was trying to ensure that she and her brother would be able to rejoin their ailing parents as soon as possible. Speaking with Mr. England, a WCCA representative working at the sparsely outfitted government office hastily established at a Main Street storefront near the Mission Inn, Sumi was promised that families would not be separated by the removal process. She and Harold believed they would be able to reunite with their parents as soon as they settled their affairs at home.[9]

On Wednesday evening, March 11, the same day General DeWitt launched the WCCA, fifty-nine-year-old Toranusuke Fujimoto, the Haradas' Issei neighbor who had recorded in his diary his attendance at Jukichi Harada's trial in 1918, was once again making his daily diary entry. However, instead of writing at the table in his comfortable farmhouse on Chase Road north of town, he was now sitting in a jail cell, describing his arrest earlier that day by the FBI.

> This morning I took care of the chickens and finished breakfast around 8 a.m. . . . The FBI came and searched the house, taking lots of things. They gathered some of my clothes and took me to jail . . . This is the first time I've been in jail. This is a very difficult experience for me. God sent me this experience as a lesson, so I shouldn't complain that this is happening to me. I shouldn't be sad. I should appreciate this precious life that God gave me.

Observing his father's many years of diligence, taking time each day to add thoughtful passages to a daily diary, Mr. Fujimoto's twenty-two-year-old son, George, began keeping his own new diary the very same evening: "Went to school as usual. Shok [his older sister, Mabel] at work in packing house. Came home about 5 PM and was shocked to learn that Pop was taken into custody by federal officials today. Twenty-eight Riverside Japanese aliens were rounded up in today's raid; Mr. Sanematsu & Pop included. Fortunately Pop was partially prepared."[10]

In the wake of the apprehension of more than two dozen local Issei, hushed rumors suggested that members of Riverside's Japanese American community, perhaps someone with an old score to settle or ties to the city's police department, might have provided information used to make some of their arrests. Harumi Ohmura, wife of the Reverend Masayoshi Ohmura of Riverside's Japanese Union Church, was sure she knew who was doing the talking, but Chief of Police Nestor Brule was keeping his sources a closely guarded secret.

Just a week after the elder Fujimoto and several other Riverside Issei found themselves in jail, President Roosevelt issued Executive Order 9102. The new order established the War Relocation Authority, empowered to remove from designated areas "persons whose removal is necessary in the interests of national security." The WRA was given the authority to "provide for the relocation of such persons in appropriate places, provide for their needs in such manner as may be appropriate, and supervise their activities." The order included the authority to arrange work for those expelled from their homes and to safeguard the public interest in their future employment. It also said that the new program "shall not undertake any evacuation activities within military areas . . . without the prior approval of the Secretary of War or the appropriate military commander." Milton Eisenhower, brother of the future commanding general and US president Dwight D. Eisenhower, was soon appointed WRA director.[11]

Developments began to happen quickly, sweeping through Pacific coast Nikkei communities like a California wildfire in the dry chaparral. On its front page on March 19, in "Mass Evacuation to Begin Next Week," the *Riverside Daily Press* explained the details of the coming removal of the state's Japanese Americans. On page six of the same paper, in "Another Jap Arrested for Alien Detention," the *Press* reported the apprehension of local resident Toramatsu Ito. Each article about the arrest of another local Issei, as reported in scores of community newspapers throughout the West, fanned the flames of hysteria and fear licking around the edges of hundreds of Japanese American homes, farms, and businesses along the Pacific coast from Seattle to San Diego. From the press and racist neighbors, otherwise calm and respectful people now had the impression their communities had been infiltrated and were surrounded by Japanese spies and saboteurs.

On March 21, Roosevelt signed another new public law making it a federal crime to refuse to leave military areas if so ordered. At the end of the month General DeWitt issued Public Proclamation No. 4, ending voluntary departure as of March 29. It was now against the law for persons of Japanese ancestry to leave the restricted military zone. Hosokawa described the paradox facing those who had not already left the region on their own: "From that day, . . . it became illegal for Japanese to leave the area and soon it would be illegal for them to remain; they had to sit tight and wait for the Army to move them."[12]

On Santa Ynez Avenue in Sacramento, perhaps missing the familiarity of her former home and routine on Lemon Street and the helpful daily presence of her youngest son, Shig, and his sister, Sumi, mother Ken Harada was sometimes confused and distressed by her recent move to an unfamiliar setting. Because of her earlier stroke, Mrs. Harada was unable to comprehend details of the current difficulties faced by others in her family and community. In these conflicted circumstances, with worried faces all around her, Ken suffered another significant decline. Probably from the effects of another stroke, Mrs. Harada's ability to speak was damaged and she was "unable to express words properly."[13]

At about the same time in Berkeley, Ken's oldest daughter, Mine Harada Kido, her three children, and a young family friend from Hilo, Violet Ishii, began making preparations to temporarily leave family breadwinner Saburo Kido in the Bay Area. Violet was a recent business college graduate now unable to return to her home in Hawaii, stranded in California because of the war. Also staying at the Kido residence on Stuart Street was Saburo's older cousin from Hawaii, Mr. Sakamoto, president of the House of Mitsukoshi department store in Honolulu. Part of the Kido family was soon ready for departure to the small town of Lindsay near Visalia, packing some of their household belongings into the truck of one of Saburo's lawfirm clients. Ready to head inland with other Nikkei families and out of the coast's restricted military zone, Mine explained her upcoming trip from Berkeley and the unexpected help she received from Mitsukoshi's Sakamoto-san:

> Kido's cousin was staying with us . . . because he couldn't go back to Hawaii
> because he was an alien . . . He was considered an enemy alien, so they wouldn't

13.1. Construction in progress, Poston, Arizona, April 10, 1942. (Clem Albers photograph, War Relocation Authority Photographs of Japanese-American Evacuation and Resettlement, Series 1, Volume 1, Section A, WRA no. A-321; courtesy of the Bancroft Library, University of California, Berkeley)

let him on the plane. He was supposed to go back . . . but . . . wasn't allowed to go . . . At that time, he was the President of the Mitsukoshi. That's that department store . . . He was the president of Mitsukoshi of Japan in Hawaii . . . So he . . . did all my packing for me because he said he knew how to do it, so he did a wonderful job . . . He threw away all our collection of . . . Japanese writings . . . magazines and anything that he thought, ah, would be considered suspicious in any way. He'd read them and put them into the fireplace, one page after the other.[14]

With the faint smell of smoke from the fireplace still lingering in the air, the Kidos' ten-room house in Berkeley was emptied of its contents. Mine and her three children, eight-year-old Rosalind, five-year-old Laurence, and baby Wally, just under two years of age, prepared to begin their exodus to rural Tulare County. Daughter Rosalind still remembers leaving her nice house in a comfortable Bay Area urban neighborhood to find very different circumstances awaiting her in the family's new temporary home in a strawberry patch in Ivanhoe: "The house we lived in was in the middle of a strawberry field which was bordered by orange trees. The house had no running water. I remember that people moved the out-house from one hole to the other, consequently there was no smell . . . I remember taking a bath in a big washtub with water that had been heated over a fire. I had the chickenpox while we were living there and I also went to the local school."[15]

As time for the forced departure drew ever closer, Masa Atsu and Martha quickly sold their corner bungalow on Santa Ynez Way in Sacramento at a financial loss, making arrangements to store their belongings at a nearby storage company. Their family's simple household possessions would have been familiar to many other middle-class Americans of the early 1940s. Two trunks and barrels of dishes, boxes of kitchenware, medical supplies, and personal effects were packed and added to a truckload of family furniture. A cedar chest, wardrobe trunk, card table, electric sewing machine, bedroom set, chest of drawers, vanity with base and mirror, nightstand, bed, springs and mattress, and Kimiko's baby crib, box of dolls, two toy baby carriages, and a doll stand were carried out to the curb and loaded into the truck. Also taken from the house was their General Electric refrigerator and vacuum cleaner, Thor washing machine, clothes dryer, and a baby's bathtub, all removed for long-term storage at A. G. Boone's Transfer and Storage warehouse on Third Avenue. Boone was "a personal friend of many years standing." Although they had no idea how long they would be away, the Sacramento Haradas believed he would be able to safely care for their things until they returned home. His family's household furniture and other possessions now taken care of, Doc drove his 1940 Windsor Model Chrysler sedan and trailer to a local garage for long-term storage.[16]

The new Marysville Assembly Center, developed after only a few weeks of hasty construction at a former migrant workers' camp on flat agricultural land at the edge of Clark Slough near the small settlement of Arboga, was eight miles south of the Sacramento Valley farming town of Marysville. With construction nearly completed, the temporary holding center was finally ready to accept its first incarcerees. One of sixteen facilities dubbed "assembly centers" by government officials, the interim gathering locations were established in California, Arizona, Oregon, and Washington to house Japanese Americans prior to their removal to ten more isolated and permanent concentration camps in seven states. The temporary assembly center north of Sacramento was expected to be ready for occupancy in mid-April. Because of late rains, standing water, and the need for further site preparation, however, the earliest arrivals were delayed until the beginning of May.

Finally, on Friday, May 8, Arboga's 100 one-story barracks buildings, five dining halls, and two structures serving as makeshift hospital facilities became a temporary home for its first arrivals. Records of the War Relocation Authority indicate that among the many future incarcerees arriving that busy Friday were Dr. Masa Atsu Harada and his family from Sacramento, wife Martha, daughter Kimi, and Dr. Harada's elderly parents, father Jukichi and mother Ken. At Arboga the Sacramento Haradas joined just over 2,400 others, most from nearby Sacramento County and all now living at the converted migrant camp under the watchful eyes of military police stationed at a small headquarters near its entrance. The incarcerees would remain here until the end of June, awaiting transfer to the more distant and long-term concentration camp facilities of the new Tule Lake Relocation Center, the soon-to-be-completed camp in the far northeastern corner of the state.[17]

In the hurried weeks before departure, two of Roy Hashimura's four orphaned sisters—Toshiye, age sixteen, and Sumiko, age fourteen, adopted by others more than a decade before—rejoined their older brother at the only real home he had ever known, the Harada house in Riverside. Toshiye, originally sent to Japan to live with her grandmother when her parents died in 1928, had returned to California when her grandmother died in the late 1930s. Sumiko, raised by relatives in the San Joaquin Valley, came south to the house on Lemon Street after Roy returned from Berkeley. Roy had been living with Saburo and Mine Kido on Stuart Street for some time, working with Clark Harada at different offices of Oakland optometrist Dr. Russell Hisao WeHara. Born in Japan in 1899, WeHara had come to the United States as a child and, like Dr. Masa Atsu Harada, remained an alien ineligible for citizenship. As a registered alien, Dr. WeHara had been locked out of his chain of Bay Area optical offices immediately after the Pearl Harbor attack, throwing his numerous employees, including both Clark and Roy, out of work. Roy explained: "They put a padlock on the optometrist's offices because he was foreign-born, born in Japan. He was ineligible for citizenship, so he wasn't a citizen, so they padlocked all his offices. So nobody could work anymore . . . So I went back to Riverside." Clark remained in the Bay Area until removal to the Tanforan Assembly Center and subsequent transfer to the Topaz Relocation Center with Dr. WeHara's family. Roy believed he would be better off returning home to Riverside for a later departure with Sumi and Shig.[18]

From the Presidio of San Francisco on May 19, General DeWitt issued a series of numbered Civilian Exclusion Orders to more than 100 communities on the coast. Each order was intended to address the uprooting of about 1,000 people. Individual sets of instructions were distributed for specific "evacuation" areas, providing community information about the coordination of the expulsion process. The accompanying Instructions to All Persons of Japanese Ancestry issued with Exclusion Order No. 83 was directed to those living in designated areas of Riverside and San Bernardino Counties. Sumi and Harold Harada received their copy of the order and learned that they had less than a week to prepare to leave home. The Harada family's instructions declared that in the affected "prohibited areas" of Riverside and San Bernardino Counties, ranging from Upland and San Bernardino in the north to San Jacinto and Hemet in the east, Temecula and the San Diego County line in the south, and west to the Orange and Los Angeles county lines, "all persons of Japanese ancestry, both alien and non-alien, will

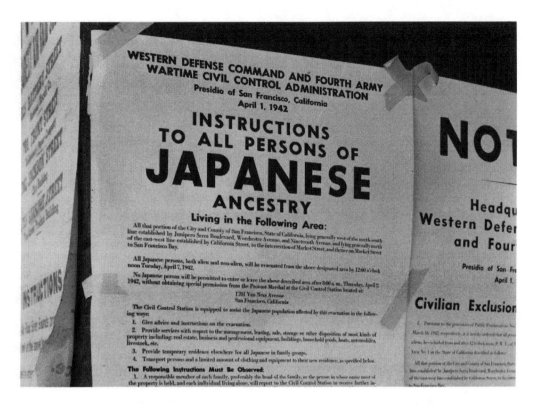

13.2. First and Front Streets, San Francisco, California, April 11, 1942. (Dorothea Lange photograph, War Relocation Authority Photographs of Japanese-American Evacuation and Resettlement, Series 14, Volume 78, Section A, WRA no. [?]-39; courtesy of the Bancroft Library, University of California, Berkeley)

be evacuated from the above area by 12 o'clock noon, P.W.T., Monday, May 25, 1942."[19]

With expulsion from Riverside and San Bernardino Counties only six days away, few had time to make the thoughtful plans suggested in the instructions of the Civilian Exclusion Order. Directions accompanying the order included references to services for "the management, leasing, sale, storage or other disposition of most kinds of property, such as real estate, business or professional equipment, household goods, boats, automobiles and livestock." In Riverside the Civil Control Station at 3557 Main Street, just half a block north of the Mission Inn and a four-block walk from the Harada house, was listed as the coordination center for the area's removal process. Persons of Japanese ancestry acting as "the head of the family" or "each individual living alone" were directed to appear at the station within two days "to receive further instructions."

Those ordered to leave their homes were also told they could take only a few essentials: "[the] size and number of packages is limited to that which can be carried by the individual or family group." The kinds of things permitted were minimal. Bedding and linens for each family member, toilet articles, extra clothing,

13.3. 1117 Oak Street, Oakland, California, May 6, 1942. (Dorothea Lange photograph, War Relocation Authority Photographs of Japanese-American Evacuation and Resettlement, Series 14, Volume 61, Section G, WRA no. C-370; courtesy of the Bancroft Library, University of California, Berkeley)

and a few personal effects were the only items listed in the instructions. No pets were allowed. Nothing could be shipped to the future incarcerees. All items taken from home were to be "securely packaged, tied and plainly marked with the name of the owner." The instructions explained that some larger items, "such as iceboxes, washing machines, pianos, and other heavy furniture," would be accepted for government storage "at the sole risk of the owner," along with smaller items like cooking utensils and other household goods, so long as those materials were "crated, packed and plainly marked with the name and address of the owner." Families were told transportation "to the Reception Center" would be furnished at no cost. Private transportation was prohibited.

The Exclusion Order also included a reminder that anyone remaining in the restricted area and failing to comply with its directions after the May 25 departure deadline would be subject to "criminal penalties." At the end of her set of instructions, Sumi Harada wrote a short list of the few things she wanted to be sure to remember: glasses, two decks of cards, and a haircut. Roy Hashimura recalled his feelings about the situation: "We were all upset about the war but we couldn't do anything about it. We were helpless . . . I didn't expect anything like the evacuation, but when it was announced, you had to face it . . . There was not much you could do. You could only take what you could carry. I didn't have much of value. Just took clothing. So, personally, I didn't have much to lose since I didn't have anything."[20]

13.4. Waiting for baggage inspection, Turlock, California, May 2, 1942. (Dorothea Lange photograph, War Relocation Authority Photographs of Japanese-American Evacuation and Resettlement, Series 14, Volume 61, Section G, WRA no. C-310; courtesy of the Bancroft Library, University of California, Berkeley)

On Friday evening, May 22, Sumi, Shig, and the three Hashimuras spent what must have been a fitful last night at home, trying to get a little sleep before rising early the next morning to leave the house on Lemon Street. The family had already made arrangements with Jess Stebler to move into the house soon after their departure. He most likely remained in his downtown hotel room for a few more days, perhaps until his monthly rent payment was due on the first of June. Still upstairs early Thursday morning before joining the others from Riverside making their way to the government's hired buses downtown, eighteen-year-old Harold paused for a moment and grabbed a pencil, almost as an afterthought. Standing near the tall dresser next to the iron-framed bed in his small room, not knowing when—or if—he would ever return, Shig approached the south wall. Leaning gently on the smooth plaster adjacent to his bedroom window, he began writing on the wall, inscribing a message to the future:

EVACUATED ON MAY 23, 1942 SAT. 7 AM
Shig
HH   DYI

Shig included his own "HH" and another set of initials, "DYI," for Dorothy Yoneko Inaba, a local Riverside girl from the family with the chicken ranch outside town, who may or may not have known that high school classmate Shig Harada thought of her as his girlfriend. And in a last flourish, Harold signed his

name, "Shig," as a farewell gesture to Lemon Street. Perhaps glancing briefly out the window of his bedroom door to the sleeping porch out front and looking through the heavy branches of the curbside pepper trees down toward the lower houses across the street, the teenaged boy turned away from his message of departure, leaving his childhood behind forever at the house on Lemon Street. He stepped into the hallway landing and down the narrow wooden staircase. At the foot of the stairs Harold probably ran a comb through his dark hair and took one last brief look at the handsome young man in the mirror over the dresser in the kamitoku room before heading through the parlor and out onto the front porch.[21]

13.5. Shig's message on the bedroom wall, Harada House National Historic Landmark. (Courtesy of the Riverside Metropolitan Museum, Riverside, California)

Joining his sister Sumi and the Hashimuras just a few minutes after 7:00 a.m., Shig and the others checked for anything they may have forgotten. With mixed feelings of worry and anticipation, they stepped off the porch one by one with what they could each carry. Making their way from Lemon Street to the corner of Eighth and Main, just steps down the sidewalk from the original location of the Washington Restaurant, the family group approached the line of Santa Fe Trailways buses waiting at the curb. Harold explained the hour between seven and eight:

> I remember . . . that we could only take what we could carry in our two hands. And I remember carrying . . . a suitcase and . . . a bag like a barracks bag . . . We stuffed both with as much clothing as we could. And with as many things as we thought might be necessary . . . It's a hard decision to make and was . . . hard to decide just what to take, and we weren't really sure where we were going. We didn't know that we were going out to the middle a' the desert . . . We went to . . . Eighth and Main . . . The buses were lined up at that corner and . . . we boarded them there . . . And, ah, not surprisingly, there weren't too many . . . people there to see us off.[22]

Similar departures were imposed in cities and towns all along the coast. Few if any of the thousands of people forced to depart knew their next destination

13.6. Bus lineup, Centerville, California, May 9, 1942. (Dorothea Lange photograph, War Relocation Authority Photographs of Japanese-American Evacuation and Resettlement, Series 14, Volume 60, Section G, WRA no. C-237; courtesy of the Bancroft Library, University of California, Berkeley)

when they left home. The Haradas, Hashimuras, and some 230 other Japanese Americans then living in Riverside avoided temporary roundup in a WRA assembly center and were instead taken directly by bus into the lower Sonoran Desert to what the government called the Poston Relocation Center. The new center had been built on the lands of the Colorado River Indian Reservation in what was then Yuma County, near Parker, Arizona.

Had any Santa Fe Trailways brochures remained on the buses lined up at Eighth and Main, their wary Riverside passengers could have learned they would be riding on "America's finest bus service between the Great Lakes and the Pacific." The bus company brochures said riders would be heading for a scenic vacationland of "Romance, Mystery and Beauty." Its highways were mapped with pictures of dramatic mountains and rocky canyons filled with Indians, boulders, cactus, gold miners, and Mexicans with wide sombreros riding burros in the southwestern desert sands between Los Angeles and Albuquerque. Some of the younger Americans on the bus surely would not have missed the now darkly humorous lines in the travel brochure: "Santa Fe Trailways buses across America travel the finest of all transcontinental highways; yet a short dis-

tance off this beaten path are countless intensely interesting places to see . . . unusual things to do."[23]

Just two days after the Haradas and Hashimuras left Riverside, the *Daily Press* published a photograph of a dozen Japanese Americans boarding the Main Street buses near the Mission Inn on Saturday. The paper reported incorrectly that just over 500 "aliens" from western Riverside and San Bernardino Counties would "be held for the duration of the war" in "the alien detention center" at Parker, Arizona. Preoccupied with its hometown promotion of wartime propaganda, the Haradas' local paper had neglected to mention that most of the West Coast's Japanese Americans were not aliens but were, in fact, citizens of the United States of America.[24]

After a slow trip through the desert lasting four or five hours, the crowded Riverside buses finally arrived at Poston. Harold remembered: "We drove out to the desert and . . . when we reached our destination [it] was really hot . . . The wind was blowin' and it was dusty and . . . we were given . . . mattress bags and . . . there were bales of hay, or straw they called it, and . . . we were made to stuff our . . . mattress bags . . . with straw, and those would be our mattresses . . . for the duration."[25]

The former Riversiders were assigned to rustic barracks surrounded by barbed-wire fences. Along with the hundreds of others arriving by bus at the camp each day, all fully occupied "off the beaten path" with "unusual things to do" in Indian Country, they became part of a peak population of 17,814 housed in three separate incarceration camps at Poston. Some 2.5 miles east of the Colorado River, the new Arizona camps were officially called Poston I, II, and III. Later, trying to make the best of a bad situation, incarcerees nicknamed them Roasten, Toasten, and Dustin.

In a matter of hours the Haradas and Hashimuras, assigned WRA identification numbers 34018 A–E, began adjusting to their new living quarters at Poston I in Barracks 4-1-B: Block 4, Building 1, Apartment B. Roy Hashimura described Family 34018's new home: "Those barracks were just tar paper on top. [When they built the camp] they uprooted all the mesquite trees, so it was really dusty when the wind blew there. The soil was loose and, when the wind blew, it would go through these tar papers and right into the rooms . . . We were in a single room with . . . the beds and a pot-bellied coal stove. That's about it—no room for anything. So there was no privacy to speak of."[26]

New camp neighbors stood uncomfortably close together in the loose dirt at Poston as the desert night fell and families stared into their first Arizona sunset with worried eyes. One by one, the lights were extinguished and the unweathered black tar-papered walls of long, low redwood barracks at the incarceration camp vanished into the darkness beneath the stars, from a short distance looking as if they were never even there.

FOURTEEN

CAMP

Still fond of California road trips to places he had never been before, early one morning in Riverside, Jess Stebler no doubt double-checked the level of the gas tank in his 1927 Cadillac coupe before heading out alone across the desert. The old blacksmith's white hakujin face was about the last one anyone expected to see at the main gate of the Poston Relocation Center. Little is known about his strange desert journey to Poston, but it must have come within a week or two after the Haradas and Hashimuras spent their first afternoon standing in the Arizona dust, pushing dry yellow straw into the long white cloth bags that would become their bedding. At age sixty-six the former citrus machine blacksmith with the strong jaw, rumpled clothing, moustache, and hearing aid, probably comfortable with his independence and status as a loner, was likely still seen as a black sheep within Riverside's prominent Stebler family. Perhaps the cause of some embarrassment to his more well-to-do relatives in town, he was living in and caring for the home of a Japanese American family, folks whom most white people viewed as a sinister threat to national security.

On this summer day Jess may have filled a couple of burlap water bags before he left the house on Lemon Street, hooking them carefully over the radiator of his aging Cadillac to have them on hand if the day got too hot. Thinking about his longtime friends now far from home and missing these people who had become like family to him, the old man headed southeast into the dawn. Long morning shadows of tall palm trees and telegraph poles flashed across his stalwart face and down the backs of thickly upholstered Cadillac seats as the car gained speed, leaving Riverside's abundant orange groves far behind. After a 200-mile trip, perhaps stopping overnight along the way among the desert's plantations of date palms, Mr. Stebler found his way to Poston, making contact with Sumi and Harold to deliver a gift from Riverside. Harold explained:

> Mr. Stebler drove down in his 1927 Cadillac . . . to Poston . . . in the middle of . . . the desert. Brought us six dozen donuts. And he being a bachelor, living alone, . . . probably really . . . loved donuts; brought them to us and . . . we really appreciated it. But six dozen donuts for the two or three of us was . . . quite a number, so . . . we distributed them to our . . . friends . . . in the same block as we were, in camp, and . . . they relished it and appreciated it very much.[1]

Sumi, Shig, and the Hashimuras soon began finding their way around their new Arizona home. Like other able-bodied incarcerees, they found work inside the camp to distract them from their worries. With his year of pre-medical education at Riverside Junior College, Harold found a job paying $16 a month, working as an orderly at the Poston hospital. Sumi applied her restaurant skills, working as a camp kitchen helper for $12 a month. Sumi also worked briefly during the summer at Poston's adobe-brick factory, where bricks to build the camp's elementary and high school buildings were being manufactured by incarcerees, but she apparently quit that hot, dirty assignment before receiving her first paycheck. Brother Roy Hashimura volunteered to teach at Poston's new elementary school, but the camp's primitive facilities and lack of school supplies failed to provide a productive educational setting for the hastily trained teachers and restless young students:

> They were short of teachers for the kids so they asked for volunteers to teach. I had two years of junior college so I thought, gee whiz, those poor kids, you know. Maybe I can help them. So I volunteered. They sent us to two weeks teacher training course and [I] didn't learn much there.
>
> I started teaching a class of forty-something sixth grade students. That was a mistake because there were no books, nothing to work with . . . So I ended up not teaching them much of anything. They had a physical education teacher coming around, music teacher coming around, but nothing to help teach the kids anything . . . Really a poor class.
>
> . . . There was this girl that was handicapped . . . The kids were picking on her, so I lectured to them and straightened them out. One day the mother came up to me and thanked me for doing what I did to get the kids to stop teasing her daughter . . . It was more or less lecturing to the kids about what was right and wrong and that's about it. There wasn't much to do.[2]

Like the others forced into the camps, those in the extended Harada family began adjusting to the unfamiliar pressures and effects of the disruptive removal process.

To the north, at the Marysville Assembly Center, shortly after 6:30 p.m. on Friday evening, May 29, Jukichi Harada was admitted to the center's makeshift hospital with a severe nosebleed. The immediate care of Dr. George Kambara stopped the bleeding, but Harada remained in the center hospital for observation overnight. The next afternoon, still in the infirmary, Mr. Harada was examined yet again by young medical assistant Edwin Takayasu Nishimura. A recent University of California graduate and future physician and medical professor, assistant Nishimura completed a written report about Harada's condition; Nishimura observed that patient Jukichi Harada is a "[v]ery cheerful and cooperative elderly man apparently somewhat younger than stated age." After recording information about Harada's blood pressure, high at 180 over 100, and other objective symptoms, Nishimura noted that Mr. Harada had been suffering from high blood pressure for the last three years. He also added that the patient's mother and several of his siblings had already died "from stroke," concluding in his clinical record that Harada's nosebleed had been caused by high blood pressure related to heart disease and arthritis.

The same Saturday afternoon, Nishimura also examined Ken, whom he described as a "[p]leasant woman of stated age with marked dysarthria in no apparent distress." Nishimura noted Mrs. Harada's paralysis on her right side, indicating that it was most likely the result of an earlier stroke, hypertension, and heart disease. The medical assistant explained further complications in Ken's condition, describing the incident involving her speech loss that had occurred three months earlier. Because of their deteriorating health, Ken and Jukichi were monitored closely by their physician son and his Sacramento medical friends, now held under military guard at the Marysville Assembly Center.[3]

The following Monday, just a day or two after his elderly in-laws had been examined at the makeshift hospital in Marysville, Saburo Kido was sitting by himself at a typewriter in the little ranch house in a strawberry field in Ivanhoe. Kido was carefully rolling a blank page of JACL stationery into the typewriter carriage to compose a two-page letter to Rex Lee at the War Relocation Authority office at the Whitcomb Hotel in San Francisco. Lee was a current WRA officer and would one day become governor of American Samoa. Saburo had recently closed down his Berkeley law office and moved inland out of Military Area No. 1, the restricted zone along the coast and in southern Arizona, finally rejoining his wife, Mine, and their three children at the rustic ranch house in Area No. 2 in Tulare County. Voluntary migration into Area No. 2 had been encouraged by the army, and some, like the Kidos and their friends from the Bay Area, had moved inland with the understanding from General DeWitt that, "in all probability," they would not be forced to move again. Recovering from a recent minor operation that had left a prominent scar on his nose, Kido said friends told him to keep the scar because it gave him "a semblance of certain toughness by taking away [his] 'angelic' appearance." So at the isolated ranch house in Ivanhoe, a somewhat tougher-looking Saburo Kido was now trying to help shape his organization's approach to the next phases of the mass expulsion.[4]

Already reflecting the new inland location of the JACL's headquarters in Salt Lake City's Beason Building, the letterhead asserted the Japanese American Citizens League was "An All American Organization of American Citizens." Lately accustomed to the more sophisticated urban amenities of Berkeley and San Francisco, Kido also explained the current limitations of his life at his new home in rural Ivanhoe. He suggested to Lee that it would be nearly impossible to help manage the national affairs of the JACL from the middle of nowhere:

> It sounds funny to call a new place your "home" but I guess I shall have to be accustomed to using this term as long as my family continues to reside here. We are living nine miles out of the town of Visalia. There is no bus service so either I have to go out on a truck we brought from San Francisco . . . or ask for a ride from a neighbor who has a strawberry patch and goes to town about twice a day. The mail man comes once a day. And so if we receive any urgent letter and desire to reply immediately, we must take it to town.

Kido explained to Lee, "Tulare County is the hotbed of agitation to evacuate the Japanese out of this Zone 2 . . . The talking point seems to be the possibility of sabotage; that is, starting of brush and forest fires in the hillsides." Kido told Lee that the owner of the house in which his family was staying had observed that summer brush fires in Tulare County were, in wartime or not, a routine occurrence there. Should any fires happen to ignite in the current summer fire season, however, Kido probably understood that someone other than Mother Nature would be blamed for any resulting losses.

Trying to improve public perceptions of the Japanese Americans remaining in the so-called free zone inland, Kido explained that those still living near Visalia were "voluntarily giving up trips to the hillsides for fishing or picnics." He also added that he and a few others had recently met locally with civil defense representatives from San Francisco who were visiting Tulare County "to investigate the possibilities of sabotage." Apparently still retaining some level of optimism, Kido explained to Lee that he had told the civil defense representatives, "[W]e would encourage voluntary cooperation if those who are agitating would reciprocate by acknowledging the sincerity of the Japanese residents to create better understanding and harmonious relationship of all living in this area."

Planning a trip to the new JACL headquarters in Salt Lake City in two weeks, Kido concluded his letter by asking Lee how he could arrange personal visits to three of the ten new incarceration camps now nearing completion: California's Manzanar, on the eastern side of the Sierra Nevada between Lone Pine and Independence; Minidoka, north of Twin Falls, Idaho; and Topaz, in central Utah near the little town of Delta, 140 miles southwest of Salt Lake City. As the Kidos began making plans for the next leg of their journey and later incarceration at the Poston Relocation Center in the coming weeks, Saburo asked Mine to begin keeping a diary. Mine refused. "I told him, 'No, I want to forget—I don't want to keep a record of these sad days.' "[5]

Contrary to General DeWitt's earlier comment that those living in the inland communities of Military Area No. 2 would not likely need to move again, word soon came that all persons of Japanese ancestry remaining there would now be required to leave the inland area. Knowing this new requirement, Saburo wrote to Cavalry major Herman Goebel of the Wartime Civil Control Administration at the end of June to say that many in Tulare County "are now ready to be evacuated." Kido asked Goebel to allow him to leave Visalia voluntarily for a move to Arizona, where he and Mine planned to join other family members. At the time, the Kidos believed that most of the Harada family would soon be reunited at Poston. Kido explained to Major Goebel: "Inasmuch as this region is to be evacuated eventually, I am now hoping that permission will be granted for me to go to Poston, Arizona, where my wife's unmarried sister and brother are. Also, Dr. M. A. Harada of the Marysville Assembly Center is expected to go as surgeon to the same place. My wife's parents are with Dr. Harada, the eldest of the children of six."[6]

As summer began, any sense of cohesiveness within the Japanese American community was gone. Abandoned produce farms, closed businesses, and empty houses, some already sold at bargain-basement prices and occupied by new owners, others watched over by a few sympathetic friends, were all that remained of the once vibrant and productive West Coast Nikkei community. Grass grew tall and dried to golden brown in neglected gardens and yards once tended each day with diligence and pride.

For their decision to cooperate with the mass removal, JACL president Saburo Kido and other JACL leaders were now also faced with growing anger and resentment from within the fragmented detainee settlements and from many of those adjusting to difficult lives behind barbed wire. In conversations with WRA director Milton Eisenhower and others at the highest levels of the removal process, Kido had been assured that the expulsion from the West Coast would be handled with great care, sensitivity, and support for the families forced to leave their homes. Those assurances helped convince Kido and others that the best the JACL could hope for was an orderly removal process. He soon learned, however, that the realities of the primitive "assembly centers" and the more isolated and poorly equipped frontier incarceration camps would not match the statements of perhaps well-intentioned but ill-prepared government bureaucrats. Kido explained many years later:

> The restrictions we had imposed on us at the assembly or relocation centers were unexpected. In fact, when discussions were held . . . the relocation centers were supposed to be a "haven of refuge" during the war years. We were supposed to be protected from the outside, but with free going in and out of the centers. Industry and farming were to be developed so that the residents of the relocation centers would have a trust fund which would help them to relocate after the war . . . The public hysteria created an atmosphere which made such a friendly haven impossible. We became virtual prisoners contrary to the original understanding and promises.[7]

Isolated and with the criticism against him and the JACL increasing, Kido was no longer optimistic. Not having seen his mother and father since they left Hawaii to return to live permanently in Japan decades earlier, Saburo may have welcomed the idea of moving closer to Mine's Issei parents and those in her extended family, people who would always respect his accomplishments, enjoy his company, and continue to honor him as family. Connections to family members were the only significant aspect of Japanese American life still intact for those fortunate enough to remain close to their relatives in camp.[8]

At the end of June, as the Kidos planned their move to Poston, the temporary Marysville Assembly Center was emptied of its incarcerees and turned over to the military for housing soldiers. Most of its 2,465 former residents were moved by train nearly 300 miles farther north to the desolate Tule Lake Relocation Center, near the railroad line, little post office, and crossroads settlement of Newell, California. Not sent to Poston as the Kidos previously believed, Dr. Masa Atsu Harada and his family, including his elderly parents, left the Marysville Assembly Center, arriving instead at Tule Lake on Monday, June 29. Doc began working at the new incarceration camp hospital the following day. The Haradas already at Tule Lake were soon reunited with Dr. Yoshizo Harada and his wife, Sumiye. Brother Yosh and Sumiye, assigned to Barracks 818-D, came to Tule Lake from the Walerga Assembly Center, just outside Sacramento, where they had been sent in the middle of May.

From July through September, Dr. Masa Atsu Harada was paid $19 a month, the highest rate of pay for incarcerees, who worked in the camps in a variety of jobs paying monthly wages of $12, $16, or $19, intentionally less than the lowest wages generally received by those serving in the military. On average working more than 80 hours a week and more than 300 hours per month, Doc made just over a nickel an hour, working in the primitive camp hospital as a surgeon with little time for anything else but sleep. Separated from the younger Haradas after coming from Marysville, Jukichi, age sixty-six, and Ken, age sixty, were admitted immediately to the Tule Lake hospital, where they remained in Ward H for the next 118 days.

14.1. Assignment of living quarters and bedding, Tule Lake, Newell, California, July 1, 1942. (War Relocation Authority Photographs of Japanese-American Evacuation and Resettlement, Series 11, Volume 31, Section D, WRA no. D-65; courtesy of the Bancroft Library, University of California, Berkeley)

In the hospital shortly after her arrival, Ken Harada's breathing became difficult, her lungs congested. Her declining health and lack of mobility were slowly taking their toll. Taken in for X rays, she was examined again by medical assistant Edwin Nishimura, her aide from Marysville who had also just been sent to Tule Lake. Nishimura offered a preliminary diagnosis of hypostatic pneumonia, often observed in the weak, elderly, and bedridden. Like all arrivals at Tule Lake, particularly in official settings like the camp hospital, Jukichi and Ken were known by their War Relocation Authority incarceree numbers, 6507-D and 6507-E, respectively.[9]

On Wednesday, July 15, Saburo and Mine's first son, Laurence Mineo Kido, turned six years old. Many years later his mother keenly remembered the muted observance of Larry's sixth birthday because it was also the day that the Kidos left the little ranch house in the strawberries near Lindsay to travel some 400 miles south to relinquish their freedom at the gates of the Poston Relocation Center. Saburo had finally received permission from the War Relocation Authority to move from inland Zone 2 to the camp at Poston, and he and Mine had already stored some of their possessions in a Fresno warehouse. The Kidos left Tulare County with several other families from Lindsay also on their way to Poston. They soon shipped additional household goods in railroad freight cars to the Arizona camp. Armed with their family travel permit from Major Goebel, addressed "To All Peace Officers and All Other Persons Concerned," and accompanied by an escort assigned by the WRA, the five members of the Kido family were authorized "to travel from

Visalia, California, to the Parker Relocation Center, Poston, Arizona, where [they] will be admitted." The Kidos arrived at Poston II on July 17. Assigned incarceree numbers 39660 A–G, the family group comprised parents Saburo and Mine; their three children, Rosalind, Laurence, and Wally; and family friends Violet Ishii, the young friend from Hawaii stranded in California, and Peter Aoki, Saburo's friend and associate from the JACL. The Kido family was assigned to camp barracks in Poston II, Block 215, Building 2, Apartment D, just a few steps from the women's and men's latrines and their new block's laundry room.[10]

After three weeks of her strange new life at dusty Poston I, where midsummer temperatures routinely rose to 115 degrees, Sumi Harada wrote a brief letter to the camp's administrative director, Wade Head. Sumi was seeking permission to join her parents at the Tule Lake Relocation Center. A month later, learning more about the application process required for a transfer from Poston, Harold submitted a more formal request on behalf of himself, Sumi, and the three Hashimuras, asking for a family transfer to Tule Lake, where the Poston Haradas hoped they would soon be reunited with their ailing parents. Using stationery of the Field Service of the Department of the Interior, Office of Indian Affairs, Poston social worker Mary Kirkland supported the Harada family request, explaining that "the physical condition of the parents is such that we believe it adviseable to have them transferred there."

Because of earlier assurances from the Wartime Civil Control Administration in Riverside that families would not be separated, Sumi and Harold believed they would have already been reunited with their parents. However, with Doc, his family, and the elder Haradas now some 650 miles away at Tule Lake, Sumi and Shig began to understand that their anticipated family reunion might be long in coming. The elder Haradas' move to Sacramento before their later incarceration at Tule Lake may have calmed family worry over their health care, but it complicated the promise of an early reunion. It would take eight more months for camp bureaucrats to process the family's request. This separation weighed especially heavy in Sumi's mind. When later recognized as time forever lost, the next several months would become more difficult than the Poston Haradas could have anticipated in the summer of 1942. Sumi observed, "During the last few hurried weeks prior to evacuation, we had to make hasty decisions and live to regret them."[11]

In September and October, construction at the last of the nation's ten new incarceration centers neared completion. At the end of this period, transfer of the West Coast's 110,000 persons of Japanese ancestry to America's concentration camps was complete. A shortage of physicians at the newest camps suggested to an often sleepless and exhausted Dr. Masa Atsu Harada at Tule Lake that he might be transferred with his family from the camp in Northern California to some other camp facility, perhaps the newer War Relocation Authority center in western Utah. Thousands of Bay Area Nikkei from the Tanforan Assembly Cen-

14.2. Family living quarters, Tanforan Racetrack horse stall, Tanforan Assembly Center, San Bruno, California, June 16, 1942. (Dorothea Lange photograph, War Relocation Authority Photographs of Japanese-American Evacuation and Resettlement, Series 15, Volume 64, Section H, WRA no. C-598; courtesy of the Bancroft Library, University of California, Berkeley)

ter, established the previous April at Tanforan Racetrack in San Bruno, soon were sent by train to the new Utah camp still under construction. Additional medical personnel would be needed there when its population increased.

The makeshift facilities at Tanforan, established in only a few days at the old racetrack just twelve miles south of San Francisco, had been home to about 8,000 men, women, and children housed in 130 barracks buildings, some fashioned from existing odorous horse stables and others newly built and arranged in neat rows within the oval racetrack's infield. The San Bruno track had once been home to San Francisco Buick dealer Charles Howard's favorite American racehorse, *Seabiscuit.* By the summer of 1942 it was bulging with exiled Japanese Americans. In September, after five months of difficult adjustment, nearly all of Tanforan's 7,600 Bay Area incarcerees were taken away from California and sent far inland to Utah's new Topaz Relocation Center.[12]

Recently free and on her own in Paris, Riverside native and artist Mine Okubo stared out a train window at Tanforan, her keen eyes absorbing every detail. A school friend of Sumi Harada and contemporary of Sumi's younger brother Yoshizo, Okubo was born in Riverside in 1912. Like Clark Harada, Mine Okubo had been accepted and supported by her teachers at the city's Polytechnic High School. Before they came to Riverside, her immigrant Issei mother and father had both been involved in the arts in Japan. Her family's strong artistic heritage supported her development as a young artist growing up in California in the 1920s and early 1930s. "My artistic talent was recognized early in the grade schools," Mine said, "but I received my first encouragement at the Polytechnic High School." Mine's high school art teacher, Althea B. Williams, encouraged the young artist to believe in herself: "For three years I had a very understanding art teacher . . . who took a keen interest in my work and . . . entered many of my works in the International High School competitions and other local shows . . . At Riverside Junior College . . . my art teacher thought University of California at Berkeley would be the best place to continue my art studies so I left Riverside in 1933."[13]

After leaving home to attend the university, Mine had also spent time studying art in Europe, living in France in the late 1930s until she returned to Southern California to be with her mother, Miyo, who was gravely ill. When her mother died in April 1940, Okubo once again returned to Berkeley.

At 7:45 on Wednesday evening, September 16, 1942, Mine Okubo and her younger brother, Toku, most recently together as incarcerees at the Tanforan Assembly Center, were seated aboard the train for Topaz. Joining them were about 500 other Tanforan incarcerees and 50 military police escorts. As night fell, the Okubos and their fellow passengers watched small gatherings of other incarcerees still standing behind the fences at Tanforan. Those left behind waved farewell from high atop the rooftops of the racetrack's horse stables as the train pulled away and headed east into the darkness toward the Nevada desert. After a tiring forced exodus in creaking railcars with drawn shades, failing old-fashioned gaslights, and vomiting passengers, with the monotony broken only by the distribution of boxes of oranges and lemons to the weary passengers and by a well-aimed brick flying through one of the train windows, the closely guarded railroad caravan finally arrived in Salt Lake City at 4:00 a.m. Four hours later the rail trip ended at the little railroad station in Delta, Utah, sixteen miles east of the new Topaz Relocation Center near the smaller settlement of Abraham.[14]

Still on the train, with the sun now over the horizon, tired families received the first edition of the *Topaz Times,* the old mimeographed *Tanforan Totalizer* newspaper renamed for the new incarceration center in Utah. Its premier issue drew muffled chuckles from those with stiff necks and sleepy eyes now looking out the train windows at their stark new surroundings when they read the little paper's hand-drawn stenciled masthead asserting that Topaz, bearing the name of Utah's state gemstone and a nearby mountain, was the "Jewel of the Desert." Beneath a simple line drawing of a radiant multifaceted topaz gem hovering among puffy clouds billowing high in the western sky, "Welcome to Topaz," the paper's front-page feature story, explained that the camp was "soon to be the fifth largest city of Utah." Leaving the train and climbing into buses, the Okubos and other weary travelers were driven from Delta to Topaz for their first look at their new home, described succinctly by the ever-observant Mine as "desolate." Laid out around a central square-mile area about the same size as Riverside's original downtown neighborhood, the new community comprised thirty-four residential blocks with twelve barracks each, a mess hall where meals were served to incarcerees in a large communal setting, several recreation halls, and a big washroom with showers and toilet and laundry facilities. Along its northern border, eight additional blocks housed the camp's administrative staff, military police, and hospital in a series of long, low, and freshly painted white buildings heated by a huge coal-fired boiler vented by a tall metal smokestack.

Secured by a sentry post at its entrance, the incarceration camp was surrounded by a long fence. When construction was finally completed a few weeks later, the new camp was overlooked by military police stationed in seven guard towers around the perimeter of the camp. Although some had claimed the government's "Relocation" program would protect the Japanese American incarcerees from assaults outside the camps, none housed inside believed the tall guard towers, staffed around the clock with armed military personnel, were designed to watch anything other than life inside the barbed-wire fence.

Just as Mine and Toku Okubo had traveled by train from San Bruno a few days earlier, several members of the extended Harada family faced the same rail journey from Tanforan to Topaz. Clark Kohei Harada, now twenty-six, had joined the family of his former employer, optometrist Dr. Russell WeHara, during the early stages of the Bay Area expulsion. Clark arrived at Topaz with the WeHaras on Tuesday, September 22. Mary Yoshiko Harada, first wife of Dr. Masa Atsu Harada, before her removal to Tanforan living as a single mother in San Francisco with her son Calvin, seventeen, and daughter Lily Ann, thirteen, arrived with her two children at Topaz the following day.[15]

A month after the trains came from Tanforan, back in California word arrived at Tule Lake that the War Relocation Authority had indeed decided to reassign some of its medical personnel to other incarceration camps. Dr. Masa Atsu Harada was scheduled for transfer to the Central Utah Project at Topaz. Three other Tule Lake physicians were sent to camp medical facilities at Manzanar in eastern California and then on to other WRA camps in Arizona and Colorado. In its English- and Japanese-language sections, English on its front page, the *Daily Tulean Dispatch*, the camp's small newspaper, offered a parting word of thanks to the four physicians leaving Tule Lake, including a brief editorial comment about camp life: "These medical men are truly sacrificing everything to meet the emergency situation we are all facing today; thus living up to the humanitarian ideal of their profession. To them we owe our physical well-being without which no group of humanity can long stand the kind of life we lead in these relocation centers. We wish them God-speed!"[16]

In preparation for the family journey to Topaz, Jukichi and Ken Harada were formally discharged from the Tule Lake hospital. As they left the camp medical facility, Dr. Tetsui Watanabe processed the old couple's discharge papers. Dr. Watanabe summarized Jukichi's physical health, diagnosing "hypertension" and "aortic insufficiency." By Saturday, October 24, Doc, Martha, Kimi, Ken, and Jukichi, accompanied by a War Relocation Authority escort, were on their way to Utah, traveling by train from Newell north to Klamath Falls, Oregon, and then east to Salt Lake City for later arrival at the railway depot in Delta. Just a few days earlier, the *Topaz Times* had reported that doctors at the new camp hospital were "overworked," so the tired staff at the primitive Topaz medical facilities likely warmly welcomed Doc Harada's arrival. By Teletype from Topaz, project director Charles Ernst contacted Elmer Shirrell, his counterpart at Tule Lake, asking when Doc's train would arrive at Delta. Ernst arranged for Topaz camp staff to meet the Harada family at the train to welcome Dr. Harada as the camp's new chief surgeon and to provide transportation to the Topaz camp because of the age and poor health of the elder Haradas.

Shortly after leaving the train at Delta, Family 6507 from the Tule Lake Relocation Center was escorted to their new home at Topaz, arriving just ten days after the dedication ceremony for the camp's new hospital. Construction had begun at Topaz a couple of weeks after Doc and his family first arrived at Tule Lake at the end of June. The newer Utah camp's 623 buildings, finished in only two months, lacked many important features and had few amenities when the earliest incarcerees arrived on September 11. However, with only half the population of Tule Lake, Doc might have hoped that the community's health needs and the work hours at Topaz would be a little easier to manage.

The Haradas were gradually converging on Topaz, inching toward their long-awaited family reunion. Yoshizo was still at Tule Lake, but Sumi and Harold at Poston had already changed their earlier transfer request and were now seeking an immediate transfer to Topaz. Before long, they hoped to be there too.[17]

FIFTEEN

BLUE BANDANAS AND
AN IRONWOOD CLUB

Throughout the fall of 1942 the losses and humiliation of the forced removal set in for the thousands of incarcerees at all ten concentration camps. For many, life inside the camps became more difficult with each passing day. At Topaz, Mine Okubo remembered: "A feeling of uncertainty hung over the camp; we were worried about the future. Plans were made and remade, as we tried to decide what to do. Some were ready to risk anything to get away. Others feared to leave the protection of the camp." Fretting over the uncertainties at Poston and distressed by her parents' absence and failing health, Sumi Harada worried every day about how long it would take to finally obtain permission from the government to rejoin her ailing parents at Topaz. With nearly everything else gone and her parents hospitalized in a camp far away in Utah, the family reunion meant more to her than ever before.[1]

Conflict arose early among some of the younger citizen Nisei and the non-citizen Issei forced into the temporary holding facilities at places like the Tanforan and Santa Anita Racetracks, and it did not take long for other community factions to express discontent. Packed mess halls symbolized the dramatic changes forced on the Nikkei community as communal dining in shifts of hundreds eating mass-produced and sometimes unfamiliar food eliminated the once routine intimacy of the family dinner table, one of the last places members of busy Nikkei families

eight209

could make regular contact with one another before the war. Mine Okubo observed of Tanforan: "Table manners were forgotten. Guzzle, guzzle, guzzle; hurry, hurry, hurry. Family life was lacking. Everyone ate wherever he or she pleased. Mothers lost all control over their children." Later at Topaz, Okubo added further details about the food, mentioning bread twice. "Each mess hall fed from two hundred and fifty to three hundred persons. Food was rationed, as it was for the civilian population on the outside . . . Often a meal consisted of rice, bread, and macaroni, or beans, bread, and spaghetti. At one time we were served liver for several weeks, until we went on strike."

Roy Hashimura also described his experiences with limited food choices at Poston: "There was not too much variety in the food. In fact, [sixty-five years later] I still won't eat apple butter because we got sick and tired of it. But the food was edible . . . I can't complain. It was food. We weren't starving."[2]

Along with the diminished strength and guidance of Issei parents within individual family units, most of the other more traditional social systems once defining the Nikkei community before the war had nearly vanished inside the temporary concentration centers. Crowded living conditions and daily embarrassments from the lack of privacy added to the stresses on family and community solidarity. After the move to the more permanent incarceration camps, more open and dangerous conflict erupted. Some within the camps worked cooperatively with government authorities to develop productive social opportunities for the incarcerees, but others viewed any cooperation as the activity of potential informants spying on behalf of camp administrators.

Activities like Nisei dance bands and sports teams soon competed for community attention with more sedate and, to the younger generation, less engaging opportunities like Issei tea societies and *ikebana* flower arranging classes. Like many children of immigrants, the Nisei had naturally drifted away from their immigrant parents and cultural ties to "the old country" as they became more integrated in US society through the public school system. As the years passed, involvement by young Nisei in everyday American life and popular culture became more important to them than knowledge of an unknown ancestral homeland.

At camps like Poston and Topaz most of the camp incarcerees' former daily patterns were gone. However, some aspects of pre-war community life were maintained inside the camps, albeit in limited ways. Small groups living in camp-block neighborhoods developed new relationships based on things like community origins, former occupations, religious affiliations, and family ties. In some of the camps the incarcerees created attractive Japanese landscape features in the desert dust, inventing personal responses to the severe limits imposed by camp life. Within a month of the forced exodus, at the end of June 1942, the new camp newspaper at Manzanar announced Kay Tamada's evening *shakuhachi* flute lessons and reported that Mrs. Yoshiko Shin of Block 14 had transported "her 50 varieties of cactus plants . . . from Los Angeles in a suitcase, along with her clothes." Some incarcerees turned to the soothing sound of the bamboo flute or a lifelong passion for horticulture, and others explored traditional dance, crafted barracks furniture from scrap lumber, and made smaller utilitarian or artistic objects to balance the pain and pass the time. Like Mine Okubo, who soon found work producing the newspaper at Topaz, other professional artists detained in camp occupied themselves by observing every detail. With precious art supplies, some began sketching, drawing, and painting scenes of their new lives in captivity.[3]

Berkeley art instructor Chiura Obata, born in Japan in 1885, had lost his job as an assistant professor at the University of California because of the government expulsion. Obata's art studio had been less than a mile from Mine and Saburo Kido's home on Stuart Street in Berkeley, a stone's throw from the big house "Potato King" George Shima had purchased, upsetting his white neighbors back in 1909. At Tanforan in 1942, Obata was joined by Bay Area artists George and Hisako Hibi and Riverside native Mine Okubo. Within a few days of his arrival at the San Bruno racetrack, Obata founded the Tanforan Art School. After his later transfer to Topaz, Obata and other artists and teachers continued their involvement in the arts through the camp's adult education program, developing art curriculum and classes for students of all ages.

Joining Obata, Hisako Hibi, a former student at the California School of Fine Arts in San Francisco, also taught painting classes at Topaz. Like the other former residents of the squalid horse stalls at Tanforan, Hisako was just settling in at Topaz in November 1942 after several hectic weeks in Utah. The first snow had fallen there on October 13, coating the surrounding mountains and low roofs of the black tar-papered barracks with icy white powder. For the sensitive and observant Bay Area artists, most of whom had never lived in a cold winter climate, the earliest snow at Topaz defined the surrounding mountains and nearby landscape outside the fences, as well as the stark contrasting shapes and sharp outlines of the structures and forms within the camp. Before long, Hibi had completed her second painting at Topaz, a dark and somber image of a row of residential barracks retreating toward the bleak horizon. Little smokestacks pointed toward gray skies overshadowed by a darker mountain looming in the distance. At the edge of a vacant Topaz street, Hibi painted an agitated cloud of smoke or dust spinning like a black tornado and spiraling over two barely recognizable human figures stooping over bare ground at the far left of the scene. The swirling dark cloud twists around and upward above them into the darkened sky, higher than the distant mountaintop.[4]

Although everyone in camp was annoyed by the pervasive dust, extreme weather, lack of privacy, and the many smaller indignities of their new living conditions, some were attempting to balance their lives through social activity and creative expression, but others hotly resented the situation in which they now found themselves. A few acted upon their frustration by directing their anger toward camp officials and other camp incarcerees, particularly those they identified as cooperating with camp authorities or others linked to the leadership of the Japanese American Citizens League. Although its membership had increased soon after Pearl Harbor, most incarcerees did not belong to the JACL. Many viewed the organization's leaders with doubt and disappointment because of their compliance with the government's expulsion plan, particularly as the stark limits of life in confinement set in. With colder weather on the way, in one of the earliest confrontations at Poston II, on September 13, 1942, just before midnight, JACL president Saburo Kido was roughed up by four or five assailants.

Earlier in the evening, Saburo and Mine had been visiting with fellow Poston incarceree Harry Yamamoto, who also lived in Block 215, two barracks away from the Kidos. Mine had already gone back to the family's apartment for the night. Walking back alone in the dark a little after 11:00 p.m., Saburo left a few minutes after Mine, after he finished reading the newspaper at Yamamoto's. First stopping briefly at the men's latrine, Kido approached his apartment at the end of the block and turned to avoid a muddy spot in front of the Kita family's barracks. Without warning, several men suddenly jumped him in the dark. Stuffing a handkerchief into his mouth to muffle his shouts for help, the attackers struggled to overpower Kido until one knocked him down. Kicking him once in the head, Kido's unknown attackers ran off into the night. Saburo tried to chase after one of his assailants, but the man vanished in the darkness. "Since it was so dark, I gave up the chase," Kido said.[5]

As painter Hisako Hibi added the finishing touches to her foreboding street scene at Topaz, Saburo made his way back to camp at Poston, Arizona, from an emergency national JACL conference he had just attended in Salt Lake City. The league's conference addressed a variety of topics concerning conditions in the incarceration camps, opportunities for students, agricultural work, organizational finances, and the future of its newspaper, *Pacific Citizen*. Beyond the rather mundane interests of the organization, however, JACL national secretary Mike Masaoka, always known for freely expressing controversial positions, put forth the idea that the JACL should support Nisei military service. "Somewhere on the field of battle, in a baptism of blood, we and our comrades must prove to all who question that we are ready and willing to die for the one country we know and pledge allegiance to," Masaoka asserted. Conference delegates reacted with what Bill Hosokawa said was "an intense, emotional, sometimes agonized outpouring on both sides of the issue as doubts and resentments were aired." Some supported the Issei parents who did not believe their sons should be required to serve in the military of the country imprisoning them all in camps. Others were concerned about a growing public outcry calling for the permanent removal of all Japanese Americans from the United States.[6]

As if the forced exodus and its losses were not enough, some of the more racist groups in the West were promoting the idea that resident aliens and the nation's citizens of Japanese ancestry should be deported as soon as possible, echoing the past. Earlier in the year, former California attorney general Ulysses S. Webb, co-author of the state's Alien Land Law in 1913 and the Harada family's nemesis in their challenge to the same law so many years before, now joined the American Legion and Native Sons of the Golden West, key players in the earlier passage of California's Alien Land Law of 1920, to once again challenge the very existence of the Japanese American community. Ending his unrivaled career as California's longest-serving attorney general, Webb had been succeeded in 1939 by Nikkei expulsion advocate Earl Warren, the future chief justice of the US Supreme Court. Attorney General Warren, mindful of maintaining potential sources of statewide political support, would become the Golden State's next governor in the upcoming election.

Old U. S. Webb, now in his late seventies and still as contrary to the Constitution as ever, argued in separate suits filed in federal court that the children of aliens ineligible for citizenship should not be allowed to become American citizens simply because they were born within US borders. Although Webb's courtroom efforts were unsuccessful at the time, with the West Coast's Japanese Americans forced into the camps and unable to muster much legal or popular support in the early months of their incarceration, many Japanese Americans feared that expulsion from the coast might be the first step leading to further government action against their community. Profoundly distressed by these developments, some of the anxious conferees in Salt Lake City were convinced that they needed to take bold action to counter the new expressions of old racist prejudices now being proclaimed against them in Congress and throughout the country.

JACL president Kido recalled that the group in Salt Lake City made a distinction between the possibility of supporting a call for Japanese American volunteers to serve in the military and what he felt was the more appropriate option for American citizens denied their rights in camp, the restoration of selective service requirements, which had been modified after the attacks on Pearl Harbor.

> We were opposed to . . . volunteering because we thought that that was unfair . . . We knew the sentiment of the people within the [camps] and . . . most of the Nisei felt that they were deprived of their citizenship rights, therefore why should they be obligated to . . . discharge the duties of a citizen?
>
> So, under those circumstances, to expect the people to volunteer, I thought, was . . . expecting too much. And, . . . if the volunteering was not successful, then we would be accused of not being loyal. I was afraid of that . . . So we said volunteering should not be encouraged. But, instead, we should have the selective service instituted on an equal basis, same as everybody else. And that's why we went for selective service.[7]

After hours of impassioned discussion and debate over this complicated and emotional issue, at the end of the conference the JACL endorsed a resolution calling for Nisei military service. Meeting in Salt Lake City with Dillon Myer, the new director of the War Relocation Authority who in June had replaced an often-sleepless Milton Eisenhower upon his resignation after only three months on the job, the JACL asked Myer to reclassify selective service requirements for Japanese Americans "on the same basis as all other Americans." To the dismay of many of the men and women sitting in the desolate incarceration centers, the JACL was now supporting the military draft of the young men locked up in camp. Worried for his safety if he returned to Poston, Mine Harada Kido wrote to her husband in Salt Lake City, "Don't come home . . . to camp." Rejecting Mine's plea, Kido said, "I decided to go home anyway," and Saburo soon returned to Poston.[8]

Shortly after Pearl Harbor, the government had discharged many of the Nisei already serving in the armed services before the war began. In addition, for young Nisei male citizens, the routine 1-A classification indicating acceptability for military service was changed to 4-C, alien ineligible for service, or 4-F, unfit for service. California-born Harold Harada remembered that he had been classified 1-A when he turned eighteen in 1941 but he was reclassified 4-C soon after the Pearl Harbor attack. By the time they arrived at Poston, Shig and his Riverside high school friends, still American citizens according to the Constitution, were all deemed unfit for service in the US military. Shig's sister, Mine, recalled her husband's thoughts on the matter, explaining why, as JACL president, Kido supported Nisei military service: "He said, 'That's . . . one of our rights, you know. Unless we get that right back, . . . we'll never be considered . . . first-class citizens.' " However, like her outspoken sister Sumi, father Jukichi, and others in the Harada family known for independent thinking, Mine Kido was never slow to express herself at awkward moments. Echoing the growing protests against the JACL leadership and others supporting Nisei service in the armed forces, Mine also challenged the JACL president, adding her discontented voice to those questioning the idea of Nisei military service: "I felt the same way, too . . . Why should we go and fight if they don't want us around?"[9]

Understandably, many believed the change in service classification to 4-C for the young men in camp was an insult to these patriotic citizens who, like other loyal Americans at the time, were anxious to serve their country in war. Most also understood the paradox of living in a government incarceration camp one day and serving agreeably in the US military the next. On November 11, the *Topaz Times* reported that Armistice Day, the commemoration of the end of World War I, would be observed at the camp high school, with "piano and violin selections and community singing," and also that 150 swine would soon be added to the Topaz hog farm, expanding camp food production. But the lead article, published a few days before the JACL conference in Salt Lake City began, informed surprised incarcerees that the military was now poised to reverse its earlier prohibition of Nisei military service: "In an effort towards amelioration of its rulings under the Selective Service whereby enlistment of Nisei personnel has been suspended since the outbreak of the war, and in response to urgent requests from Nisei circles pleading that Nisei men of Draft age be granted the opportunity to prove their loyalty by enlisting in the Armed Services of the United States, the War Department has now inaugurated a plan whereby such an opportunity is now presented to Nisei personnel."[10]

The "Nisei circles" mentioned in the *Topaz Times* article suggested to some that the JACL was speaking on their behalf without their permission. Angered by the league's outspoken support for the restoration of the draft and the impression that the group was perceived by the government and perhaps some of the wider American public as speaking for all Japanese Americans, many of whom did not belong to the organization, members of militant camp factions once again turned their anger toward JACL president Saburo Kido. As soon as he returned to Poston, Kido began distributing petitions supporting the call for Nisei military service. Some in camp found the petitions an affront to their compromised status as American citizens. They refused to jump on the JACL bandwagon as it slowly gained momentum, rolling toward the restoration of the draft for Japanese American boys still detained in camp. Others were willing to express their disagreement more forcefully. Kido explained: "The people in the relocation centers . . . thought we wanted to drag all the Nisei into the army. And, so, as a result, . . . I was a marked man." With concern for his safety at Poston growing daily, Saburo received an offer from camp authorities.

> While I was back at camp, I was called from the administration . . . and they asked me if I wanted to go. And they said in twenty-four hours I could leave if I want to go. But I asked them, "How about my family?" They said the clearance hadn't come for my family.
>
> . . . My thinking was this: I was the national president . . . Somebody's going to be the scapegoat. And I thought that if anybody was going to be the scapegoat, . . . I was the logical person and why should I let somebody else take my place? . . . I thought that if I left the camp under threat, then it'd be a disgrace to the JACL to have its leader . . . run away because he's threatened or because he's afraid that something may happen to him . . . I felt, from the Japanese community standpoint, . . . that I had to remain there. So, I refused . . . the leave clearance.[11]

Because of mounting threats, Saburo's friends in Block 215 installed extra lights near his family's barracks. Poston police were now stationed regularly near the Kido apartment. Mine explained: "It was terrible. It was terrifying . . . Maybe because they didn't know where else to . . . vent their wrath . . . that it just turned on us."[12]

Despite Kido's intent to remain in camp to participate in the incarceration process, it soon became clear to Mine and Saburo that their continued presence at Poston might jeopardize their family's safety. On the first anniversary of the Pearl Harbor attack, December 7, 1942, they submitted an Application for Leave Clearance, WRA Form 126, asking that their family be permitted to leave Poston to move east. Mine explained the steps required to obtain a leave:

> We wanted to leave as soon as possible but . . . you . . . needed two or three . . . sponsors or guarantors, and they had to be Caucasian . . . So I said, "Well, all right," and . . . I wrote down several names and then they said, "Well, the more the merrier," so you better put down . . . some more of your friends' names. And, so, what did I do? I put down six of my friends' names. And do you know, the government had to wait for all six to come in before they would consent to let me leave?
>
> [The sponsors had] to write in and say that we were . . . responsible, safe, loyal, . . . people . . . My friend that . . . held up the whole thing was in Iowa and she was snowed in. She said she was snowed in for six weeks, or something like that, and she thought since it was a government paper, it had to be typed. And she wanted to go to the church to type it, because that was . . . the only typewriter she could get to. So that's why . . . our . . . leaving . . . Poston was delayed.[13]

From JACL headquarters in Salt Lake City, Secretary Mike Masaoka sent a letter to Saburo Kido in Poston with an "offer of employment under the terms of the WRA leave regulations of October 1, 1942." Such job arrangements and formal employment offers were required for incarcerees seeking to relocate outside the West Coast's restricted military zones and away from the government concentration camps. Masaoka explained that the JACL was "prepared to hire Saburo Kido as a special staff member, the conditions of his work with us to be determined by mutual consent . . . Mr. Kido will serve as a paid member of our staff. Up to this time he has not been [a] paid worker as the office of national president has been merely a honorary one."[14]

As Mine's Riverside high school and Sunday school friend, Pauline Hunnicutt, her husband in the military and stationed at a nearby air base, waited patiently in Iowa for the snow to melt so she could reach her church typewriter in ·Sioux City, others began sending their reference letters on behalf of the Kidos to the War Relocation Authority in Washington. Back at Poston, threats against Saburo Kido increased. On December 11, bowing to pressure from those opposing the JACL call for military service, he agreed to sign a statement saying those who supported the JACL resolution at the November meeting in Salt Lake City "did not represent anyone but ourselves. The resolution pertaining to Selective Service Class 4 C which was passed therefore did not apply to the people of Poston, Arizona."

15.1. Saburo Kido (*right*) with other Poston legal staff (identified in the original WRA photograph as, *left to right*, Cap [Kosaku Steven] Tamura, Franklyn Sugijama [Sugiyama], Tom Masuda, [Ignatius] Elmer Yamamoto, Saburo Kido), Poston, Arizona, January 4, 1942. (Francis Stewart photograph, War Relocation Authority Photographs of Japanese-American Evacuation and Resettlement, Series 1, Volume 2, Section A, WRA no. A-825; courtesy of the Bancroft Library, University of California, Berkeley)

The following day Kido told a fellow JACL official of the mounting pressures at Poston. "This life in camp sure is getting to be a nervous strain on the family. The heat is on me right now on this selective service resolution . . . In a sense we were not the official delegates from Poston so what they are asking of me is not out of reason," Kido said. A week later, he explained that when he attended block meetings to discuss the resolution, he was accompanied by police guards. "I am on the verge of nervous prostration. Not only that, Mine is now sick . . . One nite, I had to have guards when I went to the showers," Kido said.

The last ten days of January saw more agitation against those who had expressed support for the JACL and government plans for Nisei military service. At Poston, acts of public humiliation founded in rural Japanese folkways sent an unequivocal—and unpleasant—message when human excrement was "thrown upon the doorstep or into the rooms of Issei or Nisei leaders." At the end of the month, when the War Department announced its plans for a Nisei volunteer combat unit, former Watsonville truck farmer Oritaro Kobayashi approached Saburo Kido, warning him to soon expect much more serious trouble.[15]

Shortly after Kobayashi's warning, just after the conclusion of the evening's *shibai* public performance at Poston II on Saturday night, January 30, Mine Harada Kido was walking back home to Block 215, returning to her barracks after taking a bath. Mine reached Apartment D shortly before 10:30, joining her husband who had already gone to bed earlier in the evening. "You had to go quite a ways to go to take a bath . . . I came back and I went to sleep," Mine said. "Funny thing, . . . Kido felt awfully sleepy, so he went to bed at eight-thirty, but I didn't go to bed 'til around ten-thirty that night."[16]

As Mine joined husband Saburo, their three children and Hawaiian friend already asleep in narrow beds nearby inside Apartment D, a few blocks away a group of eight young men gathered anxiously at the apartment of Kiichi Kawahira, an Issei resident of Block 208. Like many in the camp, most in the group meeting at Kawahira's blamed the JACL for the mass expulsion because of its early cooperation with the government. In the last few weeks, since the JACL meeting in Salt Lake City, many more young men at Poston had grown increasingly upset over JACL efforts to remove the Selective Service 4-C designation of alien ineligible for service. If successful, these young men would be eligible for the draft even though they were still being held in camp. Perhaps prompted by the lead article in the Japanese-language section of the *Poston Chronicle* on Friday announcing the formation of a volunteer Nisei combat unit for service in the military, and impatient with the older camp residents asking them to wait for a better moment to take revenge, James Tanaka, Miyoshi Matsuda, James Toya, and five other young men, most in their late teens or early twenties, together decided to make their move now, taking their chances with the consequences.[17]

An hour or so after midnight, they separated into three groups. Some, perhaps all, concealed the lower halves of their faces with blue-and-white bandanas. Moving silently in the night and nearly invisible against the black tar-papered walls of Poston's darkened residential barracks, one group carefully removed the mess hall gong and turned off the lights in the laundry room and latrines in the middle of the block. Unknown to the group, two camp police officers were out of sight nearby, just steps away from the Kidos' Apartment D in Barracks 2 of Block 215, stationed in the laundry's boiler room at the end of Barracks 1. Bored with their graveyard-shift guard assignment, one of the two Poston cops was fast asleep; the other was paying scant attention to what was going on outside.

Some of the young men, working as quickly and quietly as possible, wedged four-inch wooden pegs into the latches of all eight apartments in Barracks 1 and 2, the two long buildings just behind the block's recreation hall. With the lights out in the locations nearby, the area was in nearly total darkness, as another group slowly approached the exterior door to the apartment at the end of Barracks 2 and began unfastening its hinges. Still new, the bolts securing the hinges on the door were easy to remove without making much noise.

One of the men standing in the shadows was clutching the square handle of a two-foot-long ironwood club. Fashioned from a thick branch of the hard and heavy desert wood growing in scattered patches outside the camp, the dark weapon had a round body with a knob at its end, adding a little extra weight. Another man stood nearby, nervously holding a flashlight. Tanaka and Matsuda, both in their early twenties, glanced briefly at one another for their final silent nod of agreement to move in quickly as soon as their accomplices lifted the apartment door from its loosened hinges. Inside the darkened room, Saburo and Mine were in bed and asleep, but hearing strange sounds outside his barracks, Saburo began to stir. "I'm a light sleeper," Saburo remembered. "So when I heard a little rustling sound outside, . . . I thought that's funny . . . somebody walking outside . . . maybe something unusual is happening."[18]

Mine explained what happened next. "The men rushed in . . . They unfastened the hinges on both of our doors, . . . and came right through . . . One of the men had a huge . . . ironwood club . . . They went right to him." Mine thought it was Matsuda who first struck Saburo with the flashlight, its lens breaking and shards of glass falling to the floor. It made sense that it might have been Matsuda who had taken the flashlight to enter the apartment first, identifying Kido sleeping in the darkness and confirming his location inside the small apartment. Matsuda was the member of the group who probably knew him best. Despite their blue bandana facemasks, at the beginning of the invasion Kido recognized Matsuda immediately because they had worked together at the *New World Sun* newspaper in San Francisco, the place Kido had spent most of the day after the Pearl Harbor attack. "You are Matsuda, aren't you?" Kido exclaimed, as he jumped out of bed, struggling to pin Matsuda down. Matsuda was so surprised at Kido's recognition in the darkness that he quickly lost his edge. "We grappled when they came in," Saburo said. "We had six people in one room so there wasn't much room to move around . . . The lamp fell down; the radio fell down . . . and made a lot of noise."[19]

When Kido identified Matsuda, Tanaka, wielding the heavy ironwood club, struck Kido in the head and shoulders, smashing Kido's fingers as he tried to deflect Tanaka's blows. Bleeding from cuts on his bare feet from stepping on the broken flashlight lens, his two-year-old son in a child's bed only steps away, Kido struggled to defend himself, fearful his assailants might next attack members of his family. Nine-year-old daughter Rosalind, waking to the noise of the scuffle and her father's shouts, instantly remembered her mother's instructions; because of worries over the earlier incidents and threats to Kido, Mine had instructed her kids on what to do if something like this happened. "My bed was up against the wall that separated us from the neighbors," Rosalind recalled. "I remember my mom saying . . . that if anything happens, I'm to bang on the wall and yell as loud as I possibly can." In seconds, Mine and Violet were wide awake. They both screamed for help, joining Rosalind, pounding on the thin barracks walls to rouse the neighbors in Apartment C next door. Terrified by the attack, Violet fainted and collapsed as Mine kept calling for help. Young Rosalind listened intently to the unforgettable and frightening sounds in the night as her parents tried to beat back the intruders. "Above my bed was . . . a little hanging closet with clothes hanging in it so I was somewhat hidden back there . . . I could hear a lot of noise; I could hear my dad shouting and my mom screaming."[20]

Because of the wooden pegs stuck in their door latches, the Kidos' neighbors were prevented from coming quickly to their aid. "None of our neighbors could come out to help us," Mine explained. "All of our friends' doors . . . couldn't be opened . . . Our friends couldn't get out of their barracks . . . One of our friends jumped out of his window. He was a great big, . . . more than six-foot-tall man. He jumped out of his window to come but, by that time, it was too late." Struck again with the heavy ironwood club, adrenaline flowing, Kido fought the two men as best he could but soon began losing his strength, his legs weakening. Five feet, four inches tall and 145 pounds, at forty years of age Kido was no match for his two armed and much younger assailants. Alerted by Mine's shouts, a few neighbors finally rushed to her aid as six of Kido's attackers ran off into the darkness. Dropping the ironwood club and losing one of his brown oxfords, Tanaka took off, hobbling out into the night with just one shoe. Two neighbors who had escaped the blocked doors of their barracks, one tearing off a screen and jumping out his window and another breaking down his door, came to Kido's aid, helping him to restrain Matsuda. Delayed because one had spent a few moments in the laundry room rousing his sleepy partner after hearing shouting outside, the two Poston cops finally arrived, but a little too late to do much good.[21]

As the commotion from the attack subsided, Rosalind remained hidden near her clothes closet, listening intently. "Suddenly everything got quiet. My next recollection was seeing my dad on the ground . . . a couple of barracks beyond, lying on a mattress." Scattered nearby on the blood-spattered floor of Apartment D were two blue bandana facemasks, Tanaka's ironwood club and brown oxford shoe, and Matsuda's broken flashlight, all evidence of the nighttime attack. Semiconscious on the ground outside in the darkness and surrounded by family and sleepy-eyed neighbors from nearby barracks, Kido was lifted hurriedly into the back of a camp ambulance for a quick ride out of Poston II's gates. Jumping in as the vehicle pulled away, neighbor Dr. Harry Kita, a dentist from Salinas, tended to Kido in the ambulance as it raced three miles northeast, paralleling the Colorado River in a straight shot along Mojave Road and passing between the War Relocation Authority's agricultural fields and Poston's big hog farm.[22]

In a few minutes the ambulance pulled up to the entrance of the camp hospital at Poston I. Kido arrived at about 2:20 a.m., carried in on a stretcher. Employed there since December and working the night shift, Kido's nineteen-year-old brother-in-law, hospital orderly Harold Harada, recalled the next few hours:

> I was . . . working as an orderly in the men's ward of the . . . Poston hospital . . . I was on the night shift . . . when I heard . . . whispering amongst the . . . nursing personnel . . . in the hospital, that Saburo Kido had been attacked and was in the hospital. The minute I heard that, . . . and most a' the people weren't aware that he was my brother-in-law, . . . I went over to the surgical ward where I heard that he . . . had been admitted. And went there and . . . found that . . . the ward was heavily guarded.

. . . There were two men by his door, . . . Poston policemen, and I asked if I could . . . go in to see him, for he was my brother-in-law, they admitted me immediately and, . . . Mr. Kido was laying on his side . . . with his back exposed, . . . towards me as I entered. And he was in a fetal position, and his back looked like, ah, well it was bloody red . . . It wasn't bleeding—like a mound of hamburger that had been freshly ground and placed on a . . . metal enamel tray . . . at the butcher shop . . .

He was semi-conscious. He . . . acknowledged me when I told him who I was, and I think he sort of grunted, and that was about it. He was . . . probably heavily sedated . . . He had a bump on the back of his head.[23]

Fearing a concussion and more serious internal injuries, camp physicians assessed Kido's condition. They administered codeine for the pain and observed contusions on his scalp and back and lacerations on his hands. X rays revealed no broken bones. Later, sedated with Nembutal, Saburo did not regain consciousness for a couple of days and remained in the hospital fourteen more. Because of the attack on Kido and another unrelated disturbance the same evening, when the FBI arrested several camp residents early Sunday morning, Poston project director Wade Head asked Captain Holn of the nearby military police unit to post twenty-five soldiers at the Poston II police station. Armed with rifles with bayonets, the soldiers remained at the station until just before noon on Sunday, when they were ordered to return to their quarters as the situation quieted down.

Back at Poston II, Matsuda was restrained and surrounded by a neighborhood block group wielding improvised clubs and canes; several incarcerees had been deputized by the two Poston police officers to watch Matsuda while they left to report the attack. The lone captured assailant was soon interrogated with the help of a camp interpreter because Matsuda did not speak English well. American citizen Miyoshi Matsuda had been born in California in 1920 but he was also a Kibei (a child of Issei parents who was born in the United States but educated in Japan). Like others with firsthand exposure to life in the Japanese homeland in the few years before the war, Matsuda was more sympathetic to Japan than most of his Nisei contemporaries. When he was forced to leave his home in Monterey County, Matsuda was initially sent to the Salinas Assembly Center and then to Poston. After the assault Matsuda insisted he was the only one involved in the attack on Kido but, according to camp authorities, the crowd of incarcerees from Block 215 "became unruly and an angry voice accused: 'You're lying. We saw two or three others running away.' Upon this without any third degree being imposed on him Matsuda confessed that he had two accomplices—Tetsuo Inokuchi of block 214 and James Tanaka of 227. He was then taken to the police station for further questioning while the two named were picked up in their homes."[24]

When Inokuchi was brought to the police station, Matsuda said, "There were just the two of us, weren't there?" At Matsuda's question to Inokuchi, an annoyed camp security chief Miller ordered Matsuda "to speak only when questioned." With Matsuda silenced, Inokuchi offered several contradicting versions of the circumstances. Later on, as other accused attackers were apprehended for questioning and detained separately, each told a differing version of the story. By the time the last of the young men had been interrogated, a more complete picture of the evening attack emerged. During the questioning, according to the government's report, one man who had named another accomplice urged him, "They know all about it already so you might just as well spill everything." Asking for several glasses of water, the last man nervously named the rest of the assailants and offered additional details about the evening meeting at Kawahira's apartment. He also drew a diagram to show the location of each man during the attack.[25]

Camp officials said signed confessions had been easy to obtain from the eight young men, "since all of them were proud of the role they had played in the attack on Kido whom they considered a disturbing influence in Camp II." Poston project attorney Ted Haas observed, "[A]ll of them firmly believed that they had beaten Kido 'for the welfare of the community' and only when they were informed that a sentence of one to ten years might be passed upon them did they begin to look at it from Western standards and waiver in their convictions." Others in camp explained that the group was certain they would be kept under the authority of Poston's limited legal system, as had been the case with the incarcerees who had taken part in a serious camp strike the previous November.[26]

Just after 4:00 a.m. Sunday morning the Poston II Judicial Commission was called hastily to order at an emergency meeting to determine whether any subsequent proceedings could be handled within Poston's law enforcement authority. When the group reached its conclusion that the attack would be considered a felony, a War Relocation Authority administrative instruction required further legal action to take place outside the camp and jurisdiction of the Poston commission. As a result, after obtaining the signed confessions from each of the men involved in the attack, all eight were quickly transferred to the custody of Yuma County sheriff Pete Newman. Accompanied by a detail of deputy guards, Sheriff Newman drove the men ninety miles south to the county jail in Yuma for trial in Arizona Superior Court.

With signed confessions and the men in custody, things moved quickly. Defended by camp attorney Tom Masuda, in just a few weeks three of the eight, including Matsuda and Tanaka, received sentences from Yuma Superior Court judge Kelly of three to four years. Two others received sentences of twelve to eighteen months. At one point during the proceedings, several women at Poston approached Mine Kido, asking her to support lenience for one of her husband's attackers. Always direct, Mine related the circumstances and her succinct reply: "Before they had the hearing . . . a group of women . . . came over to me and asked me to . . . plead for leniency or freedom for one of the men because his wife had just had a baby. And I said, 'Well, how about my children?' That's all I said to them. They went away." By early March, the last three assailants had been released. One was freed because of lack of evidence; the other two received suspended sentences with conditions of future good behavior. All three had been formally released by the US legal system, but they were returned to confinement behind the fences at Unit II of the Poston Relocation Center.[27]

Shortly after the beating, on February 3, FBI director J. Edgar Hoover reported to War Relocation Authority director Dillon Myer in Washington, telling Myer the Poston attack was originally organized as a plot to kill Kido. "Investigation reflects that one Kiichi Kawahira, a Japanese alien, held a meeting in his barracks, attended by ten individuals, at which time plans for the assault and killing of Kido were drawn up by Kawahira," Hoover said. Earlier in the report Hoover explained to Myer, "The purpose of the assault was to eliminate Kido because of his activity in fighting against the Selective Service classification in 4-C of American-born Japanese." Describing most of Kido's attackers as "alien enemies," Hoover also included a synopsis of the activities of several other Poston residents involved in recent agitation inside the camp. If killing truly was the intent of Kido's eight attackers, they had been armed with the wrong weapons. Despite Hoover's enthusiasm for the murder plot, it was more likely that the men anxious enough to attack Kido with an ironwood club and flashlight had no intent of killing him. If he could be "eliminated" by other means, beaten so badly that he would be out of commission and serve as an example for others, that might be more than enough to satisfy some with less sinister motives in mind. Whether or not they intended to kill Kido, the attack's breach of safety inside their family's camp barracks confirmed how dangerous it had become for them to remain at Poston. Mine would remember that frightening night for the rest of her life, telling me in 1982: "Oh, tell ya, I was scared. You know, after we moved to . . . Salt Lake? All the time I was living in Salt Lake, no matter how hot the house got, I couldn't open the windows. That's how scared I was."[28]

Meanwhile, in Sioux City the snow had finally melted for Pauline Hunnicutt to get to town. The Kidos' slow progress with obtaining character references to support their December request for leave clearance, now made much more urgent by the January attack, resumed as she finally reached the church typewriter on February 5. Carefully typing her reference letter on behalf of Mine Harada Kido and posting it to the attention of War Relocation Authority director Dillon Myer in Washington, Mrs. Hunnicutt explained that she had known Mine since her high school years in Riverside and they had gone to church and Sunday school together. Writing that she had "complete confidence" in Mrs. Kido, Pauline offered support for her childhood friend's interest in leaving the Poston camp: "Mrs. Kido's life has been identical with that of any other American girl. In school everyone thought well of her and I can recall nothing which would lead me to feel that she felt herself as anything but another American. Her way of living has been our way of living and I am positive her thinking and her loyalties are the same."[29]

Written only a few days earlier, letters from several other references from the Kidos' past offered additional praise for the couple. Longtime friend, San Francisco attorney and Alien Land Law expert Guy C. Calden, with whom Kido had worked as an associate in the early 1930s, explained that Saburo had once been affiliated with his law firm, adding, "In my opinion there is not the slightest question as to his loyalty as an American citizen. I trust that his application to leave the relocation center will be favorably acted upon." Other letters soon followed from the Kidos' former Bay Area community, including Berkeley residents and friends of the Kidos for nearly twenty years, Perry and Dagmar Evans. The Evanses had known Saburo and Mine since Saburo's early days as a law student at Hastings College. Dr. Alfred Fiske, chairman of the Department of Psychology and Philosophy at San Francisco State College, also sent a letter to Washington on behalf of the Kidos. Dr. Fiske had worked with Saburo as codirector of the International Institute in San Francisco.[30]

In his letter of support, attorney Evans observed, "[W]e have no reason to suspect their loyalty to this country." Mrs. Evans, in her own letter, explained Saburo's interest in Japanese literature and the story of the *Ronin*, the traditional tale of wandering samurai and their practices of honor, sacrifice, loyalty, and persistence. Perhaps this story still inspired the injured Kido as he recovered at the Poston hospital. Mrs. Evans also mentioned Kido's awareness of the "economic difficulties of the common people of Japan." In a conversation she remembered from 1939 or 1940, Dagmar said Saburo "showed grave concern over the possibility of war between U.S. and Japan and deep fear that the U.S. underestimated the strength and determination of the powerful military party of Japan. We got the impression at this time that he considered war inevitable between U.S. and Japan."

Mrs. Evans also explained that Kido had earlier expressed interest in making affiliations with the Japanese Consulate in San Francisco, "but these had come to nothing because of the unfriendliness of the Japanese in that office to the U.S." After mentioning her admiration for Kido's work with the founding and subsequent activities of the Japanese American Citizens League, Mrs. Evans said, "I know he gave of his time without thought of personal comfort—in other words he sacrificed himself for its organization and welfare." Dagmar then added her memories of Saburo from her earlier days as a fellow college student at Berkeley. She said he was "modest, . . . honest and generous." She described her friend Mine as "a lady of culture and education, a devoted mother, and a hard worker in her house" and mentioned that she knew Mine's brother was also a graduate of the University of California in medicine. In her conclusion, Mrs. Evans appealed to Myer to allow the Kidos to leave Poston as soon as possible: "Mr. Evans and I feel convinced that they are dependable. They follow the Christian religion. They have been friends of ours for eighteen years. We are eager (1) to help our government and (2) in helping the Kidos. We feel their position at Poston, where Mr. Kido has been attacked, is to say the least difficult and even pitiable."[31]

Saburo Kido was still in the camp hospital recovering from his injuries. As his Bay Area friends sent their letters of support to the War Relocation Authority, Kido's character was being challenged from an unexpected and entirely different direction—the Federal Bureau of Investigation. Along with the several positive references from Bay Area friends, the Kidos' application for leave clearance was supplemented by a more pessimistic report from the FBI. The bureau's report asserted that, along with his activities with the JACL, Saburo might somehow be supporting Japan in its war against the United States. If he read the report, Kido would have shaken his sore head, feeling that he was in a no-win situation, with contradictory accusations coming at him from all sides. There was little he could do now to help him remain on the tightrope strung tightly in the vast breach separating those who believed he was doing his best under impossible circumstances and others who might have wanted him dead.

Peppered with inferences describing Kido's activities before the war, the FBI report asserted, "Kido has been reported to be pro-Japanese and to have been in close contact with the Japanese Consulate in San Francisco," apparently never considering Dagmar Evans's more enlightened version of the story. "Another source has reported that Kido was a lobbyist in California for Japanese interests in that state, and that he was sympathetic toward Japanese policy in the Far East," the FBI report continued. Kido's involvement as a shareholder and columnist with the *New World Sun* newspaper in San Francisco was also briefly described and the report mentioned the paper's "consistently pro-Japanese . . . tone prior to the declaration of war on Japan." His association with the JACL was also now held against him: "[U]ntil the summer of 1941 the J.A.C.L. was affiliated with the Japanese Association of North America. It has been reported that the Japanese Association of North America acted as an agent for the Japanese Government and was under the domination of the Japanese Consuls in the various West Coast cities."

One apparently positive reference for the FBI indicated that "the Japanese-American Citizens League did a great deal toward informing the Japanese population of the West Coast concerning the mechanics of the evacuation order and that the organization expressed a willingness to cooperate with the Wartime Civil Control Administration in any way possible." Kido just could not win.

The report also referred to Saburo's role as an attorney with the Japanese Committee on Trade and Information before the war. According to the FBI, in 1938 the committee was registered "as an Agent of the Japanese Government" and had "financed, in part, the activities of David Warren Ryder and Ralph K. Townsend, convicted Japanese agents." Before the war, both Ryder and Townsend had produced pro-Japanese propaganda for the Japanese government, working secretly through the Japanese Committee on Trade and Information. However, the report added, "Kido has denied any knowledge of the financial arrangements between the Committee and Ryder and Townsend." Finally, in its conclusion the FBI included word that in June 1942, Kido had reportedly written an article for the JACL's *Pacific Citizen* newspaper, described in the report as "the official organ of the Japanese-American Citizens League." Explaining that he had made negative comments about life at the Poston Relocation Center, the FBI review included Kido's reported statement, "From this 'hell-hole of America' we raise our voices to bring a true picture of conditions here." The FBI report said Kido's news article "continues in this vein and protests against conditions in the Poston Project. The article declares, among other things, that alien enemies are treated better than United States citizens in the Relocation Camps and that this condition is particularly true in the Poston Project." One wonders what Kido's attackers and the others opposing him so vehemently at Poston and elsewhere would have thought of the FBI's representation of his character. Despite the several negative inferences from the FBI, the Kido family was granted a leave clearance for February 23 and they soon moved to Salt Lake City, where Saburo began working at JACL headquarters as a paid employee for the Japanese American Citizens League.[32]

Back in Arizona on January 21, 1943, just a few days before her brother-in-law was attacked at Poston, Sumi Harada had paid a visit to the administrative office at Poston I. At the Poston office Sumi submitted a newly completed War Relocation Form 149, Request for Transfer. Changing her earlier application, in which she had asked to join her parents at Tule Lake, Sumi was requesting that the Haradas at Poston be transferred immediately to Topaz instead because Jukichi and Ken Harada were now there with Doc and his family. "I openly appeal to you that we may be united with my parents," Sumi said. Sumi explained that prior to her removal to Poston, she was led to believe that families would remain together: "[officials at the Wartime Civil Control Administration office in Riverside] advised us that there would be no family separations and personally promised us that families would be united."

Sumi also described the state of her parents' health: "[My parents] are critically ill in the Relocation Hospital, and we would like to be with them. Since they are not able to join us due to their condition, we would want to go to them." She asked that her brother Harold and the three Hashimuras, all still living in confinement at Poston, be allowed to leave the Arizona camp for the one in Utah as quickly as possible. Sumi explained the details of her parents' failing health as the reason for her request and pleaded for a speedy transfer approval: "My father's heart is in such a condition that he would die at any moment. My mother is a hopeless paralytic with the next stroke to be fatal. If they were in robust health, it would be of no consequence. Please let us join them before it is too late."[33]

SIXTEEN

FROM ISSEI TO NISEI

"The only time I see the sun is through the kitchen window," Ken Harada used to say when she was hard at work from dawn to dark at the Washington Restaurant. Looking west across Utah's empty high-desert flatlands, beyond snow-capped mountains toward their lost homes on the Pacific coast, those now living in winter's sticky alkaline mud below the tall guard towers at Topaz sometimes saw a beautiful sunset. On this Wednesday evening, March 10, 1943, high clouds skated across the vast horizon. The temperature dropped from a daytime high of 50 to a nighttime low of only 26 degrees. Standing water in buckets, rain barrels, and little puddles around the barracks began to freeze. From her Topaz hospital bed waiting for sleep, Mrs. Harada might have caught just a glimpse of the beauty of the western sky above the freezing earth.

As Ken Harada rested in her bed at Topaz City Hospital, painter Chiura Obata was busy completing his latest watercolor landscape, capturing the bright colors of the sweeping orange sunset high above the dark redwood water tanks at the camp's eastern border. Obata's painted brushstrokes looked very much like thousands of struggling koi, strong orange fish swimming upriver against the current in the windy sky. Wednesday night, as darkness overtook the camp, after months of waiting and worry, Sumi, Shig, and the three Hashimuras were finally on their way, en route by train from Poston to points north. Their transfer request

16.1. Wade Head, Poston project director (*right*), with CBS radio reporter Chet Huntley, Poston, Arizona, May 26, 1942. (Fred Clark photograph, War Relocation Authority Photographs of Japanese-American Evacuation and Resettlement, Series 1, Volume 2, Section A, WRA no. A-371; courtesy of the Bancroft Library, University of California, Berkeley)

had been approved by Poston project director Wade Head only days before. Now, carrying a few bags and their group travel permit and joined by four members of the Watanabe family and War Relocation Authority chaperone Mrs. Barrett, Sumi, Shig, Roy, Toshiye, and Sumiko proceeded by rail on their journey north through two restricted military zones.[1]

Riding the train toward Salt Lake City, each with $3 provided by the government for travel expenses, the small party soon made its way to Topaz. Sumi described their trip:

> When . . . the order came through, it was in March, and we . . . went on train to . . . Utah . . . The car that we were on, they . . . kept the blinds down, even in daytime. And we got off at Barstow for . . . lunch. And we had a guard with us. She . . . took head count. And, as if a most odd feeling . . . that . . . we weren't allowed to stray away from this group . . . I kept thinking people were staring at us. But they weren't. They probably thought it was an ordinary thing, you know, that they herded us along . . . And then we were herded back to the train, got back into the train and got to Salt Lake City . . . We went by train, I guess, to Fillmore. And, in Fillmore . . . these army trucks came and met us. And we piled on that, and then . . . went into camp.
>
> . . . The guards at the . . . camp gate . . . wanted to inspect our luggage . . . And, he opened my—I had a little . . . cheap suitcase, and had all of our medical things in it, you know, bandages, and so forth, and then, . . . a bottle of witch

hazel had broken. You know, it was glass. So he says, "Ah, this is what I'm looking for. It's whiskey." We tried to explain to him it's not whiskey. It's a little tiny bottle of witch hazel.

16.2. Topaz, Utah, March 14, 1943. (Francis Stewart photograph, War Relocation Authority Photographs of Japanese-American Evacuation and Resettlement, Series 4, Volume 10, Section A, WRA no. B-280; courtesy of the Bancroft Library, University of California, Berkeley)

. . . You know, going into camp, I really thought that was funny . . . I mean, opening up our luggage . . . just like we were coming into a foreign country . . . at . . . customs . . . [to] inspect all a' your stuff. No kidding.[2]

Like Mine Okubo's observations upon arriving there several months before, or painter Hisako Hibi's seeing an omen of darkness in its vacant, dusty streets, Sumi also regarded Topaz as something less than a "Jewel of the Desert." Compared to Poston, which, despite its many hardships, Sumi thought of as a "warm and friendly" community after her nine months there, she saw her new home in Utah as "cold and forbidding."

Shortly after their baggage was searched at the camp gates, Sumi and Shig were taken to their mother's bedside. "My mother and father were both in the hospital," Sumi said, "and, we saw my mother and we hugged her." Nearly a year had passed since their last time together, when Shig drove his parents from Riverside to Doc's in Sacramento. He was happy to finally see his mother again. Her eyes brightening, Ken Harada was happy too. Shig explained:

We got together again ten months later. Mother was in the hospital at Topaz . . . and we were able to finally get back to her . . . And when we arrived there . . . Mother hugged me. I was the baby of the family, so I knew that I was the apple of her eye. She hugged me and—tears welled in her eyes, and she recognized me in spite of her . . . hemiplegic condition. And after a brief fifteen minute or so visitation—we were told not to stay too long . . . we went back to our barracks . . .

And . . . in an hour or two the ambulance came after us and [we were told] that Mother had had her third stroke and was in a coma, so please come back to the hospital.

So we went—and she lived through the night but died the next morning.

She died bravely, perhaps crushed under the circumstances, but she was gallant.

"The shock of seeing us, I guess, was what . . . caused her to die . . . I guess it was just the shock, you know—emotional . . . She passed away the next day. Can't be helped. You know, it's sad to think about those things," Sumi would say thirty years later—as if it had just happened the day before.[3]

With Mine's family now living in Salt Lake City and Masa Atsu, Sumi, Clark, Harold, and Roy all close by in the camp at Topaz, the Haradas' second surviving son, Yoshizo, the former reservist with a first lieutenant's rank in the Army Dental Corps still working as a dentist at the Tule Lake Relocation Center, was the only one now separated from the family. On Friday, as Mrs. Harada lay dying, Topaz medical social services clerk Margarette Fujita sent urgent word to the Tule Lake Relocation Center, asking camp officials there to allow Yoshizo and his wife, Sumiye, to leave Tule Lake immediately to reach his critically ill mother at Topaz.

Before Yoshizo and Sumiye could leave Tule Lake, at Topaz City Hospital at 5:50 p.m., attending physician Dr. Paul Yamauchi officially observed the death from a cerebral hemorrhage of incarceree 6507-E, age sixty-one years. Ken Indo Harada, the samurai's daughter from Aichi, mother of four sons and two daughters, and a quiet, strong, and dedicated woman who fought for her home and worked honorably in Riverside's Washington Restaurant for so long, ended her life far from home, in the middle of the desert behind the barbed-wire fences of an American concentration camp.[4]

Defeated and depressed on this sad day, Doc looked into Martha's eyes, confirming their resolve to leave Topaz as soon as possible. His mother now gone and Martha nearly three months pregnant with their second child, one life ending as another began, a pensive and determined Dr. Masa Atsu Harada turned his attention to getting his family out of camp as soon as he could. A Saturday afternoon Teletype message from Topaz project director Charles Ernst informed Tule Lake project director Harvey Coverly of Ken Harada's death. Ernst asked that Dr. Yoshizo and Sumiye Harada, incarcerees 27378-A and B, be granted a temporary leave from Tule Lake for a brief trip to Topaz as soon as possible. Within hours, authorized to travel for a short-term leave "in the company of a Caucasian escort appointed by the War Relocation Authority," Yoshizo and Sumiye left the Northern California camp, making railroad connections from Newell through Klamath Falls to Salt Lake City. They arrived at the Delta train station the following Monday in plenty of time to attend Ken Harada's funeral at Topaz at the end of the week.[5]

When the Topaz Relocation Center had been completed six months earlier, along with its new barracks, guard towers, hospital, and barbed-wire fences, a small cemetery had also been established southeast of the camp's center, never to be used. For the Haradas and more than 100 other Topaz families faced with the loss of family members in camp during the war, it was simply inconceivable to leave their loved ones behind in the Utah desert. Shig explained that the family wanted to be able to visit his mother's grave in the future and did not want her remains "buried out in the desert, or someplace that's far or remote from where we wouldn't be able to pay tribute." He also explained: "It was not my . . . parents' desire to be cremated . . . They're Christians and they wanted to be . . . buried." However, like others in the incarceration camps faced with heartrending choices, the Haradas accepted cremation reluctantly, making arrangements with the War Relocation Authority and mortician L. N. Nickle, proprietor of the local funeral parlor in nearby Delta, to return Mrs. Harada's ashes to the family sometime after her memorial service at Topaz on Friday, March 19. Taking a few moments away from his duties at the camp hospital, Doc completed the WRA form asking "that the Government make the necessary funeral arrangements."[6]

In the unfamiliar and bleak setting of her new and sparsely furnished barracks apartment in Block 13, her suitcase perhaps still unpacked on Wednesday, March 17, less than a week after her arrival at Topaz and just two days before her mother's funeral, Sumi Harada spent some time reflecting on her family's loss. She composed a letter to Poston's Wade Head. Expressing her "deep appreciation" to him for approving the family's transfer to Topaz, Sumi explained: "We arrived here from Poston on Thursday, March 11 and saw Mother alive. The shock of seeing us caused her to have a stroke from which she never recovered." Sumi thanked Poston's director for the transfer from Arizona: "If it were not for the Administration we would never have seen her. I cannot tell you enough how kindly, understanding, sympathetic and sincere you people have been to us." Anticipating a future loss, Sumi also told Head, "My father is seriously ill with a cardiac heart and is not expected to live." She ended her handwritten letter with the comment, "He, my brother Harold and the three . . . Hashimuras . . . thank you from the bottom of their hearts for all that you have done for us."[7]

Also on Wednesday, perhaps only an hour or so after yet another fiery Topaz sunset disappeared from the vast sky above the camp, in a few quiet moments Sumi wrote of the samurai's daughter from Aichi:

My Mother, March 17, 1943

Today, more than ever I am
thinking of her.
Her sharp bright eyes, full
of memories of the past that
would light up when you
caught her attention. Her wavy
hair brushes back to produce a
clean cut face. Her hands soft
and gentle. I remember them
so often, when in sickness and
in pain.
O, thy loving hands.
The memories are so hard to bear.
Your loving gracious presence,
To me will never be forgotten.
O, thou were so willing to forgive
Which made thee more gracious
In my sight.
I can only ask forgiveness
When it is too late.
O kindly spirit who
Guided me,
Your goodness shall never
Leave my mind.
I see you everywhere. I
can see you at the old Eighth Street restaurant. I can
remember you at Ninth Street. I
can remember at Eighth Street, and there at the Lemon
Street house. The rides on Sunday
you were so alive.

On the train from Tule Lake, Lieutenant Yoshizo Harada either believed it would be wise for a Japanese American man on a public journey to the Topaz Relocation Center to be dressed in his US Army uniform, or he changed into it not long before his train pulled in to the Delta depot. With his wife, Sumiye, Yosh soon arrived by truck at Topaz to meet brother Shig at the camp's front gate. Shig recalled:

> I went out to the main gate to greet him, and waited for him. And he was brought in on a . . . truck from Delta into Topaz . . . I asked the guard if I couldn't go out to help him in with his bags. And the guard said, "If you cross that line, I'll shoot you." And so I said, "OK, I, I, you know, I won't help him."

And, so, my brother walked in, and walked up to the guard, and the guard checked his papers, came to attention, saluted him, and my brother [saluted the guard and] walked into camp. And I said . . . to my brother, . . . "How come you saluted him?" And he said, "Well, I have to." And I said, "Well, you know that he was gonna shoot me?" And my brother sorta' chuckled, and, I don't think he believed it but, but that was the truth . . .

. . . [Yoshizo] had his full uniform on. He had his . . . lieutenant's bars and . . . you just knew he was an officer . . . You look back at all a' these things and they seem so ironic and, and almost humorous, you know? But, here was this guy, seriously, I'm sure that he was a rookie guard and he would have . . . itched to pull his trigger.[8]

All of Ken's children were finally together again. Too ill to attend, his heart failing and protected by his family from the stress of her funeral, Jukichi Harada, Ken's husband of nearly fifty years, remained confined to his bed at Topaz City Hospital. After Mrs. Harada's Christian memorial service on Friday, her family and friends gathered outdoors alongside a drab one-story building hastily built and covered in tar paper only a few months before. Adjacent to a small tree not yet tall enough to extend its leafy green branches above the building's low roofline, just over 100 Topaz incarcerees joined the Harada family in paying their respects. With her sons serving as pallbearers, Ken's casket was taken outdoors and into the sunlight as a granddaughter and a grandson walked slowly with the others from inside the crowded recreation hall. Standing in the dirt a few yards away, a photographer carefully adjusted his camera lens, opening the shutter on a wide panorama of those gathered around the flower-covered casket.

Moving his camera closer to the center of the group for a few more exposures, the photographer captured the sad faces of those standing resolutely nearby. Dignified men dressed in suits, white shirts, and ties, once packed quickly in bags light enough for one person to carry, stood alongside strong women wearing their best dresses, fur-trimmed coats, and hats. Sprays of calla lilies rested atop Mrs. Harada's casket. Clusters of springtime daffodils, carnations, and perhaps even a few paper flowers handmade by some of the women at Topaz were arranged with flowing ribbons and dark greenery woven into wreaths. The floral arrangements framed the foreground, creating momentarily a small desert garden, an uncommon sight inside the fences of the otherwise desolate concentration camp where few flowers grew. Standing squarely behind his mother's coffin and feeling great sadness and defeat at his family's loss, his expectant wife Martha at his side, just as he did in his first family portrait, taken with his mother and father in Japan forty years before, oldest son Dr. Masa Atsu Harada stared straight into the camera, his glasses glistening in the sun.

With Shig standing right behind her and remembering her mother's gentle hands and kind spirit, Sumi joined younger brother Yoshizo, their heads bowed

16.3. Funeral of Ken Harada, Topaz, Utah, March 19, 1943. (Courtesy of the Harada Family Archival Collection, Riverside Metropolitan Museum, Riverside, California)

slightly, looking down and away from the camera toward their mother's closed casket. Opposite Sumi and Yosh, near brother Clark, stood Mine and Saburo with their two oldest children. Rosalind, with her grandmother's "sharp bright eyes" and long dark hair tied back neatly at the sides, and brother Laurence, his new trousers rolled up at the cuffs, were the only children there, standing with worried expressions near an elderly white-haired minister in long vestments. One row back, just over Doc's right shoulder, Roy Hashimura stood alone, recalling his memories of "the most beautiful Japanese lady in Riverside" and acknowledging his deep appreciation for Ken Harada's many years of dedication to her adopted son.

Within a few days, reading Ken's obituary printed in the Riverside newspaper, Harada house caretaker Jess Stebler and Ken Harada's other friends in town were saddened to learn of her passing. Explaining her nineteenth-century origins in Japan, her arrival in Riverside in 1905, and the many educational accomplishments of her children, the paper added a brief conclusion: "Mrs. Harada, the last few months of whose life were spent amidst the barren surroundings of the Topaz Relocation center, remembered with pleasure the beauty of Riverside and longed to return to the place she had called home for many years."

Just two weeks after her mother's funeral in the cold and isolated setting of the Utah camp, Sumi received an encouraging note from Jess Stebler writing from her family home in Riverside. Mr. Stebler told Sumi that her backyard peach tree at the house was starting to blossom. With the momentary happiness from a reunited family brought quickly to an end by their mother's passing and their ailing father still confined to the camp's hospital bed, the older Harada children began planning the next chapter of their lives in exile. To keep herself occupied and earn a little money at Topaz, in April, Sumi started a job as a mimeograph operator working inside the camp. At the end of May, Stebler wrote once again to his friend Sumi, saying he could see the family's roses in full bloom just outside their kitchen door. And, just two months later, on Independence Day 1943, Jess told Sumi of peaches on the tree back home.[9]

A few days after the formation of the army's all-Nisei volunteer combat team was announced in January, brother Yoshizo at Tule Lake completed his application for leave clearance, listing his only choice for employment as "active duty in grade." Yosh was volunteering for service as a lieutenant in the US Army. After attending his mother's funeral and meeting with military recruiters at Tule Lake when he returned from Topaz, Yosh wrote three times, asking to volunteer for active duty. Hearing nothing from the authorities, Yosh sought help from former Tule Lake director Elmer Shirrell, now relocation supervisor at the WRA regional office in Chicago. On April 10, thinking of his father's early guidance about patriotism, service, and doing what he thought was right, Yosh told Shirrell: "My heart is set on getting into the Army and I will do anything to get my orders for active duty for this nisei combat team at Camp Shelby. I believe I am one of the very few nisei dentists who hold a commission in the Dental Reserves. If I am ordered to Active Duty, both my father and myself would be one of the happiest people in the United States . . . Please help me, Mr. Shirrell."

Writing from Chicago, Shirrell contacted Elmer Rowalt at the WRA head office in Washington to see if he could help expedite Yosh's request, adding, "I knew him quite well at Tule Lake and have absolute confidence in him. He is not only a loyal citizen but a very good dentist as well. I can testify to this personally because he did some work for me. I would like, if at all possible, to see him achieve his desire and be allowed to serve his country."[10]

Rowalt forwarded his own request to Colonel William Scobey at the War Department. On May 3, Rowalt received word saying, as long as Dr. Harada passed his physical examination, he would be called to active duty within a few weeks. By the middle of June, Yoshizo's character references had been reviewed by the FBI. Friends and associates from Sacramento and San Francisco testified to Yosh's loyalty as an American citizen and supported his request for military service. Sacramento dentist and college classmate Dr. F. Vern Nelson told Dillon Myer at the WRA, "I have always regarded him as a loyal friend who could be trusted on all occasions." Writing from her apartment on Powell Street in San Francisco, Mary Kenetick explained she had known both Yoshizo and his wife, Sumiye, who had worked for Miss Kenetick before the war. "He was a successful Dentist," Kenetick said, "and his wife was devoted to me and very kind to me when I was ill and needed her. I have kept in touch with them since leaving for Camp . . . Yosh has told me all along that he tried to get in the American Army but was sent to Camp instead . . . I believe Dr. Harada will make an excellent soldier."

The couple's former landlady on S Street in Sacramento, Mrs. J. Fernandez, was much less sympathetic, offering her concerns about the sentiments of Yosh's wife. To landlady Fernandez, Sumiye, a Kibei, appeared too sympathetic toward Japan, and her feelings about the war seemed to worry Mrs. Fernandez:

> I don't know [Yoshizo] very long but as long as I've known him he seems o.k. But his wife I wouldn't trust her out of my sight. She is all for Japan. I heard her say so more than once. They were my tenants + I was in contact with her daily. She should be kept interned. Prior to the Pearl Harbor attack they were out every night till one + later attending meetings. They knew what was coming + said they hadn't expected it so soon. I rec'd a letter from Mr. Harada saying he is going to Camp Shelby Miss. + is taking his wife. I can not understand this as she was always outspoken as to the outcome of Japan in taking over this country. Hoping this is of some help to our beloved country.

Despite the concern from Mrs. Fernandez, Yosh's request to rejoin the army was approved. On July 12, 1943, just a week after Jess Stebler wrote to Sumi about the peaches in the backyard, Lieutenant Yoshizo Harada, still citizen 27378-A at the Tule Lake Relocation Center, received approval to leave the camp and report for duty with the US Army. Relieved to finally depart from Tule Lake, Yosh and Sumiye left California for Camp Shelby, Mississippi, where training of the army's 100th Infantry Battalion and the new 442nd Regimental Combat Team was already under way.[11]

As a native of Japan, Lieutenant Harada's older brother, Topaz chief surgeon Dr. Masa Atsu Harada, was still ineligible for American citizenship and military service. More committed than ever to make a change, Doc and Martha were determined that their next child would not begin life incarcerated behind barbed wire. At Ken Harada's funeral in March the couple was likely looking forward to the birth of their next child in the fall. By the beginning of summer, however, his immediate future was still unclear, and Doc was frustrated with conflicts among the staff and other difficulties at the primitive Topaz hospital. On June 8, Doc offered his impassioned resignation to Dr. J. A. Simpson, Topaz chief medical officer. Doc's resignation letter was published in the *Topaz Times* a few days later. He explained his concerns to Simpson and the entire Topaz community:

> The whole process of evacuation has been a terrible blow. The suffering of each and everyone of us cannot be measured purely in a sense of mental or physical anguish. The evacuation on the contrary has affected an indelible blot on our minds and has left us in a more or less bewildered condition.

. . . The requirements of the community can now be adequately cared for by the number of doctors now on this Project. Thus at the present time I do not feel that my leaving will jeopardize the health of the community.

During the past twelve months due to worries, the death of my mother, and to persistent misunderstandings my general health has become gradually undermined so much that now due to nervous disability I have been troubled with insomnia, anorexia, and a constant feeling of fatigue. The mental affliction has also progressed to the immediate members of my own family, and so it has become extremely necessary that I move them at once to more suitable surroundings. Therefore it is with deep regret that I deem it necessary to resign at once from the staff of the hospital and take steps for my departure from this Project.

Just below Doc's letter in the *Topaz Times*, Project Director Charles Ernst offered a public response to Dr. Harada's departure: "I must say that I have mixed feelings—I am sorry to see you go and, yet, at the same time, I want to congratulate you for having the opportunity to reinstate yourself and your family in circumstances to which you are all entitled. As I look back on the contribution which you have made to the welfare of the residents of Topaz, I feel a great sense of gratitude to you."[12]

With no certain prospects for landing a job outside camp, Doc sought employment on the East Coast and, not waiting for an answer, accepted an offer from Chicago, where he soon began work assisting in surgery at Martha Washington Hospital. Connecting with former Tule Lake project director and brother Yoshizo's onetime dental patient, Elmer Shirrell in Chicago, Doc hastily arranged to leave Topaz at the end of June. With no personal cash resources listed in his formal request asking the War Relocation Authority for assistance, Doc was provided a grant of $186.44 to cover his family's resettlement expenses. Traveling with Martha and Kimi from Utah to Martha's relatives living outside the western military zone in Colorado, Doc left his wife and daughter with Martha's brother, Frank Nakagawa, in the small farming community of Brighton, twenty miles northeast of Denver. There Martha joined her ailing mother, Tome Nakagawa, and her sister, Rose Suyeyasu, both also recently released from Topaz. Like Martha, sister Rose was expecting a baby in the fall, and the two young women helped one another in the coming months as they each awaited the birth of a child. Rose's son, Dennis, was born on September 6. Just a week later, true to Doc and Martha's wish to have their new baby born in freedom outside camp, their last child, son Warren Haygen Harada, like his half-brother, Calvin, named for a former US president, was born safely in a Denver hospital on September 13. His unusual Japanese name had been chosen at Topaz by widowed grandfather Jukichi to signify peace.[13]

Remaining in the hospital ward at Topaz for the rest of the year, his heart weakening slowly each day, Jukichi Harada spent most of his time in bed, his

16.4. Charles Ernst, Topaz project director, Topaz, Utah, October 19, 1942. (Tom Parker photograph, War Relocation Authority Photographs of Japanese-American Evacuation and Resettlement, Series 4, Volume 10, Section A, WRA no. E-6; courtesy of the Bancroft Library, University of California, Berkeley)

labored breathing sometimes assisted with an oxygen tent. Jukichi's two daughters and youngest son all recalled their father's last days. "They said my father's heart was in bad condition," Sumi explained. "And all the months that he was there, . . . when . . . his breathing became . . . bad, . . . we had to have oxygen for him . . . He kept saying he wanted to walk. See, he was bedfast. And he kept saying get him slippers so he could walk, and . . . he could become a human being again." Because Sumi and Harold lived close to the camp hospital in Block 13 and Harold was working there as a laboratory technician, they saw their father often. "We'd visit him every day," Harold said. "He loved coffee . . . I don't think the doctors recommended too much a' that. But, we used to give him a cup of coffee, . . . perhaps every time we visited him. And I don't think that was bad . . . In fact, I think he's probably smilin' now, . . . sayin', 'Thanks for the coffee,'" Harold remembered.[14]

Living in Salt Lake City with her family a few hours away, oldest daughter Mine traveled south to visit her father at Topaz as often as she could, sometimes accompanied by her daughter, Rosalind. Visiting her father as he rested uncomfortably in his narrow camp hospital bed while still detained behind the high fences at Topaz, Mine had trouble reconciling Jukichi's current situation with his continued strident support for the United States of America. On Mine's last visit with her father at Topaz, she complained to him about the incarceration and life in camp. "I was knocking it, you know, for all we were going through," Mine said. She understood, however, that her ailing father, perhaps at times as strong-willed, outspoken, and independent as his oldest daughter, still had no intention of giving up on his adopted country. "Oh, he was a patriot," Mine recalled, "he was all for America all the time. I remember the last time I talked to him, too. He said, 'In spite of what we're going through, . . . don't ever forget, . . . this is a great country.'"[15]

Still believing in his United States of America, patriot Jukichi Harada died at the Topaz camp hospital on Sunday, January 30, 1944. His youngest son, Shig, then just twenty, was with him at his bedside:

> It was less than a year after my mother passed away that Dad passed away . . .
> He was crushed. He was broken. He had encouraged . . . all of us to serve the United States of America and . . . he also . . . told us to . . . be brave and courageous, . . . and do what . . . we thought would be right.
> . . . He had nothing but faith in this country. And he was . . . really, a broken man . . . I really can't say what his absolute feelings were about . . . being put into this kind of situation, but I don't . . . think he had any misgivings or hard feelings about it.
> And I think that he understood well what the situation was and how necessary it was for us to . . . cooperate with the . . . United States government, by all means, . . . right or wrong.
> And . . . I'm sure that . . . he must have felt that we would return and justice would be done.[16]

With the cause of death of incarceree 6507-D listed in hospital files as total heart failure and his age recorded at sixty-eight years, five months, and eight days, a brief article in Thursday's *Topaz Times* reported Jukichi Harada's passing and announced his funeral for the following Sunday at 2:30 p.m. at the Protestant church in Topaz Recreation Hall 22. Mine arranged for flowers to be delivered to Topaz from Salt Lake City. By the time his father died, Lieutenant Yoshizo Harada was back in the army at Camp Shelby, Mississippi. The day after Jukichi's passing, Yosh wrote to Sumi and Shig, explaining he would not be able to make it to their father's funeral because of his military responsibilities. "I grieve with you in the loss of our father and pray that he and mother are together somewhere in the hereafter," Yosh wrote. He remembered his last visit with his ailing father at Topaz City Hospital. Knowing he might not ever see his son again, old father Jukichi expressed reassurance to Lieutenant Harada. Yosh explained to his brother and sister, "On my last emergency leave I told father the [unlikely] probability of my attending his funeral or being at his side at the last and he laughed and said that he would see me in Heaven."

On the day of the funeral, Topaz counselor Claud Pratt offered sympathy to the Haradas on behalf of the camp's community welfare department: "We . . . find it difficult to find proper words that would be consoling to you for losing your father at this time. We recall that it was only a short time ago you lost your beloved mother. With deepest feelings of sorrow, may our expressions of sympathy be added to those of your many friends."

For the afternoon memorial service on Sunday, February 6, a second funeral photograph taken in the cold February air outside the camp recreation hall mirrored the sadness of Ken Harada's memorial less than a year before. Among the six pallbearers, their black armbands worn in mourning, stood three of Jukichi's sons, Clark, Harold, and Roy Hashimura, orphaned again as a young man of twenty-four, and son-in-law, JACL president Saburo Kido. The family's list of honorary pallbearers included familiar names from Riverside like George S. Kaneko and Issei patriarchs Risaburo Inaba and Yasuichi Teshima. A pal of Harold's back home in Riverside, Mr. Teshima's youngest son, Michio, was now a star basketball player at the Poston Relocation Center.

Jukichi Harada's memorial service was officiated by the Reverend Jiryu Fujii, a former leader of Oakland's Japanese Methodist Church. The memorial included a Bible reading, printed in Japanese, emphasizing forgiveness, Psalm 32:5, which, according to the service program, was Jukichi Harada's favorite: "I acknowledge my sin unto thee, and mine iniquity I have not hid. I said, I will confess my transgressions unto the LORD; and thou forgavest the iniquity of my sin."

Perhaps at the end of his life, like many, Jukichi believed he should seek forgiveness for some regretful aspects of his past. Some of those sitting respectfully at his afternoon funeral might have also thought Harada's fondness for forgiveness might now help them through their own solitude and reflection of the transgressions, injustices, and sin of Relocation.

An uplifting song from Yukiko Oishi followed other Bible readings and Christian prayers. After the service, two cars were provided for the family by the War Relocation Authority and Nickle's funeral parlor in nearby Delta. Jukichi Harada's remains were transported for cremation to Salt Lake City and his ashes were returned to Shig in a week by the Topaz Community Welfare Department. The WRA required that Shig sign a Receipt for Urn, authorizing the transfer of his father's remains from the government back to the Harada family. Shig gave his father's urn to his sister, Sumi, who was already caring for her mother's ashes. Back in Topaz's chilly Barracks 13-1-D, Sumi dutifully kept her parents' remains safely in her custody until she could carry them back home to Riverside.

Western Union telegrams of sympathy and *okoden* condolences with modest monetary contributions arrived at Topaz from friends still detained in other camps. Back at the Poston Relocation Center in Arizona, the Reverend Masayoshi Ohmura and other friends from Riverside's Japanese Union Church held a memorial service on February 9 in remembrance of Mr. and Mrs. Harada. The following day Reverend Ohmura wrote to Sumi, telling her a small shipment of artificial flowers made by the "ladies of Riverside" still incarcerated at Poston had been sent to the Haradas. A few days later, symbolically closing the story of a generation for the one family closest to him, son-in-law Saburo Kido, writing for the *Pacific Citizen*, offered a brief memorial to Jukichi Harada. Kido mentioned Harada's early involvement with the test of California's Alien Land Law, adding that in his view his father-in-law was a "typical pioneer Issei." With both Ken and Jukichi now gone, the remaining members of the Harada family still in camp now turned away from their recent losses, setting their sights on new beginnings.[17]

SEVENTEEN

QUESTIONS OF LOYALTY

Ever since her brothers had entrusted her parents' urns to her at Topaz, Sumi had made certain they were always close by. In lonesome moments in her cold and dimly lit barracks apartment in what some might have regarded as unlucky Block 13, having them near had provided Sumi with a strange sense of comfort. Now, in the middle of May 1944, she was finally carrying them away from Topaz, traveling by train from Delta to Chicago. Sumi still worried about what lay ahead but she was also curiously optimistic about leaving the desolation and sadness of her family's recent past far behind. Unexpected feelings of freedom began to surface as the train rattled along the railroad tracks snaking out of Utah east toward Chicago.

Thinking of more practical matters for the moment, Sumi wondered how she would establish herself in Chicago with what remained of the $65.82 in resettlement expenses provided by the War Relocation Authority. She had just spent more than half that amount on train fare. Starting over would not be easy. In her application for assistance, filed with the WRA at Topaz on May 6, Sumi reported that she had had no earnings during the previous six months. She said she was starting this next episode of her life with a grand total of $5 of her own money, the only savings she had after twenty-four months in camp.[1]

The last year had gone by quickly. In the nine months between the passings of her parents at the Topaz Relocation Center, Sumi and her brothers had joined thousands of others facing the consequences of the shift in policy now urging incarcerees to resettle in non-restricted areas outside camp and allowing Japanese Americans to join the military. With mixed feelings about the meaning of loyalty, patriotism, personal responsibility, and family honor, ideals Issei parents had worked hard to instill in their children in the United States, each had responded to the situation differently. Shortly before their mother's death at Topaz, with brother-in-law Saburo Kido still in the hospital at Poston recovering from the attack spurred by his support for Nisei military service, the War Relocation Authority had required the Haradas and all others in camp over the age of seventeen to complete a questionnaire seeking new information about their personal backgrounds and beliefs. In contrast to the earlier individual surveys conducted upon admission to the incarceration camps—rather ordinary registration forms used to record things like date and place of birth, previous places of residence, education, physical condition, religion, employment skills, and hobbies—the latest survey included questions designed to assess the loyalty of each incarceree.

The new questionnaires were initially intended to evaluate the status of male citizens who might become eligible for future military service. However, expanding its scope, the survey was soon distributed in every camp to all those eighteen or older, citizen Nisei and non-citizen Issei alike. Males and females received slightly different versions to complete. Respondents were asked to report their political party affiliation, the year they first registered to vote, and whether they had any immediate relatives living in Japan. Other questions sought information about community financial contributions, language skills, and membership in civic organizations. One question asked respondents to "[l]ist magazines and newspapers to which you have subscribed or have customarily read." In her response, handwritten at Poston just a few days before she left for her mother's bedside at Topaz, Sumi Harada had listed herself as a Republican and a member of the Methodist Church. She replied that she had no immediate relatives living in Japan, adding she had recently donated $2 to Riverside's Community Chest. Sumi also reported that she subscribed to or read the *Atlantic Monthly*, *Riverside Enterprise*, and the Japanese American Citizens League's *Pacific Citizen*. Responding to another question asking for a list of five personal references, Sumi provided names and addresses of three unmarried women friends from Riverside, teacher Margaretta Finley and retirees Sue Caldwell and Zella Jones. Sumi also added Jess Stebler's name to her list of references. Mr. Stebler's current address was listed as her own house at 3356 Lemon Street. She included a note saying she had known Stebler for thirty years. Sumi added that her knowledge of spoken Japanese was "good," but her reading and writing skills in the language of her ancestors were "poor." Listing no interests in sports or hobbies, Sumi responded to other questions asking for details of foreign investments and whether respondent had been "subjected to any disciplinary action since your evacuation." Sumi answered negatively to both.

If inquiries about political party affiliation and personal reading habits seemed like an invasion of privacy for American citizens, especially for those in camp now predisposed to mistrust the promises of the government, two controversial questions at the end of the survey pushed many incarcerees over the edge. For Sumi and other females, Question 27 asked, "If the opportunity presents itself and you are found qualified, would you be willing to volunteer for the Army Nurse Corps or the WAAC [the Women's Army Auxiliary Corps]?" Question 28 addressed a deeper matter: "Will you swear unqualified allegiance to the United States of America and forswear any form of allegiance or obedience to the Japanese emperor, or any other foreign government, power, or organization?" Sumi answered "no" to Question 27, adding "illness of parents" as a brief explanation for her negative response about her willingness to volunteer for army service. She responded "yes" to Question 28.[2]

For Sumi's brothers and the other young men in camp having trouble adjusting to life in confinement and now confronted with the possibility of leaving camp for military service, the loyalty questionnaire posed new problems. On the form to be completed by draft-age males, Question 27 read, "Are you willing to serve in the armed forces of the United States on combat duty, wherever ordered?" Question 28, as for the women, asked the men about their allegiance to the United States. With its inquiry about forswearing allegiance to the Japanese emperor, Question 28 inferred that by answering affirmatively, respondents might be acknowledging they were giving up a previous allegiance to Japan even if none had ever existed. Some believed if they answered "yes," it would mean they were admitting that at some time in the past they had sworn allegiance to the emperor and the nation now at war with the United States. Because of the confusion and anger caused by this poorly phrased inquiry, some felt Questions 27 and 28 were tricks designed to evoke hasty responses that might put those who answered positively into further jeopardy.

In some sectors there was even talk of camp incarcerees being forced to serve in segregated military combat suicide units. At the time the questionnaire was issued, it was becoming widely known that long-established racists and others hell-bent on taking over the real estate still owned by the Japanese on the West Coast were clamoring to have the camp incarcerees prohibited from ever returning home. Thus, looking out the small windows of drab residential barracks across cold desert landscapes enclosed by wire fences and monitored closely by watchful guards, some began thinking that any expression of disagreement might lead to mass deportations from camp to other more distant or foreign lands. Reinforcing these new fears, before long, many who had not expressed unequivocal support for the United States in their answers to the loyalty questions were sent to the Tule Lake camp in California, now being reorganized as a well-fortified and heavily guarded detention center, much more like a prison than the other camps, for incarcerees labeled by some as the "disloyal Japanese Americans."[3]

Oldest brother Dr. Masa Atsu Harada, considered an alien because of his birth in Japan, was still ineligible for citizenship and military service. Working at Topaz City Hospital, Doc was incorrectly given the survey for female aliens to complete, perhaps by someone who did not realize that his first name was masculine. Doc judiciously declined to answer if he would volunteer for the Army Nurse Corps or Women's Auxiliary, but he did respond positively to his form's version of Question 28. On Doc's form for aliens, the question read, "Will you swear to abide by the laws of the United States and take no action which would in any way interfere with the war effort of the United States?" "Yes," Doc replied. Along with his response saying he would abide by the law and not interfere with the American war effort, Dr. Harada mentioned his memberships in the American Medical Association, California Medical Association, and Sacramento Medical Society, adding that he had donated $5 each to the American Red Cross and Sacramento Community Chest in 1942. More than twice as old as his youngest brother, Doc, now forty-five, had tried to join the armed services several times since the war broke out and would try again the following year, but because of his legal status as a Japanese alien, his repeated requests for a commission in the US Army were apparently never acted upon.[4]

Given his pre-war status as a reserve lieutenant in the Army Dental Corps and his strong personal desire to rejoin the army as soon as possible, Dr. Yoshizo Harada was required only to complete a shortened questionnaire at Tule Lake. Yosh returned his completed survey, along with his Selective Service Form 304A, soon to be used to process his request for active duty with the new 442nd Regimental Combat Team at Camp Shelby, Mississippi. Like sister Sumi, the family's youngest son, Harold Shigetaka Harada, the boy born at the Lemon Street house in 1923, also completed his survey at Poston less than a month before his mother's death. Of draft age at nineteen but not yet old enough to list himself as a registered voter, Shig answered his questions on a form adorned with the seal of the Selective Service System. He listed his former involvement in ROTC at Riverside's Polytechnic High School, membership in the local junior college's Kappa Upsilon fraternity, interest in basketball, and job as a gardener during summer 1940. Shig also noted that his knowledge of the Japanese language was "fair" and his reading ability in Latin was "good." As has Sumi, Shig included lifelong Riverside friend and Harada house caretaker Jess Stebler on his list of references, along with Mulberry Street neighbor, truck driver Morrison Lore, another hometown friend whom young Shig would one day honor when naming his first son.[5]

For Shig, his responses to Questions 27 and 28 were unequivocal. He replied, "Yes; Yes." For others in camp, however, like Shig's own older brother Clark, these questions did not have easy answers. Shig explained what some were thinking about as they pondered how to respond:

Well, I've never sworn allegiance to the emperor of Japan, and certainly I'll swear allegiance to the United States of America. But how am I going to answer that? If I answer that "Yes," . . . you know, that means that I will have sworn allegiance to the emperor sometime in the past, which is not true . . . Well that was the question, and a lot of people were confused by that. I wasn't. I just said "Yes, Yes," . . . that I would forswear allegiance whether I needed to or not. So what if I forswear allegiance to the emperor?

. . . Those were very meaningful questions and there [was] a lot of confusion and a lot of anger and anguish . . . But it was no problem for me. It was "Yes, Yes," all the way, right or wrong.

. . . So there were many of us that answered "Yes, Yes," and we went forth . . . Since I did answer "Yes, Yes," I was subsequently drafted.[6]

In marked contrast to Shig's immediate reply of "Yes, Yes," for brother Clark the loyalty questionnaire prompted a conflicted and angry response. Elected by popular vote in October 1942 as one of the first twenty-five council members on the new Topaz Community Council, the representative body of the camp's limited self-government system authorized by the War Relocation Authority, Clark had been reelected in December as one of four councilmen representing District 5. Just a month after taking his seat on the new council, on February 10, 1943, in a small marriage ceremony performed by the Reverend Joseph Tsukamoto at the camp's Protestant church, Clark Harada, twenty-six years old, married camp sweetheart Sonoko Adachi, twenty-seven. Sonoko was a Bay Area woman from El Cerrito who had been sent to Tanforan and Topaz with her parents, brother, and sister. Even though he was still in camp, Clark was finally feeling some sense of purpose and personal stability.

However, just ten days after his wedding, with a deep commitment to his personal beliefs at the time, growing resentment over his situation at Topaz, and perhaps just a measure of characteristic Harada independence, Clark responded to Questions 27 and 28 with a "No" and a "Yes." Swearing allegiance to the United States, Clark's positive answer to Question 28 was matched with a resounding "No" regarding his willingness to serve in combat with the armed forces. Like the others angered over the forced removal from their homes and those considering resistance to the draft until the government changed their status as camp incarcerees, former high school ROTC officer and current Topaz community councilman Clark Harada registered his strong feelings, objecting to being drafted for military service. How could his country ask for unbridled loyalty from incarcerated citizens to whom it had shown no loyalty whatsoever?[7]

In other camps, like Manzanar in California and Heart Mountain in Wyoming, organized resistance to the draft and violent protests soon followed. Young men who answered Questions 27 and 28 with an unequivocal "No, No" response were soon labeled as "No-No Boys," and some would eventually be sent to prison.

At Topaz, however, where Clark Harada had been confined for the last five months, the response was less strident. Nevertheless, shortly after the new questionnaires were distributed there, the Resident Council for Japanese American Civil Rights was soon established at the Utah camp. Councilman Clark Harada supported its call for the restoration of Nisei rights as a condition for draft registration. In mid-February, anxious Topaz block meetings were held to discuss the issues. A resolution was authorized by a group called the Committee of 33, composed from a larger group of 152 camp representatives, asking President Roosevelt to recognize "only one class of citizenship in this country."

The resolution acknowledged the Nikkei community's early and orderly cooperation with the army's expulsion orders, saying that "a loyal citizen of one race should not be treated any different from another." It also expressed a desire to "prevent in the future, the mass evacuation or confining of citizens without trial," claiming some of the issues included in the measure "constitute a violation of our civil rights." Calling on Roosevelt and Secretary of War Stimson to respond by protecting the rights of the non-citizen Issei and disbursing citizen "nisei soldiers into the Army at large rather than by forming a separate combat team," the resolution concluded with a request asking a spokesman of the government, "preferably the President of the United States," to respond with "satisfactory answers" so the citizens of Topaz could "go and fight for this country without fear or qualms concerning the security of our future rights." It took just two days for another camp faction, identified in the camp newspaper only as "Other Residents of Topaz," to take exception to the conditional resolution of the block committee.

The new group published its comments about loyalty in the *Topaz Times*. With no indication of how many "other residents" the new statement represented, on Wednesday, February 17, their comments, wired from Topaz project director Charles Ernst to War Relocation Authority director Dillon Myer in Washington, appeared in a *Times* article printed in the center of page one. "We feel that loyalty to our country is something to be expressed without reference to past grievances or wrongs," the new group said. They concluded their opposing views with a challenge to the earlier committee resolution, ending with their own pledge, "We shall register, we are loyal, we shall fight for the United States."[8]

The day before the new loyalty statement appeared in the camp newspaper, on Tuesday morning, February 16, WRA director Myer wired officials at Topaz, offering his reply to the Topaz block committee's loyalty resolution. Myer said the WRA was trying to offer an opportunity "by which the good faith of the Japanese Americans could be dramatized in such a manner that it might be brought quickly and clearly into the consciousness of the American public." Myer continued: "This is not the time to quibble or bargain. This is the crucial test. It is the time for thoughtful consideration and decision. Secretary Stimson cannot give the answers to the resolution. That answer will be provided in a large measure by the residents of Topaz and the other relocation centers. It is my hope and my belief that they will not fail this crucial test."[9]

At the end of the week the *Topaz Times* also printed Secretary of War Stimson's response:

> It is only by mutual confidence and cooperation that the loyal Japanese Americans can be restored their civil rights. The present program is not complete rehabilitation but is the first step in that direction. The United States government has evidenced its faith in the loyal Japanese American by giving them the opportunity to serve their country. This is their opportunity to demonstrate to the American people that they have faith in America.[10]

To the secretary of war, asking those confined behind barbed wire to willingly come forward to demonstrate their "faith in America" seemed appropriate at the time as government officials in Washington told the incarcerees they were each on their own in deciding how they should respond. It was now up to them.

Clark Kohei Harada's reaction was no real surprise to some within his family, who knew him as an independent and sometimes contrary thinker. In some ways Ko's support for the idea that the government should fully restore his freedom and his rights as an American citizen before he would serve willingly in the military reflected what he had learned in his high school ROTC and social studies classes. His independence even mirrored some aspects of his father's challenge to the Alien Land Law so many years before. And now, in marked contrast to the strident patriotic beliefs of his late father and three brothers, all of whom had already expressed strong support for military service with the United States in its war against Imperial Japan and Nazi Germany, Clark found himself increasingly isolated at Topaz. Moreover, he was also becoming estranged from some in his own close-knit family.

Clark's mounting concerns about registration for the draft and military service would overwhelm his outlook in the coming months. At the end of April he wrote another appeal from Topaz to his Berkeley draft board, clarifying his position about military service: "Kindly restore me to my former state as was prior to May 6, 1942, with all restitution. Protect my family and relatives. Give me my civil rights, equality, justice and freedom as any other citizen, and I shall only be too happy to serve."[11]

Clark's brother-in-law, JACL president Saburo Kido, representing the views of the Japanese American Citizens League, disagreed with the draft resisters' stance. Writing in his column in the *Pacific Citizen* in March 1944, Kido said:

> Any person who incites or encourages any citizen to evade the draft is assuming a grave responsibility. It is needless to say the offense constitutes sedition. One must remember that one of the most serious offenses a person can commit is to become a "draft dodger." A nation will not easily forgive or quickly forget any-

one who refuses to serve when his country calls in a national emergency. It will be a tragic mistake to have young men who are 18 or thereabouts to become stigmatized as "draft dodgers" for the rest of their lives.[12]

The reinstated draft had been in effect for citizens of Japanese American ancestry since the beginning of the year. Now, as the thin green shoots of wild desert grasses carpeted the ragged edges of the muddy camp at Topaz, just a few months after their father's passing, both Shig and Sumi left the Utah camp to join their oldest brother in Illinois. With his work experience in the hospitals at both Poston and Topaz, Shig left camp first. He departed at the end of April to take a job in Chicago, working as a lab technician for Dr. Israel Davidsohn at Mt. Sinai Hospital. Without lining up a job first, sister Sumi followed a few weeks later, first shipping a few possessions from Topaz back to Jess Stebler in Riverside. In Chicago for the next fifteen months, Sumi eventually found clerical work, earning a small salary at a Baptist publishing house. Brother Roy Hashimura also left Topaz in May, first living with the Kidos in Salt Lake City. Roy worked there briefly as a laborer at a meatpacking plant. Later, Roy moved to New York, where he would remain for a few months more until he was drafted, sharing an apartment with Saburo Kido's friend Peter Aoki, who had already left Poston and was working at the JACL office in New York City.[13]

In the summer of 1944, Clark Harada, his parents both gone, brother Yosh in the army, and his other siblings temporarily resettled in cities outside the restricted military zone, was the last member of his childhood family still remaining in camp. Soon after the loyalty controversy surfaced, he had explored resettlement in Detroit and a possible job offer for work in an optical shop, but those plans fell through. By October, as the Japanese American soldiers of the 100th/442nd were engaged in heavy battle in eastern France, Clark's anxieties about the future had grown to the point that camp officials were describing him as "embittered" and "neurotic." In his confidential report about Harada's situation, Topaz relocation advisor J. Hugh Turner said Clark was suspicious and belligerent, adding that he had likely been "sending characteristically poisonous letters to his brother who as a result imagines Clark to be an object of persecution."

Another camp officer had already prepared a similar review based on his interview with Clark. He offered a few more details about what some now viewed as Clark's deteriorating psychological state. "Mr. Harada says he quit his job at the Co-op last month because he was classified 1-A for the draft and expects to be inducted any day now. Man's father and mother have died since coming to Topaz," the report began. Complaining of ill health, having paid multiple visits to the camp hospital for a variety of minor injuries and ailments during the spring and summer, Clark met with the interviewer for more than an hour and was reportedly "allowed to talk and express his opinions freely." Although some of his comments were focused inward, revealing a nearly overwhelming personal anguish, the depressed but still outspoken twenty-seven-year-old rallied to express other strong thoughts and opinions well ahead of his time. Clark said he was "feeling very bitter about evacuation and feels that the United States should reimburse evacuees for financial losses sustained." When asked about his plans for life after the war, the interviewer reported, Clark told him that "he may not return from the war. He cannot tell if he will want to return."

The interviewer added that Clark, like other incarcerees worrying about their future if they returned to the West Coast, was concerned that upon his possible return at the war's end "he might not be acceptable to the community." Clark said he might not report for induction if called and he believed "the evacuation of a United States citizen was unconstitutional." Prepared a few days after the interview, Turner's confidential report claimed Clark was becoming more difficult with each passing day: "He regards everything with intense suspicion, constantly baits and insults others, and carries a very large and easily-knocked-off chip on his shoulder. He undoubtedly is intelligent and has ability. With a less suspicious and belligerent attitude, he would have a good personality. His appearance is excellent. He has a skilled trade at which he could earn a good living. In view of his early leave clearance, it is surprising he has not resettled."

In hindsight, Turner's analysis of Clark Harada also offered a rather understated conclusion that could have applied to nearly everyone else still in camp who was having trouble crafting a positive outlook on what life might be like in the future. "Definitely it can be said," Turner ended his report, "that other than the fact of evacuation, he has received entirely fair treatment."[14]

In a few days, Topaz project director Luther Hoffman wrote a confidential letter to Lieutenant Colonel Joseph R. Byerly at Camp Blanding, Florida, responding to Byerly's earlier inquiry sent to Hoffman on behalf of Clark's brother, rookie US Army private Harold S. Harada. By now in basic training at Camp Blanding and preparing to join the 442nd Regimental Combat Team in Europe, Shig met with the lieutenant colonel to ask for help in addressing his older brother's concerns back at Topaz. Luther Hoffman had taken over leadership at the Utah camp from its first director earlier in the year. The camp's second chief administrator, the new director was remembered by some as a former government bureaucrat from the Bureau of Indian Affairs "who saw Topaz as just another Indian reservation to be pacified." Hoffman offered Lieutenant Colonel Byerly his thoughts about Clark Harada:

> Clark has full civil rights, is eligible to leave the center at any time he wishes
> and reestablish himself any place in the United States outside of the West
> Coast and will be given certain financial assistance by WRA to enable him to
> relocate if and when he makes up his mind to do so.

. . . [L]ike some others he feels he has been mistreated by evacuation and is endeavoring to keep out of the Army, which naturally we do not support.

We are making every effort to help him work out or talk out his resentments over what is past and begin to do his part towards assuring that the future will be better than the immediate past. That, as his brothers so well know through doing their part[,] is mostly up to Clark himself.

. . . [T]ell Clark's brothers we will be glad to have their suggestions as to any way in which we can help Clark work out his own plans for the future.

Amid increasing concerns from Topaz officials and with new support from his brothers and sisters, who no doubt believed he too should escape the rising pressures of life in camp as soon as he could, Clark was finally able to arrange a quick departure from Topaz at the beginning of November. Like others in his family, Clark left the Utah camp for work in Chicago. He left his wife, Sonoko, with the rest of the Adachi family at Topaz until she joined him in Illinois nine months later. Clark's confrontation with patriotism was over for the moment as he left camp to begin a civilian job in Chicago. However, Clark's youngest brother, Shig, would soon be facing these challenges across the Atlantic in wartime Europe.[15]

EIGHTEEN

IT'S UP TO YOU, MEDIC

As Clark Harada wrestled with his worries and plans for the future, believing strongly in his fervent convictions of how loyalty and patriotism should be expressed, word had come to brother Shig that he had passed his military physical examination. Shig's brief civilian job at Dr. Israel Davidsohn's medical laboratory at Mt. Sinai Hospital in Chicago came to an abrupt and unceremonious end:

> The director of the hospital said that due to my unstable future since I passed the examination, he would have to relieve me of my duties, and he fired me on the spot . . . So I went to work in an assembly plant assembling . . . air coolers for the army hospitals . . . I'd never wielded any tools to speak of before, but I quickly learned how to assemble these sheet metal air coolers for the good of the cause. And from there . . . I was sent to Camp Blanding and took my basic training, in infantry, . . . and passed as a rifleman.[1]

After basic training in Florida in fall 1944, Shig was sent overseas in January with some 1,200 new Nisei soldiers. Many of the young recruits had been drafted from the incarceration camps and transported across the Atlantic to reinforce the seasoned Hawaiian veterans in the 100th Battalion. Just as the D-day invasion by the Allies in Normandy began turning the tide in the liberation of the European mainland in June 1944, the men of the 100th were added to the more recently

18.1. US Army medic Harold S. Harada, circa 1944. (Courtesy of the Harada Family Archival Collection, Riverside Metropolitan Museum, Riverside, California)

arrived volunteers of the larger 442nd Regimental Combat Team. For the first time at full force, the new regiment suffered high battle casualties, joining other Allied troops fighting against the Germans at Cassino south of Rome, liberating Bruyères in eastern France, and rescuing the 200 American soldiers of the "Lost Battalion," trapped by the Germans in the Vosges Mountains in October. By the end of 1944, the weary Japanese Americans had lost more than half their brothers through death or injury in combat. Troops of the 100th/442nd were now stationed in the south of France, awaiting stateside reinforcements to bring the regiment back to its full strength before its next major deployment back to Italy.

Californian Shig Harada was first assigned as a medic with the 100th Battalion's medical detachment. Even in the relatively mild Mediterranean climate of Provence and the French Riviera, winter temperatures were so low in early 1945 that, despite extra blankets and sleeping for warmth next to his army buddy Paul Hasegawa, Shig remembered, "It was so cold you could hardly sleep." In contrast to the heavy fighting they had experienced the previous year, the young soldiers of the 100th Infantry Battalion were now patrolling a comparatively quiet area along the southern French coast in what many informally dubbed the "Champagne Campaign." Relishing a break to recuperate from heavier combat, some of the boys even had time to steal a few moments watching the girls walking along the beachfront at places like the Promenade des Anglais in Nice. Just to the east, the 442nd Regimental Combat Team patrolled the Alpes Maritimes, the mountains along the French border with Italy.

Medic Harada was not really sure exactly where he was in France, but he soon saw combat for the first time in the mountains near the southern coastal town of

Menton, just five miles from Monaco and Monte Carlo, and a mile or two west of the Italian border:

> Near Menton, they loaded us into big cattle trucks, huge trucks, . . . and we had to go by night . . . They only had their night lights to use . . . I don't know how these drivers went around the curves, but they did, and they went at break-neck speed because . . . I guess, they felt that . . . the faster they drove, the less apt they were going to be hit . . . So . . . we took this ride and we finally . . . joined the 100th Battalion and [I] was assigned to the medical detachment of the 100th Battalion . . . And we got our . . . first taste of combat by going up from Menton, where we had our forward aid station, up to the line.
>
> . . . It was a good hike up the mountains . . . We were assigned . . . as medics and got our first taste of combat . . . There was hardly any fire—artillery fire would go over our heads. Occasionally one would land closely, but it was a good way to get broken in.
>
> When we would go from the line position down to take a shower, with the engineer battalion they'd set up a shower, a huge gang shower, where the men would come down and take a shower . . . and get back up to the line. And coming down from there, the Germans would have target practice with us as we'd come off the hill. And we'd run from . . . tree to tree, . . . trying to guess where the next round might land. And then we would . . . try to figure it out. But there was really no figuring. It was just your chance. But if you thought that you're running correctly, it gave you a little more impetus to go that way than any other. So that was our philosophy. And it would have been terrible if we were killed going to take a shower, but I think we'd still be heroes.[2]

After his first brief "taste of combat," Shig and the other recently drafted American soldiers were awaiting further orders in southern France by March 1945. They were all adjusting to life in the army with an odd mix of battle-hardened Hawaiians, the 442nd's early volunteers, and the green draftees from the mainland incarceration camps. With their different cultural backgrounds and wartime experiences, the disparate members of the combat team's three subgroups did not always see eye to eye, but the regiment's motto, "Go for Broke," united them through their willingness to risk everything to succeed. Reflecting on his time with the 442nd half a century later, Shig explained the motto's layered meanings:

> This "Go for Broke" spirit comes from many ways—from our Issei parents who inculcated Japanese culture into us as much as they could, as much as we would accept, maybe. And then on top of that, the American phrase for gambling "Go for Broke" would mean to shoot the works.
>
> . . . The fact that our parents and siblings . . . , our friends, were in these internment camps behind barbed wire and behind armed guards, . . . we knew that . . . I think that when we went into attack, that was probably uppermost in our minds. Not . . . so much about killing the German enemy, but more to

absolve us of any thought of disloyalty; to try to have our families released from these kinds of places, and to not ever have this kind of experience be undergone by any ethnic group because of their ethnicity.

. . . The Go for Broke spirit of my comrades—they were protecting me. I didn't carry any weapons, and they protected me and they watched me . . . like I have always been watched, the baby of the family.

They took care of medics . . . like you wouldn't believe. And they knew that we were out in the open trying to help them, . . . and that is the Go for Broke spirit too, that they would Go for Broke . . . for a medic. They would Go for Broke for their comrades. They'd Go for Broke for all of . . . their friends and relatives in relocation centers, and they'd Go for Broke for their buddy next to them fighting alongside. They would die.[3]

Between skirmishes in the Alpes Maritimes it was rumored the troops would soon be sent back to the States on a six-week extended pass and then, perhaps, to combat in the Pacific. When Shig and the others reached their port of departure, they were surprised to see a fleet of small landing craft awaiting their arrival. "When we got down to Marseilles . . . to embark, we saw that the ships that were waiting . . . for us were LSTs, or landing ship tanks, . . . so we knew that we weren't going to cross the Atlantic in these little things. So, then, the next guess was, 'Where were we going?' . . . With landing ship tanks, that meant an invasion . . . It was an ominous sign," Shig recalled.[4]

After a roundabout trip at sea, planned to avoid submarine attack in the Mediterranean, the troops arrived at the Tuscan port town of Livorno. Known to the English-speaking troops as Leghorn, Livorno was some 160 miles north of Rome at the edge of the Ligurian Sea on the northwestern Italian coast. The men soon transferred to a staging area not far from the ancient city of Pisa, where General Mark Clark joined them to explain their secret mission to break the German Gothic Line with a surprise attack in northern Italy. Harold remembered:

Mark Clark came out to greet us in his Cadillac limousine with . . . motorcycle escort, drove right up to our battalion formation . . . The entire battalion was there . . . and he drove right up to the middle of it, stepped out, . . . no public address system, nothing. His voice was tremendous . . . He said . . . he was inviting us back to spearhead his Fifth Army, and chase the Germans all the way back to Germany, and he brought us in for the kill. And I could hear murmurings of . . . the old timers, the old Hawaiian veterans murmuring, "You mean, we going to be killed."[5]

North of Pisa, about six miles southeast of the famous marble quarries of Carrara near the base of Mount Folgorito on the morning of April 5, 1945, Shig Harada and some of the other more recently arrived mainland "Katonks" were waiting anxiously just behind Company A. The somewhat more refined and largely untested troops from the states were labeled "Katonks" in jest by their "Buddha-

18.2. Private Sano and members of his company in training, 442nd Regimental Combat Team, Camp Shelby, Mississippi, 1943. (Charles E. Mace photograph, War Relocation Authority Photographs of Japanese-American Evacuation and Resettlement, Series 12, Volume 42, Section E, WRA no. H-59; courtesy of the Bancroft Library, University of California, Berkeley)

head" brothers from Hawaii in honor of the sound their mainlander heads made hitting the floor in fights with the tough Hawaiians. Whether Katonks or Buddhaheads, the young soldiers waiting near the mountainside village of Serraveza were wondering what lay ahead for them.

The medic from Southern California was watching the time closely. Shig checked his bandages and other medical supplies and began thinking about scrambling up the sides of the Italian mountains the US Army had code-named Georgia, Florida, and Ohio. Checking his wristwatch one more time and recalling the muffled and ominous remarks of the observant Buddhaheads in response to General Mark Clark's comment about bringing them in "for the kill," Shig briefly thought again about how just a few hours earlier he had run into old Riverside neighbor and high school buddy Mitch Teshima.

Wide awake before sunrise, Shig was still recalling last night's chance encounter with Mitch, happy at having spotted him unexpectedly in the evening chow line. The two twenty-one-year-old soldiers from California had not seen each other in months, not since they were both in training back in the States at Camp Blanding. Now here they were together again in northern Italy, catching up on news of family and friends from hometown Riverside and happily recalling their high school days together and Mitch's unrivaled basketball scoring record at the Poston Relocation Center. Like Shig, Mitch had been taken from Riverside to

Poston in 1942, and he had distinguished himself there as the ace forward on the camp's basketball team.

It was by sheer coincidence that we met each other, because he was in Company C and I was in the medics.

The kitchen crew of the 100th Battalion prepared a hot meal for us that evening . . . knowing that . . . we were going into attack the following morning. And . . . so they brought up a hot meal . . . on trailers drawn by jeeps . . . We had a hot meal of . . . rice . . . cooked Japanese style, . . . pork chops and canned sliced pineapples. Pork chops and pineapples were a favorite of the Hawaiians, and . . . a favorite of ours, too.

And we enjoyed a nice meal . . . together, . . . very pleased that we were able to meet . . . We sat on our steel helmets on this roadside, and had our mess kits filled with this meal. And we ate, and talked, probably for forty-five minutes. And we reminisced about, ah, old boyfriends, girlfriends, sports . . . Mitch, . . . in Poston, was . . . basketball's highest scorer. I think he scored forty-seven points in a game. And he was quite an athlete, although he wasn't . . . big of stature, but he was quick. And he was an excellent athlete, good basketball player. And we talked about those kinds a' things and, oh, we just had a great time.

And we bid each other farewell . . . and good luck, . . . "Gonna see ya again."[6]

With thoughts of home still at the top of his mind, Shig might have also remembered his late father's childhood guidance about loyalty and the duty of warriors as he looked down at his wristwatch one last time, just seconds before 5:00 a.m.

I was . . . in line just in back of A Company . . . with our litter bearer team . . . I watched . . . the time very closely and . . . precisely at 5 a.m. [came] a huge barrage from down in the valley up towards . . . the peaks just above us. And, these humungous shells were goin' over us. It sort of reminded me of Fourth of July, the rockets and all that, and . . . our . . . small machine gun fire throwing tracers up towards the peaks . . . There was . . . a cruiser, I believe, either a cruiser or a destroyer, in the Mediterranean, firing up into . . . the mountain peaks there, too. And it was just a tremendous barrage for fifteen minutes. And I looked down at my watch and . . . at exactly, . . . 5:16, the . . . call came down to us . . . , "Litter bearers up!"

. . . So we moved up at . . . 5:16, started moving up towards the front a' the line. And . . . we got up to the top and asked, . . . "Where were the injured?" And they said, . . . "There's one guy over here, with . . . part of his leg off. And there's another guy over there with part of his . . . arm gone." And . . . so, we had a choice to make of picking either one of the two up. We couldn't take the two. So . . . we picked the guy up . . . with the foot half off . . . and carted him off.

. . . We did that . . . from 5:15 until 10:30 at night, until it was so dark that we couldn't see the person ahead of us. And . . . we were able to haul four

wounded off that hill, . . . during that . . . sixteen-and-a-half hours . . . four men.
Took us a tremendous amount a' time because of terrain . . . Sliding down shale
. . . where we had to slide the litters down.

In near-total darkness, after what seemed like an endless day of trying to res-
cue the wounded from the battlefield, Shig Harada and the other exhausted young
medics with him returned to the forward aid station for the night. Settling in for
a well-earned rest in a hayloft above the commotion of those still treating the injured soldiers below, the men were joined by the battalion's chaplain, Israel Yost.

At the end . . . we . . . were told to . . . go back to the forward aid station and
. . . get rest there. So we went to the forward aid station, and it was in . . . a barn,
. . . Italian farmer's barn—pretty huge thing. Had a big loft—hay up there, and
that's where we were told to go to sleep. And, below, was the aid station—men
were being treated. And, so I climbed up there and started to go to sleep.

. . . As we were trying to sleep . . . Chaplain Israel Yost yelled up into the
loft and asked us if we wanted to hear the names of the casualties for the day.
And we all said, "Yes." And, amongst the names, was Michio Teshima. And
when I heard, "Michio Teshima," well I, I can't begin to tell ya what I felt like.

. . . To me, it was something that I'll never forget. And, ah, couldn't believe
that somebody with a belly full of pork chops, rice, and pineapples, . . . and his
brain swimming with . . . reminiscence of . . . Riverside and all of our friends
and all that, how could this guy be killed, you know?

But, he was—amongst five others. One . . . barrage. Six Japanese Americans killed in one shot. And there were many that were killed and many that
were wounded that morning.[7]

Nineteen Japanese American soldiers died during the first day of battle near
Serraveza. Nine, including Shig's hometown hero, Private Michio Teshima, were
from "Charlie" Company, Company C. Four were from Company A, the unit followed by Harada and the other litter bearers who transported only four wounded
men off the mountain in sixteen hours. Five of the nine killed in Charlie Company
were from California, including Mitch Teshima from Riverside. Three others were
from Hawaii, and one was from Fife, Washington, just east of Tacoma. Within
the first half hour of battle on April 5, one of the soldiers fighting in Company A,
Private First Class Sadao Munemori from Glendale, California, his mother and
other family members incarcerated at Manzanar, also lost his life when he threw
himself over an exploding grenade to save two soldiers nearby. For his heroism in
battle, PFC Munemori was posthumously awarded the only Congressional Medal
of Honor presented to a Japanese American soldier during the war in recognition
of combat actions. Later in the month, in the same campaign near San Terenzo
and just eighteen miles northwest of where Private Mitch Teshima of Company C
had been killed on April 5, Company E's second lieutenant and future United

States senator from Hawaii Daniel Inouye, a year younger than Shig Harada, was wounded by a sniper's bullet as he destroyed two enemy machine gun nests, his right arm shattered by an exploding German grenade.[8]

Joining thousands of other soldiers in heavy fighting during their successful campaign in the Po River Valley in April, as the warriors of the 442nd Regimental Combat Team "went for broke" one last time, driving the Germans "all the way back to Germany" in just a month. With each new day of battle, the Allies became ever more assured that the Axis powers were on the run and the end of the war in Europe was at hand, and medic Shig Harada and the other young soldiers around him continued to confront each new assignment as best they could. In each situation, Shig learned life lessons he would never forget. Like the other young men of World War II who would hold their combat experiences well below the surface for the rest of their lives, after many years of remaining silent about his encounters during the war and approaching the end of his life, Shig would finally decide his wartime lessons might be of some value to others. "It's tough to recall these things," Shig told us half a century later, breaking his silence about the battles in northern Italy. Shig was standing once again before his childhood message on the cracked plaster wall of his bedroom upstairs inside the house on Lemon Street. Holding his old medic's red-cross armband in his hands, Shig said: "I didn't like to talk about it too much before. But, now, I think that these things should be known to everybody."

He told about reencountering the men of Charlie Company, the former unit of his late friend, Mitch Teshima. To avoid being targeted by German snipers, who had previously fired on and killed unarmed medics, medic Shig Harada had hidden his red-cross armband in his jacket pocket:

> We were resting in sort of a draw and, on the mountainside to the left of us, we could see our guys dug in. And it was the men from C Company. And, as we were resting, and waiting to move forward, a call for medic came down from the hill . . . The section leader . . . was Sergeant Masao Suzuki . . . and this young punk medic comes up . . . and I go to him, and I say, . . . "Suzie, what do you want me to do? Do you want me to go after the guy or stay with you guys?"
>
> . . . You know what his answer was? Without blinkin' an eye, he said, "It's up to you, Medic." He wasn't going to send me up to my death and have it on his conscience, you know. It was up to me.
>
> So, what did I do? I picked up my medical bag and went toward the hill. First guy I go to is dug in. I said, "What hit him?" And he says, "Sniper, I think." And, boy, that frightened me. So I ran to the next guy and got down next to him, because I figured I better not expose myself too much, and I said, "What hit him?" And he said, "Sniper." And I got to thinkin', and I knew that . . . we decided and voted not to wear these [red-cross armbands] in combat, and not to paint our helmets with the red cross because, by then, snipers were hittin' . . . the red cross pretty well, so we decided not to wear 'em. But I kept

mine in my jacket pocket, and I had it folded. Had it in there. And, by the third hole, I said, "Well, you know, what have I got to lose? If this German sniper's got a conscience, he will obey the Geneva rules and not shoot on the medic."

So I got it out, and waved it towards where I thought the shots were coming ... from ... and then nothing happened, so I kept it in my hand and ran to the next hole—crept and crawled—ran, alternated so I'd throw 'em off target, hopefully. And ran from hole to hole, waving this thing 'til, after about seven or eight holes, I finally got to the victim.

Waving his armband in the air in the direction of the heavily armed Germans he knew were in hiding nearby, Shig ran breathlessly from foxhole to foxhole until he reached a rocky hillside and was staring into the boyish face of another young California soldier felled by a sniper's bullet. Although he looked more like a boy than a man to some, Charlie Company's Private First Class Michiru Sumida, wounded but conscious when Harada arrived, was five years older than Shig. Sumida hailed from Marina, a little seaside settlement just a few miles up the coast from the bustling fishing port of Monterey. He was one of eleven children in a hardworking farming family known and respected on the peninsula for growing the produce that did so well along the coast: strawberries, artichokes, broccoli, and cabbages. His parents, father Toraichi and mother Setsuyo, had both come to California from the prefecture of Hiroshima in southern Japan. In 1942, like those in the family of the twenty-one-year-old medic now catching his breath at his side, some in Michiru's family had also been sent to the Poston Relocation Center. PFC Sumida helped the medic assess his injuries as Harada worked as quickly as he could to administer first aid on the battlefield.

He was a nice lookin' young Japanese American kid, sort of baby-faced, and he was still alive and conscious when I got to him, and I said, "Where are you hit?" He pointed to his belly. I cut open his trousers, and looked and, about two inches below his navel ... was a little black hole ... And there was no bleeding. And I checked his backside and he appeared to be OK.

So I dressed that wound, and called for the litter bearers to come up. And loaded him on the litter, and wished him luck and sent him on his way. And, I thought, this guy's gonna make it. And never heard from him, or anything again, until I got back. Then I talked to some guys from Charlie Company, I said, "Hey, remember that guy that got hit on the hill there?" ... I said, "Whatever happened to him?" And they said, "Oh, he died." ... He was killed in action.

In the days after the sunrise artillery barrage and with machine gun tracers sailing over Shig Harada and his medic partners, who were waiting for orders to move their pairs of litter bearers up to the front line, the young American soldiers of the 442nd Regimental Combat Team took part in some of the deadliest fighting any had yet faced. Lutheran chaplain Israel Yost offered comfort and prayers for the dying to growing numbers of casualties. Yost had joined the battalion in

18.3. Medic Harold Harada's army boots. (Courtesy of the Harada Family Artifact Collection, Riverside Metropolitan Museum, Riverside, California)

its earlier sojourn in Italy and had been with the unit at the battle of Cassino in 1944. Medic Harada remembered Chaplain Yost's contribution to the regiment's exhausted medical teams:

> He used to come out and greet our litter teams. He'd run out—he didn't have to be at the forward aid station—he could have been at the rear aid station— but he wanted to be up at the forward aid station. And he wanted to come out and greet almost every litter bearer team.
>
> A hundred yards out . . . from the forward aid station, he'd get a hold a' the front end a' the . . . litter, and we with short legs behind this big 6-2 or 6-4-inch chaplain would have to run, almost, behind him, to bring them in, in their last hundred yards.
>
> But it was such a relief to see him because we would get relieved. Because we would sort a' change off, and he would pack the front end—Great man.[9]

After a couple of days of continuous battle with German gunners, endless rounds of ear-splitting artillery bursting across the hazy smoke-filled sky overhead, and machine gun fire and persistent bombardment rumbling the ground beneath and shaking him to the bone, Shig "drew the short straw" and was assigned as a medic with the heavy weapons machine gun section of D or "Dog" Company. Harada was replacing another medic who had just been wounded. Thirteen medics with the 100th/442nd had been killed in the fighting in the Vosges in 1944, and by spring it was common knowledge that unarmed medics were just as much a target for the desperate Germans as anyone else. Not far from an Italian farmhouse, taking a break from hiking all day in the April rain, Shig was finally at rest, putting on a fresh pair of socks and retying the thick laces of his heavy combat boots. His brief moment of reflection was shattered by "a loud pop and a scream for Medic."

> I . . . picked up my medical pouch, ran to where I thought the medic call was coming from; saw four men down. And I took a quick survey of the situation to see if I could tell which one was the most seriously wounded . . . and took a glance at the three men.
>
> . . . One had shrapnel in both legs and in the chest. The one had . . . shrapnel right between the eyes. The other . . . had just one shrapnel wound in his leg. But without any hesitation I knew that the worst was the fourth guy—a gaping hole in his lower right quadrant. I told him that I was the medic, that he was going to be okay. And I took out this huge compress that I carried with me. It was a 10 by 10 abdominal compress. It folded down into a very compact size and it was at the bottom of my pouch . . . I put the 10 by 10 compress on . . . His femur was fractured and was . . . sticking up out of his thigh, . . . and his femoral vessels, the abdominal vessels were all bleeding.
>
> And just by looking at him I knew that he wasn't going to make it. But I told him that he was going to be okay. I put those compresses on him. I pushed down as heavily as I could. And as I told him that he was going to be okay his eyes were open, but in a couple of minutes or less, his eyeballs sort of twirled around in his skull. His eyelids closed for eternity, and he shivered, and that was it.
>
> . . . The next morning, we got up and had breakfast, and went in front of . . . this farmhouse in which this accident had taken place, and . . . the Italian pisano farmer had a long extended pole, looked like there was a block of wood at the end of it, and he was scraping the front of his house—scraping the blood and guts of a hero off of that wall.
>
> It seems so funereal to me, . . . that this was the final benediction. So . . . I repeated to myself the 23rd Psalm and tried to send this brave hero to heaven.[10]

With the differences among the experienced Hawaiian veterans, mainland volunteers, and green draftees set aside for the moment, youthful Japanese American soldiers fought together bravely and died side by side in the Po Valley campaign to defeat the Germans and break the Gothic Line in record time. However, along with their proud efforts meeting immediate military objectives in the mountains of Italy, many of the Japanese American soldiers fighting there at the end of the war in April 1945 had another purpose in mind.

Casualties mounted each day from German gunfire flying at them from all directions from fortified gun emplacements hidden among the rocks in the rugged countryside. Their friends and combat buddies were falling all around them. Keeping their heads down and climbing as quickly as they could over the broken shale of the Apennine Mountains' steep slopes, some could not forget that their

18.4. Manzanar Relocation Center, July 3, 1943. (Dorothea Lange photograph, War Relocation Authority Photographs of Japanese-American Evacuation and Resettlement, Series 8, Volume 78, Section C, WRA no. [?]-838; courtesy of the Bancroft Library, University of California, Berkeley)

comrades had lost their lives or were severely wounded fighting for a nation still holding their families and friends under guard at places like Poston, Topaz, and Manzanar. With their red, white, and blue uniform arm patches depicting the lighted torch of Liberty, symbolic protection now drenched with sweat and stained with the blood of young Japanese Americans, the men fighting in the 100th/442nd in service to their country had answered their own questions of loyalty on a much deeper level than most would ever comfortably admit. Shig himself explained:

> Not for any particular person, or American, or any ethnic group, but, above all, we wanted to get . . . siblings and parents returned from internment camps, and back to normal. And . . . I think that was the reason why the 100th/442nd Regimental Combat Team was so great in its combat mission. Because, I think, topmost in their minds were their friends and families in internment camps. [We remembered what was] said by General DeWitt, that "A Jap is a Jap. Once a Jap, always a Jap." And I think that was what motivated some of us to do what we had to do.[11]

On April 12, as members of the 100th/442nd worked their way north along the western coast of Italy, advancing toward Carrara, and other Allied troops pursued the Germans inland, President Franklin Roosevelt died of a cerebral hemorrhage at Warm Springs, Georgia. Harry Truman assumed the presidency. On April 28, Italian Fascist leader Benito Mussolini was murdered and strung up by the heels on public view in northern Italy. Two days later, on April 30 in Berlin, Nazi Germany's Adolf Hitler committed suicide in a bunker with Eva Braun as Soviet troops overtook the German capital. Also on April 30, medic Shig Harada, now out of harm's way, took a few moments to write of simpler matters to sister Sumi back home in the States:

> I took my first shower in about 27 days yesterday so I feel pretty clean today. But it will take more than one shower to get me real clean. We also got a change of socks and since I had your wool socks on I was going to throw them away as they were dirty. I gave it a second thought and decided that if I threw them away I would have heck to pay so I got a helmet full of water and washed them. Good home training!
>
> The people in this part of Italy seem to be better off than those down there where we started from. We trade cigarettes and candy for rice, onions and eggs so we make "okazu" out of our canned C and K rations whenever we get a chance. The people line the streets of the towns that we have liberated and clap and throw flowers at us. They are really happy to see us. If we should stop they give us water or wine. The race baiters and all those that are anti-Japanese should see this and the sacrifices that our men have made to receive this joyous welcome. I have seen what the Partisans do to the Fascists and that is just what I would do to anyone that calls me a Jap.[12]

Just days after the Japanese Americans and the other Allied soldiers around them had defeated the Germans in the Po River campaign, the Germans surrendered and the war in Europe was over. One hundred one Japanese American soldiers had died in the campaign in northern Italy and another 874 lay wounded. Medic Shig Harada was soon transferred with other troops to the Ghedi airstrip in northern Italy, where, housed in a small city of pup tents, the Americans would now help to process hundreds of German prisoners of war. A few months later, on September 2, 1945, aboard the battleship USS *Missouri* in Tokyo Bay, with the small American flag flown by the flagship of Commodore Perry when his fleet entered the same bay in 1853 displayed above them nearby, and just days after the Americans dropped atomic bombs on Hiroshima and Nagasaki, somber representatives of the Empire of Japan signed the articles of unconditional surrender to the Allies, officially ending World War II. For those still lucky enough to be alive, it was finally time to think about going back home.

NINETEEN

HOME

Sumi Harada had been away from California for three chaotic and difficult years. In contrast to other incarcerees who had lost their family belongings, homes, and businesses because of the forced removal from the West Coast and were now thinking seriously about resettling permanently among friendly people in eastern cities and towns, Sumi hoped to return to Lemon Street as soon as she could. Jess Stebler's willingness to care for her house while she was away meant that, unlike many others, Sumi still had a place to call home.

Staying in a small apartment on South Blackstone Avenue in the Hyde Park neighborhood of Chicago's South Side, Sumi worked during the week at a religious publishing house. In early 1945 she was anticipating a return to California one day soon, but she knew she still needed to accumulate the funds required to make the move. Still, she had little trouble mustering the courage to decline an unexpected offer from a Japanese American friend who knew Sumi still had the house in Riverside, although it might have provided the money she needed to reestablish herself after the war:

> One of my friends . . . called me one day and said she wanted to ask me if I
> wanted to sell this house on Lemon Street . . . because one of her friends living
> in Riverside wanted to buy it. She named a ridiculously low price.

I told her, "I don't want to sell the house." She said, "Why? You can't ever go back to the West Coast." I said, "Well, that's the last tie I have with Riverside, . . . I'm not going to sell it." I said, "All of our possessions are in that house." They were valueless to anyone else I guess, but they meant something to me. I said, "No. By no means."[1]

Sumi worried about her friend's claim that she might not ever be allowed to return to California. She was extremely anxious and uncertain about her future but she refused to see the psychiatrist offered during her interview at the War Relocation Authority office in Chicago. At the end of May, just a month or so after hearing of Mitch Teshima's combat death in Italy and hoping her brother Shig was safe and coming home soon, Sumi was so distressed about her future she thought she might even be mentally disturbed.

Seeking assistance from the WRA, Sumi was also having trouble finding a better job that paid enough to help cover the cost of transportation home and starting life over again in California. She believed her health limited her potential for factory work; therefore, as long as she remained in Chicago, Sumi knew her earnings from menial clerical jobs would likely be limited. Of no relief to her immediate concerns about her financial situation and the effort it was going to take to reestablish herself with little money, one day in Chicago she was summoned to the offices of the Federal Bureau of Investigation. Responding to a notice requiring her to appear to retrieve contraband material confiscated by the FBI from the Harada home in 1942, Sumi was concerned about what costly arrangements she might now have to make to accept it. "They told me to come to the FBI office. I was given . . . a notice, and I was sort a' worried. I didn't know what sort of thing . . . they had taken from the house. I kept wondering, . . . it must be something large. And how will I get it home? Because, you know, in Chicago, I thought well, maybe I'll have to call a cab, and, and cart it back. And I was surprised when it was just . . . this little tiny box."

Sumi nervously took the box from the table before her. Opening it carefully, she was relieved and even somewhat amused to find an old familiar object from her childhood small enough to carry back to her Chicago apartment in her coat pocket—her father's Japanese Red Cross donation pin, awarded to Jukichi Harada for his gift to the victims of the Great Kanto Earthquake in 1923. With this small token of her late father's generosity safely back in her care and holding on to it so tightly it would never be lost again, Sumi went back to her flat on Blackstone Avenue. Along with the two boxes holding her parents' ashes, she added the little box to the growing collection she was gathering in anticipation of going back home.[2]

When paying another visit to the WRA office in July, Sumi explained she believed the $45 monthly income from her family's two rental properties in Riverside would provide enough support to allow her to resume her life on Lemon Street. Sumi told the WRA she now had $150 in cash set aside to help support her move. She also described her ten-room furnished house in California, explaining that the Reverend Masayoshi Ohmura, her Congregational minister at the Japanese Union Church in Riverside, had asked if her childhood home could be used as a temporary hostel for Japanese American families needing a place to stay. Without homes to return to, many of the incarcerees planning to come back to their former communities were seeking resettlement help from friends and religious organizations. In cities and towns throughout the West, reaction to the thousands of Japanese Americans planning to come home was mixed. Those Japanese Americans whose homes and businesses had been sold at a loss and erased from the map, their stored possessions vandalized or stolen, found it extremely difficult to start life over again, especially in places where angry neighbors did not welcome their return: "Threats, night riders, burnings, beatings, were the lot of the gutty little evacuees who returned to the acres they legally owned. With the great camps closing behind them, with expulsion in reverse, they had no other choice . . . To start again took a desperate sort of courage."[3]

Soon after the war, the War Relocation Authority reported, not surprisingly, that community receptivity was playing an important role in determining resettlement patterns for those former incarcerees returning from the camps. The WRA explained the "movement of evacuee population at the close of the centers was greatest to areas which offered least resistance." With encouragement and assistance from the WRA, like those in the extended Harada family, some 30,000 incarcerees had left the camps in 1943 and 1944, moving away from the West's restricted military zones to temporary homes in colder climates in midwestern and eastern communities. When the military ban against Japanese Americans living on the West Coast was finally lifted at the beginning of 1945, many believed they might now be able to return home.

Those still in the camps had few resources and little choice. Some incarcerees with the greatest worries about reestablishing themselves after the war were even hoping that the security of camp life would be extended for as long as possible. Whether they had resettled in the East or had remained in camp, many of the older Issei who were comfortable with hard work, familiar with farming on the coast, and lucky enough to retain their small tracts of agricultural land out west during the war believed a return to their own farmlands and the only way of life they had ever known seemed like a good idea. In some California agricultural areas in the Salinas, Santa Maria, and Imperial Valleys, however, it was said local hostility actually prevented the return of significant numbers of former Japanese American residents. In Lompoc, on the central coast of Santa Barbara County, the WRA reported one returning incarceree "found his small farm stripped of everything inside and out." At the Takedas' ranch in Santa Clara County near San Jose, phone lines were cut, their house set afire, and shots fired at the returning family as they fought to extinguish the blaze. Farther north, in Hood River, Oregon, some sixty miles up the Columbia River from Portland, local citizens angrily removed the names of sixteen Nisei soldiers from the American Legion war honor roll at city hall until a nationwide condemnation forced their restoration.

In the San Francisco Bay Area several communities were much more receptive. Hearing of the hostile situations in other places along the coast, some of the former incarcerees decided to make new homes there. Down south in Riverside County's Coachella Valley, the WRA said, "[C]ommunity sentiment was favorable, and in many ways the people helped the relocated farmers get started." In Coachella, the agency reported, "a greater number of the prewar number had returned, nearly 400 individuals as compared with a prewar 552." In the area around nearby Riverside, a few former residents had returned home early in the resettlement process. Their reports of a relatively favorable reception helped to encourage others to return. Despite some local problems with theft, June Nakamura remembered that Riverside provided a much warmer welcome than some of the other areas in the state. "Well, a lot of people had places to come to, homes and things like that . . . Some things were stolen, and in some places, like up north, places were burned down. But where we were it wasn't that bad," she recalled.

Some Riverside old-timers within the white community almost certainly remembered Frank Miller's support and enthusiasm for his Nikkei neighbors and no doubt recalled their own positive relationships with at least a few local Japanese American families before the war. Riverside's Edwin Hiroto had been sent with his family to Poston, and he spoke of the warm welcome his family received upon their return after the war. "People who had been residents of Riverside for a long time were very warm and cordial," Hiroto said. "The neighbors were very cordial. They thought it was great that we were home." No fewer than ten Japanese American families occupied the same addresses in Riverside both before and after the war. Others would soon find new housing within their former Riverside community.[4]

By the end of the summer in 1945, Reverend Ohmura had already established a temporary hostel at the Japanese Union Church parsonage but he still needed more room for others needing his help. As a small but steady stream of those now returning home began making their way back to Riverside, Reverend Ohmura, personally acquainted with most of the returnees, was busy doing his best to assist them in their search for shelter. Knowing about the Harada house on Lemon Street, Ohmura believed that if Sumi would be kind enough to make spare bedrooms in her home available, he would be able to help a few more former incarcerees find temporary housing until they could get their feet on the ground. With a now-empty house, even before she returned to California, Sumi decided to support Reverend Ohmura's request. She also began packing her things for the

19.1. Main Street, Riverside, California, circa 1946. (Courtesy of the Riverside Metropolitan Museum, Riverside, California)

trip back to Riverside, hoping life might soon return to normal. In Chicago on Thursday, August 23, Sumi received approval for her resettlement plan from WRA assistant relocation officer Elizabeth Beck. Just five days later, she completed a WRA Request for Transfer of Property, making arrangements for the WRA to ship one box and one trunk from Miss Sumi Harada in Chicago to Miss Sumi Harada at 3356 Lemon Street in Riverside. After three years in exile, her family never to be the same again, Sumi was finally on her way home.[5]

Back in California at the end of the month, Sumi offered thanks to wartime Harada house caretaker Jess Stebler as he made plans to move elsewhere, most likely to simple rented lodgings somewhere downtown. Alone but pleased to finally be home again, Sumi noticed a few things around her old house that needed attention. Loose windowpanes and weathered paint told Sumi years had passed since she had paid any attention to such details. Simple matters that had never seemed very important to her before now took on new meaning. With both her parents gone and their presence missed at the family home on Lemon Street, Sumi could not bring herself to sort through their personal effects, leaving many of their

19.2. The Reverend Masayoshi Ohmura, Japanese Union Church, Riverside, California, September 7, 1945. (Hikaru Iwasaki photograph, War Relocation Authority Photographs of Japanese-American Evacuation and Resettlement, Series 16, Volume AX1, Section K, WRA no. [?]-286; courtesy of the Bancroft Library, University of California, Berkeley)

things right where they had been before the war. Her mother's simple hats and dresses and her father's last suit, all left in the house at the time of the incarceration, were still hanging in the closets where they could remain for now. Sumi also knew she needed to contact the cemetery to make arrangements for the burial of their ashes, but for the time being, she kept them at home, waiting for other family members to return and help her with a memorial service.[6]

In the dining room near the sideboard, still catching the afternoon sunlight from the window along the driveway, Sumi was pleased to find the venerable potted houseplant Mr. Stebler had carefully watered and kept alive throughout the war. The plant had appeared in the background of family snapshots taken at the house in happier times in the 1930s. Its survival through so much loss and turmoil made Sumi feel a little better, reminding her some things had not changed inside her house on Lemon Street. Filling a cup from the spigot at the kitchen sink and taking a moment to pour fresh water around the roots beneath the old plant's broad green leaves, Sumi once again felt some small purpose in being back home. She would turn thirty-six on Christmas Day and was now thinking about how she might support herself living alone. Sumi started looking for work in those early weeks and was gradually joined by several former incarcerees needing a place to stay.[7]

> I was living here by myself. And . . . I thought about looking for work. I went around . . . and . . . they'd look at me and they'd say, "Well," you know, "you're too old." So . . . I tried to get a job at the library. You had to take tests, you know. And I took tests. And then they said they wanted to interview me,

and then, I—maybe I didn't have enough education . . . But I thought maybe that I could get a job in filing or something. But I didn't get it.

19.3. Sumi Harada, circa 1945. (Courtesy of the Harada Family Archival Collection, Riverside Metropolitan Museum, Riverside, California)

So . . . I was staying home, and . . . then a young boy came . . . and he stayed with me for a while . . . I knew him in camp. We lived in the same block. And he . . . was either passing through, or he asked me if he could stay a few days. And I said, "Yes. You can stay here." And he stayed about a month. He was looking for work, too . . . He was a nice, . . . well-behaved . . . boy.

Haruto "Pluto" Shimazu was the first to arrive for a temporary stay at the Harada home. From nearby Colton before the war and sent with his family to Poston from San Bernardino, Pluto Shimazu, nicknamed by friends for Walt Disney's popular cartoon character of the 1930s, turned nineteen on September 8. He stayed at the house on Lemon Street for about a month, looking for work and helping Sumi with a few long-overdue maintenance chores, such as puttying those loose windowpanes, in exchange for a place to live. Within the month Reverend Ohmura renewed his contact with Sumi and she began accepting additional boarders, most of whom she had become acquainted with at Poston. "They didn't have houses to go back to. That's why they came . . . They had no place to go. So they asked if they could stay 'til they found . . . a place that they . . . could . . . go to," Sumi said. For the next few months, no fewer than eleven people from four different families stayed at the Harada house with Sumi.[8]

With referrals from Reverend Ohmura, among those coming to the house on Lemon Street were three members of the Takanabe family. Removed to Poston from nearby Upland, the Takanabes had once worked in agriculture there before the war, managing a peach orchard. Father Isaku, born in Japan on the southern island of Kyushu in 1881, came to the United States in 1899. Like other Issei men his age, Mr. Takanabe had married late in life. His wife, Yasuno, also from Kyushu, arrived in the United States from Japan shortly before the Immigration Act of 1924 stopped Asians from coming to the United States. Mrs. Takanabe was nearly fifteen years younger than her husband. The couple's youngest daughter, Ruthie, was born in California in 1931, so she was just fourteen when they came to live with Sumi until the family could reestablish itself, finding local work doing housework or gardening.[9]

In addition to the three Takanabes were four members of the Kobayashi family. Issei widower Ishinosuke Kobayashi was sixty-nine years old and, like Sumi's late father, slowed by heart trouble. Mr. Kobayashi was joined at the Harada house by his eldest daughter, Katsuko or "Kay," twenty-nine; son Jinnosuke, age twenty-five, whom Sumi and his close friends called "Gene"; and the elder Kobayashi's married third daughter, Tomiko Mayeda. All three of the Kobayashi children were born in California. Tomi and her new husband, James, were expecting their first baby. In some ways, the bustling and vibrant Kobayashi family reminded Sumi of her own. Even with strangers living at the house on Lemon Street, it was good to have the old family home full of life once more.

Gene Kobayashi lined up work as a gardener for a few well-to-do Riverside families. James Mayeda was lucky to find a job at the Santa Fe railroad yards in San Bernardino. James spent his days doing train engine maintenance, driving back and forth to work from the Harada house in Riverside. His parents, Matsutaro and Miye Mayeda, forced from Kern County to Poston when the war began, joined their son and his expectant wife at the Lemon Street house for a month or two. The elder Mayedas lived there until they established a new strawberry farm across the river beyond Mount Rubidoux in West Riverside. One more single man from the Poston Relocation Center, Sam Ogawa, born in California in 1924 and also originally bussed to the Arizona camp from Riverside, came to stay briefly but unhappily at the Harada house. With her characteristic honesty, Sumi described Ogawa's short stay with a chuckle: "He was a sloppy person . . . He didn't like the set-up. So he . . . moved out."[10]

The busy returnees filled Sumi's old house with the lively sounds of family life, staying in different rooms upstairs and down. Every bed in the house was occupied at night. Still without a job, Sumi was concerned about her financial situation, but reluctant to charge her temporary boarders rent, she let them remain at no cost until they could establish themselves elsewhere. Sumi said all she needed was a little help buying groceries. "I know that you people don't have too much money, . . . If you could just help with the food," Sumi told them. With so much traffic inside her house and only one bathtub, Sumi tried to bring some order to the often-unavailable bathroom downstairs by asking the boarders to keep their towels separate from hers. She glued a small typewritten paper sign to the gray wainscot above the towel rack: "Please use these towels and leave towels on other racks alone."

Before long, brother Clark and his wife, Sonoko, also came back from Chicago to live temporarily at Clark's childhood home. Sonoko began helping Sumi look after things at the busy Harada house. With so many people more than filling the several bedrooms at her house and colder weather on the way, Sumi arranged to have the open sleeping porch upstairs enclosed with siding and six new windows so everyone might have a little more room in the crowded living quarters. Sumi said those in the disparate group demonstrated a willingness to adapt to difficult circumstances, sharing a sense of camaraderie. "It was like a boarding house . . . We all chipped in and did it . . . My sister-in-law . . . helped me, too, you know . . . I had asthma badly so I was sick so, a lot a' times, my sister-in-law took over, . . . getting the breakfast going . . . There weren't practically any complaints about the food," Sumi explained.[11]

Despite the general cooperation, not everyone got along all the time. Brother Clark, apparently just as opinionated and contrary as ever, soon found himself in a disagreement with fledgling landscape gardener Gene Kobayashi. The two young men tried to work together to find local gardening jobs, but Sumi remembered that Clark could not get along with Gene and the pair had a "falling out." In two or three months, the Takanabes, Kobayashis, Mayedas, and Clark and Sonoko were gone. Eventually, they all found their own places to live and moved away. Sumi was once again the sole occupant of the house on Lemon Street, still thinking about how she would support herself. As the weeks went by, the old two-story house in Riverside became the family's touchstone for a return to what they all hoped would be a normal life in California. Coming back to the West Coast from different wartime experiences, each member of the Harada family returned to Lemon Street at one time or another to visit sister Sumi and to gather their thoughts about what to do next.

Brother Roy Hashimura had remained in Germany for a year or two after the war ended before eventually returning to California for a brief stay at the house on Lemon Street. Drafted at about the same time as Shig, Roy took his infantry training in Georgia and was still enrolled in officer candidate school when the war ended. Asked by the military if he would be interested in further training in Japanese language school for an assignment in occupied Japan, Roy decided on service in post-war Europe instead. At the beginning of 1946, Roy was still in the army, serving as a provost marshal at a prison interrogation center in Germany. "There were six thousand German SS prisoners there," Roy recalled. "There was a Polish captain with a company of Polish guards that actually did the guarding of the prison, and the captain reported to me." The irony of serving as a provost marshal in charge of security at a German prisoner interrogation camp was not lost on Roy. "There I was in charge of security of a prison and just a short time before I was a prisoner myself in Poston and Topaz for a couple of years," Roy said.

Later transferred to 9th Infantry Division headquarters in southern Germany, Hashimura worked in Augsburg for a time, supervising the division's gas and coal supply. There he caught the attention of Annie Becker, a pretty twenty-year-old German woman from Kerzenheim, fifty miles southwest of Frankfurt. Annie was working in the kitchen at the officers' mess in Augsburg. "I saw her walking with a girlfriend who she roomed and worked with," Roy remembered. "Since I spoke German, I introduced myself, and that's how we met," he added. Although Roy Hashimura was prohibited from fraternizing with German civilians, the twenty-seven-year-old Japanese American soldier from California and Anna Elizabeth Becker were soon nearly inseparable. Annie began learning English from Roy, and they did their best to get around what they viewed as unreasonable military restrictions.

In a few weeks Roy was transferred from Augsburg thirty miles southeast to the former Nazi concentration camp at Dachau, heading a platoon guarding a new courtroom recently established there as a forum for war crimes trials. Japanese American soldiers of the 522nd Field Artillery Battalion, separated from the 442nd Regimental Combat Team earlier in the year and assigned to other Allied units fighting in Germany, had been among the liberators of Dachau subcamps in 1945. Roy was stationed at Dachau for a few months in early 1946. His platoon provided security during the trial of sixty-one men associated with the operation of the notorious Mauthausen concentration camp in Austria. Assigned to Dachau for several months, American soldier Hashimura, who had himself been living behind barbed-wire fences in his own country just a year and a half earlier, saw remnants of the German concentration camp crematorium. He also spoke with one of the first American soldiers who had taken part in the camp's liberation at the end of April 1945. Roy recalled: "It was unbelievable. These huge ovens—they must have had four or five of them. And all kinds of weapons that they beat the prisoners with. I talked to one First Lieutenant who was there when they first went in. He said that bodies were all over the place and the stench was unbelievable. Terrible place."

After the Mauthausen trial ended in May, Roy was discharged from the armed services. He lined up a new civilian job supervising concessions at an army post exchange back in Augsburg. Still with Annie, Roy provided her with fine new clothing from his German friend Rudolph, the dressmaking concessionaire at the post exchange. Former military officers were eligible to visit the local officers' club, so Roy and Annie would sometimes go dancing there together. Roy recalled one of their visits when an American army captain was so angry to see the two of them dancing in the officers' club that he had to be restrained by two other officers:

> Each had an arm around that captain. He was glaring at me. I guess he didn't like the fact that Annie and I were dancing in the officers club. I guess he was prejudiced . . . I wasn't in uniform; I was a civilian at the time. Maybe he didn't know that I was an ex-officer . . . I guess he was just prejudiced against Japanese. I don't know. Nothing happened. He was taken out of the club. That was the only instance of prejudice that I'd seen among officers.

Despite their treatment from those having trouble with the courtship and romance of the handsome Japanese American man from California and the attractive German woman from Kerzenheim, Roy and Annie were soon married. Before long, the young couple and their first daughter, Alitza, their new American family with both Japanese and German roots, were on their way from Annie's girlhood home in Germany to Roy's boyhood home in California. After waiting a week in New York for the ship that would deliver the American-made Studebaker Roy had purchased in Germany in a complicated deal involving the sale of an army jeep, the Hashimuras drove across the country to Riverside. Roy recalled his memorable reunion with sister Sumi: "I was short on funds and I didn't want to stay in a motel so we got to Riverside early in the morning. I knocked on Sumi's door. Well, that was a bad mistake. She was mad as hell. She told me and Annie, 'Go back to Germany!' But she let us stay there and with the funds I had left I went to the horse races at Del Mar. I would win some and lose some and finally lost all my money."

After a trying time for Annie and Roy at Sumi's house, the Hashimuras moved to nearby Los Angeles, where they lived for a time at a place on Vermont Avenue purchased by Saburo and Mine Kido when they moved their family back to California from Salt Lake City. As Saburo slowly built his new law practice in the Los Angeles Little Tokyo neighborhood downtown near city hall, the Kidos moved to a house on Dalton Avenue not far from the Los Angeles Coliseum. Mine helped brother Roy find a job at a local Japanese produce stand where he would work for the next year, sixty hours a week for a dollar an hour, until he could finally put something more promising together to support his family.

Brothers Masa Atsu and Yoshizo both returned home to Sacramento to reestablish their medical and dental practices. A few years later, in the early 1950s, just as soon as national legislation was passed allowing Japanese immigrants the right to be naturalized, Doc jumped at the chance to finally become an American citizen. Doc was the only sibling in the Harada family still considered an alien because of his birth in Japan in 1899. However, the long-awaited milestone in Masa Atsu's difficult life was bittersweet. As his family gathered to celebrate his new US citizenship, his wife Martha baking a cake and decorating their house with American flags and daughter Kimi describing the moment as the realization of her father's "biggest dream," Doc suffered a devastating heart attack and stroke, ending his medical career and leaving him an invalid for the rest of his life.[12]

Youngest brother Shig also came home to California to plan his next move, staying with his older sister at their family home in Riverside. Hauling his heavy olive-green army duffel bag up the narrow staircase at the house on Lemon Street, Shig moved back into his childhood bedroom on the second floor at the front of the house. Emptying his pockets and tossing a wallet stuffed with his draft registration card, worthless Italian lire, and a coupon for drinks from the "Go for Broke Club" in Leghorn into the top drawer of his old dresser, Shig also left a few snapshots, military patches, and his medic's red-cross armband in another dresser drawer. In the darkness of a nearby closet upstairs, assuming he would return for them in due time, Shig also stashed his army uniform and the worn-out pair of scuffed-up combat boots he had worn on the run up into the mountains with the 100th/442nd in the rain and foxholes of Italy.

Like most young American soldiers recently discharged from the service, who were thinking less of the past and more about the future each day, Shig kept most of his wartime combat memories to himself. Turning his thoughts to more pleasant dreams, Shig was happy to stay in touch with his attractive girlfriend from the nursing staff at Topaz City Hospital, Chiye Yoshimori. If things went well, he might ask Chiye for her hand in marriage, finish school, and become a dentist like his older brother Yosh.[13]

Not long after the war had ended, slowly putting the pieces of her life back together, Sumi was pleased to find old friend Henry Teshima standing at her front door. Thinking of his youngest brother, Mitch, Henry had dropped by the house on Lemon Street to say goodbye to Sumi. The third son of Issei parents Yasuichi and Kameno Teshima, Henry, along with his three brothers, had lived with his family less than a mile from the Haradas on the east side of town on Park Avenue near Reverend Ohmura's Japanese Union Church before the war. Recalling Yasuichi's friendship back home, the Harada children had included the elder Teshima's name on their list of honorary pallbearers for father Jukichi's funeral at Topaz. On one of his last visits in town, Hisao Teshima, "Henry" to his younger friends, spoke to Sumi of his youngest brother, Michio. Sumi and Henry recalled happier times and spoke of Mitch's death in service with the 100th/442nd just weeks before the end of the war. Henry told Sumi that his folks were fairly certain they would never return to California because Riverside simply held "too many memories" that they thought best to leave behind forever.

Henry's father had earned a modest income, working as a gardener at the community hospital before the war. He and Henry's mother were incarcerated at Poston with their three youngest sons: Harry, Henry, and Mitch. The elder Teshimas, still at Poston in 1944, decided to move east to Detroit. At the end of the year they would be joined in Michigan by their oldest son, John. After high school and two years of junior college in Riverside, John Yasuyoshi Teshima left his home in Southern California for college up north in the 1930s. John followed in the footsteps of Dr. Masa Atsu Harada and graduated from the University of California medical school in San Francisco just before the war began.

When the bombs fell at Pearl Harbor, young Dr. Teshima was working as an intern at City and County Hospital in San Francisco. In 1942 he was sent to Tanforan. After moving to Utah with the thousands of other former Tanforan incarcerees, Dr. Teshima joined former Riverside neighbor Doc Harada at the Topaz Relocation Center in the fall and spent the next two years working long hours as the youngest of the four camp physicians at Topaz City Hospital. Part of his routine duties at Topaz had included tending to his Riverside neighborhood friend Clark Harada during Clark's several visits to the infirmary in the spring and summer of 1944. "Tesh," as his friends at Topaz called him, eventually left Utah to join his parents in Detroit. Thus, it was now up to brother Henry to settle the family's affairs in Riverside.[14]

It was just a few days before Henry moved away from Riverside for good. Before he left, however, he wanted to leave something with Sumi. With both his hands outstretched before her, Henry presented Sumi with a small package wrapped in plain brown paper and securely tied with string. Not knowing what was inside, Sumi sensed it was best to simply accept it without asking any questions. With no indication from Henry that she should open the parcel and his somewhat strange parting words to her that she should "dispose of it any way she wished," Sumi got the impression it was time to move on. She added the unopened package to the several other things she was taking out to store in the garage, locking its doors securely with a padlock.

On a hot July afternoon in the summer of 1948, some fifty miles inland from Southern California's famous Pacific shoreline and the waters touching the coast of their ancestral homeland far across the sea, the time had finally come to say farewell to her parents. Joined by sister Mine's family from Los Angeles, a small gathering shared a meal at the house on Lemon Street and took the ashes of Jukichi and Ken for one last car ride to Olivewood Cemetery on Central Avenue. Brother Yoshizo had not been able to attend his father's memorial service at Topaz in 1944, but he made it back to Riverside four years later to join Sumi, Mine, and Shig at the simple graveside service.

Friends and family rested for a moment on a wooden bench as colorful sprays of gladiolas, chrysanthemums, and sword ferns were placed with care on the lawn nearby. Overhead, California sunshine filtered through the lush green foliage of a thick canopy of tree branches. Gathering quietly in the shade for their final goodbye, the remaining members of the Harada family commemorated the love and the struggles of Ken and Jukichi Harada. Just a few steps from the dark granite tombstone marking the resting place of their son Tadao, the two small boxes containing their ashes were carefully laid to rest side by side in a single grave, forever closing their half-century-long American journey. They were home at last.[15]

Just before dusk at Olivewood, a few hours after the long-postponed graveside service, the desert air began to cool. Shimmering fronds of Mexican fan palms and fragrant, dark green cypresses stood alone, towering over the freshly turned earth and bouquets of flowers resting on the new grave not far from the entrance to the cemetery. Back at the house on Lemon Street, a close-knit group of relatives and perhaps a friend or two offered tentative hugs, releasing awkward embraces to pile into their secondhand automobiles. Waving hands offered faint goodbyes out the windows as the stuffy cars drove off. Gray exhaust filled the stale air behind each car as it passed through the long, low shadows of the stucco-covered Mission Revival towers of the highway bridge beneath the great wooden cross still standing high atop the rocky slopes of Mount Rubidoux. Crossing the bridge above the dry riverbed of the Santa Ana and passing the healthy strawberry plants growing in neat, well-tended rows at new farms in West Riverside, the cars joined others in a small parade heading northwest toward Los Angeles, scooting like dark stink bugs across the sandy edges of the Mojave. By early evening the cars were gone and Sumi Harada was again alone at the house on Lemon Street.

SUMI'S HOUSE

3356 LEMON STREET, RIVERSIDE, CALIFORNIA
Early evening, sometime in August 1948

Standing on the front porch of her modest family home in Riverside, Sumi adjusted her glasses and squinted briefly into the setting sun, turning slowly to enter her empty house. As the screen door closed, Sumi shut and locked the front door behind her. Perhaps she was thinking about the last few turbulent years—of her invalid parents traveling uncomfortably from Riverside to Sacramento to Tule Lake and Topaz. She might have also contemplated her curious legacy contained in the two boxes holding their ashes, the boxes she carried from the desolate camp in Utah east to Chicago and then all the way home to California. Memories of young friend Mitch Teshima dying bravely for his country on a springtime morning in faraway Italy or of the small kindnesses expressed by old Jess Stebler might have occupied her mind in the stillness of this summer night. Sumi could also have been thinking of her sister, brothers, and their families and the new lives they were beginning in other California communities. Or perhaps, at age thirty-eight, alone and unemployed, she was simply wondering about her next step, one that might help to put recent sad days behind her.

Many young Americans who returned from wartime homes elsewhere were banking on a future of security, prosperity, and peace. However, Sumi's next steps took her closer to the past. For the next fifty years, Sumi Harada would live alone in the house on Lemon Street with the shades drawn, her refuge filled with family

20.1. Harada House front door, 3356 Lemon Street, Riverside, 1977. (Mark Rawitsch photograph, collection of the author)

belongings and memories to keep the now absent people of her childhood close at hand. Once crowded and noisy, filled with voices and the daily activities of a growing family and, later, the friends from camp who stayed there after the war, the old house now seemed quiet, huge, and vacant to its sole resident. Moving downstairs to be cooler in the summer and warmer in winter, Sumi slept on a narrow metal cot nudged up against the dining room wall, adjacent to the kitchen stove and the bathroom with the big claw-foot tub. She had left the rest of the house just as it was in the years before the war. Behind the garage, tendrils of morning glories clung tenaciously to the fence, their blue flowers turning bright round faces toward the sun.

Upstairs the clocks stopped and, in a way, time stood still. A 1942 calendar with the handwritten notation "Left May 23rd" still hung on the wall behind a door to the laundry room, a permanent reminder of that day in late spring when Sumi and Shig hastily departed their childhood home for an early morning bus ride to the Poston Relocation Center in the Arizona desert. Sumi's parents' clothing, reflecting the style of the early 1930s, hung neatly in bedroom closets among a few long-forgotten possessions of other local Japanese American families, stored in the house for safekeeping during the war. Inexpensive turn-of-the-century dressers with graceful mirrors and tarnished knobs, their thinly veneered wooden drawers lined with 1940s *Rafu Shimpo* newspapers, held secrets known only to Sumi.

Frugal by family tradition and her own limited economic circumstances, a young adult of the Great Depression with narrowing dreams and memories of doing without in camp, Sumi rarely, if ever, threw anything away. Graying to white as the years went by, her hair a little wild at unguarded moments, and somewhat frightening to the few neighborhood children living nearby, Sumi became known as a cranky Nisei packrat, as some unkindly said behind her back. Living alone, she had filled her old house with a vast accumulation of family letters, photographs, documents, yellowed newspaper clippings, magazines, paper bags, holiday greeting cards, school portraits of nieces and nephews, a few unopened Christmas presents, and a growing sense of personal responsibility for everything she had inherited or collected and kept over the years. Her domestic skills squarely on the back burner, cobwebs had accumulated throughout her old house. Recycled cardboard boxes overflowed with family photographs and utility bill receipts.

Failing to secure the job at the library, Sumi struggled to find steady work in Riverside. By word of mouth, she finally patched together various part-time jobs, working weekdays as a housekeeper for several prominent Riverside residents, including the city's mayor. Sumi walked or took the bus to work at some of the nicer homes scattered throughout the city. She cleaned for white families living in big old Queen Anne Victorians, with the intricate gingerbread woodwork and dusty banisters, and in the newer hillside Spanish Revival mansions, always needing wax for their shiny handmade floor tiles made of orange clay from Mexico. Once in a while, Sumi earned a few extra dollars by babysitting for local Japanese American families. She worked as a housekeeper from the 1950s until her retirement in the mid-1970s, when her high blood pressure, asthma, and age began taking their toll.

Sumi never learned to drive well, despite her younger brothers' multiple attempts to teach her how to shift gears without popping the clutch along the verdant palm-lined country roads in nearby orange groves, and she gave up driving altogether sometime around 1960. Sumi's discomfort behind the wheel and her resulting lack of mobility put her at a disadvantage in Southern California, a place where the automobile is essential for independence, personal freedom, and success. Sumi had lived a restricted life within walking distance of her birthplace, typically going places only as far as the Riverside municipal bus line, a friend, a visiting relative, or her own two feet would carry her. Sumi's many years living alone in an aging downtown neighborhood without much money or a car revealed a different side of what some still call the California Dream, a darker side of personal ambitions unrealized because of the perceptions of others that were, especially for the first half of Sumi's life, routinely reinforced by the larger society around her and by those who could not see past her gender, skin color, and ethnicity.

Shaped by her early experiences as a non-white child in a white neighborhood, Sumi Harada was one of only a few children of Japanese heritage in public school, where she had to face the prejudices held by many in the community. Her character and outlook also developed from personal experiences at home and was influenced by her position as the younger of two daughters in her Japanese American family. In her twenties during the Great Depression, with sister Mine and oldest brother Masa both married and gone from home, Sumi found herself a young single woman obligated to her aging Issei parents, both by Japanese family tradition and the limited opportunities of the depressed 1930s economy. Dutifully caring for her increasingly infirm and elderly mother and father, Sumi left college after only a year to manage her family's downtown restaurant. She helped to support her younger brothers and parents and maintained the family business until the military order to evacuate came so abruptly in spring 1942.

At five feet, one inch tall, Sumi Harada never commanded attention by her physical stature. Early photographs reveal a young, attractive Sumi, outfitted in fashionable ensembles of the late 1920s. Sumi may have been aware of her physical beauty, but she often seemed a little wary of the Kodak's prying eye. Her niece Rosalind Uno, "Michan" to the family, recalled a memorable day soon after the war in the mid-1940s when her auntie Sumi took her as a teenager shopping for dress clothes in one of the nicest department stores in Salt Lake City and a later visit to a Pasadena dressmaker. "She bought me a beautiful outfit with lace on it, a pleated skirt, . . . very good quality stuff. I remember my mom was not very happy because she said they were not very practical clothes. But I loved them," Michan says.[1]

Other family members and a few friends remembered their extreme caution in approaching Sumi, who displayed a conflicted and even bitter side, according to some. Despite her personal strength and intelligence, evident in her quick wit and sharp tongue, Sumi Harada was deeply influenced by her personal insecurities, limited social and economic circumstances, and inability or unwillingness to forget the indignities she suffered as a child and young woman surrounded by those who wanted people like her to live somewhere else. When I knew Sumi in later life, she was always dressed neatly in plain cotton housedresses, some perhaps homemade. Most of her everyday clothing was worn at the edges, and some of her nicer outfits were often covered with a protective apron. A few displayed muted floral patterns vaguely suggesting the South Pacific. The colors of her clothing, for her dresses and her practical walking shoes with their thick dark laces and low rubber heels, were usually various shades of brown, not vivid at all. Sumi Harada did not want to stand out in a crowd and, consciously or unconsciously, may have relied on her diminutive physical presence and modest dress to purposely fade into the background in most public settings. The frames of her glasses, silver with rounded outer rims like the shiny eyes of a big red snapper, complimented her graying hair. And whenever she tilted her head at one of my questions or comments, even if only to hear or see me more clearly, she seemed nearly always skeptical of everything I said.

20.2. Sumi Harada, 3356 Lemon Street, Riverside, 1977. (Mark Rawitsch photograph, collection of the author)

I first met Sumi when she was nearly seventy and I was in my twenties, soon after calling her on the telephone to make an appointment to interview her about Riverside history. Working as a graduate student at the nearby University of California campus, studying the history of the American West in community settings, I was also involved in an architectural survey of the city's old Mission Revival and Craftsman bungalow neighborhoods. Born of an interest in community history that was prompted, in part, by the national observances of the American Bicentennial in 1976, the building survey recorded information about the construction dates and architectural styles of the houses in the community's oldest residential districts. Walking along the once prosperous thoroughfares of Riverside's downtown neighborhoods and a little bored by the repeating scenery of gnarled front-yard orange trees, drab city streetscapes, and the little checkboxes of the bright white survey forms, my mind wandered. I started thinking about how the stories from within each house are rarely evident in architecture, about how I found much greater inspiration when avoiding the rats when exploring the dank and empty performance stage of the city's abandoned Loring Opera House or trespassing in the dust under a chain-link fence and through a dark and mysterious hole knocked into the crumbling back wall of vacant Chinatown's last brick storefront.

A grant from the National Endowment for the Humanities and a university internship at the Riverside Municipal Museum supported my research on the academic and social activities of Riverside's Japanese American high school students before and after World War II. The museum at the corner of Orange and Seventh, a stately civic building once housing the town's post office and, in later years, the city police department, was kitty-corner to Riverside's derelict grand hotel, the old Mission Inn. Once a fashionable and widely known California roadside attraction before the war—and the place Richard Nixon wed Patricia Ryan in 1940 and Hollywood actress Nancy Davis spent her honeymoon night with actor Ronald Reagan on their way to Phoenix in March 1952—the Mission Inn was struggling for survival, a forgotten California landmark perhaps nearly gone forever.

The hotel's cavernous and sparsely furnished lobby had been stripped of its Mission Revival furniture and most of Frank Miller's eclectic art collection in the late 1950s. Twenty years later, some folks in town tried desperately to save the old place. When I arrived in Riverside the inn's untended gardens were dotted with broken fragments of overturned Japanese stone lanterns. Huge, deformed cacti loomed overhead and dry, raggedy weeds grew between the cracks of Mexican pavers lining walkways to nowhere. The huge hotel, then owned by the city redevelopment agency, was crumbling like a beached *Titanic* amid a sea of vacant storefronts and other empty buildings. Some of its former guest rooms had been converted into cheap apartments, and dusty wilting vines clung to stucco-covered walls like the twisted veins on the fragile hands of a ninety-year-old. Despite these clear signs of neglect and decay, however, it was still possible to imagine that the old hotel might, with great luck and many millions of dollars, still see better days.

As in other California communities thirty years after World War II, books about Riverside's history did not mention the forced removal of Japanese Americans; only a few held faint references to the roots of the nation's civil rights struggles of the mid-twentieth century. I first became interested in the wartime expulsion of the Nikkei as a high school junior in teacher Daniel Nay's US history class at California High School in nearby Whittier. Captivated by artist Mine Okubo's finely rendered drawings and her personal story of the wartime expulsion in *Citizen 13660,* the earliest illustrated narrative of camp life, which was published soon after the war, I had borrowed her book at the Whittier Public Library for a term paper in Mr. Nay's class in 1967.

My sense of history was heightened the following year when our high school sponsored its annual American Heritage Tour to the East Coast during the Easter break in 1968. Visits to Jamestown, Williamsburg, Capitol Hill, and the White House were planned. However, just a few days before our group was scheduled to leave Whittier, our trip was nearly cancelled when Dr. Martin Luther King Jr. was assassinated in Memphis. Subsequent uprisings (the news media called them "riots") in Washington, DC, and many other places across the country led to a curfew in the nation's capital. During our visit there, I found it haunting to see military jeeps manned by soldiers carrying rifles patrolling the vacant evening streets.

On one of our few days in Washington, we stood on the Capitol steps, listening to a presentation by California senator Thomas Kuchel as he spoke to us about Dr. King's death and the riots, pointing out across the city toward smoke still rising faintly in the distance from smoldering Washington neighborhoods. Telling no one, our teachers adjusted the heritage tour itinerary, convincing our bus driver to drive us through the devastated neighborhoods so we could see something more of history than smoke rising in the distance.

A month after our return, on June 3, my friend Brian Anderson and I bought 50 cents' worth of gasoline and drove his funky white Plymouth Valiant from Whittier to South Central Los Angeles the day before the California primary election, hoping to see Senator Robert F. Kennedy as he campaigned for president. Although South Central was less than fifteen miles from our safe Whittier suburbs, it seemed as if Brian and I had landed on another planet as we parked his car on a nearby side street. Our two white faces were outnumbered by the faces of hundreds of others waiting anxiously for Kennedy's campaign swing through the heart of the African American neighborhood around Central Avenue. In an hour or so, the excitement was palpable as the senator's motorcade cruised into view. Men and women shouted and waved. Children ran together holding hands, passing chain-link fences and vacant lots along the sidewalk. A spirited blues band played on a nearby street corner. Hope was in the air. Senator Kennedy stood in an open convertible, his shirtsleeves rolled up, steadied in the back of the vehicle by athletes Rosey Grier and Rafer Johnson. From both sides of the street, people surged around him. When I ran up alongside his moving car, Kennedy reached down and we shook hands as he passed triumphantly through the crowded—and electrified—streets of South Central.

I was one of only a very few white boys running along Central Avenue that day, and remembering the fear among the parents in my suburban Whittier neighborhood over the Watts riots three years before and the unsettling images I had seen for myself in the streets of Washington just a few weeks earlier, I was moved deeply by the welcoming smiles and friendly responses from other young people in the crowd who offered their hands in friendship to Brian and me after Senator Kennedy's motorcade passed by. His assassination a night later in the kitchen pantry at the Ambassador Hotel crushed all of us who had believed the country was finally on the verge of realizing some of its tarnished promises and dreams.

Later the same summer, on another much longer road trip after graduating with the Class of '68 in June, I talked some of my high school buddies into what they thought was an odd idea to drive out to the east side of the Sierras to see Manzanar firsthand. Even though we all had vague notions from our fathers and mothers about their "ancient" experiences and romances during World War II, even though we might have been born as a result of those hasty wartime relationships, and with the war in Vietnam dominating our thoughts about the future, most of us knew nothing about America's concentration camps. Driving into the California desert, I remember having to spend part of our journey explaining why I was interested in going to Manzanar. "We need to see this place," I said. "It's not in our history books." We found only a few remains of the forgotten camp among the weeds at the desolate and abandoned prison. Scrawled on the walls of a stone gatehouse, we discovered angry graffiti blaming President Franklin Roosevelt for what had happened to the Japanese Americans once held there. "May Roosevelt rot in his grave for what he did to us here," one of the messages proclaimed.

In graduate school at the university a few years later, now focused on researching the Japanese American experience in Riverside, I found myself wanting to know much more about how the forced removal during World War II had affected people there, but I could not find much in print. A colleague at the university, doctoral candidate Morrison "Morri" Wong, generously offered copies of oral history interviews and other materials that had been gathered to create the Japanese Americans in Riverside Research Project, housed at the university library. Through this material, I learned of Riverside's Harada family and their involvement in the first Japanese American court test of the California Alien Land Law of 1913. Also through Morri, I heard that one of the few remaining spokespersons for local Japanese American history, Sumi Harada—and one of the three children involved in the Alien Land Law court case some sixty years earlier—lived just a short walk from my tiny windowless office in the cramped and airless basement of the city museum.

I looked up Sumi in the telephone book, called to introduce myself, and made an appointment to visit her at the house on Lemon Street. A few days later, walking from the museum four blocks northwest along the cracked pathway of Lemon Street's sidewalk and passing a few aging Mission Revival city monuments along the way, I searched for addresses on a hodgepodge of old houses. Many were divided into duplexes or even smaller apartments with mismatched address numbers tacked on multiple doorways of once stately single-family homes. All were hunkered down like dry, scaly lizards hiding in the golden winter crabgrass growing out of the cracks and over the edges of the sidewalk beneath towering palm trees among overgrown garden shrubbery in the smoggy downtown neighborhood.

Approaching a tilting cement street lamp sheltered under the thick branches of a spreading pepper tree, I spotted the number 3356 in the shade above the front door of a tall and boxy two-story house on the right side of the street in the middle of the block. I paused for a moment to observe the old house standing much taller than its neighbors. Its ancient wooden siding and thick layers of cracked paint were baked to a chalky yellow like the dull surface of a long-forgotten earthenware pot left sitting in the garden sun. Taking the few steps up the short concrete sidewalk, I quickly climbed the couple of front stairs to what felt to me like a soft landing on the brittle porch. I noticed that its fragile boards, perhaps made more

20.3. Harada House front porch detail, 3356 Lemon Street, Riverside, 1976. (Mark Rawitsch photograph, collection of the author)

20.4. Harada House sleeping porch detail, 3356 Lemon Street, Riverside, 1976. (Mark Rawitsch photograph, collection of the author)

20.5. Harada House back roof detail, 3356 Lemon Street, Riverside, 1976. (Mark Rawitsch photograph, collection of the author)

20.6. Harada House first-floor window detail, 3356 Lemon Street, Riverside, 1976. (Mark Rawitsch photograph, collection of the author)

of termites than of cellulose, seemed to sag under me as I leaned forward to open the black screen door and knock a couple of times on the wooden door behind the screen. In a few moments, Sumi Harada pulled aside a faded gauzy white curtain, unlocked and opened the door, and invited me in to take a seat. She asked me to avoid sitting in the old Mission-style chairs occupying her parlor, the first room entered off the front porch. "The seat's split on that one. I don't think you should sit in it," she said.

Still standing and shifting uncomfortably at Sumi's oblique welcome, I stepped away from the dark oak chair and instead sunk deeply into the soft cushion of a dusty blue-striped sofa. Feeling I had little time to make a good impression, I sensed Sumi sizing me up, scrutinizing my bell-bottom pants and shoulder-length graduate student hair as I explained nervously my interest in learning more about Riverside history from her. I told her that I was seeking information about the local community generally and, at first, did not mention my particular interest in Japanese American history. Responding to an early question from Sumi, who I think determined quickly I was speaking to her because she held a perspective about life in Riverside that was different from most, I explained that I first became aware of Japanese American history as a Southern California teenager by reading artist Mine Okubo's book, *Citizen 13660*. Sumi nodded and listened as I also told her of my unusual summer road trip out to Manzanar in 1968.

For the first time since my arrival, Sumi offered a faint but knowing smile. She told me that Mine Okubo was born and grew up in Riverside, adding she was one of her younger friends at school. She also mentioned offhandedly that she had been keeping a set of Okubo family dishes in an upstairs bedroom, left in the Lemon Street house when Riverside's Japanese Americans were ordered to move from California in 1942. Astonished by this connection, I asked Sumi if I could see the Okubo dishes. She agreed. Leading me from the parlor sofa and into the dining room, passing scattered piles of papers covering the surface of her dining room table adjacent to an old Victorian sideboard stocked with boxes of Kleenex and buried in more papers, she reached the end of her small metal sleeping cot and years of cheap calendars hanging on a nail, one after the other, on a gray door leading to the kitchen. Turning slowly to the left through another small room, passing her mother's old foot-powered Singer sewing machine on the right; a bedroom dresser; a single bed filled with an odd assortment of straw hats, umbrellas, and cardboard boxes; and a disconnected radio standing like a miniature Gothic cathedral on the smooth and well-worn linoleum floor beside the bed, I followed Sumi up the steps of a narrow wooden staircase. I chose my route carefully to avoid stumbling over the small boxes and other miscellaneous items stored along the walls at the edges of each of the lower stairs. "Now be careful here," Sumi warned, "there's no railing to hold on to."

20.7. Harada House interior detail, upstairs bedroom, Harada House National Historic Landmark. (Dana Neitzel photograph, courtesy of the Riverside Metropolitan Museum, Riverside, California)

At the top of the stairs, we turned to enter a dark bedroom. Just inside the small room, Sumi slowly rotated an antique electrical wall switch, clicking on an ancient incandescent lightbulb suspended from the ceiling in a tarnished brass light fixture. Its etched glass shade was covered in a thin layer of dust. Sumi pointed to a brown paper shopping bag sitting on the bedroom floor. "They're in there," she said. Inside the paper bag I saw what I remember now as a set of finely decorated ceramic Japanese *jubako* dishes stacked one atop another. Reaching into the paper bag, I lifted the delicate lid off the first dish, and my memories of Mine Okubo's drawings of life at Tanforan and Topaz came rushing back to me. Holding that fragile piece of the Okubo family's forgotten past, I was connected to the artist's hand and history, back through the familiar pages and drawings of *Citizen 13660* to history alive in my own hands.

In the few moments before Sumi unceremoniously shut off the light, I briefly observed the details of the room's furnishings. Intrigued by what I saw, I expressed interest in seeing more of Sumi's house. "Is it OK if we look around a little?" I asked. "I guess so," Sumi agreed quietly, and we maneuvered our way past long-unused family relics to explore other rooms in her dark old house. Upstairs bed-

rooms were neat and tidy, although apparently unoccupied for many years. The air was still but plaster walls displayed long cracks shooting up from

20.8. Harada House interior detail, upstairs bedroom, Harada House National Historic Landmark. (Dana Neitzel photograph, courtesy of the Riverside Metropolitan Museum, Riverside, California)

the floor and across the ceiling like black bolts of lightning. All the windows were closed, latched, and covered with dark blinds and limp curtains, some with a gaudy pattern of fading red, pink, and blue roses.

Every room upstairs was sparsely furnished with an old-fashioned iron-framed bed or two, most without sheets or blankets. One of the rooms contained a child's empty rocking chair and two straw-colored woven trunks, the smaller placed squarely on top of the other on a worn area rug rolled out on the bare wooden floor between the beds. A round Chinese sewing basket with silk tassels and green glass beads attached to its delicate lid rested on a nearby dresser top. On a bureau in another bedroom, a fancy, blood-red Japanese jewelry box adorned with golden birds and flowers stood alone, its lacquered pagoda-style rooftop reflected in a large oval mirror above. A lonesome mourning dove cooed outside the bedroom window. The last room we visited upstairs contained just one bed and a painted wicker bedside table with an unplugged electric lamp and a 1930s radio. On a small wooden writing desk in the corner, a man's pipe and an open package of loose tobacco looked as if someone had just left them there a few moments

20.9. Harada House interior detail, 1942 Sun Life of Canada calendar, laundry room, Harada House National Historic Landmark. (Dana Neitzel photograph, courtesy of the Riverside Metropolitan Museum, Riverside, California)

before. Closer to the bedroom door, a nineteenth-century side chair with a sturdy caned seat seemed poised for a former inhabitant's return.

Downstairs in the kitchen, beneath a bare lightbulb hanging from a long electric extension cord strung overhead, was where Sumi fixed simple meals for one and most often dined alone at a squatty painted table with solid wooden legs and a shiny vinyl tablecloth. Dual flames of blue pilot lights fluttered at one another in a hand-me-down gas range and sooty water heater, offering a faint sense of life in the otherwise quiet room. Standing before her old kitchen stove, Sumi would one day show me how to make *dashi* broth for *miso* soup, teaching me how to add a piece of dark green *kombu* seaweed to clear tap water boiling in a battered aluminum pot and sprinkling delicate dried bonito fish flakes on the surface of the water to let them sink slowly into the fragrant hot water after turning off the heat.

Across the tiny room, a wooden cupboard stuffed with mismatched cups, saucers, silverware, and dishes stood against the wall behind the backyard door. Its fragile cupboard curtains struggled to keep outdoor dust away from the crockery and random kitchen utensils in drinking glasses on the crowded shelves inside. Over at the kitchen sink along the wainscot trim, a foot or two above the hot- and cold-water faucets, hung a row of simple pots and pans. A few steps away in the pantry near a big laundry basket and enameled metal dish pan hanging on the wall, a collection of forty or fifty rusty skeleton keys on rings tied together with cotton string dangled from a single nail near rows of canned goods, tins of tea, sugar, shoyu, and other kitchen supplies. "All those keys are from my father's rooming houses," Sumi said. "I guess they don't open anything now. I should throw them out," she added.

Not far from an oversized sink in a back laundry room off the kitchen, two or three big steamer trunks sat against the wall beneath high wooden shelves lined with dusty boxes. Near the trunks I was surprised to find a long-forgotten 1942 calendar still hanging there in the darkness behind the laundry room door. Some of the months were missing but Seiichiro Nagamori's blue-and-gold insurance company calendar from Los Angeles was still in pretty good shape. Before the war Nagamori managed a successful insurance business, selling policies to struggling Japanese and East Indian farmers in Southern California. Born in Japan in 1893, he had come to the United States as a silk merchant and later found work with Sun Life Insurance Company of Canada. By the late 1920s his insurance business in Little Tokyo had become so prosperous he was able to build a new house in Hollywood. Like Jukichi Harada, alien Seiichiro Nagamori had placed the ownership of his family's home in the name of his five-year-old citizen daughter, Toshiko. By 1942 the Nagamoris had been sent from California to the Heart Mountain Relocation Center in Wyoming. Unable to find work after his difficult return to Los Angeles at war's end, Nagamori was refused a job by his former employer. Isolated, depressed, and unable to sleep because of his lack of a job and income, Nagamori committed suicide in 1945. His grandson, Lance Ito, only daughter Toshiko's boy born five years after Nagamori's death, would one day become a Los Angeles County Superior Court judge. Looking again at this calendar on the wall, upon closer inspection in the dim light of the laundry room I noticed the handwritten note, "Left May 23r.d." I asked Sumi about the date. "What's May 23, 1942?" I inquired. "Ooohhh, that's the day we went into camp," she replied.[2]

In the front of the house, hanging on the parlor wall above the sofa, a framed poem in black ink on a long sheet of bright white paper displayed the expert hand of Sumi's paternal grandfather. "That was sent to me from a relative in Japan a few years ago," Sumi said. "It's my grandfather's Japanese calligraphy. Grandfather Harada was known as a very good calligrapher in Japan," she added proudly. Just off the parlor, opposite a small bookcase crammed with books and a few outdated magazines, on the west side of the house facing the street, the one downstairs bedroom was piled high with cardboard boxes stacked on the big double bed adjacent to a tall and delicate bamboo nicknack shelf. Random objects on the dusty shelf were overseen by a dark portrait of an elderly couple dressed in Japanese clothing. Grandfather and Grandmother Harada stared intently through the wavy glass, scrutinizing me like an unwelcome intruder standing there in the golden light.

As Sumi led me cautiously from room to room, I was fascinated by what was unfolding gradually before my prying eyes. With no stretch of my imagination, it seemed as if the old house was speaking to me. I thought of myself as an archaeologist in a time warp, discovering something between a place in the Twilight Zone and the King Tut's tomb of Japanese American history. Thinking again of Nagamori's 1942 calendar and the thoughtful drawings in Mine Okubo's book, I realized that I had never before knowingly spoken to anyone who had lived in an American concentration camp. I also sensed that Sumi might be willing to provide me with a unique personal view of what was, to me at the time, a commonly ignored or, at best, poorly understood facet of recent American history.

Back in the parlor and sitting on the sofa, Sumi and I continued our conversation about her memories of hometown Riverside. Taking a break for her to look after something in the kitchen, I asked to use the downstairs bathroom. Still amazed by the contents and condition of the inside of Sumi's house and alone for a moment in the small bathroom at the back of the house, I noticed a narrow wooden shelf, high out of Sumi's reach without a step ladder, crowded with ancient bath or medical supplies and a couple of dusty boxes marked with labels printed in Japanese. Glued to the gray wainscoting of the bathroom wall below the shelf was a cracked and flaking brown paper sign above the towel rack, its neatly typewritten message asking that the towels be kept in order, but Sumi was living here alone. I wondered why nothing had changed.

Over time and in subsequent visits, Sumi and I developed mutual trust and respect for one another. Meeting weekly over milk and cookies, usually store-bought chocolate chip or Oreos, we never missed our appointments together. I always arrived at the scheduled hour, and my consistency apparently impressed her. Later, though, aware of Sumi's legendary cantankerous side, her niece Naomi teased me, saying she could not understand why her auntie Sumi ever opened her door to me, a total stranger with wire-rimmed glasses, a moustache, and hair down to his shoulders. After a couple of visits, suppressing her prejudices about young men with long hair and kindly setting aside any qualms spurred by my physical appearance, Sumi began showing me family photographs to illustrate her memories. Each of the black-and-white images, some cracked and well worn at their edges, others carefully pasted chronologically in a thick family album with a dry leather cover, prompted Sumi's recollection of more stories and expanded details about the lives of the people in her many photographs.

I listened carefully to Sumi's stories of moving to the Lemon Street neighborhood as a child in 1916. She offered thoughts about her family's involvement in the Alien Land Law court case, early life in the new neighborhood, and what it was like to grow up living near the Mission Inn with her parents, brothers, and sister. Sumi remembered the abundance of a backyard apricot tree and the scent of orange blossoms wafting through the air from groves surrounding her Southern California city, neighbors who were nice and others who were not so nice, work after school in her family's Washington Restaurant, and the difficult decisions of a young woman confronted with the forced removal in the early 1940s.

I asked about the little paper sign glued to the bathroom wall and Sumi explained she put it there to remind the incarceration camp returnees who lived in her house for a few months after the war to keep their towels in order. As with the spiritual and sometimes magical places celebrated in Native American creation stories or those of an epic poem, I began seeing the time capsule of Sumi's dark and dusty old house as a place with a rich and lesson-filled story to tell, a Japanese American family story with small threads connecting to the much larger weave of American history and even to the entire history of the human spirit.

When I explained to Sumi that I had heard rumors about a city redevelopment project slating the old Lemon Street neighborhood for urban renewal, she told me some people in town also believed the Mission Inn would soon be scheduled for demolition. I worried that Sumi would be forced to move away again when her house was torn down. With this likely outcome in mind, our work together became much more urgent. We started working more methodically, continuing to gather her family photographs and other materials from scattered locations throughout her house. We found a portrait of President Woodrow Wilson in a dark closet beneath the stairs and the Canadian Pacific Railway Company steamship ticket held by her mother when she came to the United States in 1905. Each time I visited, Sumi had another small collection of materials assembled for our review.

As she became more comfortable and open with me, Sumi's wry sense of humor began to surface. When I suggested we might be able to save her house from demolition by declaring it a historical landmark, she laughed, offering her characteristic "ke, ke, ke" chuckle and teasing that I was comparing her family and house on Lemon Street to the Kennedys and their compound in Hyannis Port. After all, if they were planning to raze the famous Mission Inn, why would anyone want to save Sumi Harada's plain old house on Lemon Street?

Always moved by her stories and encouraged by our progress together, early one morning I returned to Lemon Street with a heavy reel-to-reel tape recorder. As I fumbled with the microphone, setting it on a side table in her old-fashioned parlor, Sumi let me capture her memories and mixed emotions about her house and life in her old neighborhood. She remembered a childhood fire in a grocery store across the street from her downtown rooming house and also the horse-drawn wagons, blacksmith shops, streetcars, and excitement of playing in her own backyard. On cool Riverside mornings during the warmer months, Sumi would prop open her front door with a dark chunk of ironwood saved as an odd souvenir of her days at the Poston Relocation Center. "You have to do that in Riverside to keep your house cool. I can't afford air conditioning." Presenting me with the weighty black doorstop, its shiny edges polished from years of scooting back and forth over a worn spot in her parlor carpet, she observed parenthetically, "That's the same kind of wood they beat up my brother-in-law, Mr. Kido, with—it's lots heavier than it looks."

More than once, Sumi asserted that I was wasting my time and asking her too many questions about things no one cared about. She said most people are simply too preoccupied with their own lives to think about saving old neighborhoods or historical landmarks. Sumi offered her interpretation of what she thought most Americans would say about that topic. "Let the past stay where it is," she told me. "We have to go ahead." I then asked Sumi about saving her house:

> MARK: Do you think that same way, too? . . . What are your real feelings about saving this house? After all the Haradas are gone and everything, . . . do you think this should be saved? Or do you think maybe it should just fall down with urban redevelopment? What do you think?
>
> SUMI: Well, if you have a sentimental attachment for something, sort of, um, you know, tearing at your heartstrings, to think the thing is going to be plowed under. But . . . I guess, I should accept it.
>
> MARK: No—but we have ways we can prevent it . . . Maybe we can do something about it. You know—the National Register . . . listing and all a' that. We can try, anyway.
>
> SUMI: Should I say that it's only memories that keep a person bound to a house?
>
> MARK: Well, maybe most houses, but not this one. I mean, . . . that's a good part of it.
>
> SUMI: Um hum.
>
> MARK: That's for all your family things. But, for other people—
> SUMI: Well, personally, for myself, that's what it is.
>
> MARK: Right. But for other people, in the future, it's more than that, because of what happened here.
>
> SUMI: Well, I think that . . . this . . . fight that my father put up, you know, to hold it, is . . . of great importance to me because, . . . he was just an immigrant, you know, from Japan, and he . . . tried to establish a foothold here . . . I was just a youngster, but . . . as I grew up, . . . I saw all the . . . obstacles in life that a person has to . . . go through. That it must have been . . . a hard thing for my father to do . . . without a good knowledge of the language. With his . . . limited education in English, he still hung on.[3]

With a sense of Sumi's growing interest, perhaps even pride, in telling me more about key episodes in her family's long American story, and ignoring her sly

inferences that I should simply go away and leave her alone, I kept returning week after week. I learned from Sumi that her youngest brother, Shig, served in World War II as a medic in the 442nd Regimental Combat Team and that sister Mine's husband, Saburo Kido, president of the Japanese American Citizens League during the war, was severely beaten by other incarcerees at the Poston Relocation Center for supporting Nisei military service. Sumi always called him "Mr. Kido." Sumi told me proudly that the Kidos' son-in-law, her niece Michan's husband, Bay Area activist Edison Uno, was among the first to advocate for government redress on behalf of those forced into the incarceration camps in the 1940s. She also remembered sadly the passing of her two hardworking brothers, physician Dr. Masa Atsu Harada and dentist Dr. Yoshizo Harada, who died within ten months of each other in 1963.

As the weeks passed, Sumi shared more and more. We began identifying the faces in her many family photographs, labeling each image one by one. When I finally mustered my courage to ask if she ever had experienced any difficulties because of her ancestry, Sumi recounted stories from elementary school. "Tell me about school," I asked.

"Well, I remember, I think I was in the third or fourth grade, we had to have partners in, ah, dancing. You know, little folk dancing, or something? And, ah, there was one colored girl. And I had to be partners with her. And I, I felt it right then, you know. We were two different colored skins, but the whites stayed with the whites. I always had this feeling, and it, you know, never leaves you. You won't feel it! Because you're white, see?" "I can tell you to this day about Valentine's Day," she added later. "You put all your Valentines in boxes. I think I only got two. And that's a sickening feeling. You know it's not your heart or your soul—it's the color of your skin."[4]

For someone with her countenance and personality, Sumi was perhaps wise to spend her life alone, accompanied throughout the years only by a series of small dogs with scrappy outlooks that matched hers and a visiting neighborhood cat or two. Although normally rather subdued among others, Sumi was observant, quick-witted, and sharp-tongued—never shy about expressing her opinion. As an adult she was suspicious of first encounters and stingy with affection. Some recall her now as never reticent to speak her mind, even if it hurt. Despite her reputation for being outspoken and sometimes insensitive among friends and family, I gradually came to know her as a thoughtful, intelligent woman who always tried her best to share difficult memories with me.

Sumi and her sister and brothers, especially in their early years at school or in large community gatherings in hometown Riverside, were often the only people of color in the room. This perhaps unwanted distinction shaped their individual responses to life in ways that made them retreat in some circumstances and find quiet approaches to maintaining their personal independence, dignity, and strength in others. Sumi never forgot the confrontational encounters of her childhood and, when pressed to recall these uncomfortable moments, offered what seemed to me some of her saddest and most intimate memories. "You asked me about my memory, and so I'm trying to tell you," she would say to me impatiently. Recalling her father's purchase of the family's house in a white neighborhood and the immediate reaction of their new neighbors, Sumi said, "Well, I guess at first he didn't understand the attitude of the people—that . . . they really hated us." In an unforgettable voice conjured from her distant childhood, she imitated for me the anger of a neighbor woman down the street: "You Japs stay on your side a' the street. Don't you ever walk over here." And, in the softer tone of her old voice, added almost secretly, "Even after I grew up, I used to be scared if I walked by that corner."[5]

Working together, we organized Sumi's family collections, packing the materials in museum storage boxes stacked neatly in the parlor, one on top of the other, like the Okubo family's jubako dishes in the brown paper bag upstairs. One January afternoon in 1977, Sumi's brother from Los Angeles, Clark Kohei Harada, born in the family rooming house in 1916 just before the Haradas moved to their new house on Lemon Street, paid a visit to Riverside. Sumi invited me to join them at the family home, where Clark recalled the birth of his youngest brother, Harold, born in the downstairs front bedroom of the Harada house in the summer of 1923, remembering, Clark said, a day filled with "a lot of excitement."

As the day unfolded Sumi chided her brother, seven years younger than she, for nearly burning down the family garage as a five-year-old playing with matches in the early 1920s. "I think you can still see the burned walls," Sumi added impishly. Clark was wearing a brown leather jacket, and his eyes were somewhat hidden behind a pair of cool sunglasses. He turned to me with raised eyebrows and a sheepish grin. Challenged by Sumi's claim of still being able to see the burned walls inside the garage, Clark and I asked her to prove it. Sumi accepted our challenge to visit the scene of the fire. Leaving the parlor, we walked through the kitchen and out the back door, approaching the small wooden garage at the back of the house. Sumi explained that its doors had not been opened in years because they were blocked with dirt. As Sumi went back into the kitchen, searching for the garage padlock key, Clark found a hoe in the backyard tool shed. He worked at scraping away the garden soil in front of the garage until Sumi returned to unlock the padlock. On creaking, rusty hinges one of the fragile doors finally swung wide open. Winter light flooded the inside of the tiny building. As our eyes adjusted, Sumi pointed to the evidence of Clark's 1920s fire visible on a row of blackened boards along the wall. "See, I told you so," Sumi said critically, as if Clark and I had not believed her story. Elsewhere inside the garage we discovered an old wooden Japanese rice cooker, a few household tools and garden implements, long-expired black-and-orange California license plates, and a small package wrapped in brown paper secured with neatly tied string. I lifted the package from its dusty resting place, asking Sumi if she knew what was inside. Sumi shook her head. "No," she said, almost in a whisper, as she let me gently untie the string and unwrap the brittle paper.

Sumi told me the package had been stored in the garage for thirty years, ever since the Teshima family sold their longtime home in Riverside soon after returning from camp. She said Riverside held "too many memories" for the Teshimas because of the wartime death of their son Michio, known to his Riverside teachers as Richard but to his closest friends as Mitch. After the war, when the Teshimas decided to move away from California, Henry Teshima, one of the family's three surviving sons, gave the unopened package to Sumi, telling her to dispose of it any way she wished. As with so many things entrusted to her care by others, Sumi never disposed of the package and she never knew its contents until we opened it that day. Inside the brown wrapping paper we found four hand-painted *koi nobori*, carp fish windsock banners traditionally flown high in the wind on bamboo poles for Japanese Boys' Day celebrations in early May. Colorful nobori were originally used in Japan on the battlefield to identify troops and, later, to inspire Japanese boys to honor, bravery, and discipline. They signify the strength of the carp, King of the River, swimming against the current. "These koi are probably one each for the four Teshima boys," Sumi said.

20.11 / 20.12. Sumi Harada with Teshima family koi nobori and American flag found in the Harada House garage, Riverside, 1977. (Mark Rawitsch photographs, collection of the author)

Unwrapping the thin layers of nobori, underneath the koi banners at the bundle's heart we were surprised to find a tattered but carefully folded forty-eight-star American flag. Seeing the deteriorated flag, Sumi worried that she would be held accountable for its poor condition. We spread the parcel's contents in the bright sunshine on the white cement of Sumi's backyard patio, cautiously unfolding the fragile koi nobori. The biggest banner was over sixteen feet long. One of them was labeled in pencil at its split bamboo mouth hoop as "Michio's Fish," indicating that it once had belonged to Mitch Teshima. Back in the house, Sumi rummaged through some old black-and-white photographs to find an image of the nearby Mission Inn. Its outdoor courtyard was decorated with a half dozen koi nobori flying high above for a Japanese Boys' Day celebration sometime around 1920. The parent navel orange tree planted by President Theodore Roosevelt was also visible in the picture between the hotel driveway and a string of Japanese paper lanterns hanging along the Spanish roof tiles of Frank Miller's Old Adobe. Sumi mentioned that Frank Miller was an avid supporter of Riverside's Japanese community and a friend of the Harada family.

In a few days, Sumi and I arranged for her to donate the bundle to the city museum. I completed the donation form for Sumi to sign and we soon paid a visit to the museum to make the gift. The curator discarded the string, brown paper wrapping, and part of a cloth bag used for packing. The wrinkled bag was labeled in Japanese characters and decorated with an image of rabbit-ear irises. Carefully inspecting the tattered American flag and noting its poor condition, the curator declined to accept it, explaining awkwardly that the museum could not afford to restore it. I crossed out its listing on the donation form and, with Sumi's permission, kept the old flag, never losing sight of the image of four Japanese koi nobori and a forty-eight-star American flag flying high together in the sky against the wind. A quarter century later, I finally had the chance to interview Sumi's youngest brother about his wartime life as an army medic in the 442nd Regimental Combat Team. A chill ran down my spine when Dr. Harold Harada told me his story of sharing a last supper of pork chops, hot rice, and canned pineapple one springtime evening in Italy with his Riverside hometown hero, Private Mitch Teshima of Company C of the 100th Battalion of the 442nd Regimental Combat Team, killed at dawn the following morning by a German gun barrage.

Our small and sometimes heartrending discoveries at Sumi's house provided the chance for us to open lines of conversation that are, in polite company, otherwise tightly closed. Thirty years after the war, in the 1970s, when Sumi and I were rummaging through the long-forgotten drawers, closets, cupboards, and trunks in the old Harada house, many Japanese Americans were not comfortable sharing their feelings about the staggering losses of the wartime expulsion or the difficult lives their families lived in the United States prior to the war. Only a few Issei remained, and their second-generation Nisei children, American citizens by

20.13. Dr. Harold Harada (*right*) and Mark Rawitsch at the house on Lemon Street, upstairs bedroom, Harada House National Historic Landmark, July 22, 2000. (Dana Neitzel photograph, courtesy of the Riverside Metropolitan Museum, Riverside, California)

birth, were not inclined to share their deepest feelings about their often difficult life experiences. Like the long-forgotten Teshima family bundle, with its koi nobori and tattered American flag lying in the dark for thirty years waiting for our rediscovery, or even the Harada house itself, the story of the nation's Japanese American pioneers was waiting for rediscovery too.

At the time, it was common for some, including Sumi, not to raise or deeply explore long-buried memories and to excuse the mistakes of the past as inevitable, and perhaps even shameful and best forgotten. The term in Japanese is *shi kata ganai*, "it can't be helped." "You know, it's sad to think about those things," Sumi would say. Although it was never easy for Sumi to respond to difficult questions, being surrounded by the many objects inside her old house seemed to help break the ice for us when speaking about the past. To me, each Harada family artifact was a little gift of history offering the two of us a chance to talk about difficult subjects not easily raised. For Sumi, as perhaps for anyone else, it was much easier to talk about uncomfortable topics if we could first refer to something tangible, an old object that might serve as a conversation piece and was at least one step removed from the raw emotion of recounting sad memories.

Unwrapping the Teshima family's koi nobori banners and their hidden American flag, a bundle of history—brown on the outside and red, white, and blue in the middle—Sumi and I ventured into the impossible world of talking about citizenship, patriotism, the impacts of the wartime expulsion, and the premature death of a young friend. In a closed bedroom upstairs, the wedding portrait of a dapper, young Nisei couple fashionably dressed in the style of the late 1920s—Sumi's older sister, Mine, and her youthful new husband, attorney Saburo Kido—along with the old ironwood doorstop guarding her threshold downstairs, led us down the rocky path of discussing the founding of the Japanese American Citizens League and the conflicted circumstances Mr. Kido faced as JACL president during World War II. In the back of a dark upstairs closet, brother Shig's wartime army uniform, worn-out combat boots, and duffle bag prompted stories about the "Go for Broke" spirit of the 442nd Regimental Combat Team. A sad photograph of her mother's funeral in front of the low recreation hall at the Topaz Relocation Center, with its dignified faces expressing great distress, opened the door to conversations about the sacrifices and losses of camp life and to Sumi's prescient opinion that Americans should be ever vigilant about the rights and responsibilities of their citizenship:

> Well, I'd like to say, in reference especially to camp, that even if you have citizenship, you better guard that real carefully. They just proclaim an order and tell you, "Well, you've got 1 percent some kind of foreign blood in you, we're gonna stick you into a camp." Or, you're just gonna go. Even if you're a citizen. It's all I keep telling people. They better guard that possession, because, if the military and the government tell you, "Move," you move. They say now that we could have fought it. But, I don't think so. It's too big an order.[6]

This is not so hard to believe today, seventy years after the forced expulsion of World War II but only a breath after 9/11 and the hasty establishment of an American military prison using "enhanced interrogation techniques" on "detainees" at Guantánamo.

In the 1970s, most Japanese American families, especially those significant numbers of people who lost their livelihoods, homes, and family belongings during the wartime expulsion, probably could not bear to face their losses in casual conversations about what had happened in the past. For many, it was time to move on. For Sumi, however, one of the few able to hold on and return to her family home and its humble contents, which had become even more meaningful to her after the unfathomable losses of the war and representative of the dedication, hard work, and struggles of her immigrant parents, her simple home had become her own historical landmark. The house on Lemon Street was a rare and precious touchstone of Sumi's family's history, a central ingredient for her personal identity as she approached the end of her life.

Sumi's door with the cracked yellow paint was always opened when I knocked. Whether or not she knew it, with each fragment of her family's past she shared, Sumi was allowing me to follow her gentle guidance and proceed with my questions. I am sure now she knew I was using the relics inside her house as a way to speak about the complicated feelings she had held hidden away for many years inside her heart. Nonetheless, whenever I asked Sumi for more, although she might hesitate, sound infringed upon, and be even a little crabby or embarrassed at times, she always proceeded to tell me the fragments of her family's rich American story. As was her style, Sumi routinely complained and challenged me about my questions but, without exception, she continued to offer me answers, leads, and other bits of information, taking me on a thirty-five-year-long journey of discovery about the lives and times of California's Japanese American pioneers, people who were not inclined to reveal the details of their struggles or even tell their stories out loud to anyone, even close family members.

Like so many of her generation and ethnicity who grew up in California, watching Issei parents struggle through years of hard work and social discrimination only to lose everything during the war, Sumi seemed embarrassed by the past. She routinely expressed her doubts about the value of her family's stories—and herself—to anyone else. "I'm just an impoverished old woman staying here," Sumi said to me one day. I know at times Sumi wondered if she should be talking with me about a past she felt should perhaps be forgotten: "I know you're gonna ask me those difficult things. I should never bring them up," she would say.

With the work of the city's architectural survey still in my mind, I began to think that we should nominate the Harada house as a historical landmark. Its plain and functional architecture, forlorn physical condition, and location in a less fashionable urban neighborhood were no match for Riverside's more impressive community monuments, but, to me, its history spoke volumes beyond the charming façades of Riverside's Mission Revival past. I believed that because of its long association with Japanese American history in California, particularly its role in the little-known pre-war battles over Nikkei property rights that set the stage for the wartime expulsion, the Harada house deserved the same attention as Riverside's more stately architectural monuments.

With Sumi's acceptance of the idea and assigned by the museum as an intern with the city's Cultural Heritage Board, I worked with her to prepare the paperwork nominating the house as a local historical landmark. Some people in town who seemed more interested in architecture than in the stories told by Sumi's old house told us the Harada home did not "look historical." Despite these complaints and with only a brief deliberation, the heritage board accepted our nomination with enthusiasm and made Harada House Riverside Historical Landmark #23, joining Frank Miller's Mission Inn, the site of the parent navel orange tree, and other points of community interest on the city's growing list of landmarks. Our successful nomination of the house for listing in the *National Register of Historic Places* soon followed. With the nominations accepted, I prepared a field report about the story of Harada House as part of my graduate studies program, completed my work at the university, received a master's degree in history, and moved away from Riverside to my first job as curator of a small museum near Santa Barbara.

By the early 1980s I had been away from Riverside for several years, working in a second job as director of the Mendocino County Museum in Northern California. Dr. Ronald Tobey, my former history professor at University of California, Riverside, called to ask me to prepare my graduate report for publication. I finally paid a visit to Sumi's recently widowed sister, Mine Harada Kido, at her comfortable home in a nice apartment on Anza Street in San Francisco. Mine revealed that Riverside hotelman Frank Miller was an early supporter of the Harada family in their efforts to move to the Lemon Street neighborhood. She offered tantalizing information about his behind-the-scenes role in the purchase of the Haradas' new house. Like her younger sister, Mine was never reticent when expressing herself. When I asked her to explain her feelings about the future of her childhood home as a historical landmark, she told me she felt sorry for Sumi living in such a run-down old house. "They ought to tear it down . . . That house is full of termites and it's creeping into the furniture," Mine concluded bluntly.[7]

As we completed research for the book, Riverside's Operation Paintbrush, part of a city neighborhood improvement program, provided the landmark Harada House with exterior repairs and a fresh coat of paint. I was pleased that Sumi did not have to pay for the maintenance work and was glad her old house finally looked so nice. Soon after the new paint job, in March 1983, I coaxed Sumi outside and she posed proudly for my camera on her postage-stamp-sized front lawn. Later the same year, the Department of History at UCR published *No Other Place: Japanese American Pioneers in a Southern California Neighborhood,* and the Harada family story began to receive more attention with each passing year.

Missing sister Mine, who passed away in 1984, Sumi continued to live in her landmark home, seeming to find purpose in her newfound local celebrity status as a living historical treasure. Schoolchildren visited Sumi from time to time, asking her questions about things like Japanese etiquette and requesting firsthand accounts of Japanese American history. After making one last journey to Poston for a reunion of former incarcerees in 1985, Sumi spent most of her time close to home, volunteering as a docent at the nearby Mission Inn and observing neighborhood life along Lemon Street on walks to and from the First Congregational Church most Sunday mornings. Some Riverside friends claimed that Sumi—not her house—had become the real historical landmark.

In 1988, Harada House was included in *Five Views: An Ethnic Historic Site Survey for California*, produced to launch a more comprehensive historical sites inventory for the state. Historical sites representing the heritage of Native

Americans, African Americans, Chinese Americans, Mexican Americans, and Japanese Americans are all listed, along with the landmark Harada House in Riverside. Two years later, a few weeks before Sumi received a letter from President George H.W. Bush apologizing to Japanese Americans for their wartime expulsion and incarceration—the culmination of late nephew Edison Uno's early efforts for redress—the Harada family's house was designated as a National Historic Landmark. Listed five years after the site of the Manzanar Relocation Center received the same distinction, Harada House joined Frank Miller's Mission Inn as one of only two national landmarks in Riverside. Sumi was interviewed by the local paper and the *Los Angeles Times*. "Father would be pleased about President Bush's letter," Sumi told the *Times* reporter. "He would be proud this house has been designated of historic importance to the America he loved so much."

In her last decade, Sumi gained further community prominence and recognition. In 1992 she received honors at the leadership awards banquet hosted by the Asian Pacific American Student Programs at the University of California, Riverside. The university student organization's annual Sumi Harada Service Award was named in her honor. In 1995, at the age of eighty-five, the little girl who had once received only two Valentines was named one of her city's four Women of Achievement, feted at a banquet attended by 700 admirers just a couple of blocks from home at the Riverside Convention Center.[8]

As her last years passed, Sumi slowed down more and more each year. Friends added new handrails above her old claw-foot bathtub and to the steps leading up from the sidewalk to the front porch.

Autumn

The days go by—
Since I last saw my brothers' smiling faces.
I clutched my childish joys.
I sought a warm place in the sun
And shivered as the wind blew a chilly blast.

The months go by—
They tell me, e'en the birds wing their way, south,
I must stay here, alone.
I sought a warm place in the sun
And shivered as the wind blew a chilly blast

Seasons go by—
Life and death are as one.
The wrinkled crone remains, who was afraid to venture forth.
I sought a warm place in the sun,
And shivered as the wind blew a chilly blast.

—Sumi Harada

In the late 1990s, still living alone and doing her best to maintain her fierce independence, Sumi suffered a fall at home. It took a few days for the neighbors to notice the mail piling up on the front porch and to realize that Sumi needed help. Her youngest brother, dentist Dr. Harold Harada, soon made arrangements for Sumi to move from Riverside to a Los Angeles convalescent hospital for extended care near his own home in Culver City, the same medical facility where brother Clark spent his last days before his death in 1995. Sumi never returned to the house on Lemon Street. For the next several months she lived in the hospital near her brother and he visited her often. Sumi's health gradually declined and she died of complications from cancer at the venerable age of ninety on May 8, 2000. In a phone call to me at home in Northern California, Dr. Harada invited me back to Riverside to speak at Sumi's funeral service at the First Congregational Church, just a few blocks down Lemon Street from Harada House.[9]

Pleased by the size of the crowd gathering in the foyer of the Spanish Renaissance Revival church, a place that felt like Riverside to me, I met Dr. Harold Harada in person for the first time. I remembered the thin nineteen-year-old in the sepia-toned World War II military portrait, the only image I had of Harold. "Gosh, you just aged fifty years right before my eyes," I said. Startled somewhat by my remark, Dr. Harada shook my hand warmly and told me how pleased he was to finally meet me. I returned the compliment.

A few minutes later, offering my memories of Sumi before the large group assembled for her memorial service at the First Congregational Church, I stood on the same spot where Dr. Booker T. Washington addressed the good neighbors of Riverside in 1914. Family and friends smiled knowingly and laughed politely when I stated that Sumi was never afraid to express a personal opinion. I then offered my own conclusion to Sumi's long life as the caretaker of her family's American story and of the landmark Harada House:

> Through Sumi Harada's generosity, patience, inventive good humor, lack of fear about expressing herself, and having some sense that her family story was worth sharing with a wider audience than just a twenty-six-year-old graduate student, an important American story can now be told—a California story of American civil rights and the struggle for democracy and freedom that, I think, can now comfortably take a seat along with Rosa Parks on that bus from Montgomery.
>
> A couple of weeks ago, I finally got around to carefully selecting and planting a red-leaf Japanese maple in my own backyard. I'd been wanting to do that for many years but something made me finally take care of getting it done just a week before Sumi passed away, although I had not yet heard that she would not be with us for much longer. Turns out that Japanese maple has new meaning for me now. I hope it lives on for a good long time—just as Sumi did.
>
> We love you, Sumi—Go for Broke!

After the memorial service at the church downtown, a smaller group proceeded out to the family plot at Olivewood Cemetery. At the conclusion of a brief interment service near the grave of Jukichi and Ken Harada, I took a folded piece of white paper from inside my coat pocket and, carefully opening the paper, placed a dry red maple leaf from my new backyard tree among the many flowers covering Sumi's casket.

In the months after Sumi's passing, brother Harold removed much of the more recent accumulations of papers and other materials from the house on Lemon Street. The stack of boxes Sumi and I had packed with family photographs twenty-five years before remained where we left it next to her blue-striped sofa in the parlor. Convinced of the value of his family's story and seeing the growing interest in such things from new generations of Americans, Dr. Harada began making plans to transfer the house and its contents to public ownership through a donation to the City of Riverside. At about the same time, the Southern Poverty Law Center's Teaching Tolerance Program in Montgomery, Alabama, published *A Place at the Table: Struggles for Equality in America*. The Alabama program provides "teachers with resources and ideas to help promote respect for differences." Chapter 7, "The House on Lemon Street," used the Harada family story as a voice for Asian American equality. We all were delighted when the new book was distributed at no cost to schools around the nation.

Back at the house in July, Dr. Harada met with staff from the nearby Riverside Municipal Museum and other local researchers, who conducted a digital photographic documentation of the home's interior. Sitting again on Sumi's old blue sofa, we recorded a videotaped interview with Dr. Harada, joined by a tightly packed group in the darkened and warm Harada House parlor. Just beyond Dr. Harada I noticed a crumbling green plastic window shade repaired, no doubt by Sumi, with a Sunkist orange soda pop box folded flat and taped to a gaping hole. Like some sort of ancient Japanese scroll, the window shade hung in the parlor next to Grandfather Harada's calligraphy, a curious homage to Lemon Street and Riverside's once-famed citrus industry.

With sweat dripping from his brow, Harold responded to questions about his family history and his time as a medic during the war. The interview continued for two hours as the summer temperature inside the old house climbed to nearly 100 degrees. After the interview Dr. Harada's two adult daughters, Naomi and Kathleen, joined the rest of the group, following their dad in an extended exploration of the house. Harold led us from room to room on a personal videotaped tour of his boyhood home. The camera caught him finding his World War II combat uniform in an upstairs closet and his wallet of the same era in a nearby dresser. Behind a bunch of worthless Italian lire in the old leather wallet, Harold found a faded coupon. "Hey, 'Go For Broke Club, Leghorn, Italy, 442nd Regimental Combat Team.' How about that. God—they owe me some drinks!" Harold exclaims. In one of the trunks in the laundry room downstairs, Naomi found a small box of carefully layered cotton surrounding the dried umbilical cords of each child born into the Harada family in the early 1900s, individually wrapped and labeled in handwritten Japanese with the children's names and birth dates.[10]

In the fall Harold traveled to Washington, DC, to attend the dedication of the National Japanese American Memorial to Patriotism. Michio Teshima's name is listed there, along with the other Japanese American veterans killed in action while in service to their country. In an article published in *Rafu Shimpo*, journalist Sam Chu Lin explained that the memorial was dedicated to honor Japanese American veterans who served in World War II and "members of their families who were interned and subjected to discrimination during the conflict." Lin also included a few comments from those in attendance: "'This is very meaningful,' said Dr. Harold Harada of Culver City. 'It's most touching to me. I'm very impressed.'"

In spring 2001, with thoughts of his visit to the national memorial fresh in mind and his Mercedes sedan with the "Go for Broke/442nd Regimental Combat Team" license plate holder parked in the driveway nearby, Harold once more returned to Lemon Street. Dr. Harada had local workmen install a new historical marker on the front lawn of Harada House. City officials organized a National Historic Landmark Plaque Dedication on April 19. Shig concluded the ceremony with his memories of growing up in Riverside. He introduced the crowd to Harada family members, friends, and neighbors, including his childhood Sunday school teacher Dorothy McBride, now in her nineties and sitting proudly in the front row. Harold offered thanks to the city that evening, throwing a big dinner party for us all at the now fully restored and newly fashionable Mission Inn. Dressed in a silk kimono, Frank Miller's smiling ghost presided from a nearby balcony.

For the next two years museum staff continued to work with Dr. Harada and his daughter Naomi to transfer Harada House to public ownership. However, in summer 2003 as the transfer neared completion, Dr. Harada's health began to fade. Naomi called me in mid-August to let me know that Dr. Harold Shigetaka Harada, born in the downstairs front bedroom of the Harada home on August 15, 1923—the last Harada child of his generation, "The Last of the Mohicans" as he liked to call himself—had passed away quietly at home on August 17, two days after acknowledging the milestone of his eightieth birthday.

The following May, Riverside's Harada House Strategic Visioning Workshop, supported by the City of Riverside and a grant from the Western Office of the National Trust for Historic Preservation, was coordinated by Lynn Voorheis, Curator of Historic Structures at the Riverside Municipal Museum. Historic preservation consultants, museum curators, city planners, community leaders, and Harada family members all took part in the two-day workshop. Shig and Chiye's daughters, Naomi and Kathleen, and Yoshizo and Sumiye's daughter, Rosemary, offered the group details of family history, along with their own ideas about how their family's home should be preserved and interpreted in the future. We spent time visiting the house on Lemon Street, making long-range plans for the city's new Harada House Project.

At the conclusion of the workshop Naomi and Kathleen invited me to join them and museum curator Dr. Brenda Focht for a visit to Olivewood Cemetery. We took the purple orchid bouquets from the workshop's table vases and Brenda drove us to Olivewood, where we placed the flowers on the graves of Jukichi, Ken, Tadao, and Sumi Harada. And as Sumi had done nearly every Memorial Day since his passing in 1950, we also found Jess Stebler's grave beneath a huge cypress tree and placed a small bouquet there too. Now in their forties, Naomi and Kathleen recalled the annual journeys they had made to the same cemetery as girls, remembering long pre-freeway trips in the family's blue Mercury station wagon with parents Harold and Chiye and brothers Ken and Paul, riding the sixty miles from Culver City to Riverside, the car packed with kids, food, and flowers.

In the 1960s the Haradas, Kidos, and Hashimuras would sometimes gather at Auntie Sumi's house for holiday meals. On the Memorial Day weekend at the end of May, as Naomi and Kathleen recalled, Shig and Chiye would also bring their family to Riverside for a visit to Lemon Street and an annual trip to the cemetery. The Harada sisters recalled their dad listening to the Indianapolis 500 car race on the radio in the Mercury on what seemed to them an endless road trip. Avoiding Sumi's vigilant red-and-white Brittany spaniel Tootsie, with her challenging personality that was "just like Auntie Sumi's," the family shared a potluck around the dinner table in the crowded dining room at Sumi's old house—a typical Southern California multicultural meal of sushi, teriyaki chicken, potato salad, ham, and Auntie Sumi's famous pinto beans and chicken mole. Shig and Chiye's four grown children recalled the aroma of the pinto beans as the first thing they remembered about getting out of the station wagon on those long family trips to Lemon Street. Nieces Naomi and Kathleen have never forgotten the thrill of drinking soda from the thin glass straws that Auntie Sumi let them use on special occasions if they were lucky and behaved themselves.

Back among Olivewood's tombstones the low buzz of rushing traffic from the nearby Riverside Freeway was a constant reminder of the pace of California life speeding by outside the cemetery. While we were still there, Brenda's cell phone rang and we learned that staff at the city attorney's office had the papers ready for Naomi and Kathleen to sign, transferring ownership of Harada House to the City of Riverside. Late in the afternoon we headed out of the cemetery and back downtown to the city attorney's office so the two Harada sisters could sign the papers. Waiting in the nicely air-conditioned city hall conference room for the property transfer papers to arrive, I noticed a framed photograph of Riverside's well-known Victorian house museum, Heritage House, displayed on the wall above the room's wide conference table. I recalled my time there as the museum's student intern in the 1970s, and, even though I had nearly forgotten, one last memory of Sumi flitted into the room, reminding me that Naomi and Kathleen's auntie Sumi also used to work there as a housekeeper years before it became a city landmark.

I told Naomi and Kathleen I remembered their auntie Sumi telling me that when Mrs. McDavid, the last owner of the house, asked Sumi to cut her toenails, she defiantly refused. She told me she declared to Mrs. McDavid: "I'll dust your banisters and tabletops, but I won't cut your toenails! Your feet stink!" Naomi and Kathleen just nodded their heads and smiled. A moment later the two Harada sisters signed the transfer papers, and after nearly ninety years of family ownership and an inspiring story of cultural struggle, family dedication, perseverance, and generosity spanning the entire twentieth century, Harada House was finally placed in the care of future generations. Auntie Sumi's house is now a National Historic Landmark that will tell its proud American story for many years to come—a place for teaching, learning, and personal reflection about the struggle for the American Dream; a reflection of the opportunities and responsibilities of freedom, family, and citizenship; and a story of our successes and failures as different Americans seek to find their place in the world.

At the end of the workday at city hall the four of us next made a quick trip to Magnolia Elementary School to see Sumi Harada's smiling face in the group portrait of eleven twentieth-century Riverside pioneers joined together forever in a painted mural created by artist Dr. Sam Huang to celebrate the diversity of Riverside's citizens. Sumi is only one of two women represented in the mural. She joins men like Frank Miller of the Mission Inn and World War II Congressional Medal of Honor recipient Ysmael Villegas. Eliza Tibbets, the eccentric Riverside pioneer who planted the first two Washington navel orange trees in her yard at the edge of town back in the 1870s, accompanies Sumi as the only other woman in the mural. Gracing its entrance on Magnolia Avenue, the colorful mural illustrates the elementary school's motto, "Know the Past, Live the Present, Dream the Future." Forever smiling in the mural at the elementary school, a happy expression I rarely witnessed in real life, Sumi had now earned her place in a new world of California history, mythology, and folklore. She had, it also occurred to me, finally been recognized as the teacher her ancestors would have been proud to know.

Just a year later the story of Harada House was once again shared with a large and attentive audience gathered back on Lemon Street at the First Church of Christ, Scientist, Riverside's oldest example of Mission Revival architecture, for the 30th Annual California Preservation Conference. The California Preservation Foundation's annual meeting theme in 2005 celebrated cultural diversity. Those of us working on the Harada House Project were pleased when Dr. Anthea Hartig, the new director of the Western Regional Office of the National Trust for Historic Preservation and a member of the Harada House Project team, introduced me to deliver the conference's plenary session keynote address, "Harada House National Historic Landmark: There's No Place Like Home; The Story of Sumi's House."

By way of introduction to the conference's theme, Anthea explained her recent encounter with airport personnel conducting passenger security check-in at San Francisco International Airport. Noting the remarks of her baggage inspector at SFO, Anthea explained that he complained to her, saying all the attention being paid to the many folks in line waiting to board their planes, each now "inconvenienced" by the aftermath of tragic events of the attacks on the twin towers a couple of years before—the twenty-first century's own Pearl Harbor—would not be necessary if the nation had been more careful about, as the inspector said, "all this diversity stuff." To Anthea and her listeners in Riverside, the airport inspector was inferring that if the nation had been more vigilant about controlling its cultural makeup, we might not be suffering these new challenges from outside our borders or the new "patriot acts" from within that were, once again, shaking the very foundations of our free society.

In preparation for my address, just before Dr. Hartig's introduction, I carefully unfolded the Teshima family's tattered American flag—the same one the former Riverside museum curator would not accept from the bundle Sumi, Clark, and I found in the Harada House garage in 1977—and hung it up behind the pulpit. Thanking Dr. Hartig, I opened my remarks by asking the audience to imagine they were sitting with Sumi Harada and me just up the street on the front porch of 3356 Lemon Street, turning the pages of a heavy family photograph album and listening to our stories of Harada House and the American Dream. The audience seemed moved and inspired by the Harada family story as I concluded my remarks by referring to the Teshima family flag hanging on the wall behind me and explaining my intent to come back to town to try once more to donate it to the city museum. This time the old American flag was accepted by a new museum curator and will soon be reunited with the Teshima brothers' four koi nobori banners to once again fly high together against the current in the wind.

With the inauguration of President Barack Obama and the Obama family's move to their new house on Pennsylvania Avenue, far from Lemon Street, I wondered what the Haradas would say now about the promises of the American Dream. Reviewing my own collection of materials about the Harada family story and knowing our chances to interview the last Harada children of their generation had passed, I combed through their statements, searching for observations that might help people interested in their family story to understand their ideas about their American lives and the lessons of their house on Lemon Street.

Back in 1982, when I asked Mine Harada Kido how she thought her parents' experiences as Issei pioneers affected her life as a young Nisei growing up in California and whether the Alien Land Law court case influenced her family's development, she thought for a moment and replied: "I don't know except I always want to stick up for my own rights. That's why I believed in whatever the JACL was doing . . . I don't know how much that influenced my life but every time I feel that I'm being discriminated in any way, I really want to assert my rights."

Just before we went out to the garage to prove sister Sumi's claim he had nearly burned it down playing with matches, Clark Kohei Harada had expressed his thoughts about the family's view of the significance of the court case and the preservation of Harada House as a historic landmark:

> My dad had a strong belief in the American way of life and he bought the house with the intent of having his children go to a school nearest to their home and have the advantages of our society . . . They were American citizens.
>
> Through his case we can recognize that even minor citizens have their rights protected . . . This is the way I see it . . . It's a credit to Riverside, too . . . I think the preservation of the house would be meaningful to maybe some people who could evaluate [how] an immigrant from a foreign country, who came here for the first time, never returned to his homeland, made a significant contribution and, the more I think about it, the bigger it seems to me.
>
> . . . If you could show me a man who's contributed as much as my dad has to this country, . . . I'd certainly respect him and if I could do half as much as he did, I'd be proud of myself.

On another hot day in July, once again back in the parlor and sitting on the sofa at the house on Lemon Street, at the end of my interview with Dr. Harold Harada, I asked, "If you could forever be on the front porch and seeing people come by and read the plaque, what would you like to say to them?" Shig replied:

> I would hope that this simple plaque would educate the person reading the plaque that this plaque did not come easily. If it weren't for this one man, Ju-kichi Harada, the plaque wouldn't be here. And that's all it was, . . . one man actually. And for him and his family to be so honored by a government that was forgiving and understanding, I think is Americanism in a nutshell.
>
> The fact that . . . we were ostracized, we were put in internment camps, . . . practically made to go to war, withstand all of the prejudice and discrimination that we took, and still come out on top.
>
> And look at where we are today. Look at where the Japanese Americans are today . . . On a social level we're accepted as equals now.
>
> . . . Had it not been for the 850 men that were killed [in the war], we wouldn't be here. Had it not been for Saburo Kido, my brother-in-law, speaking out for the draft and all that, I don't think we'd be here. The others that spoke up, . . . my niece's husband, Edison Uno, who was an activist and who spoke for redress for the Japanese Americans—and we received redress, apologies, I think, from two presidents of the United States . . . What more do we need to strive for?

I think that if an outsider were to view this plaque and this house, . . .
I hope that it would be more meaningful than just another piece of brass and
a couple of pieces of wood stuck together; that there's a lot more . . . to those
things than what appears on the surface. That's what I would hope.[11]

The National Historic Landmark Harada House, still and always "Sumi's
house" to me, is now recognized and celebrated in California and nationally for its
historical significance because of its association with the first Japanese American
court test of the California Alien Land Law of 1913 and for its later link to the
experiences of the forced removal and return, things we now find useful to recall
and understand as we Americans continue to search for who we are, or who we
can become, charting an uncertain future in uncertain times. Because of this recognition and acknowledgment, many hours and lots of money—much more than
immigrants Jukichi and Ken Harada ever earned in their lives—have been spent
thoughtfully analyzing the structure of the landmark Harada House and planning
in great detail for its repair, preservation, and interpretation. All this careful work
provides a stage on which to pull up a sturdy oak chair and sit on the porch in the
cool shade under the wide branches of the one remaining sidewalk pepper tree to
hear the *story* of the Harada family taking its place at the table, a seat on that bus,
with all the other American families who should be remembered.

With the ongoing need to more fully understand and embrace the meaning of
our country's many opportunities, promises, and responsibilities, I believe Sumi, her
parents, sister, and brothers, all of whom have now passed from the scene, would
like to be remembered as members of an American family who each did their best
to confront adversity and live their lives with purpose, dignity, and courage. And I
think that the Haradas would like their simple California house to be remembered
mostly for what it always meant to them, the place they called *Home*. Harada House
offers a foundation for hope and belief in a future for all the many honorable and
hardworking families still struggling with their neighbors to realize their American
Dream, regardless of their origins or the color of their skin—especially those facing
racist cowards in the night who still hang nooses in the schoolyard and spray-paint
swastikas on campaign posters, or the people on YouTube and the call-in radio stations ranting that some of us should simply give up our struggle for freedom, pack
up our things, and go back to the land of our ancestors.

Sharing her thoughts about the history of her house on Lemon Street and our
America, Sumi Harada concluded:

Sometimes I think it's just a matter of the color of your skin. You know, we
breathe the same air and drink the same water. So I'm glad I didn't sell the
place. I'm glad I had someplace to come back to. It's *home*. There's no other
place.

AFTERWORD

Located on a tree-lined street adjacent to Riverside's downtown, the historic Harada House has been recognized as one of the most significant and powerful civil rights landmarks in California.[1] Although the house is a modest two-story home from the turn of the last century, the building represents one of the most central themes in our national story: immigration, and for people of color, the subsequent struggle for inclusion, often against seemingly insurmountable odds.

Although this significance has certainly been established by the designation of the Harada House as a National Historic Landmark, *The House on Lemon Street: Japanese Pioneers and the American Dream* fills a huge gap by detailing the narrative of Asian immigrant home life. Relatively little is known about day-to-day lives of first- and second-generation families prior to World War II. The preservation of the Harada House will now change that.

Consider these facts. Ms. Sumi Harada returned from a period of forced confinement in 1945, and from that moment she kept the pre-war contents of the house intact. After the house was designated a historical landmark, Sumi and others in the Harada family became more interested in donating the family home and its contents to the Riverside Metropolitan Museum and the City of Riverside. After the gift was completed, a grant from the Getty Foundation, a philanthropic division of the J. Paul Getty Trust, supported the preparation of a conservation plan. This project enabled the museum to assemble nationally known historic preservation professionals to assess, provide recommendations, and draft a long-term conservation plan for the Harada House. When the house was recently emptied of its contents to reinforce the physical structure, museum staff removed more than 6,000 objects representing the Harada family's history in America. Each object is now being logged, numbered, and photographically digitized. The house, its history, and family artifacts are supported by an archival collection that is seventy linear feet in length, as well as by a range of unpublished and published reports and studies, including the one you now hold in your hands. If stacked one document on top of the other, the archival collection would stand more than twice as tall as the two-story Harada House itself. In sum, because Ms. Sumi Harada, a Nisei daughter of Issei pioneer parents, made extraordinary efforts to preserve the family's house and possessions, the Harada House is well on its way to becoming the most significant archive for specific and comparative study of the early Japanese American immigrant house and home.[2]

THE HISTORICAL CONTEXT OF THE HOME

The genesis of the Harada House as a literal archive of the pre-war Japanese American house begins with context, including its historical and legal matrix. As author Mark Rawitsch meticulously details, these roots demonstrate how and why a home was particularly important to Asian immigrants in the United States before World War II and why a house was a critical acquisition for a family—at once material, symbolic, and spiritual.

Like other first-generation Asian immigrants to the United States mainland, Jukichi Harada was an alien who was, by definition, ineligible for US citizenship through naturalization.[3] Since Issei immigrants were typically thrifty and upwardly mobile, they sought to acquire property even though that property might be only a small storefront or an acre or two of farmland. Like the Chinese before them, as the Issei became independent, they were often construed as undesirable competitors that were a threat to the Euro-American mainstream. Purchasing and owning a building or land, therefore, took on special significance for the Issei. It represented access to means of production and reproduction. Property ownership offered the material basis for long-term security, especially in a society that took pains to ensure that Asian immigrants provided labor but otherwise stayed in their place in the shadows. In addition, the notion of genealogical continuity cannot be overestimated in terms of the cultural values of early Asian immigrants, including the Issei. In this sense, property ownership also represented a long-term, if not permanent, stake in this country. If a man was fortunate enough to have a wife, as was Jukichi Harada, a home of one's own was a place where even a "resident alien" could shelter and raise his American children.

Although the Issei-Nisei house is quite distinctive from the Japanese house,[4] several cultural continuities are worth considering here. From the beginning Rawitsch intimates that the Issei brought practices that overtly and subtly shaped the early Japanese American home. The practice of cutting, drying, and saving children's umbilical cords, for example, seems exotic but may be as simple as affirming that one's home is the center of the children's and the family's world, as the Old Norse eponym *hus* implies.

The Japanese agricultural class during the Tokugawa period had a strong sense of the *ie*, or household, as an entity.[5] The *ie* was composed conceptually of ancestors from the past, the present holders of the house and associated land, but was also inclusive of future generations who in turn would hold and manage the property. Considering an Issei household within the context of the *ie* gives us an indication of why and how the cultural motivations for establishing and then maintaining a house were particularly intense. That intensity was magnified, at least for those who wanted to stay in the United States, because barriers to homeownership were institutionalized with the passage of the first California Alien Land Law in 1913.[6]

CONCEPTUALIZING THE HOME

What, then, does *The House on Lemon Street* offer to help us understand the nature of the pre-war Issei-Nisei household and home?[7] If a "house" can be thought of as a kind of assemblage, it has at least three intertwined dimensions.[8] In and of itself, every house necessarily references a material object, located in time and space. As a structure inhabited by a family or family-like group, a house generates specific relationships and practices that have their own palette of motifs, tones, textures, and even smells. A house also evokes a special discourse of words, symbols, and meanings that have their own logic of corporateness that generates a diffuse, enduring solidarity.[9] Thus, as J. Macgregor Wise advises, a "house" creates a space of comfort via "the arrangement of objects, practices, feelings, and affects," including memories.[10] If a home entails an entire semiotic domain of enunciated meanings and signifiers, then the Japanese American home also entails the unspoken but just as powerful kinesic cues dispensed in face-to-face interactions within the immediate family—physical movements, what Bourdieu terms *hexis*—that are significant communicators in a high-context cultural setting.[11] In terms of Rawitsch's account, what does this trifocal perspective reveal about the intricacies of the pre-war Japanese American house and household?

THE PHYSICAL DIMENSIONS OF THE HOME

Given the land as the territorial base on which the Harada House stands, one might ask about the physicality of the home. Here, Rawitsch gives us many more details than any other available account. Although the physical arrangement of the early Japanese American home has been mentioned by ethnographers such as John Embree and authors covering the Issei experience such as the Japanese journalist Kazuo Ito, no one has told readers as much about the house of their subjects as has Rawitsch.[12]

Rawitsch, in *The House on Lemon Street*, details the contents of the Harada House with references to lists and descriptions of certain furniture and family possessions. These observations will certainly be expanded by the staff of the Riverside Metropolitan Museum. Information about the precise configurations of objects within rooms, and their specific use by family members, will indicate how the Haradas as individuals and as a group were tied to the neighborhood, the city, and the world beyond. Similarly, Rawitsch's description of the household in terms of the uses of living and dining rooms, bedrooms and kitchen, is significant and will bear intensive examination. Whether the habit of a "packrat" or not, Sumi Harada's propensity for preserving things will bear evidence of more subtle correlations between the rooms, their contents, and early Japanese American domestic practices.[13]

Rawitsch's attention to the yard, front and back, also reveals key characteristics of Issei interests and skills. Flowers, from an aesthetic point of view, are part of this, as is the tiny Harada House fishpond with its "struggling goldfish" (*koi*, or Japanese carp, in a more affluent setting). For Issei who farmed as part of their livelihood, fresh fruit and vegetables were meticulously grown and provided welcome supplements to the meat and other dishes at the dinner table. A home garden, however small, required skill to create—a literal display of knowledge and ability—but tending a garden was also a practical and healthful hobby.

THE MEANING/FEELINGS OF A HOME

Jukichi and Ken's feelings about a home follow from these foundations, material and legal. The Harada House is intimately tied to a Jeffersonian sense of self-determination; "independence" in the sense that evolving an individuated self, who can make autonomous decisions, is engendered by owning one's own space.

Because they were a married couple, home for the first-generation Haradas entailed shelter and nurturing. It was the ideal place to start a family and raise children. Concomitantly, in terms of its location, a home would be ideal if it were near a good public school, as well as close to the family's preferred place of worship. Shelter and nurture were something that the Haradas could then offer kin and kith. The meaning of "home" encompasses the idea of comfort and also of well-being and security. Within the Harada House these offerings were extended most directly to immediate family, but also to extended family and to those included in family, such as Roy Hashimura (the Haradas' adopted son), coworkers in the Harada family businesses, neighbors, and significant others.

At a material level, the house also represents economic security. This is why, with the Haradas' success and prosperity, Rawitsch observes that, as time passed and family life stabilized, the Harada House felt more and more like home. Ownership for Issei entailed responsibility. Jukichi took some of his business profits and repaired, renovated, and, when possible, expanded his house. In the process of ownership, improvement, and investment, the house becomes a home—an integral setting for the growth and nurturing of the Harada family. The Harada House sheltered and also provided sanctity in a spiritual sense. Similarly, the home came to represent the Harada family's achievements, its prosperity, and eventually its honor. The articulation of property and honor takes its broadest form especially through tangible threats and the need to secure the home against them. War is the ultimate instance of threat, and second-generation Harada children willingly joined the armed forces to defend and secure their personal home but also to defend and secure their country as a whole.

The last meaning of home to explore here is tied to generational succession and death. Ken and Jukichi both passed away in camp, far from Riverside and the Harada House. Their ultimate return to the Riverside cemetery is described as a final homecoming. That Riverside, the site of their family residence, became Ken and Jukichi's final resting place reaffirms the spiritual if not holy dimension of the Harada House. In sum, for Jukichi and Ken, as for Sumi, a real home had meaning beyond money, and so it really should not be, and perhaps cannot be, sold to another. In this light, readers should note that Executive Order 9066, which allowed the forced removal of all persons of Japanese ancestry from the West Coast, was a particularly horrific experience for the Haradas and their compatriots, a fact that I will return to.

THE MATERIAL FUNCTIONS OF A HOME

The functions of, as well as practices in, a home are squarely tied to the notion of time and duration. Again, Rawitsch's meticulous history and the museum curators' careful cataloging of the Harada House and its family collection should bear much fruit for anyone who wants to ponder these themes in terms of historically and culturally framed data sets.

The House on Lemon Street informs us how ideals shape and drive the ways that the Issei-Nisei house was conceptualized and used. As a shelter for children and for the family, a home is set up in such a way as to promote their vitality, health, and well-being. This, of course, would be as much in a physical sense as it would be in terms of a psychological and emotional sense. Specialized rooms in the house played their own roles. What the family called the "*kamitoku* room" provided a space for personal grooming. Concomitantly, the kitchen and dining room were the sites for the preparation and presentation of food. But functions are not always unique and discrete: family interactions intersected with simple nourishment in these same rooms.

In terms of the Issei family, the household was also a central unit of production and consumption. The Haradas' businesses—the Washington Restaurant, the different rooming houses, and later rental properties—were intimately tied to family labor, certainly Ken's in the beginning. Then, as the children got older, each one had to assume certain responsibilities to ensure that the businesses remained operational and made some profit. So the function of a house included capital and labor and meant that the household itself was necessary to leverage different kinds of resources needed to promote economic security.

This economic functionality of the household is exemplified in the Haradas' own housing trajectory. Their initial living space was rented. To generate some extra income, however, early on, the Haradas were willing to take on roomers in whatever extra space they could free up. This was a relatively painless way to accumulate capital, although transient roomers, often unmarried men, certainly impinged on family privacy and must have eaten at the edges of a cultural sensibility that routinely differentiates family from others, and the inside (*uchi*) from the outside (*soto*).[14]

The house and the land it rests on function as a staging ground from which to access other "limited goods" represented in the local neighborhood; proximity to schools, churches, and other nearby institutional resources such as businesses can all factor in here. It is worth mentioning another functional dimension, even if it is subtle in the Harada family's case. The household is a foundation for engagement, in the sense of extending succor and aid to extended kin and kith. The most readily observable moment, when this dimension of the Harada House becomes clear, is the time of "resettlement," or Japanese Americans' post-war return to the larger society following their imprisonment in War Relocation Authority camps. Sumi Harada threw open the Harada home to her homeless compatriots. She did not even charge her roomers rent because she fully understood and appreciated the depth of their need for a home, however temporary.

THE TEMPORAL DIMENSIONS OF A HOME

The set of practices that evolve in any home is closely related to its imagined functions. From Rawitsch's account it is clear that the Harada House served as a medium for the inculcation of Japanese American culture in terms of language, customs, tastes, and rituals. From various vignettes, folklore was a part of this too. Rawitsch details how the Haradas' home was the place where Jukichi and Ken Harada took the time to talk to, teach, and interact with their children, imparting profound lessons of morality and comportment. The Harada home was the staging ground for rituals, heavily laden with symbols, marking important values and stages in the life cycle. Readers will note how Boys' Day, the Fourth of July, Christmas, other holidays, festive family gatherings, and meals marked these stages. Visiting the cemetery, cleaning the graves of the ancestors, and remembering them and thus their sacrifices are other key family ceremonies.

The house and home have their unique temporal frames, and these crisscross each other in patterned ways in the Haradas' case. Again, since there was so much struggle and risk for Jukichi and Ken—because of their status as aliens ineligible for naturalization—to find and make a real home for their family, the precious nature of the home, to be guarded and defended at all costs, is something that pervades the ethos of the Harada House for its entire history.

Through the challenges of the Great Depression, consolidation is another moment in the temporal duration of the Haradas' house. As the family experienced economic stability and upward mobility, the two generations acculturated, the Nisei gradually entered the mainstream, albeit in their own fashion, and eventually the children left their family of orientation.

The specific historical circumstances of the Japanese American experience during the 1940s mark the ethnic community's trajectory, individually and collectively, and this certainly encompasses houses and homes like the Haradas'. "Guilt by reason of race" created a huge interruption and breach in people's lives. For 110,000 persons, the forced removal from homes and neighborhoods was a painful experience of rejection and stigmatization. Although some were able to recreate a semblance of home in confinement, that was short-lived. From 1943 to 1946, Japanese Americans who returned to the larger society were often scattered from their pre-war families and communities. Upon returning to pre-war homes, if even possible, things were never quite the same. Thus, the cycle of generations—cutting of umbilical cords or apron strings, the "letting go" that occurs as children split off and move on—was a markedly different process within the Japanese American community. Many family members were subject, depending on when they left camp, to different periods of confinement. Thus, to gain release, individuals dispersed before families had a chance to consider reunification as a group.

The broad features of mass incarceration and their impact on the Japanese American family are fairly well-known. At the least, the impact involved an initial violation, as FBI raids and searches were seen as an attack on honor, as well as a violation of the sanctity of the home itself. Although many must have felt a strong need to defend their property and home, as did the Haradas, many were without the means to do so. Indeed, many Japanese Americans were only renters. Because of Executive Order 9066, more than 110,000 persons of Japanese ancestry were forced to leave their neighborhoods and homes, taking with them only what they could carry. They found themselves for approximately six months in army-run Wartime Civil Control Administration "assembly centers" and then for one to three years in more permanent War Relocation Authority camps. Normal family cohesion and rituals were shattered, and although some practices were improvised to take their place, these were piecemeal at best.

For those who engaged in politics, camp life deteriorated into a setting of terror. Pro- and anti-American factions battled each other for the hearts and minds of the prisoners; some militants were beaten, others were jailed. Still others, like Jukichi and Ken, did not survive the camp experience. Ill and infirm Issei, Nisei, and Sansei died in camp. We will never know exactly how many deaths were hastened by the pressures and poor conditions people had to endure. For at least some, the resettlement period, roughly 1943 to perhaps 1955, was a second trauma, sometimes as hurtful as camp itself.[15] Thus, we will also never be able to fully calibrate the time it took people to return home or search anew for an authentic home.

The domestic cycle ends, inevitably, in decline and death. In this case, one thing that differentiates some families is the notion of if and how they will be remembered by subsequent generations. Here, the Harada House and the Harada family story take a different turn than most of the Issei-Nisei households that were formed in this country. It is clear that the Harada House was a generative site, evoking feelings of respect, duty, obligation, and achievement in its resident family, and now in us as an audience. Many of the activities occurring in this house were practical in nature, but as time passes and the family members transition into their own lives and families in the United States of America, often in distant communities, the house evokes memories of the home that inspired generative practices that we can examine retrospectively and untangle, if only to appreciate their depth and complexity.

FUTURE ONTOLOGIES

In *The House on Lemon Street*, the history Mark Rawitsch presents shows the Harada House's temporal dynamic as it evolved from an imagined site of aspirations to a physical site that was inhabited and energized. Routines, habits, and rituals were enacted in its rooms and yards. Eventually, and in the end, the Harada House became a National Historic Landmark but also a physical structure depopulated in terms of living family members. With the house and family physical objects still intact, now enhanced by the archival and textual materials collected by the Riverside Metropolitan Museum, there is great potential for us to see with clarity how this house, and houses in general, were built layer upon layer of objects, bodies, languages, practices, rituals, values, opinions, and a panoply of feelings and emotional textures. In this fashion a house creates a stable base "to launch beginnings." As such, a house is a critical dimension of human culture.

Even as we can see the seemingly universal dimensions of the Harada House story, it is very clear from *The House on Lemon Street* that there is a great deal of historical specificity that makes the early Japanese American experience (and houses) in the United States distinctive from other ethnic or mainstream histories (and houses).

In this sense, Jukichi Harada's independence and his willingness to engage in whatever battles were necessary to prevail in his quest for land and home ownership give us the historical and legal contexts to interpret what Rawitsch foregrounds as the American Dream. The pre-war American Dream of the Issei was highly shaped by the conditions that generation of Asian immigrants faced in their American journey. Much more than the simple bourgeois attainment of middle-class security, possession of a house, storefront, or farm acreage was critically important but also subversive in its own way. These acquisitions, along with the long-cherished dream of naturalized US citizenship, were the Issei's generational assertion that they were equal to other immigrants who had come to these shores seeking new opportunities—despite long-standing European and Euro-American insistence that Asians were unassimilable, inferior, and not the materials out of which upstanding American citizens could be made. The American Dream fashioned by the Issei was not the American Dream that Sansei, or even Nisei after the war, envisioned or aspired to. Rawitsch's account shows us that a house's meaning, including its larger political significance, shifts with the historical times.

An indelible feature of Japanese American history that shaped any historical consideration of a given individual's or family's house had to do with Executive Order 9066 and the resulting experience of mass removal, mass incarceration, and resettlement. There is little to recapitulate here, other than to note that the walls and contents of the Harada House itself will long bear witness to the shock and trauma on those persons of Japanese ancestry who were unfortunate enough to live on the West Coast in the 1940s.

In sum, from Mark Rawitsch's careful history we leave with an understanding that a house is a site that has a form, contents, members, functions, feelings, cycles, aesthetics, and duration, all of which amount to a nexus of creative possibilities. As J. Macgregor Wise advises us, the house also entails a nexus of possible boundaries, limitations, and constraints. Knowing all of these will better allow us to understand the house in all of its layers and intricacies. Here, Rawitsch leaves us with one more issue that is subtly adumbrated in his text.

Given her gender and circumstances, Sumi Harada became the person who stayed in the Harada House, returning after the war to preserve her inheritance. Her life became encompassed in and by the Harada House as a site for memories and as a symbol of her family, as well as her dedication to the family. After the war, and increasingly as the years went by, Sumi lived in limited spaces of the house. She dedicated most areas and rooms to preserving its contents, as if these objects would somehow bear witness to the struggles, travails, and achievements of her parents and siblings.

Around the time that the preservation of the landmark Harada House became an issue, as various downtown redevelopment projects threatened its very existence, Mark Rawitsch entered the scene as the family's and house's historian and documentarian. In the process, the Harada House became first a city and then a national landmark. Its meanings expanded exponentially as the Harada House became a physical focus, tying the past and present, the seemingly very particular to the local and the national. The Harada House is a mnemonic serving as a vehicle to talk about complicated but also possibly hidden feelings of history and family, as Sumi Harada so aptly put it, hidden feelings that Japanese American writers continue to hear and tap as part of the ongoing dynamic within post-war families. Sumi's sacrifices, in other words, are an inherent part of the Harada House. Perhaps the ultimate gift it proffers is one question that we must ask, even though we can't really answer it: At what price was the gift given?

It is our hope that the Harada House will be as fascinating to everyone who sees or hears of it as it has been for us. It is a gift that Jukichi and Ken Harada offered to their children, and that Sumi Harada and the Harada family now offer to all of us.

LANE RYO HIRABAYASHI

George and Sakaye Aratani Professor in
Japanese American Incarceration, Redress, and Community,
Asian American Studies
University of California, Los Angeles

NOTES

CHAPTER 1: HERE IS YOUR CHANCE

1. Quotation from advertisement, *Riverside Daily Press*, December 8, 1915 (Noble's listing ran December 8–15, 1915); Sumi Harada in discussion with Mark Rawitsch, January 10, 1977; "In the Superior Court of the State of California in and for the County of Riverside, *The People of the State of California, Plaintiff vs. Jukirchi [sic] Harada, Defendant*," Reporter's Transcript, Case 7751, California Attorney General Records, California State Archives, Sacramento (hereafter referred to as Reporter's Transcript); "California Deaths, 1940–1997, Frank Colfax Noble," Ancestry.com, http://vitals.rootsweb.ancestry .com/ca/death/search.cgi (accessed March 20, 2008); "Minor Children of Japanese Purchase Residence," *Riverside Enterprise*, December 23, 1915.

2. Thomas W. Patterson, *A Colony for California: Riverside's First Hundred Years* (Riverside, CA: Press-Enterprise Company, 1971), 440; "Individual Record," June 27, 1942, United States War Relocation Authority (hereafter referred to as WRA), Sumi Harada File.

3. Quotations from Reporter's Transcript, testimony of J. Harada, 88, 13; Reporter's Transcript, testimony of J. Harada, 9, 12–15, 87–88, 92; testimony of F. C. Noble, 104, 107–108; "Japanese Buy on Lemon St.," *Riverside Daily Press*, December 23, 1915; "Minor Children of Japanese Purchase Residence," *Riverside Enterprise*, December 23, 1915. According to city directories, the Gunnersons lived at 196 North Street in Riverside. City directories also indicate that the last resident of the Lemon Street house prior to

the Harada purchase was Sarah Smith. The exact date of the construction of 356 Lemon Street is unknown but has been estimated as 1884. The earliest known photograph of the house appeared in the *Los Angeles Examiner* on January 5, 1916, and shows the house prior to the alterations of 1916. A second newspaper photograph in the *Los Angeles Times*, on October 22, 1916, shows the house after the Haradas' alterations had been completed.

4. Quotation from Reporter's Transcript, testimony of F. C. Noble, 110.

5. Quotations from "Minor Children of Japanese Purchase Residence," *Riverside Enterprise*, December 23, 1915; "Land Titles to Children; Jap Plan to Evade Law on Aliens," *Los Angeles Examiner*, December 25, 1915; Reporter's Transcript, testimony of J. Van de Grift, 69.

CHAPTER 2: THE SCHOOLTEACHER AND
THE SAMURAI'S DAUGHTER

1. Indo Family Koseki Records (hereafter referred to as Indo Koseki), Aichi Prefecture, Japan, obtained in Aichi by Valerie Harada and translated by Kayo Kaname Levenson, Willits, California, and Takashi Oda, office of the Consulate General of Japan, San Francisco, California, 2005; Kouhei Okuda, Public Relations, Kariya City Hall, Kariya, Aichi, Japan, translated by Kaori Mizoguchi, e-mail messages to Mark Rawitsch, August 7, 9, 26, and September 21, 2006; "Individual Record," September 11, 1942, WRA, Ken Harada File; Harada Family Koseki Records (hereafter referred to as Harada Koseki), Aichi Prefecture, Japan, obtained in Aichi by Valerie Harada and translated by Kayo Kaname Levenson, Willits, California, and Takashi Oda, office of the Consulate General of Japan, San Francisco, California, 2005 ; "Individual Record," September 12, 1942, WRA, Shiashi Harry [Jukichi] Harada File; Jiromaru Akira, Nagoya University Library, e-mail message to Mark Rawitsch, January 17, 2007. Jiromaru Akira, in an e-mail message to Mark Rawitsch, December 21, 2006, adds, according to the Aichi Prefectural Archives, "There was a teacher named Harada Takanori at school of Ogawa area, Anjo from 1889 (Meiji 22) to 1906 (Meiji 39)." The birthplace of Jukichi Harada has not yet been determined. Sumi Harada told Mark Rawitsch that her father was born in Ogawa in Aichi prefecture, but there is more than one community area called "Ogawa" in Aichi. Tadao Harada's gravestone at Olivewood Cemetery has several inscriptions written in Japanese, among them a reference that translates as "Aichi-ken Hekikai-Gun Sakurai-Mura aza Ogawa," another possible indication of the Haradas' community origins in Aichi.

2. Mark E. Lincicome, *Principle, Praxis, and the Politics of Educational Reform in Meiji Japan* (Honolulu: University of Hawaii Press, 1995), 1–3, 9–17; E. Patricia Tsurumi, "Meiji Primary School Language and Ethics Textbooks: Old Values for a New Society?" *Modern Asian Studies* 8, no. 2 (1974): 247–261; Ann Waswo, *Modern Japanese Society 1868–1994* (Oxford: Oxford University Press, 1996), 29–30.

3. "Individual Record," November 7, 1942, WRA, Shiashi Harry [Jukichi] Harada File; Jiromaru Akira, e-mail messages to Mark Rawitsch, November 22, 27, December 7, 11, 2006; "Alumni Association List," Aichi University of Education Library; [teaching assignments], Aichi Prefecture Library, Aichiken Koho, Official Gazette of Aichi Prefecture, and Aichi Kyoiku Zasshi.

4. "Individual Record," September 11, 1942; "Clinical Record, Family and Personal History" (various dates); "Individual Record," November 7, 1942, WRA, Ken Harada File; Harada Koseki and Indo Koseki.

5. Jiromaru Akira, e-mail message to Mark Rawitsch, December 21, 2006.

6. Quotations from Mine Harada Kido, interview by Mark Rawitsch, January 17, 1982; Clark Harada, interview by Mark Rawitsch, January 31, 1977. Sumi Harada in discussion with Mark Rawitsch, January 10, 1977; Jiromaru Akira, e-mail message to Mark Rawitsch, January 17, 2007. Harada-sensei may have even left his second teaching job shortly after it began, but records in Japan suggest that since no resignation document is on file, it is possible that Harada never began his second assignment at the school in Anjo.

7. Tsutsui Tadashi, Diplomatic Record Office of the Ministry of Foreign Affairs of Japan, Harada Jukichi Passport Record, 1898, microfilm reel #5, personal communication with Mark Rawitsch, 2007; Immigration Document #68811, Harada Family Archival Collection, Riverside Metropolitan Museum.

8. Robert Pendleton and Patrick McSherry, "The U.S. Revenue Cutter Service in the Spanish American War, Spanish American War Centennial," http://www.spanamwar.com/USRCS.htm (accessed December 10, 2007); "Muster Roll of the Officers and Crew of the United States Steamer Grant for the Month of July 1898," National Archives; Harada Koseki; see also Jukichi Harada, Personal History Notes, circa 1940, Harada Family Archival Collection, for a brief reference to the *Pensacola*.

9. Quotations from "USS *Solace* Log," Volume 5, January 1–March 6, 1901; Jukichi Harada, Personal History Notes; Mine Harada Kido, letter to Mark Rawitsch, February 24, 1977. Jukichi Harada, Personal History Notes; "Muster Roll of the USS *Solace*," December 1900, March 1901; "USS *Solace* Log," Volume 5, January 1–March 6, 1901, Volume 6, March 7–10, 1901; "USS *Solace*, Record of the Miscellaneous Events of the Day," February 24, 1901, March 4, 1901; "American Casualties," *New York Times*, July 23, 1900; Mark C. Mollan, Archivist, Old Navy/Maritime, National Archives and Records Administration, e-mail message to Mark Rawitsch, November 2, 2006.

10. Jukichi Harada, Personal History Notes; Immigration Document #68811, Harada Family Archival Collection; William Greene, National Archives and Records Service, Pacific Region, e-mail messages to Mark Rawitsch, November 8, 22, 2006; *The Baptist Missionary Magazine* (August 1903): 885; "California Passenger and Crew Lists, 1893–1957, *Gaelic*," Ancestry.com, June 18, 1903, www.ancestry.com (accessed May 8, 2009).

11. Harada Koseki; "List or Manifest of Alien Passengers for the U.S. Immigration Officer at Port of Arrival, S.S. *Doric*, October 1904," National Archives; Bill Hosokawa, *Nisei: The Quiet Americans, Rev. Ed.* (Boulder: University Press of Colorado, 2002), 120; Jukichi Harada, Personal History Notes; Hosokawa, *Nisei*, 52, 120–121; "California Passenger and Crew Lists, 1893–1957, *Gaelic*, 18 June 1903," www.ancestry.com (accessed May 8, 2009); Jukichi Harada, "Application for Reentry," Harada Family Archival Collection.

12. Quotations from "Before Board of Special Inquiry, Port of San Francisco, Cal., October 27, 1904, #455," National Archives.

13. Quotation from Jukichi Harada, Personal History Notes. Sumi Harada in discussion with Mark Rawitsch, January 10, 1977; Dr. Harold Harada, interview by Mark

Rawitsch, July 23, 2000; Harry W. Lawton, "Chronological History of Chinese Pioneers in Riverside and the Southern California Citrus Belt," in *Wong Ho Leun: An American Chinatown*, Vol. 1: *History* (San Diego: The Great Basin Foundation, 1987), 120–121.

14. Quotation from Rosalind Uno, e-mail message to Mark Rawitsch, August 26, 2006.

15. Immigration Document #18776; Canadian Pacific Railway Co. Ticket #13695, Steamer *Tartar*, July 15, 1905; Jukichi Harada, Personal History Notes; "Canadian Pacific's New Steamer Line," *New York Times*, October 3, 1898; "Canadian Passenger Lists, 1865–1935, *Princess Victoria*," August 4, 1905, Ancestry.com, www.ancestry.com (accessed May 8, 2009).

CHAPTER 3: HERE TO STAY

1. Roger Daniels, *The Politics of Prejudice: The Anti-Japanese Movement in California and the Struggle for Japanese Exclusion* (Glouster, MA: Peter Smith, 1966), 9; Harry Kitano, *Japanese Americans: The Evolution of a Subculture* (Englewood Cliffs, NJ: Prentice-Hall, 1969), 16, 55, 67, 76, 91, 134. Kitano notes, "[T]he most visible Japanese scars were from legal decisions" (p. 26). See also Milton R. Konvitz, *The Alien and the Asiatic in American Law* (Ithaca, NY: Cornell University Press, 1946), and Frank Chuman, *The Bamboo People: The Law and Japanese Americans* (Del Mar, CA: Publisher's Inc., 1976).

2. Daniels, *Politics of Prejudice*, 19, vi; Kitano, *Japanese Americans*, 14–15. For a comprehensive story of California's early development and what came to be known on the West Coast and elsewhere as the California Dream, see the several works by Dr. Kevin Starr, including *Americans and the California Dream* (Oxford: Oxford University Press, 1973); *Inventing the Dream: California through the Progressive Era* (Oxford: Oxford University Press, 1985); and *Material Dreams: Southern California through the 1920s* (Oxford: Oxford University Press, 1990).

3. Kitano, *Japanese Americans*, 10–13; Daniels, *Politics of Prejudice*, 2–3; Hosokawa, *Nisei*, 38; W. G. Beasley, *The Modern History of Japan* (New York: Harcourt School, 1963), 105–113; Daniels, *Politics of Prejudice*, 4, 7–9; Bradford Smith, *Americans from Japan* (Philadelphia: Lippincott, 1948), 202; Japanese Association of the Pacific Northwest, *Japanese Immigration: Exposition of Its Real Status* (Seattle: Japanese Association of the Pacific Northwest, 1907), 5.

4. Daniels, *Politics of Prejudice*, 3–15; Kitano, *Japanese Americans*, 3, 10, 57, 62; Hosokawa, *Nisei*, 45.

5. Daniels, *Politics of Prejudice*, 6, 13, 44; Kitano, *Japanese Americans*, 62; Chuman, *Bamboo People*, 36.

6. Quotation from Kitano, *Japanese Americans*, 61. Daniels, *Politics of Prejudice*, 7, 13–14; Kitano, *Japanese Americans*, 61–63.

7. Quotation from "Rejoices at the Fall of Schmitz in 'Frisco; Says Jap Trouble Is Only Labor Question," *Boston Sunday Herald*, June 16, 1907, "Virtual Museum of the City of San Francisco," http://www.sfmuseum.org/conflag/phelan.html (accessed May 25, 2009).

8. Quotation cited by Kitano, *Japanese Americans*, 16 (without reference to original title or date).

9. Chuman, *Bamboo People*, 8; Daniels, *Politics of Prejudice*, 16–18.

10. Patterson, *Colony*, 55, 114–116; Lawton, "Chronological History," 67–70.

11. Quotation cited by Chuman, *Bamboo People*, 9. Daniels, *Politics of Prejudice*, 18. Quotation from Chuman, *Bamboo People*, 10. Konvitz, *Alien and the Asiatic*, 2, 44; Carey McWilliams, cited by Konvitz, *Alien and the Asiatic*, 12.

12. Quotations cited by Konvitz, *Alien and the Asiatic*, 108; Chuman, *Bamboo People*, 6. Konvitz, *Alien and the Asiatic*, 108; Chuman, *Bamboo People*, 66, 183; Daniels, *Politics of Prejudice*, 50–51.

13. Quotation from Konvitz, *Alien and the Asiatic*, 148. Konvitz, *Alien and the Asiatic*, 153–154.

14. Quotations and reference from Daniels, *Politics of Prejudice*, 65–66.

15. Ibid., vi, 106.

16. Ibid., 24, 27–29, 34; Chuman, *Bamboo People*, 23–24.

17. Daniels, *Politics of Prejudice*, 31, 36, 69–70, 41–44; Chuman, *Bamboo People*, 28–29.

18. Quotation from Daniels, *Politics of Prejudice*, 48. Chuman, *Bamboo People*, 41–42. Quotation of Grove L. Johnson cited in Franklin Hichborn, *Story of the Session of the California Legislature of 1909* (San Francisco: Press of the James H. Barry Co., 1909), 206–207n90.

19. 1910 Republican Slate Platform quotation from Franklin Hichborn, *Story of the Session of the California Legislature of 1911* (San Francisco: Press of the James H. Barry Co., 1911), xxiv.

20. Chuman, *Bamboo People*, 42, 48; Daniels, *Politics of Prejudice*, 48–49; Walton Bean, *California: An Interpretive History* (New York: McGraw-Hill, 1978), 275–279; Daniels, *Politics of Prejudice*, 50. Quotation from Supreme Court of the United States, *Oyama v. California*, 332 U.S. 633 (1948), 11.

21. Konvitz, *Alien and the Asiatic*, 155–156; Daniels, *Politics of Prejudice*, 51. Daniels notes, "Many of the earlier antialien land bills were aimed at foreign corporations rather than individuals" (132n). Chuman, *Bamboo People*, 46–47; Kitano, *Japanese Americans*, 17.

22. Chuman, *Bamboo People*, 47; Daniels, *Politics of Prejudice*, 27, 58, 61–62; see also Konvitz, *Alien and the Asiatic*, 159, for the Japanese reaction to the passage of the 1913 California law.

23. Teruko Okada Kachi, *The Treaty of 1911 and the Immigration and Alien Land Law Issue between the United States and Japan, 1911–1913* (New York: Arno Press, 1978), 224n. See also Daniels, *Politics of Prejudice*, 48, 51–57; John Modell, *The Economics and Politics of Racial Accommodation: The Japanese of Los Angeles, 1900–1942* (Urbana: University of Illinois Press, 1977), 38; Kachi, *Treaty of 1911*, 229; Chuman, *Bamboo People*, 47, 49; Daniels, *Politics of Prejudice*, 49, 61.

24. Daniels, *Politics of Prejudice*, 61–62; Audrie Girdner and Anne Loftis, *The Great Betrayal: The Evacuation of the Japanese-Americans during World War II* (London: Macmillan, 1969), 59; Chuman, *Bamboo People*, 46–51; Konvitz, *Alien and the Asiatic*, 159. See also Chuman, *Bamboo People*, 49, for information about the progressives and "race."

25. Quotation from Daniels, *Politics of Prejudice*, 82. Raymond Leslie Buell, "The Development of the Anti-Japanese Agitation in the United States," *Political Science Quarterly*

38 (March 1923): 66; see also vol. 37 (December 1922): 605–638 (Buell mentions the *Harada* case briefly); Daniels, *Politics of Prejudice*, 88, 63.

26. Quotations from "Brown Yankee Potato Boss," *Los Angeles Times*, November 28, 1909.

27. Chuman, *Bamboo People*, 76; see also Kitano, *Japanese Americans*, 30. Mine Harada Kido, letter to Mark Rawitsch, March 21, 1977, noted: "Papa bought property in 1911 . . . In those days aliens could buy land. I think 1912 was the last year. I think the Fujimotos still own the property in Riverside that their alien father bought in his own name in 1912." Later examples of the difficulties encountered by Japanese in search of improved housing can also be found in Monica Sone, *Nisei Daughter* (Boston: Little, Brown, 1953), 111–116, and Daniel Okimoto, *American in Disguise* (New York: Walker/Weatherhill, 1971), 61–62. Sone's example dates from before World War II, Okimoto's from circa 1954. Quotations from Daniels, *Politics of Prejudice*, 10. Daniels also asks, "If even a millionaire had problems finding a home, what must it have been like for his less prosperous compatriots?" See also "Five Views: An Ethnic Historic Site Survey for California, Japanese Americans in California," California Department of Parks and Recreation, Office of Historic Preservation, National Park Service, December 1988, http://www.nps.gov/history/history/online_books/5views/5views.htm (accessed March 15, 2009).

28. Quotation from Hiram Johnson letter to Charles Clifford Tinckler, February 12, 1917, BANC MSS C-B 581, Hiram Johnson Papers, Bancroft Library, University of California, Berkeley.

29. Quotation of U. S. Webb cited in Chuman, *Bamboo People*, 48.

30. Quotations from Reporter's Transcript, remarks of A. A. Adair and testimony of Cora Fletcher, 51.

CHAPTER 4: IN THE SHADOW OF THE MISSION INN

1. John W. North, "A Colony for California," March 17, 1870, cited in Patterson, *Colony*, 19. See also Patterson, *Colony*, 21–29, 33–39.

2. Quotation from Patterson, *Colony*, 63. Patterson, *Colony*, 32, 44–48, 76, 187, 213.

3. Patterson, *Colony*, 140–153; Lawton, "Riverside's First Chinatown and the Boom of the Eighties," in Lawton, *Wong Ho Leun*, 1–22; and "Chronological History," 62.

4. Quotation from Patterson, *Colony*, 194. Patterson, *Colony*, 194–197.

5. Quotation from Lawton, "First Chinatown," 75. Lawton, "First Chinatown," 1–22.

6. Quotations from Lawton, "First Chinatown," 9, 39.

7. Quotations from Patterson, *Colony*, 194, 166.

8. Quotation from Lawton, "Chronological History," 80. Quotation of the Reverend George H. Deere, sermon of March 7, 1886, George H. Deere, *Autobiography by George H. Deere, D.D., Pastor Emeritus of All Souls Universalist Church, Riverside, California* (Riverside, CA: Press Printing, 1908), cited in Shelly Raven, "Red Paper and Varnished Ducks: Subjective Images of Riverside's Chinatown," in Lawton, *Wong Ho Leun*, 221–224. See Lawton, "First Chinatown," 1–22, 39, 48–49, and "Chronological History," 68, 78–80.

9. Lawton, "First Chinatown," 1–22, 48–49, and "Chronological History," 68, 78–81.

10. Patterson, *Colony*, 42–51, 155–165, 185–186, 205, 197, 75, 167–178.

11. Quotations from Patterson, *Colony*, 231, 206. Ingersol quoted in Patterson, *Colony*, 206. Patterson, *Colony*, 231, 206; H. Vincent Moses and Brenda Buller Focht, *Life in Little Gom-Benn: Chinese Immigrant Society in Riverside, 1885–1930* (Riverside, CA: Riverside Museum Press, 1991), n.p.

12. Quotations from Esther Klotz, *The Mission Inn: Its History and Artifacts* (Riverside, CA: Rubidoux Printing, 1981), 2; Patterson, *Colony*, 240. Klotz, *Mission Inn*, 2–5.

13. Quotation from Patterson, *Colony*, 239. Patterson, *Colony*, 239–244; Klotz, *Mission Inn*, 13–16.

14. Quotations and information from "Artistic, Stately, Beautiful as an Old Greek Temple," *Riverside Enterprise*, May 7, 1903; "Riverside's Enthusiasm," *Los Angeles Times*, May 8, 1903. See also "Contents of Casket in Corner Stone of the Riverside County Courthouse," May 1903, Riverside County Courthouse lobby exhibition, 2009.

15. Quotation from Frank A. Miller letter to Dr. Herbert Priestly, January 30, 1935, fF869 R6 M3, collection of material relating to Riverside and the Mission Inn, Bancroft Library, University of California, Berkeley.

16. Quotation from Patterson, *Colony*, 240.

17. Quotation from Kitano, *Japanese Americans*, 143. See Morrison G. Wong, "The Japanese in Riverside, 1890–1945: A Special Case in Race Relations" (PhD diss., University of California, Riverside, 1977); Thomas W. Patterson, "A 1905 Episode Suggests Some Ambiguities in How Riverside Once Treated Its Japanese," *Riverside Press-Enterprise*, July 8, 1979; Mark H. Rawitsch, "Japanese American Relocation: Educational Patterns and Community Receptivity" (seminar paper, University of California, Riverside, June 4, 1976). See Japanese Americans in Riverside Research Project, University of California, Riverside (hereafter referred to as JARRP).

18. Quotation from Moses and Focht, *Life in Little Gom-Benn*, n.p. Lawton, "Chronological History," 111–113. Quotation from *Pacific Rural Press* cited in Lawton, "Chronological History," 112–113.

19. Wong, "Japanese in Riverside," 19–20. Roy Ito cited in Patterson, *Colony*, 197.

20. Quotation from "Social Activity of Casa Blanca Area," *Riverside Daily Press*, December 24, 1906. Wong, "Japanese in Riverside," 19; J. Kumamoto, "Museum Lecture Series; Ethnic Minorities in Riverside," n.d., Riverside Metropolitan Museum, Riverside, in Harada Family Archival Collection; Edward K. Strong Jr., *The Second-Generation Japanese Problem* (Stanford, CA: Stanford University Press, 1934), 272–273. Nearby Redlands reported the next largest group, consisting of only 175 Japanese citrus workers; "Schmitz Ready to Die to Check Japanese," *Riverside Daily Press*, December 24, 1906.

21. Wong, "Japanese in Riverside," 27, 40, 117–118 (table 7-1); Klotz, *Mission Inn*, 40; Patterson, "A 1905 Episode"; Mine Harada Kido, interview by Mark Rawitsch, January 17, 1982; Martha Iseda, interview by Mark Rawitsch, May 9, 1977; Edwin C. Hiroto, interview with JARRP, January 26, 1976, 9; Frank T. Shintani, interview with JARRP, April 19, 1975, 4; "Asian American Riverside," University of California, Riverside, http://aar.ucr.edu (accessed March 21, 2009); Emanuel E. Parker, "Historic Site Designation Asked for Grave of Japanese-American," *Riverside Press-Enterprise*, April 16, 1980; Patterson, "A 1905 Episode"; Patterson, "Japanese in Riverside Area: New Mystery about Old Tragedy," *Riverside Press-Enterprise*, February 21, 1971; Kaneko Family Plot, Ulysses Kaneko tombstone, Olivewood Cemetery, Riverside; Sumi Harada, interview by Mark

Rawitsch, February 24, 1982; Mine Harada Kido, interview by Mark Rawitsch, January 17, 1982; Dr. Harold Harada, interview by Mark Rawitsch, July 22, 2000.

22. Patterson, *Colony*, 194–197; Patricia Riddell and Leslie Bacha, "Riverside's Chinatown: A Study of the Past" (seminar paper, University of California, Riverside, June 13, 1974), 6, 21; Wong, "Japanese in Riverside," 25 (table 2-2), 27–28 (figures 2-2, 2-3), 35; Masami Muramoto, interview with JARRP, n.d., 4, 15; Sho Takeda, interview with JARRP, February 26, 1975, 1, 7; H. Yashida, interview with JARRP, n.d., 13; Edwin C. Hiroto, interview with JARRP, January 26, 1976, 9.

23. Quotations from Lawton, "Chronological History," 81, 105, 110. Lawton, "First Chinatown," 51, and "Chronological History," 114–115, 117; "Sloe-Eyed Students; the Japanese Mission in Los Angeles," *Los Angeles Times*, November 4, 1900; the Reverend M. C. Harris, D.D., "Pacific Japanese Methodist Episcopal Mission," in Eugene R. Smith, D.D., editor, *The Gospel in All Lands* (New York: Missionary Society of the Methodist Episcopal Church, 1901), 32–34.

24. Quotations from the Reverend George H. Deere, cited in Raven, "Red Paper and Varnished Ducks," 221–224.

25. G. A. Zentmyer, ed., *The Lighted Cross: The First 100 Years of Riverside's First Church, 1872–1972* (Riverside, CA: First Congregational Church, 1972), 64; Patterson, *Colony*, 52, 247, 289; Klotz, *Mission Inn*, 39.

26. Quotation from Mabel Bristol interview cited in Wong, "Japanese in Riverside," 47. See also Sumi Harada, interview by Mark Rawitsch, February 24, 1982, and G. Fugimoto interview cited in Wong, "Japanese in Riverside," 47.

27. Quotations from Edwin C. Hiroto interview cited in Wong, "Japanese in Riverside," 48; Mrs. H. J. Craft letter to Marcella Craft, December 24, 1921, Marcella Craft Archival Collection, Riverside Metropolitan Museum.

28. Quotation from Patterson, *Colony*, 187. Patterson, *Colony*, 318.

29. Quotations from Edward Fry, *Theodore Waterhouse, 1838–1891: Notes of His Life and Extracts from His Letters and Papers* (London: Chiswick Press, Charles Wittingham and Company, 1894), 165, 168, 171.

30. Quotations from Wilson Crewdson, letter to Oscar Browning, July 28, 1879, Wilson Crewdson correspondence with Oscar Browning, King's College Archive Centre, Cambridge, Papers of Oscar Browning, OB, correspondence 1879–1912; Anna Jackson, Deputy Keeper, Asian Department, Victoria and Albert Museum, London, e-mail message to Mark Rawitsch, August 27, 2004.

31. Quotation from Ayako Hotta-Lister, *The Japan-British Exhibition of 1910: Gateway to the Island Empire of the East* (Richmond, Surrey: Curzon Press, 1999), 51. Hotta-Lister, *Japan-British Exhibition*, 57–58, 65–66.

32. Quotations from Patterson, *Colony*, 217.

33. Quotations from Klotz, *Mission Inn*, 6; *Transactions and Proceedings of the Japan Society* (London: Japan Society of London, 1941), xvi. Anna Jackson, e-mail message to Mark Rawitsch, August 27, 2004; Sandys B. Foster, *The Pedigree of Wilson of High Wray and Kendal and the Families Connected with Them* (printed for private circulation by W. H. and L. Collingridge, 1871), 66–76; King's College Cambridge, Annual Report, 1918, 4; Register of Members of King's College Cambridge, 1797–1925, 97–98; Wilson Crewdson, correspondence with Oscar Browning, King's College Archive Centre, Cam-

bridge, Papers of Oscar Browning, OB, correspondence 1879–1912; Wilson Crewdson, *The Dawn of Western Influence in Japan* (London: Japan Society, 1903); Wilson Crewdson, *The Textiles of Old Japan, Transactions*, XI, 3 (London: Japan Society, 1914); Wilson Crewdson, *Japan Our Ally* (London: Macmillan, 1915); Edward F. Strange, *The Colour Prints of Hiroshige* (London: Cassell and Company, 1925); *Catalogue of the Birds in the British Museum*, vol. 23 (London: British Museum, 1894), 100; Hotta-Lister, *Japan-British Exhibition*, 57–58, 65–66; Patterson, *Colony*, 179–187, 215–220, 246, 317–318, 321; Klotz, *Mission Inn*, 2, 62.

34. Quotation from Martha Iseda, interview by Mark Rawitsch, May 9, 1977. Patterson, *Colony*, 187–188, 219–220; Klotz, *Mission Inn*, 62. Both authors rely on information from Zona Gale, *Frank Miller of Mission Inn* (New York: D. Appleton-Century Company, 1938); Irene McGroarty Wright, interview by Mark Rawitsch, November 1976; Martha Iseda, interview by Mark Rawitsch, May 9, 1977; U.S. National Archives and Records Administration, "Japanese-American Internee Data File, 1942–1945: Masao M. Iseda, 34063A," http://aad.archives.gov/aad/series-description.jsp?s=623 (accessed November 19, 2010). See also Gyosuke Iseda, *Frank Miller* (Riverside, 1928 [printed in Japanese]), Harada Family Archival Collection.

35. Quotations from "Japanese Guests on Anniversary," *Riverside Daily Press*, November 1, 1917; Mabel Bristol interview with JARRP, March 1, 1975. Klotz, *Mission Inn*, 64; G. Fugimoto interview cited in Wong, "Japanese in Riverside," 150.

36. Quotations from Klotz, *Mission Inn*, 64. Klotz, *Mission Inn*, 62–65; Patterson, *Colony*, 256; Gale, *Frank Miller*, 164.

37. Quotations from Gale, *Frank Miller*, 102–103; "Frank Miller Hails Japan Gift; Decorated Battledore Sent to Peace Worker," *Los Angeles Times*, August 18, 1933. See also "Honor Worthily Given," *Riverside Daily Press*, August 22, 1933; Klotz, *Mission Inn*, 65.

38. Quotation from "Mission Inn, Riverside, California," n.d., circa 1935–1936, fF869 R6 M3, collection of material relating to Riverside and the Mission Inn, Bancroft Library, University of California, Berkeley. See also Iseda, *Frank Miller*.

CHAPTER 5: PILGRIM'S PROGRESS

1. Joyce Carter Vickery, *Defending Eden: New Mexican Pioneers in Southern California 1830–1890* (Riverside: Department of History, University of California, Riverside, and Riverside Museum Press, 1977), 4–26; Moses and Focht, *Life in Little Gom-Benn*, n.p.; "History of Sherman Indian Museum," www.shermanindianmuseum .org (accessed February 11, 2008); Department of Commerce, Bureau of the Census, Thirteenth Census of the United States Taken in the Year 1910, Vol. II, Population 1910, Reports by States with Statistics for Counties, Cities and Other Civil Divisions, Alabama–Montana.

2. Thirteenth Census of the United States, Reports by States, Alabama–Montana, 166, 174–175; Harada Koseki.

3. Patterson, "A 1905 Episode," and "Japanese in Riverside Area: New Mystery about Old Tragedy," *Riverside Press-Enterprise*, February 21, 1971; Emanuel E. Parker, "Historic Site Designation Asked for Grave of Japanese-American," *Riverside Press-Enterprise*, April 16, 1980.

4. Quotations from Mine Harada Kido, interview by Mark Rawitsch, January 17, 1982.

5. Quotation from "Chief of Police Starts Clean-up Crusade," *Riverside Daily Press*, February 1, 1913. Sumi Harada in discussion with Mark Rawitsch, January 10, 1977; Sumi Harada, interview by Mark Rawitsch, February 24, 1982.

6. Jennifer Mermilliod, "3643 University Avenue, Jackson Building," n.d. [circa 2004], Riverside Metropolitan Museum Collection.

7. Quotation from Wong, "Japanese in Riverside," cited at Asian American Riverside, University of California, Riverside, http://aar.ucr.edu/ (accessed January 30, 2008). Thirteenth Census of the United States, Reports by States, Alabama–Montana, 166; Raven, "Red Paper and Varnished Ducks," 260; Lawton, "Last Survivor of City's Chinatown Lives There and Refuses to Sell It," in *Wong Ho Leun*, 305–310.

8. Quotations from Mine Harada Kido, interview by Mark Rawitsch, January 17, 1982.

9. Quotations from Washington Restaurant Menu, circa 1910–1919, Harada Family Archival Collection. Mine Harada Kido, interview by Mark Rawitsch, January 17, 1982.

10. Sumi Harada in discussion with Mark Rawitsch, January 10, 1977; *Riverside City and County Directory* (Los Angeles, 1912), 103; *Riverside City and County Directory* (Los Angeles, 1913), 103; Harada Koseki.

CHAPTER 6: LITTLE LAMB GONE TO JESUS

1. Klotz, *Mission Inn*, 19.

2. Harada Koseki.

3. Quotation from Dr. Harold Harada, interview by Mark Rawitsch, July 22, 2000.

4. Quotations from "The Night President Teddy Roosevelt Invited Booker T. Washington to Dinner," *The Journal of Blacks in Higher Education* 35 (Spring 2002): 24–25.

5. Quotation from ibid., 24.

6. Mark Bauerlein, "The Tactical Life of Booker T. Washington," *The Chronicle Review* 50, no. 14 (November 28, 2003): B12, The Chronicle of Higher Education, http://chronicle.com/article/The-Tactical-Life-of-Booker-T/29240 (accessed December 17, 2010).

7. Quotation and information from Joan Hall, "Booker T. in Riverside," in *Commemorating Washington's Birthday & 1914 Visit* (Riverside, CA: The Black Voice News, 2005), 3; Thirteenth Census of the United States, Reports by States, Alabama–Montana, 174–175; Department of Commerce, Bureau of the Census, Fourteenth Census of the United States, State Compendium, California [1920], Statistics of Population, Occupations, Agriculture, Irrigation, Drainage, Manufacturers, and Mines and Quarries for the State, Counties and Cities, 11, 14, 18, 22, 31, 35.

8. Quotation from First Congregational Church, Riverside, "First Congregational Church April 26, 1914," in Estudillo Scrapbook, 161, BANC MSS 69/27, Miguel Estudillo Papers, Bancroft Library, University of California, Berkeley.

9. Mermilliod, "3643 University Avenue"; Olivewood Memorial Park Records, Riverside; "California Births, 1905–1995, Riverside County," birth record for Yone Harada, May 31, 1914, http://familytreelegends.com (accessed May 18, 2008).

10. Quotations from "'The Clansman' Motion Picture Masterpiece at Loring To-night," *Riverside Daily Press*, January 1, 1915; Loring Opera House advertisement, *Riverside Daily Press*, January 1, 1915. Robert Lang, ed., *The Birth of a Nation: D. W. Griffith, Director* (New Brunswick, NJ: Rutgers University Press, 1994), 25–30.

11. Quotation from "Suit Filed Here against Alien Has International Importance," *Riverside Daily Press*, October 5, 1916. Klotz, *Mission Inn*, 28–29; John Brown Jr. and James Boyd, *History of San Bernardino and Riverside Counties*, vol. 2 (Chicago: The Lewis Publishing Company, 1922), 740–743; Franklin Harper, ed., *Who's Who in the Pacific Coast: A Biographical Compilation of Notable Living Contemporaries West of the Rocky Mountains* (Los Angeles: Harper Publishing Company, 1913), 188; "Art Society for County," *San Jacinto Register*, n.d., Miguel Estudillo Scrapbook, 273, and "Local Lawyers and Woman Suffrage," *Riverside Enterprise*, October 10, 1911, in Miguel Estudillo Scrapbook, 90, BANC MSS 69/27, Miguel Estudillo Papers, Bancroft Library, University of California, Berkeley.

12. Quotations from Patterson, *Colony*, 263; Esther Klotz, "Victorian Elegance Now Kindling Wood," *Report of Riverside Museum Associates* 1, no. 2 (May 1964): 1; Thirteenth Census of the United States, Reports by States, Alabama–Montana, Enumeration District No. 73, Sheet 3A; Patterson, *Colony*, 347. Vandegrift Genealogy, "Generation 10, 573 Nellie Frances Vandegrift and 574 Clara Josephine Vandegrift," Ancestry.com, http://www.ancestry.com/browse/bookview.aspx?dbid=26012&iid=dvm_GenMono006771-001 (accessed October 29, 2009); "City Mourns Passing of J. Van de Grift," *Riverside Enterprise*, February 15, 1923.

13. Thirteenth Census of the United States, Reports by States, Alabama–Montana; Patterson, *Colony*, 261–269, 247, 384; Klotz, *Mission Inn*, 67; Reporter's Transcript, testimony of William Farr, 38; Sumi Harada, interview by Mark Rawitsch, December 13, 1976.

14. Remarks of Stewart Malloch, June 8, 1985, in Raven, "Red Paper and Varnished Ducks," 260; Riverside City Directories, 1915–1917.

15. Quotations from D. W. Griffith to *Sight and Sound*, 1947, cited in Lang, *The Birth of a Nation*, 3; "'The Clansman' Motion Picture Masterpiece at Loring Tonight," *Riverside Daily Press*, January 1, 1915. Patterson, *Colony*, 192, 355; Thirteenth Census of the United States, Reports by States, Alabama–Montana; Riverside City Directories, 1915–1917; see Mr. Robinson's December 26, 1913, death notice in the *Riverside Enterprise* in which he is listed as "Alvah W. Robinson"; National Archives and Records Administration, Civil War Pension Index, 1861–1934, "Alvin W. Robinson."

16. Quotations from "The Continuity Script," in Lang, *The Birth of a Nation*, 44, 103, 109; *Riverside Enterprise*, January 2, 1915.

17. Quotations from Dr. Booker T. Washington letter to Florence Sewell Bond, June 30, 1915, in *The Booker T. Washington Papers*, Open Book Edition, vol. 13: 1914–15, University of Illinois Press, 1984, http://www.historycooperative.org/btw/Vol.13/html/335.html (accessed April 6, 2008).

18. Quotation from Klotz, *Mission Inn*, 38. Bauerlein, "Tactical Life of Booker T. Washington," http://www.skidmore.edu/~mstokes/227/BTW.html link: http://chronicle.com/weekly/v50/i14/14b01201.htm (accessed March 24, 2009); Hall, "Booker T. in Riverside," 3; Klotz, *Mission Inn*, 38.

CHAPTER 7: THE PEOPLE OF CALIFORNIA VERSUS HARADA

1. Quotations from Klotz, "Victorian Elegance," 1, 4; Reporter's Transcript, testimony of Jacob Van de Grift, 69.

2. Quotations from Nellie Van de Grift Sanchez, *The Life of Mrs. Robert Louis Stevenson* (New York: Charles Scribner's Sons, 1925) 8, 14. See also Sanchez, *Life of Mrs. Robert Louis Stevenson*, 1–15.

3. Quotation from Reporter's Transcript, testimony of F. C. Noble, 107. "Minor Children of Japanese Purchase Residence," *Riverside Enterprise*, December 23, 1915; Reporter's Transcript, testimony of J. Harada, 10, 90, 93; testimony of F. C. Noble, 107.

4. Quotation from Mine Harada Kido, letter to Mark Rawitsch, March 21, 1977. "Index to Official Records, Grantees and Plaintiffs 1914–1917, A–L, Riverside County 7," 322. Watari purchased the property prior to the passage of the 1913 Alien Land Law.

5. Quotations from Reporter's Transcript, testimony of J. Harada, 91, 92, 94. Reporter's Transcript, remarks of A. A. Adair and J. Lewinsohn, 91–94.

6. Quotation from Reporter's Transcript, testimony of I. S. Logan, 82–83. It is not known if Harada consented to the withdrawal. "Japanese Buy on Lemon St.," *Riverside Daily Press*, December 23, 1915; Reporter's Transcript, testimony of A. G. Urquhart, 60; "Index to Official Records," 322.

7. Quotations from Reporter's Transcript, testimony of F. C. Noble, 109–110. Raymond Benjamin, letter to Joseph Lewinsohn, May 28, 1918, Attorney General Records, California State Archives, Sacramento (hereafter referred to as Attorney General Records); Reporter's Transcript, see remarks of A. A. Adair, 110.

8. Quotation from Reporter's Transcript, testimony of C. Robinson, 76. Reporter's Transcript, testimony of C. Robinson, 76; testimony of C. Fletcher, 51; testimony of J. G. Hansler, 55. Hansler referred to the group as a "committee." Riverside City Directory, 1898; Civil War Pension Records, "Alvin W. Robinson"; Thirteenth Census of the United States, Riverside City, listing for A. W. Robinson, 342 Lemon Street, April 20, 1910.

9. Quotation from "Minor Children of Japanese Purchase Residence," *Riverside Enterprise*, December 23, 1915.

10. Quotation from Reporter's Transcript, testimony of W. Farr, 39–40. Reporter's Transcript, testimony of J. G. Hansler, 52; testimony of A. G. Urquhart, 58–59; testimony of J. Van de Grift, 66; testimony of C. Fletcher, 47–48, 50; testimony of C. Robinson, 78. See also Reporter's Transcript, testimony of all neighbors, and Riverside City and County Directory (Los Angeles, 1915). Today's Lemon Street addresses of the houses then occupied by the majority of the members of the committee are 3385, Fletcher; 3369, Hansler; 3327, Urquhart; 3311, Farr; and 3342, Robinson. "Mr. Fritz," never specifically identified in court documents, reportedly died before the case came to trial. Carpenter Israel L. Fritz lived around the corner from the Harada house on Fourth Street. See response for expression of sympathy from Mrs. S. Jennie Fritz to Miguel Estudillo, postmarked May 25, 1917, in BANC MSS 69/27, Miguel Estudillo Papers, Bancroft Library, University of California, Berkeley.

11. Quotation from Reporter's Transcript, testimony of C. Robinson, 76. Reporter's Transcript, testimony of C. Fletcher, 49; testimony of A. G. Urquhart, 59, 61; testimony

of J. Van de Grift, 67; testimony of J. Harada, 27–29. It seems quite possible that language difficulties led to a misunderstanding by all parties. Evidence of communication problems appears throughout the Reporter's Transcript.

12. Quotations from Reporter's Transcript, testimony of J. Harada, 25, 27, 29. Thirteenth Census of the United States, Riverside City, listing for A. G. Urquhart, 327 Lemon Street, April 20, 1910; Reporter's Transcript, testimony of A. G. Urquhart, 61; testimony of J. Harada, 24–25, 41; testimony of J. Van de Grift, 68.

13. Quotations from Sumi Harada, interview by Mark Rawitsch, February 24, 1982; Mine Harada Kido, interview by Mark Rawitsch, January 17, 1982. Wong, "Japanese in Riverside," 20–22, cited at Asian American Riverside, http://aar.ucr.edu/ (accessed March 30, 2009).

14. Quotation from Mine Harada Kido, letter to Mark Rawitsch, February 24, 1977. Mine Harada Kido, letter to Mark Rawitsch, February 2, 1982; Mine Harada Kido, interview cited in Wong, "Japanese in Riverside," 146; Mine Harada Kido, interview by Mark Rawitsch, January 17, 1982. No additional evidence of Miller's offer has been found. It is probable that no other written evidence exists. Miller's indirect support is suggested by his 1917 banquet for Riverside Japanese, during which the *Harada* case was discussed by attorney Purington. Of Miller's offer, Mine Harada Kido told me: "It was all talk. I don't think they had any papers or anything." A photographic portrait of Ed Miller, circa 1920, is in the Harada Family Archival Collection.

15. Quotations from Patterson, *Colony*, 339, 210, 349. See also Patterson, *Colony*, 300, 339, 389–390; Miguel Estudillo letter to J. W. McGrath, January 11, 1916; Miguel Estudillo letter to Hon. H. L. Carnahan, March 25, 1916, BANC MSS 60/27, Miguel Estudillo Papers, Bancroft Library, University of California, Berkeley; Brown and Boyd, *History of San Bernardino and Riverside Counties*, 740.

16. Quotation from Miguel Estudillo letter to Hon. H. L. Carnahan, February 28, 1916, BANC MSS 69/27, Miguel Estudillo Papers, Bancroft Library, University of California, Berkeley.

17. Quotation of Henry Coil, cited in Patterson, *Colony*, 294.

18. Quotations from Klotz, *Mission Inn*, 90, 12, 19, 43. Riverside City Directory, 1898. For more on Ed Miller, see Patterson, *Colony*, 112 (photograph), 217.

19. Quotation from "Wholesale Purchase of California Farm Property by Nipponese for Children Predicted," *Los Angeles Examiner*, January 5, 1916. See also "Land Titles to Children." Roger Daniels, 74, notes in *The Politics of Prejudice*: "With the onset of the First World War, in which Japan was an associate rather than an enemy of the United States, the yellow peril continued to thrive. Its chief exponents were the Hearst press and the German propaganda machine within the United States."

20. Quotation from Reporter's Transcript, testimony of J. Harada, 90. "Contract for Construction," January 8, 1916, Clerk of the Superior Court, Riverside Civil Files C-114, 7736–7809, Case 7751.

21. Quotation from "Jap Foe Is Now Here Says Phelan," *San Francisco Examiner*, January 19, 1916; see also "Preparedness Essential to U.S. Says Phelan; Japanese Ever-Present Menace to This Coast," *San Francisco Examiner*, January 10, 1916; "Phelan Reveals Pacific Peril," *San Francisco Examiner*, January 22, 1916. Harry Carr, "Japan vs. America in a Riverside Suit," *Los Angeles Times*, October 22, 1916; U. S. Webb, letter to F. G. [*sic*]

Noble, January 17, 1916; U. S. Webb, letter to J. G. Hansler, January 17, 1916; U. S. Webb, letter to Robert M. Clarke, January 17, 1916, Attorney General Records; James D. Phelan, letter to Hiram Johnson, January 24, 1916, BANC MSS C-B 581, Hiram Johnson Papers, Bancroft Library, University of California, Berkeley.

22. Quotation from James D. Phelan, letter to Hiram Johnson, February 22, 1916, BANC MSS C-B 581, Hiram Johnson Papers, Bancroft Library, University of California, Berkeley. Hiram Johnson, letter to James D. Phelan, February 8, 1916; Hiram Johnson to James D. Phelan, February 11, 1916, BANC MSS C-B 581, Hiram Johnson Papers, Bancroft Library, University of California, Berkeley. Newspaper references to the Santa Barbara case suggest it was delayed on "technical grounds." See Attorney General clipping file on the *Harada* case, Attorney General Records. The *San Francisco Chronicle*, October 6, 1916, reported that a Santa Barbara case had been filed "a year ago by the State against a Chinese. It has dragged through the courts since that time and trial of it has been delayed on various technical grounds." See references in the Attorney General letter files referring to the *Gin Fook Bin* case in Santa Barbara: U. S. Webb, letter to Francis Price, February 22, 1918; U. S. Webb, letter to J. L. Lewinsohn, February [illegible date], 1918; U. S. Webb, letter to J. L. Lewinsohn, March 22, 1918: "The case of People vs. Gin Fook Bin, in which judgment was recently ordered in favor of the State, involves the constitutionality of the Alien Land Act, and I assume that appeal will be taken, so that we may have a reasonably early determination of that question. If the statute be upheld, as I assume it will be, then with the light of that decision we can commence the action in the Riverside case." The *Harada* case went to trial two months later, apparently before further judgment was rendered in the *Gin Fook Bin* case. *Harada* was the first to involve a Japanese.

23. U. S. Webb, letter to Messrs. Richards, Carrier, and Heaney, January 27, 1916, Attorney General Records.

24. Quotations from the undated witness list for *The People of California v. Jukichi Harada*, Attorney General Records; "Condemns Jap Sale," *Los Angeles Times*, January 9, 1916. Miguel Estudillo, letters to U. S. Webb, February 17, 1916, and March 28, 1916, BANC MSS 69/27, Miguel Estudillo Papers, Bancroft Library, University of California, Berkeley.

25. Quotations from Washington Restaurant Menu, Harada Family Archival Collection; Mine Harada Kido, interview by Mark Rawitsch, January 17, 1982; "Jap Alien Law to Be Tested," *Los Angeles Times*, October 6, 1916. See also Harada Koseki; Harada House contents, Harada Family Artifact Collection, Riverside Metropolitan Museum.

26. Quotation from Sumi Harada, interview by Mark Rawitsch, December 13, 1976. Sumi Harada in discussion with Mark Rawitsch, January 10, 1977; see contract with Harp Brothers in Reporter's Transcript, 32–33. The original 1916 paint is observable on the exterior walls of the enclosed upstairs front porch of the Harada house.

27. Quotation from Sumi Harada, interview by Mark Rawitsch, December 13, 1976. Dr. Harold Harada, interview by Mark Rawitsch, July 22, 2000; see Jess Stebler's letters and cards to Sumi Harada, 1943–1945, quoted in Kurt Russo, "The Harada House" (unpublished research paper, University of California, Riverside, 2006), 8; see family photographs in Harada Family Archival Collection; visits by Mark Rawitsch with Sumi, Clark, and Dr. Harold Harada at Harada House, 1977–2000.

28. Quotations from U. S. Webb, letter to Robert M. Clarke, September 6, 1916, Attorney General Records; "To Test Anti-Alien Land Law Here," *Riverside Enterprise*, October 5, 1916. Miguel Estudillo, letter to U. S. Webb, August 24, 1916, Attorney General Records; Miguel Estudillo, letter to Raymond Best, July 21, 1916, BANC MSS 69/27, Miguel Estudillo Papers, Bancroft Library, University of California, Berkeley; Robert M. Clarke, letter to Miguel Estudillo, September 28, 1916, Attorney General Records; Riverside Superior Court Civil Files, Case 7751, Item 8 (microfilm). No concrete reasons for Webb's delay in responding to Estudillo have been found. It may have been that Webb saw where the case led and did not want to pursue the matter. In Riverside, it seems that when Miguel Estudillo agreed to handle the case, the neighborhood committee felt assured of action and did not press for a swift conclusion to the lawsuit. Webb discussed the delay in the letter to Clarke on September 6, 1916: "Some time ago we had up for consideration the matter of commencing action against a Japanese in Riverside . . . it was then practically determined that such action would be commenced, though for some reason its commencement was deferred." Estudillo mentioned to Raymond Best, on July 21, 1916, that the matter had waited so long that he was "not . . . sure what the committee would do," and that he had "dismissed the matter" from his mind.

CHAPTER 8: WORLD WAR AND A BASKET OF APPLES

1. Quotation from Miguel Estudillo, letter to Robert M. Clarke, October 6, 1916, Attorney General Records.

2. Quotations from Miguel Estudillo, letter to Robert M. Clarke, October 11, 1916, Attorney General Records. "Alien Land Law Suit Brought in California," *New York Times*, October 6, 1916; see also "First Test for Alien Land Law," *Sacramento Bee*, October 5, 1916; "Anti-Alien Law under New Test," *San Francisco Examiner*, October 6, 1916; "Confiscation of Japanese Realty Purpose of Suit," *San Francisco Chronicle*, October 6, 1916; "State Test of Its Alien Land Law Is Started," *Los Angeles Examiner*, October 6, 1916; "Jap Alien Law to Be Tested," *Los Angeles Times*, October 6, 1916; "California to Test Alien Land Ownership," *Atlanta Constitution*, October 6, 1916; "California Anti-Alien Test," *Christian Science Monitor*, October 6, 1916; "Jap Government Stirred over Harada Case," *Riverside Enterprise*, October 7, 1916; "Japanese Land Case Up," *Washington Post*, October 8, 1916; Adair and Winder, letter to J. Harada, March 17, 1919, Harada Family Archival Collection.

3. Quotations from Harry Carr, "Japan vs. America in a Riverside Suit," *Los Angeles Times*, October 22, 1916, and Harry Carr, letter to Miguel Estudillo, October 21, 1916, BANC MSS 60/27, Miguel Estudillo Papers, Bancroft Library, University of California, Berkeley. Carr said that the Japanese newspaper he quoted was the "North American Herald."

4. General Catalogue of Bates College and Cobb Divinity School, 1863–1915 (Lewiston, ME: Bates College, 1915), 246; Universalist Church of America, *The Universalist Register: Containing the Statistics of the Church, With an Almanac for 1875* (Boston: Universalist Publishing House, 1875), 116; Maine Memory Network, Maine Historical Society, www.mainememory.net (accessed March 17, 2008); DAR, *Directory of the National Soci-*

ety of the Daughters of the American Revolution (Washington, DC: National Society of the Daughters of the American Revolution, 1911), 50.

5. Quotation from "Japanese at Trial," *Los Angeles Times*, December 5, 1916. "Jap Alien Case Ready for Trial," *Los Angeles Times*, November 19, 1916; "Harada Case Is on Today," *Riverside Daily Press*, December 4, 1916; Miguel Estudillo, letter to Robert B. Camarillo, December 6, 1916, Attorney General Records.

6. Quotations from Miguel Estudillo, letter to Robert M. Clarke, December 26, 1916; Robert M. Clarke, letter to Miguel Estudillo, December 28, 1916, Attorney General Records. "Harada Case Is on Today," *Riverside Daily Press*, December 4, 1916.

7. Quotation from "The Japanese Cloud," *Sunset* 37 (Holiday Number, 1916): 34.

8. Quotation and information from Hugh H. Craig, *In the Superior Court of the State of California In and For the County of Riverside, The People of the State of California, Plaintiff, vs. Jukichi Harada, et al.*, Defendants, Opinion of Hon. Hugh H. Craig, Judge [1917], Harada Family Archival Collection.

9. Quotations and information from ibid., 4–5, 10. "Anti-Alien Land Law Upheld by Decision," *Los Angeles Times*, April 5, 1917.

10. Quotation from U. S. Webb, letter to Robert M. Clarke, April 9, 1917, Attorney General Records. Webb also added, "I suggest that a like disposition be made of the case pending in Santa Barbara."

11. Quotation of Theodore Roosevelt, cited in Daniels, *Politics of Prejudice*, 143n; other quotations from Daniels, *Politics of Prejudice*, 79; California Attorney General, Proceedings, California Land Title Association, 38th Anniversary Conference, 1944, 97.

12. Quotations from Robert M. Clarke, letter to Miguel Estudillo, April 11, 1917, Attorney General Records. Oyama to Hugh H. Craig, April 19, 1917; Riverside Superior Court Civil Files, Case 7751, Item 42 (microfilm); Robert M. Clarke, letter to Miguel Estudillo, April 28, 1917; Miguel Estudillo, letter to Robert M. Clarke, April 30, 1917, Attorney General Records.

13. Quotation from Miguel Estudillo, letter to Robert M. Clarke, June 25, 1917, Attorney General Records. Robert M. Clarke, letter to Miguel Estudillo, June 14, 1917, Attorney General Records. See also "Second Round Won by State," *Los Angeles Times*, July 1, 1917.

14. Quotations from "Japanese Guests on Anniversary," *Riverside Daily Press*, November 1, 1917. "Japanese Pledge Gladly Received," *Riverside Daily Press*, October 1, 1917.

15. Quotations from Sumi Harada, interview by Mark Rawitsch, February 24, 1982; Mine Harada Kido, letter to Mark Rawitsch, February 24, 1977; Mine Harada Kido, interview by Mark Rawitsch, January 17, 1982.

16. Quotations from Mine Harada Kido, interview by Mark Rawitsch, January 17, 1982; Sumi Harada, interview by Mark Rawitsch, February 24, 1982.

17. Quotation from "Minor Children of Japanese Purchase Residence," *Riverside Enterprise*, December 23, 1915. Waswo, *Modern Japanese Society*, 30; Mine Harada Kido, letter to Mark Rawitsch, March 21, 1977.

18. Mine Harada Kido, interview by Mark Rawitsch, January 17, 1982; Mine Harada Kido, letter to Mark Rawitsch, March 21, 1977.

19. Quotations from U. S. Webb, letter to Robert Clarke, December 17, 1917, Attorney General Records; Miguel Estudillo, "A History of Riverside County Bar by Atty

Miguel Estudillo; Anti-Alien Law," *The Riverside Law Recorder*, June 21, 1940, BANC MSS 69/27, Miguel Estudillo Papers, Bancroft Library, University of California, Berkeley. A recent search of name indexes and other likely State Department correspondence index sources at the National Archives, Washington, DC, including Japanese consul files from the time, failed to identify any specific references to the *Harada* case. See Warren S. Hower, e-mail messages to Mark Rawitsch, December 11, 2009, to January 28, 2010, and February 1, 2010: "The entries I reviewed are the Name Index in RG 59, Entry 10. I looked for all of the names listed and didn't come across any communications from the time frame in question. I then reviewed RG60 Entry 95 card index, again looking for names of the individuals listed in your email 4 roles of microfilm in RG 59, M30, and Japanese Consul files from the time period in question."

20. Quotation from Miguel Estudillo, letter to Joseph Lewinsohn, February 12, 1918, Attorney General Records. U. S. Webb, letter to Hon. Benjamin F. Bledsoe, January 26, 1918; U. S. Webb, letter to Robert M. Clarke, February 1, 1918, Attorney General Records.

21. Quotations from Joseph Lewinsohn, letter to U. S. Webb, March 1, 1918; U. S. Webb, letter to Joseph Lewinsohn, March 2, 1918, Attorney General Records. Miguel Estudillo, letter to Joseph Lewinsohn, February 28, 1918; Joseph Lewinsohn, letter to Miguel Estudillo, March 9, 1918, Attorney General Records.

22. Quotations from Miguel Estudillo, letter to Joseph Lewinsohn, March 18, 1918; U. S. Webb, letter to Joseph Lewinsohn, March 22, 1918, Attorney General Records. Joseph Lewinsohn, letter to Miguel Estudillo, March 9, 1918; Miguel Estudillo, letter to Joseph Lewinsohn, March 18, 1918, Attorney General Records. See also Joseph Lewinsohn, letter to U. S. Webb, May 2, 1918, Attorney General Records.

23. Quotation from U. S. Webb, letter to Joseph Lewinsohn, March 22, 1918, Attorney General Records. See also Biennial Report of the Attorney General of the State of California, 1916–1918 (Sacramento, 1919), 18. The report of the attorney general described the *Gin Fook Bin* case in Santa Barbara as a "Chinese escheat case," adding that it had been "tried and closed. Sale of property pending. Suit to declare escheat under alien land law. Judgment of escheat as to part of property. Sale to divide same." The same report also described incorrectly the *Harada* case as a "Chinese escheat" and added that the case had been tried: "Judgment went for defendants. Motion for new trial by people pending. Suit to declare escheat under alien land law." See also "Supreme Court May Decide It," *Los Angeles Times*, February 8, 1916.

24. Quotation from "Death of W. A. Purington Casts Gloom over Entire Community," *Riverside Daily Press*, April 19, 1918.

25. Quotation and information from Elmer Wallace Holmes et al., *History of Riverside County, California, with Biographical Sketches* (Los Angeles: Historic Record Company, 1912), 480–482. Joseph Lewinsohn letter to U. S. Webb, May 2, 1918, Attorney General Records.

26. Quotations from Joseph Lewinsohn, letter to U. S. Webb, May 2, 1918, Attorney General Records; U. S. Webb, letter to Miguel Estudillo, May 8, 1918, Attorney General Records. Webb's response of May 8, 1918, outlines most of Estudillo's letter of May 3, 1918, which apparently no longer exists. See Attorney General Records and Estudillo Papers at Bancroft Library; see also U. S. Webb, letter to Joseph Lewinsohn, May 8,

1918; Joseph Lewinsohn, letter to Miguel Estudillo, May 11, 1918; Miguel Estudillo, letter to Joseph Lewinsohn, May 13, 1918, Attorney General Records.

CHAPTER 9: FACE-TO-FACE

1. Quotation from "Diary of Toranosuke Fujimoto," University of California, Riverside, via e-mail and translation from Akiko Nomura to Mark Rawitsch, January 26, 2007; "The Fujimoto Family and the Japanese American Community in Riverside," Asian American Riverside, University of California, Riverside, http://aar.ucr.edu/ (accessed February 22, 2007).

2. Miguel Estudillo to Joseph Lewinsohn, May 24, 1918, Attorney General Records; Holmes et al., *History of Riverside County,* 437–439; "Keokuk Mourns Death of Judge Hugh H. Craig," *The Daily Gate and Constitution Democrat* (Keokuk, IA), September 9, 1922.

3. Quotation from Reporter's Transcript, remarks of J. Lewinsohn, 18. Miguel Estudillo was appointed Riverside City attorney on January 7, 1918; see Record of Common Council, City of Riverside, Volume 16, Riverside City Hall Archives, 32. Although Estudillo added a few comments from time to time during the trial, he did not participate actively in the courtroom proceedings.

4. Quotations from Japanese Consulate, *Documental History of Law Cases Affecting Japanese in the United States, 1916–1924* (San Francisco: Consulate General of Japan, 1925), 702–703, 706; see also 701 and 712.

5. Quotation from Reporter's Transcript, remarks of H. Craig, 20.

6. Quotations from Reporter's Transcript, remarks of M. Estudillo, H. Craig, and J. Lewinsohn, 46.

7. Adair and Winder letter to J. Harada, March 17, 1919, Harada Family Archival Collection. Quotation from Mine Harada Kido, letter to Mark Rawitsch, February 24, 1977.

8. Quotation from Reporter's Transcript, testimony of C. Fletcher, 51.

9. Quotation from Reporter's Transcript, remarks of A. A. Adair and M. Estudillo; testimony of C. Robinson, 78.

10. Quotations from Reporter's Transcript, testimony of J. Harada, 91–92.

11. Quotation from Reporter's Transcript, remarks of J. Lewinsohn, 99. Reporter's Transcript, testimony of F. C. Noble, 110.

12. Quotation from Hugh H. Craig, In the Superior Court of the State of California In and For the County of Riverside, The People of the State of California, Plaintiff, vs. Jukichi Harada, et al., Defendants, Opinion of Hon. Hugh H. Craig, Judge, Riverside Superior Court Civil Files, Case 7751, Item 25 (microfilm) 2, 6. See also "Japanese Born Here May Own Real Estate," *San Francisco Chronicle,* September 18, 1918; "Japanese Wins Right to Land," *San Francisco Examiner,* September 18, 1918; "Japanese Born Here May Own Real Estate," *Los Angeles Times,* September 18, 1918; "Japanese Wins Land Suit," *Washington Post,* September 18, 1918; "Court Construes Anti-Alien Law," *Christian Science Monitor,* September 20, 1918.

13. Quotations from Craig, *Opinion,* 3, 5, 7. See also *Opinion,* 8. The Japanese Mission was located at the southeast corner of Fifth and Mulberry Streets. The public school

occupied the block across Mulberry to the west. Both sites were a three- to four-block walk from the Harada house. The site of the Japanese Mission is now occupied by the Riverside Freeway.

14. *Opinion*, 8–9; "Judge Craig Decides that Native Born Japanese May Own Land Here," *Riverside Daily Press*, September 17, 1918.

15. Quotation from Joseph Lewinsohn, letter to Miguel Estudillo, September 19, 1918, Attorney General Records. Miguel Estudillo, letter to Joseph Lewinsohn, September 25, 1918; Katherine L. Scott, letter to Joseph Lewinsohn, September 21, 1918; Miguel Estudillo, letter to Joseph Lewinsohn, September 24, 1918; U. S. Webb, letter to Joseph Lewinsohn, September 26, 1918, Attorney General Records. See also "Japanese Wins Right to Land," *San Francisco Examiner*, September 18, 1918; "Anti-Alien Land Law in California," *Christian Science Monitor*, October 1, 1918.

16. "Notice of Intention to Move for New Trial," October 25, 1918, Riverside Superior Court Civil Files, Case 7751, Item 6 (microfilm). Ujiro Oyama, letter to Robert M. Clarke, October 30, 1918; Joseph Lewinsohn, letter to Ujiro Oyama, November 9, 1918; Joseph Lewinsohn, letter to Miguel Estudillo, September 26, 1918, Attorney General Records; "Harada Case Again," *Los Angeles Times*, January 19, 1919; "No Evasion of Anti-Alien Law," *Los Angeles Times*, January 22, 1919.

17. Quotation from "Denies Motion for New Trial," *Riverside Daily Press*, January 21, 1919. "Japanese Buy Land in Tulare County," *Riverside Daily Press*, January 21, 1919. Quotation from U. S. Webb, letter to Raymond Buell, September 8, 1920, Attorney General Records. A survey of city directory listings for nine square blocks surrounding the Harada house indicated that immediate migrations of residents did not take place as a result of Judge Craig's decision. In fact, some of the members of the neighborhood committee remained in the neighborhood for the rest of their lives.

18. Quotation from U. S. Webb, letter to Frank Noble, in Reporter's Transcript, testimony of F. C. Noble, 110.

19. Quotation from Miguel Estudillo, letter to Joseph Lewinsohn, February 12, 1919, Attorney General Records. See also "Japanese Wins Land Suit," *Washington Post*, September 18, 1918; "Japanese Born Here May Own Real Estate," *Los Angeles Times*, September 18, 1918; "Judge H. H. Craig Leaves Bench," *Riverside Daily Press*, September 1, 1921. Judge Craig resigned his position in late 1921 to become general counsel for the Southern Sierras Power Company. It was reported at the time that "it is universally regarded as certain that he could hold the office without opposition as long as he desired," thereby suggesting that Craig's decision in the *Harada* case had no lasting effect on his role as superior court judge. Quotation from Miguel Estudillo, BANC MSS 69/27, Miguel Estudillo Papers, Bancroft Library, University of California, Berkeley.

20. Quotation from Mine Harada Kido, interview by Mark Rawitsch, January 17, 1982.

CHAPTER 10: KEEP CALIFORNIA WHITE

1. Quotation from Daniels, *Politics of Prejudice*, 74. See also Daniels, *Politics of Prejudice*, 78, 81–82; Modell, *Economics and Politics of Racial Accommodation*, 38.

2. Quotation and information from Daniels, *Politics of Prejudice*, 85.

3. Daniels, *Politics of Prejudice*, 88; Chuman, *Bamboo People*, 79–80.

4. Quotations from "Japanese Question Discussed in Calm and Friendly Manner," *Riverside Daily Press*, February 24, 1920. See also Wong, "Japanese in Riverside," 138.

5. Quotation from remarks of Senator James D. Phelan in *Japanese Immigration; Hearings Before the Committee on Immigration and Naturalization, House of Representatives, Sixty-Sixth Congress, Second Session, July 12, 13, and 14, 1920*, Part I: *Hearings at San Francisco and Sacramento, California* (Washington, DC: Government Printing Office, 1921), 18–19, http://books.google.com/books (accessed August 24, 2009). See Sidney L. Gulick, *Should Congress Enact Special Laws Affecting Japanese?* (New York: National Committee on American Japanese Relations, 1922).

6. Quotation from remarks of John E. Raker, George Shima, and Chairman Albert Johnson in *Japanese Immigration*, 65–66.

7. Quotations from *Japanese Immigration*, Exhibit A, 1023. See also testimony of Albert Chapelle, *Japanese Immigration*, 904–917.

8. Quotations from Mine Harada Kido interview with JARRP, undated and unpaginated; Mine Harada Kido, interview by Mark Rawitsch, January 17, 1982. Mine believed that the poster, printed in English, was produced and distributed by the Japanese Association. Daniels notes in *The Politics of Prejudice* that the Japanese Association of America campaigned actively against the 1920 measure.

9. Quotations from Daniels, *Politics of Prejudice*, 88; Chuman, *Bamboo People*, 76. See Chuman, *Bamboo People*, 79.

10. Quotations from Reporter's Transcript, testimony of F. C. Noble, 109–110; U. S. Webb, Brief of U. S. Webb, As Attorney General of California, On Order of Court for Resubmission of Case—In the Matter of The Estate and Guardianship of Tetsubumi Yano (a minor), December 1921, Attorney General Records; U. S. Webb letter to Raymond Buell, September 8, 1920, Attorney General Records.

11. Chuman, *Bamboo People*, 203–214. See also Konvitz, *The Alien and the Asiatic in American Law*, 161–167, and Saburo Kido, "Story of a Typical Pioneer Issei," *Pacific Citizen*, February 19, 1944.

12. Quotation of Justice William Francis Murphy in U.S. Supreme Court, *Oyama v. California*, 332 U.S. 633 (1948) 651, 657, 660–662, http://supreme.justia.com/us /332/633/case.html (accessed November 29, 2009). Greg Robinson, *A Tragedy of Democracy: Japanese Confinement in North America* (New York: Columbia University Press, 2009), 259.

13. Quotation of Judge Thurmond Clarke cited in Chuman, *Bamboo People*, 221. Chuman, *Bamboo People*, 201–202, 218–221. Lua Thurmond Safwenberg (niece of Robert M. Clarke and cousin of Thurmond Clarke) in discussion with Mark Rawitsch, 1977.

14. Quotation cited in Chuman, *Bamboo People*, 222.

15. Quotation from "Ku Klux Klan Seeks Members in Riverside," *Riverside Enterprise*, January 18, 1923, in Kevin Hallaran, e-mail message to Mark Rawitsch, August 22, 2006.

16. Quotations from "Closed Lecture on the Ku Klux Klan," January 21, 1924, Evans Archival Collection, Riverside Metropolitan Museum, in Kevin Hallaran, e-mail message to Mark Rawitsch, August 22, 2006.

17. Quotations from "Do You Know that the Ku Klux Klan Is Organized in Riverside?" Knights of the Ku Klux Klan, letter to S. C. Evans; S. C. Evans, letter to W. J. Reynolds, May 9, 1919, Evans Archival Collection, Riverside Metropolitan Museum, in Kevin Hallaran, e-mail message to Mark Rawitsch, August 22, 2006.

18. Quotations from Reporter's Transcript, remarks of A. A. Adair and testimony of C. Robinson, 78; Mine Harada Kido, letter to Mark Rawitsch, March 21, 1977. Sumi Harada, interview by Mark Rawitsch, December 13, 1976.

19. Quotations from Sumi Harada, interview by Mark Rawitsch, December 13, 1976; Mine Harada Kido, interview by Mark Rawitsch, January 17, 1982.

20. Dr. Harold Harada, interview by Mark Rawitsch, July 21, 2000. Quotations from Rosalind Uno, in Mark Rawitsch's interview with Rosalind Uno, Wally Kido, Kimi Klein, Naomi Harada, Dr. Ken Harada, and Paul Harada, October 29, 2005.

21. Mermilliod, "3643 University Avenue"; Sumi Harada, interviews by Mark Rawitsch, February 24, 1982, and December 13, 1976. See also Gregory Clancey, *Earthquake Nation: The Cultural Politics of Japanese Seismicity, 1868–1930* (Berkeley: University of California Press, 2006), 113.

22. Quotations from "Chief of Police Starts Clean-up Crusade," *Riverside Daily Press*, February 1, 1913.

23. Quotation from Dr. Harold Harada, interview by Mark Rawitsch, July 22, 2000. Mine Harada Kido, interview by Mark Rawitsch, January 17, 1982; Dr. Harold Harada, interview by Mark Rawitsch, July 23, 2000; Nestor Brule, letter to War Relocation Authority, March 26, 1943, WRA, Shiashi Harry [Jukichi] Harada File; Sumi Harada, interview by Mark Rawitsch, February 24, 1982; Jukichi Harada, Personal History Notes.

24. Quotations from Sumi Harada in discussion with Mark Rawitsch, January 10, 1977; Mine Harada Kido, interview with Mark Rawitsch, January 17, 1982. "Individual Record," November 6, 1942; M. A. Harada, MD, letter to Edward M. Joyce, March 10, 1945; "Form WRA-12 29," June 1942; WRA, Dr. Masa Atsu Harada File.

25. Naomi Harada, e-mail message to Mark Rawitsch, January 26, 2007; Lily Ann Inouye, e-mail messages to Mark Rawitsch, April 8, July 12, 16, 2007; "Application for Leave Clearance" [first page missing], February 20, 1943; M. A. Harada, MD, letter to Edward M. Joyce, March 10, 1945; "Form WRA-12, 29," June 1942; Howard C. Naffziger, MD, letter to D. D. Myer, March 15, 1943; WRA, Dr. Masa Atsu Harada File.

26. "Individual Record," August 17, 1942; Paulene Hunnicutt letter to War Relocation Project, February 5, 1943; WRA, Mine Harada Kido File; Mine Harada Kido, letter to Mark Rawitsch, February 24, 1977; Bill Hosokawa, *JACL: In Quest of Justice* (New York: William Morrow and Company, 1982), 38; Wally Kido in Mark Rawitsch's interview with Rosalind Uno, Wally Kido, Kimi Klein, Naomi Harada, Dr. Ken Harada, and Paul Harada, October 29, 2005.

27. Mine Harada Kido, interview by Mark Rawitsch, January 17, 1982; Mine Harada Kido, letter to Mark Rawitsch, February 24, 1977; Bill Hosokawa, *JACL*, 125; Saburo Kido, "Individual Record," August 17, 1942, WRA, Saburo Kido File; Hosokawa, *JACL*, 38; "Application for Leave Clearance," December 7, 1942; "Application," n.d.; WRA, Saburo Kido File.

28. Quotation from Mine Harada Kido, interview by Mark Rawitsch, January 17, 1982. Mine Harada and Saburo Kido, Engagement Announcement, December 15, 1927, Harada Family Archival Collection.

29. "Application," n.d. [circa 1942]; "Application for Attorney Positions," December 10, 1942, WRA, Saburo Kido File; Mine Harada Kido, interview by Mark Rawitsch, January 17, 1982; Mine Harada Kido, letter to Mark Rawitsch, February 24, 1977; Sumi Harada in discussion with Mark Rawitsch, January 10, 1977; Smith, *Americans*, 258; Hosokawa, *JACL*, 30–47; quotations from Hosokawa, *JACL* , 46; Mine Harada Kido, letter to Mark Rawitsch, March 21, 1977.

CHAPTER 11: THE ONLY TIME I SEE THE SUN

1. Quotations from "Japanese Kills Wife and Self," *Los Angeles Times*, August 11, 1928; Dr. Harold Harada, interview by Mark Rawitsch, July 22, 2000.

2. Quotations from Roy Hashimura, interviews by Wally Kido, December 7, 2006, January 8, 23, 2007; Dr. Harold Harada, interview by Mark Rawitsch, July 22, 2000. Mermilliod, "3643 University Avenue"; [War Relocation Authority], Central Utah Final Accountability Report, October 1945, 29; Sumi Harada in discussion with Mark Rawitsch, January 10, 1977. See portrait photograph of Mr. Hashimura, circa 1910–1920, in Harada Family Archival Collection.

3. Mermilliod, "3643 University Avenue"; Kitano, *Japanese Americans*, 20; Sumi Harada in discussion with Mark Rawitsch, January 10, 1977. Quotation from interview with Dr. Harold Harada, July 22, 2000.

4. Quotation from interview with Mine Harada Kido, January 17, 1982. "Application for Leave Clearance," February 26, 1943, WRA, Shiashi Harry [Jukichi] Harada File.

5. Quotation from Sumi Harada, interview by Mark Rawitsch, February 24, 1982.

6. Quotation from Roy Hashimura, interview by Wally Kido, January 8, 2007.

7. Quotation from ibid.; see Mark Rawitsch's interview with Rosalind Uno, Wally Kido, Kimi Klein, Naomi Harada, Dr. Ken Harada, and Paul Harada, October 29, 2005.

8. Quotation from Dr. Harold Harada, interview by Mark Rawitsch, July 23, 2000.

9. Photograph of Washington Restaurant interior, 541 Eighth Street, circa 1930, Harada Family Archival Collection; Patterson, *Colony*, 351. See spiral notepad records of daily restaurant supply purchases in the Harada Family Archival Collection.

10. Mermilliod, "3643 University Avenue"; quotation from Dr. Harold Harada, interview by Mark Rawitsch, July 23, 2000; H. Nakajima, *The Japanese Telephone and Business Directory of Southern California*, Number 25 (1936), 28–29.

11. Quotation from Dr. Harold Harada, interview by Mark Rawitsch, July 22, 2000. Nakajima, *Japanese Telephone and Business Directory*, 28; Roy Hashimura, interview by Wally Kido, January 8, 2007.

12. Klotz, *Mission Inn*, 97, 90–91, 22, 50–52, 93–95; "Japan Occupation Essays: Albert O. Nakazawa," The National Japanese American Veterans Council, http://www .njavc.org (accessed February 11, 2007). Quotations of Chandler, Hirota, and Saito from Fred Hogue, "Last Honors Paid Miller; Rites Conducted at Mission Inn," *Los Angeles*

Times, June 18, 1935; Ed Ainsworth, "Honor Paid to Memory of Miller," *Los Angeles Times*, September 23, 1935.

13. Quotation from Klotz, *Mission Inn*, 99. Klotz, *Mission Inn*, 97–99.

14. Quotations from Dr. Harold Harada, interview by Mark Rawitsch, July 23, 2000. Dr. Harold Harada in discussion with Mark Rawitsch, July 22–23, 2000.

15. Clark Harada, Grade Records 1937–1938, Riverside School Records, Riverside Polytechnic High School, 1919–1960, Riverside Municipal Archives; *The 1938 Orange and Green*, Riverside Polytechnic High School (Riverside, CA: Riverside Polytechnic High School, 1938), n.p.

16. Naomi Harada, e-mail to Mark Rawitsch, January 26, 2004; Roy Hashimura, interview by Wally Kido, January 8, 2007; "Statement of United States Citizen of Japanese Ancestry," DSS Form 304A, February 22, 1943, WRA, Clark Harada File; quotation from Betty Finley, "Prophecy," *The 1938 Orange and Green*, n.p.; Riverside School Records.

17. Quotation from Mine Harada Kido, letter to Mark Rawitsch, March 21, 1977.

18. Quotations from Mine Harada Kido, letter to Mark Rawitsch, February 24, 1977, and Mine Harada Kido, interview by Mark Rawitsch, January 17, 1982.

19. Quotation from Dr. Harold Harada, interview by Mark Rawitsch, July 22, 2000. See also Roy Hashimura, interview by Wally Kido, January 8, 2007.

20. Quotation from Dr. Harold Harada, interview by Mark Rawitsch, July 22, 2000. Patterson, *Colony,* 263–266; Roy Hashimura, interview by Wally Kido, December 7, 2006; "California Deaths, 1940–1997, Jess Stebler," February 15, 1876, to December 4, 1950, Ancestry.com, http://vitals.rootsweb.ancestry.com/ca/death/search.cgi (accessed March 20, 2008). Sumi reported in a WRA Application for Leave Clearance, March 1, 1943, that she had known Stebler for thirty years prior to the wartime expulsion.

21. Quotations from Sumi Harada in discussion with Mark Rawitsch, January 10, 1977; Dr. Harold Harada, interview by Mark Rawitsch, July 22, 2000.

22. Quotation from Roy Hashimura, interview by Wally Kido, December 7, 2006. Harada family photographs and negatives from circa 1935–1940, Harada Family Archival Collection.

23. Sumi Harada in discussion with Mark Rawitsch, January 10, 1977; Jukichi Harada, Personal History Notes.

24. Quotation from Sumi Harada, interview by Mark Rawitsch, December 13, 1976. See Riverside city directories, circa 1935–1940.

25. Quotations from "Eulogize Craig during Session," *Riverside Daily Press*, September 11, 1922. "Judge Craig Is Stricken," *Riverside Daily Press*, September 7, 1922; "All Riverside Today Mourns Death of Judge Hugh H. Craig," *Riverside Daily Press*, September 9, 1922; "Sorrowing Friends Pay Last Tribute to Judge Hugh H. Craig," *Riverside Daily Press*, September 11, 1922; "Condition Is Still Grave," *Riverside Enterprise*, January 18, 1923; "No Improvement in the Condition of Injured Couple," *Riverside Enterprise*, January 18, 1923; "Accident Held Unavoidable," *Riverside Enterprise*, January 23, 1923; "City Mourns Passing of J. Van De Grift," *Riverside Enterprise*, February 15, 1923. According to her death notice in the *Riverside Enterprise*, Cynthia Robinson died in Riverside on September 25, 1922, at the age of seventy-eight.

26. Quotation from Lily Ann Inouye, e-mail messages to Mark Rawitsch, April 8, 17, July 12, 2007. Warren Harada, e-mail messages to Mark Rawitsch, November 20, 21,

2006; Kimi Klein, e-mail messages to Mark Rawitsch, March 19, 20, 2007; Naomi Harada, e-mail message to Mark Rawitsch, March 19, 2007; Rosemary Hayashi, e-mail message to Mark Rawitsch, May 26, 2007.

27. "Individual Record," June 27, 1942, WRA, Sumi Harada File; "To whom it may concern," July 25, 1939, unsigned letter describing Jukichi Harada's medical disabilities, Harada Family Archival Collection; Roy Hashimura, interviews with Wally Kido, December 7, 2006, January 8, 2007; "Individual Record," November 18, 1942, WRA, Clark Harada File. See Clark Harada, correspondence to Sumi Harada, circa 1937–1942, Harada Family Archival Collection.

28. Dr. [Yoshizo] Harada, letter to Elmer L. Shirrell, April 10, 1943; "Individual Record," August 28, 1942, WRA, Dr. Yoshizo Harada File. Quotations from Rosemary Hayashi, e-mail message to Mark Rawitsch, May 26, 2007; Rosalind Uno, e-mail message to Mark Rawitsch, November 17, 2006.

29. Jukichi Harada, Personal History Notes.

30. Jukichi Harada, Draft Registration Card, 1918, National Archives; Masa Atsu Harada, Draft Registration Card, 1918, National Archives. See Hosokawa, *JACL*, 51–56, 293–299.

31. Edwin Nishimura, "Clinical Record, Objective Symptoms, and Clinical Record, History of Present Disease," May 30, 1942, WRA, Ken Harada File; Ken Harada Alien Registration, February 8, 1942, with photograph, Harada Family Archival Collection; Mine Harada Kido, interview by Mark Rawitsch, January 17, 1982; "A Tour of the Harada House with Dr. Harold Harada," videotape, July 22, 2000; Dr. Harold Harada, interview by Mark Rawitsch, July 22, 2000.

32. See Jess Stebler, letters and cards to Sumi Harada, 1943–1945, quoted in Russo, "The Harada House," 8; Harada Family Archival Collection; visits by Mark Rawitsch with Sumi, Clark, and Dr. Harold Harada at Harada House, 1977–2000.

33. Katherine Howland Ranck, letter to Priscilla Howland, December 22, 1941, Mark H. Rawitsch Collection.

CHAPTER 12: FAREWELL TO RIVERSIDE

1. Quotation from Hosokawa, *JACL*, 130; "Application for Leave Clearance," December 7, 1942, WRA, Mine Harada Kido File.

2. Quotation from Dr. Harold Harada, interview by Mark Rawitsch, July 22, 2000.

3. Quotation from Hosokawa, *JACL*, 130.

4. Quotation of Saburo Kido; the first paragraph is cited in Girdner and Loftis, *Great Betrayal*, 10; the second paragraph is cited in Hosokawa, *JACL*, 130–131.

5. Quotation from Dr. Harold Harada, interview by Mark Rawitsch, July 22, 2000. See Matthew T. Estes and Donald H. Estes, "Hot Enough to Melt Iron: The San Diego Nikkei Experience, 1942–1946," *The Journal of San Diego History* 42, no. 3 (Summer 1996): 1.

6. Quotations of President Franklin D. Roosevelt, "Day of Infamy," audio recording, December 8, 1941, http://www.radiochemistry.org/history/video/fdr_infamy.html (accessed November 7, 2010).

7. Quotations from "Scare on the Coast," *Time*, February 16, 1942.

8. Quotations from Joe Vargo, "Shooting Enemies in the Night; Target Was Fear in 'Battle of L.A.,'" *Riverside Press-Enterprise*, August 10, 1995; Hosokawa, *JACL,* 144, 142.

9. Quotations from Hosokawa, *JACL,* 142–144; Mine Harada Kido, interview by Mark Rawitsch, January 17, 1982; Konvitz, *The Alien and the Asiatic in American Law*, 241; Keith Aoki, "No Right to Own? The Early Twentieth-Century 'Alien Land Laws' as a Prelude to Internment," *Boston College Law Review*, 40 B.C.L. Rev. 37 (1998): 9.

10. "Saburo Kido's Address at the Emergency JACL Meeting, San Francisco, March 8, 1942," cited in Hosokawa, *JACL,* Appendix B, 364–369; Saburo Kido, interview with Joe Grant Masaoka and Robert A. Wilson, January 4, 1967.

11. Quotations from Dr. Harold Harada, interview by Mark Rawitsch, July 22, 2000.

12. Quotations from Sumi Harada, interview by Mark Rawitsch, December 13, 1976.

13. Quotation from Dr. Harold Harada, interview by Mark Rawitsch, July 22, 2000; "WRA Evacuee Property Report," April 7, 1945, and other file correspondence, WRA, Harold Harada File.

14. Quotation from Sumi Harada, interview by Mark Rawitsch, December 13, 1976.

15. Quotations from Hosokawa, *JACL,* 144. Deborah K. Lim, "Meeting with Governor Olson," Research Report Prepared for Presidential Select Committee on JACL Resolution #7, 1990, http://www.resisters.com/study/LimPartICID.htm#ID3 (accessed November 7, 2010); Saburo Kido, interview with Joe Grant Masaoka and Robert A. Wilson, May 9, 1966; Hosokawa, *JACL,* 146; "Olson Tells Japanese Here They Must Help or Get Out," *Los Angeles Times*, February 7, 1942.

16. Quotations from "Scare on the Coast," *Time*, February 16, 1942.

17. Quotation from Lily Ann Inouye, e-mail message to Mark Rawitsch, April 17, 2007.

18. Lt. Gen. J. L. DeWitt to the Chief of Staff, US Army, June 5, 1943, in US Army, Western Defense Command and Fourth Army, Final Report; *Japanese Evacuation from the West Coast 1942* (Washington, DC: Government Printing Office, 1943), vii–x.

19. Quotations from "Executive Order 9066," *Japanese American Internment Curriculum*, http://bss.sfsu.edu/internment/executiorder9066.html (accessed April 16, 2009); "Immediate Evacuation of Japanese Demanded," *Los Angeles Times*, February 25, 1942; "Ouster of All Japs in California Near," *San Francisco Examiner*, February 27, 1942. "Submarine Shells Southland Oil Field," *Los Angeles Times*, February 24, 1942; "Coast Alert for New Raids," *Los Angeles Times*, February 25, 1942; "Army Says Alarm Real," *Los Angeles Times*, February 26, 1942.

20. Quotations from "A Tour of the Harada House"; Mine Harada Kido, interview by Mark Rawitsch, January 17, 1982.

21. Quotation from Sumi Harada, interview by Mark Rawitsch, February 24, 1982.

22. "To Government of United States of America," March 2, 1942, Harada House Inventory Notes, Harada Family Archival Collection.

23. Dr. Harold Harada, interview by Mark Rawitsch, July 22, 2000; "Individual Record," November 6, 1942, WRA, Dr. Masa Atsu Harada File; Central Utah Final Accountability Report, 26; "Application for Leave Clearance," retitled "Questionnaire," February 26, 1943, WRA, Ken Harada File; photographs of 1567 Santa Ynez Way, Sacramento,

from Patty and Warren Harada in e-mail message to Mark Rawitsch, August 2, 2007, and earlier images of the Sacramento house in Harada Family Archival Collection.

CHAPTER 13: LEAVING LEMON STREET BEHIND

1. Quotation from Dr. Harold Harada, interview by Mark Rawitsch, July 23, 2000.

2. Quotation from Dr. Harold Harada, interview by Mark Rawitsch, July 22, 2000.

3. Mike Masaoka, "To Whom It May Concern," December 14, 1942, WRA, Saburo Kido File; Hosokawa, *JACL,* 170.

4. Quotations from Hosokawa, *JACL,* 108.

5. Quotations from ibid., 155.

6. Quotations from Saburo Kido's JACL speech here and below from Hosokawa, *JACL,* 364–369; quotations regarding the discussions of the removal process and the FBI encounter in San Francisco from Saburo Kido, interview with Joe Grant Masaoka and Robert A. Wilson, January 4, 1967.

7. Quotation from Hosokawa, *JACL,* 161.

8. See the entire text of Kido's speech in Hosokawa, *JACL,* 364–369; other quotations come from Hosokawa, *JACL,* 152–168. The pre-war stance of the *JACL,* difficulties caused by its collaborative position after Pearl Harbor, and how that position affected the organization's ability to address the government claim that "military necessity" required the mass expulsion are explained in Stephanie Bangarth, *Voices Raised in Protest: Defending North American Citizens of Japanese Ancestry, 1942–1949* (Vancouver: UBC Press, 2008), 121–126.

9. Jeffery F. Burton et al., *Confinement and Ethnicity: An Overview of World War II Japanese American Relocation Sites*, Western Archaeological and Conservation Center, National Park Service, US Department of the Interior, Publications in Anthropology 74, 1999 (revised, July 2000), http://www.cr.nps.gov/history/online_books/anthropology74/index.htm (accessed March 17, 2007); Sumi Harada, letter to [Wade] Head, January 21, 1943, WRA, Sumi Harada File.

10. Quotations from "The Diaries of George Fujimoto," Asian American Riverside, University of California, Riverside, http://www.asianamericanriverside.ucr.edu/Notable AsianAmericans/Japanese/Fujimoto/index.html (accessed April 20, 2009).

11. Quotations from Executive Order 9102, "The American Presidency Project," "Franklin D. Roosevelt XXXII President of the United States: 1933–1945, 37, Executive Order 9102 Establishing the War Relocation Authority, March 18, 1942," http://www.presidency.ucsb.edu/ws/index.php?pid=16239 (accessed November 7, 2010). Sumi Harada in discussion with Mark Rawitsch, January 10, 1977; Hosokawa, *JACL,* 184; Nestor N. Brule, letter to Claude E. Corwall, December 9, 1942, WRA, Clark Harada File.

12. Quotation from Hosokawa, *JACL,* 172.

13. Quotation from Edwin Nishimura, "Clinical Record, Objective Symptoms, and Clinical Record, History of Present Disease," May 30, 1942, WRA, Ken Harada File.

14. Quotation from Mine Harada Kido, interview by Mark Rawitsch, January 17, 1982. Saburo Kido, letter to Rex Lee, June 1, 1942, WRA, Saburo Kido File; Rosalind Uno, e-mail message to Mark Rawitsch, March 31, 2007.

15. Quotation from Rosalind Uno, e-mail message to Mark Rawitsch, December 17, 2006. See "Individual Record" of Rosalind Mitsuye Kido, August 17, 1942, WRA, in Mine Harada Kido File.

16. Warren Harada, e-mail message to Mark Rawitsch, December 4, 2006; "WRA Form 156, List of Personal Property," March 25, 1944; "Evacuee Property Report," March 25, 1944; "Request for Transportation of Property," various dates in March 1944; Dr. M. A. Harada, "Special Power of Attorney," 1943; quotation from M. A. Harada, MD, letter to Mr. O. B. Wilt, March 4, 1944; "Individual Record," November 6, 1942, WRA, Dr. Masa Atsu Harada File.

17. "Individual Record," November 7, 1942, WRA, Shiashi Harry [Jukichi] Harada File; "Individual Record," November 7, 1942, WRA, Ken Harada File; "Individual Record," November 6, 1942, WRA, Dr. Masa Atsu Harada File; Burton et al., *Confinement and Ethnicity.*

18. Quotation from Roy Hashimura, interview by Wally Kido, December 7, 2006; Central Utah Final Accountability Report, 29–30; Hosokawa, *JACL,* 94–95; Ray D. Johnston, letter to Charles F. Ernst, June 28, 1943, WRA, Sumi Harada File; "Japanese-American Internee Data File, 1942–1945: Dr. Russell H. WeHara, #20607L," http://aad.archives.gov/aad/series-description.jsp?s=623 (accessed November 21, 2010); Clark Harada, letter to Jukichi Harada, April 23, 1942, Harada Family Archival Collection. Clark's letter to his father on April 23, sent to the house on Lemon Street, suggests that Jukichi and Ken may not have left Riverside for Sacramento until sometime at the end of April.

19. Quotations and information from "C.E. Order 83, Instructions to All Persons of Japanese Ancestry," Harada Family Archival Collection.

20. Quotations from ibid.; Roy Hashimura, interview by Wally Kido, January 8, 2007.

21. Quotation of Harold Harada's wall message, Harada House National Historic Landmark, upstairs west front bedroom, west wall. Riverside School Records, Riverside Municipal Archives.

22. Quotation from Dr. Harold Harada, interview by Mark Rawitsch, July 23, 2000.

23. Quotations from Santa Fe Trailways brochure, "Grand Canyon and the Indian Empire," Wichita, Kansas, circa 1940, The University of Arizona Libraries, http://www.library.arizona.edu/exhibits/pams/pdfs/75grtrai.pdf (accessed August 12, 2009).

24. Quotations from "Japanese Families Leave Riverside," *Riverside Daily Press,* May 25, 1942.

25. Quotation from Dr. Harold Harada, interview by Mark Rawitsch, July 23, 2000. See Poston Relocation Center WRA photographs, Bancroft Library, University of California, Berkeley, Poston bus arrivals: Vol. 1, Sec. A, WRA #A-76 and Vol. 2, Sec. A, WRA #397; and an image of a family putting straw into mattress covers at Poston: Vol. 1, Sec. A, WRA #A-147.

26. Quotation from Roy Hashimura, interview by Wally Kido, January 8, 2007. Sumi Harada, letter to "Mr. Wade" [Wade Head], June 16, 1942, WRA, Sumi Harada File.

CHAPTER 14: CAMP

1. Quotation from Dr. Harold Harada, interview by Mark Rawitsch, July 23, 2000.

2. "Application for Private Employment," April 6, 1944, WRA, Harold Harada File; "Employment Record," 1943[42] to 1944, WRA, Sumi Harada File; Burton et al., *Confinement and Ethnicity*, "Chapter 10: Poston Relocation Center." Quotation from Roy Hashimura, interview by Wally Kido, January 8, 2007.

3. Quotations from "In-Patient Card," May 29, 1942; "Clinical Record," May 30, 1942, WRA, Shiashi Harry [Jukichi] Harada File; "Clinical Record," May 30, 1942, WRA, Ken Harada File. "Japanese-American Internee Data File, 1942–1945: Edwin T. Nishimura, #06509A," http://aad.archives.gov/aad/series-description.jsp?s=623 (accessed November 19, 2010).

4. Quotation from Hosokawa, *JACL,* 169. Saburo Kido, interviews with Joe Grant Masaoka and Robert A. Wilson, January 4, 1967, and May 9, 1966. Quotation from Saburo Kido, letter to Rex Lee, June 1, 1942, WRA, Saburo Kido File.

5. Quotations from Saburo Kido, letter to Rex Lee, June 1, 1942, WRA, Saburo Kido File; Mine Harada Kido, letter to Mark Rawitsch, May 22, 1977.

6. Quotations from Saburo Kido, letter to Major Herman Goebel, June 26, 1942, WRA, Saburo Kido File.

7. Quotation from Hosokawa, *JACL,* 16.

8. Wally Kido, e-mail message to Mark Rawitsch, September 12, 2007; Rosalind Uno, e-mail messages to Mark Rawitsch, September 13 and 16, 2007.

9. "Identification and Summary Sheet," [Date of Disposition] October 25, 1942, WRA, Ken Harada File; "Identification and Summary Sheet," [Date of Disposition] October 25, 1942, WRA, Shiashi Harry [Jukichi] Harada File; "Individual Record," August 28, 1942, WRA, Dr. Yoshizo Harada File; "Individual Record of Cash Advances," June 4, 1942, to October 21, 1942, WRA, Dr. Masa Atsu Harada File; "Clinical Record X-Ray Report," July 9, 1942, WRA, Ken Harada File.

10. Mine Harada Kido, interview by Mark Rawitsch, January 17, 1982; "Individual Record," Laurence Mineo Kido, August 17, 1942, WRA, in Mine Harada Kido File. Quotation from Herman P. Goebel Jr., "To All Peace Officers and All Other Persons Concerned," [Travel Permit] July 1942, WRA, Saburo Kido File. "Individual Record," August 17, 1942, WRA, Saburo Kido File; Hosokawa, *JACL,* 219, 277; "The Beating of Saburo Kido," BANC MSS 67/14, Frames 0257–0277, Reel 239, 1–6, Japanese American Evacuation and Resettlement Records, Bancroft Library, University of California, Berkeley.

11. Quotation from Sumi Harada, letter to Wade [Head], June 16, 1942, WRA, Sumi Harada File. "WRA Application for Special Transfer" [to Tule Lake], n.d. [probably 1942]; Sumi Harada, letter to [Wade] Head, January 21, 1943; Mary M. Kirkland, letter to Robert A. Petrie, August 5, 1942, WRA, Sumi Harada File.

12. [War Relocation Authority] Central Utah Final Accountability Roster, October 31, 1945; Laura Hillenbrand, *Seabiscuit: An American Legend* (New York: Random House, 2001).

13. Quotation from Mine Okubo, letter to Mark Rawitsch, March 11, 1976.

14. Mine Okubo, *Citizen 13660* (Seattle: University of Washington Press, 1983), 113–122; "Japanese-American Internee Data File, 1942–1945: Mine Okubo, 13660A" and "Toku R. Okubo, 13660B," http://aad.archives.gov/aad/series-description.jsp?s=623 (accessed November 19, 2010).

15. Quotations from "Welcome to Topaz," *Topaz Times*, September 17, 1942; Okubo, *Citizen*, 122. Okubo, *Citizen*, 113–122; Burton et al., *Confinement and Ethnicity*, "Chapter 12, Topaz Relocation Center"; [War Relocation Authority] Central Utah Final Accountability Report, 26; Kimi Klein, e-mail message to Mark Rawitsch, March 19, 2007; Lily Ann Inouye, e-mail message to Mark Rawitsch, April 17, 2007.

16. "4 Doctors to Leave," *Daily Tulean Dispatch*, October 24, 1942. Quotation from "Thanks to Medical Profession," *Daily Tulean Dispatch*, October 24, 1942.

17. Quotations from "Identifying Summary Sheet," [disposition date] October 25, 1942, WRA, Shiashi Harry [Jukichi] Harada File; "Hospital," *Topaz Times*, October 14, 1942. "Briefs and Bulletins," *Topaz Times*, October 30, 1942; Central Utah Final Accountability Report, 26; "Consent to Care at Hospital," October 27, 1942, WRA, Ken Harada File; "Individual Record," November 7, 1942, WRA, Ken Harada File; [file correspondence chronology], January 21 to March 11, 1943, WRA, Sumi Harada File; Charles F. Ernst, letter to Elmer L. Shirrell, October 24, 1942, Community Welfare Medical Division, letter to C. F. Ernst, October 23, 1942, "Employment Record," October 27, [1942,] to June 23, [1943], WRA, Dr. Masa Atsu Harada File; War Relocation Authority Photographs, Series 4, Bancroft Library; Central Utah Relocation Center (Topaz, Utah), Volume 10, Section A, WRA No. E-30, Topaz City Hospital dedication ceremony photograph by Tom Parker, October 17, 1942; Burton et al., *Confinement and Ethnicity*, "Chapter 12, Topaz Relocation Center."

CHAPTER 15: BLUE BANDANAS AND AN IRONWOOD CLUB

1. Quotation from Okubo, *Citizen*, 139.

2. Quotations from ibid., 89, 143; Wally Kido interview with Roy Hashimura, January 8, 2007.

3. Quotation and information from *Manzanar Free Press*, January 20, 1942. Edward H. Spicer et al., *Impounded People: Japanese-Americans in the Relocation Centers* (Tucson: University of Arizona Press, 1969), 61–64; see also the recent work of Shirley Muramoto Wong in "Hidden Legacy: Tribute to Teachers of Japanese Traditional Arts in the War Relocation Authority Camps," event program, Koyasan Buddhist Temple, Los Angeles, April 20, 2010.

4. Kimi Kodani Hill, *Topaz Moon: Chiura Obata's Art of the Internment* (Berkeley, CA: Heyday Books, 2000), 2; Central Utah Relocation Center Final Accountability Roster, 32; Okubo, *Citizen*, 145; Hisako Hibi, untitled painting, Topaz, Utah, November 1942, Japanese American National Museum Collection, Los Angeles, Accession Number 96.601.9.

5. Quotation and information from "Via Saburo Kido," September 14, 1942, Japanese American Evacuation and Resettlement Records, Bancroft Library, University of California, Berkeley.

6. Quotations from Hosokawa, *JACL,* 198. Hosokawa, *JACL,* 197–198, 201; Estes and Estes, "Hot Enough to Melt Iron."

7. Quotation from interview with Saburo Kido by Joe Grant Masaoka and Robert A. Wilson, May 9, 1966.

8. Quotation from Hosokawa, *JACL,* 201. Hosokawa, *JACL,* 190–194; Dillon S. Myer, "War Relocation Authority: The Director's Account, An Interview Conducted by Amelia R. Fry, November 6, 1969," in *Japanese-American Relocation Reviewed*, Vol. 2: *The Internment* (Berkeley: Regional Oral History Office, Bancroft Library, University of California, 1976), 2a. Quotation from interview with Saburo Kido by Joe Grant Masaoka and Robert A. Wilson, May 9, 1966. Eric L. Muller, *Free to Die for Their Country: The Story of the Japanese American Draft Resisters in World War II* (Chicago: University of Chicago Press, 2003), 44–46.

9. Quotation from Mine Harada Kido, interview by Mark Rawitsch, January 17, 1982.

10. Quotations from *Topaz Times*, November 11, 1942; "The City: Reveal Plan to Enlist Nisei in Army," *Topaz Times*, November 11, 1942.

11. Quotation of Saburo Kido, interview with Joe Grant Masaoka and Robert A. Wilson, May 9, 1966.

12. "The Beating of Saburo Kido." Quotation from Mine Harada Kido, interview by Mark Rawitsch, January 17, 1982. Saburo Kido, interview with Joe Grant Masaoka and Robert A. Wilson, May 9, 1966.

13. Quotation from Mine Harada Kido, interview by Mark Rawitsch, January 17, 1982.

14. Quotation from Mike Masaoka, "To Whom It May Concern," December 14, 1942, WRA, Saburo Kido File.

15. Quotations of Saburo Kido, from Edward J. Kirby, "Subversive Activities at War Relocation Centers," Federal Bureau of Investigation, [declassified] File No. 100-4483, January 9, 1943, US National Archives and Records Administration; Norris James, letter to Chief, WRA Reports Division, February 1, 1943, WRA, Saburo Kido File. "Japanese-American Internee Data File, 1942–1945; Oritaro Kobayashi, 13344A," http://aad .archives.gov/aad/series-description.jsp?s=623 (accessed November 19, 2010); see also Eric L. Muller, "A Penny for Their Thoughts: Draft Resistance at the Poston Relocation Center," *Law and Contemporary Problems* (Spring 2005).

16. Quotation from Mine Harada Kido, interview by Mark Rawitsch, January 17, 1982.

17. [Untranslated article printed in Japanese], *Poston Chronicle*, January 29, 1943; see "War Department Plans to Organize Japanese American Combat Team," *Topaz Times*, January 29, 1943.

18. Quotation from Saburo Kido, interview with Joe Grant Masaoka and Robert A. Wilson, May 9, 1966.

19. Quotations from Mine Harada Kido, interview by Mark Rawitsch, January 17, 1982; Philip M. Glick, letter to John H. Provinse, February 6, 1943; Norris E. James, letter to John Baker, January 31, 1943, WRA, Saburo Kido File; Saburo Kido, interview with Joe Grant Masaoka and Robert A. Wilson, May 9, 1966. "Japanese-American Internee Data File, 1942–1945: James J. Tanaka, 34414A"; "Miyoshi Matsuda, 13249B," http://aad.archives.gov/aad/series-description.jsp?s=623 (accessed November 19, 2010).

20. Quotations from Rosalind Uno, from Mark Rawitsch's interview with Rosalind Uno, Wally Kido, Kimi Klein, Naomi Harada, Dr. Ken Harada, and Paul Harada, October 29, 2005.

21. Quotations from Mine Harada Kido, interview by Mark Rawitsch, January 17, 1982.

22. Quotation from Rosalind Uno, from Mark Rawitsch's interview with Rosalind Uno, Wally Kido, Kimi Klein, Naomi Harada, Dr. Ken Harada, and Paul Harada, October 29, 2005.

23. Quotation from Dr. Harold Harada, interview by Mark Rawitsch, July 23, 2000. "Application for Private Employment," April 6, 1944, WRA, Harold Harada File; "The Beating of Saburo Kido," 1–6; "Individual Record," August 17, 1942; "Clinical Record," January 31 to February 15, 1943; "Clinical Record, Ward Surgeon's Progress and Treatment Record," January 31 to February 4, 1943; "Clinical Record, Brief," February 15, 1943; Norris E. James, letter to John Baker, January 31, 1943, WRA, Saburo Kido File.

24. Quotation from "The Beating of Saburo Kido," 6–7. "Japanese-American Internee Data File, 1942–1945: Miyoshi Matsuda, 13249B," http://aad.archives.gov/aad /series-description.jsp?s=623 (accessed November 19, 2010).

25. Quotations from "The Beating of Saburo Kido," 7–8.

26. Quotations from ibid., 9.

27. Quotation from Mine Harada Kido, interview by Mark Rawitsch, January 17, 1982. "Eight Held for Felony Charge; State Court to Try Men for Assault on JACL Head," *Poston Chronicle*, February 2, 1943; "Kido Attackers Sentenced; Five to Serve in State Penitentiary," *Poston Chronicle*, February 19, 1943; "Last Two Kido's Attackers Released on Suspension," *Poston Chronicle*, March 7, 1943; "Kido Well after Recent Beating," *Topaz Times*, March 2, 1943; Saburo Kido, interview with Joe Grant Masaoka and Robert A. Wilson, May 9, 1966.

28. Quotations from J. Edgar Hoover, letter to Dillon S. Myer, February 3, 1943, WRA, Saburo Kido File; Mine Harada Kido, interview by Mark Rawitsch, January 17, 1982.

29. Quotations from Pauline Hunnicutt, letter to Dillon Myer, February 5, 1943, WRA, Mine Harada Kido File.

30. Quotation from Guy C. Calden, letter to D. S. Myer, January 28, 1943, WRA, Saburo Kido File. Dr. Alfred Fiske, letter to Gentlemen, no date [circa January 1943], WRA, Saburo Kido File.

31. Quotations from Perry Evans, letter to Director, War Relocation Authority, January 29, 1943; Dagmar A. Evans, letter to Director, War Relocation Authority, February 5, 1943, WRA, Saburo Kido File.

32. Quotations from "Re: Saburo Kido," February 20, 1943, WRA, Saburo Kido File. The reference to this report in Kido's file as coming from the FBI can be found in Mine Harada Kido's WRA file; "Exhibit XV, War Relocation Authority Indefinite Leave," n.d., WRA, Saburo Kido File.

33. Quotations from "Request for Transfer," January 21, 1943, WRA, Sumi Harada File.

CHAPTER 16: FROM ISSEI TO NISEI

1. Quotation from Sumi Harada, interview by Mark Rawitsch, February 24, 1982. "Weather Report," *Topaz Times*, March 11, 1943; Chiura Obata, "Sunset, Water Tower,

March 10, 1943" [Topaz, Utah], painting, watercolor on paper, 15.5 × 20.5 inches, collection of the Obata Family.

2. Quotation from Sumi Harada, interview by Mark Rawitsch, December 13, 1976. [Correspondence summary], January 21 to March 17, 1943; "Form WRA-149, Request for Transfer," January 25, 1943; W. Wade Head, letter to Miss Nell Findley, March 9, 1943; Mark H. Astrup, letter to W. Wade Head, February 25, 1943; Ray Ashworth, communication to "All Peace Officers and All Other Persons Concerned," February 24, 1943; Sumi Harada, Harold Harada, and Roy, Toshiye, and Sumiko Hashimura, letter to Leave Office Travel Bureau, April 10, 1943, WRA, Sumi Harada File; "Brief Beats," *Poston Chronicle*, March 11, 1943; "Transit," *Topaz Times*, April 1, 1943; Sumi Harada, letter to Wade Head, January 21, 1943, WRA, Sumi Harada File.

3. Quotations from Dr. Harold Harada, interview by Mark Rawitsch, July 22, 2000; Sumi Harada, interview by Mark Rawitsch, December 13, 1976. Sumi Harada, letter to Wade Head, March 17, 1943, WRA, Sumi Harada File.

4. Dr. Harold Harada, interview by Mark Rawitsch, July 23, 2000; Sumi Harada, interview by Mark Rawitsch, December 13, 1976; Margarette E. Fujita, letter to George LaFabregue, March 12, 1943, WRA, Ken Harada File; "Deaths," *Topaz Times*, March 20, 1943; State of Utah, Certificate of Death for Ken Harada.

5. Charles A. Ernst letter to Masa Atsu Harada, "Notice of Action on Application for Leave Clearance," October 1, 1943, WRA, Dr. Masa Atsu Harada File; Kimi Klein, e-mail message to Mark Rawitsch, April 18, 2006; Charles F. Ernst, letter to Harvey Coverly, March 13, 1943. Quotation from "WRA Form 133, Citizen's Short-Term Leave," March 14, 1943, WRA, Dr. Yoshizo Harada File. J. O. Hayes, letter to Charles F. Ernst, March 14, 1943, WRA, Dr. Yoshizo Harada File.

6. Quotations from Dr. Harold Harada, interview by Mark Rawitsch, July 23, 2000. Burton et al., *Confinement and Ethnicity*, "Chapter 12, Topaz Relocation Center"; [Funeral Arrangements] Form, WRA, March 16, 1943; George Lafabregue, letter to Gilbert L. Niesse, March 16, 1943, WRA, Ken Harada File.

7. Sumi Harada, interview by Mark Rawitsch, December 13, 1976. Quotations from Sumi Harada, letter to Wade Head, March 17, 1943, WRA, Sumi Harada File.

8. Poem by Sumi Harada, "My Mother, March 17, 1943," Harada Family Archival Collection, and Gayle Wattawa, ed., *Inlandia: A Literary Journey through California's Inland Empire* (Santa Clara, CA: Santa Clara University and Heyday Books, 2006), 199–200. Quotation from Dr. Harold Harada, interview by Mark Rawitsch, July 23, 2000.

9. Quotation from "In Memoriam, Mrs. Ken Harada," undated newspaper clipping, no original source, in Harada Family Archival Collection. Eralia V. Gonzales, "To Whom It May Concern," May 10, 1944, Harada Family Archival Collection; Russo, "The Harada House," 16.

10. Quotations from Yoshiyo [Yoshizo] Harada, DDS, letter to [Elmer] Shirrell, April 10, 1943; Elmer L. Shirrell, letter to E. R. Rowalt, April 19, 1943, WRA, Dr. Yoshizo Harada File.

11. E. M. Rowalt, letter to Colonel William P. Scobey, April 23, 1943; Captain John M. Hall, letter to Elmer Rowalt, May 3, 1943; [Leave Status Report], July 12, 1943, WRA, Dr. Yoshizo Harada File. Quotations from F. V. Nelson, DDS, letter to Dillon S. Myer, March 4, 1943; Mary R. Kenetick, [letter #2] to D. S. Myer, n.d. [circa Febru-

ary 1943], and Mary R. Kenetick, [letter #1] to D. S. Myer, February 22, 1943; Mrs. J. Fernandez, letter to D. S. Myer, n.d. [circa February 1943]; [Leave Authorization], July 12, 1943; "War Relocation Authority Enlistee Service and Payment Record Card, Fiscal Year 1944," WRA, Dr. Yoshizo Harada File; Rosemary Hayashi, e-mail message to Mark Rawitsch, July 31, 2007.

12. Kimi Klein, e-mail message to Mark Rawitsch, April 18, 2006. Quotations from "A Letter of Resignation," M. A. Harada, MD, letter to Dr. J. A. Simpson, June 8, 1943, and Charles F. Ernst, letter to Dr. [M. A.] Harada, n.d., in *Topaz Times*, June 12, 1943. "Hospital," *Topaz Times*, October 14, 1942; see also Gordon H. Chang, *Morning Glory, Evening Shadow: Yamato Ichihashi and His Internment Writings, 1942–1945* (Stanford, CA: Stanford University Press, 1996), 228: May 24, [1943]: "Yamato wrote from Topaz, Utah project: Chiura was beaten a month ago but no culprit arrested as yet; a bokushi [minister] was hit with a stone, but no serious damage. The most serious case is the fight between two doctors, Harada, formerly of Tule Lake[,] and Ito, rather popular with the people. Professional jealousy."

13. M. A. Harada, MD, letter to Robert Cullum, June 14, 1943; Charles F. Ernst, letter to WRA Chicago, June 10, 1943; M. A. Harada, MD, letter to Edward M. Joyce, March 10, 1945; Charles F. Ernst, letter to Elmer L Shirrell, June 15, 1943; "Computation of Grant," June 19, 1943, WRA, Dr. Masa Atsu Harada File; Central Utah Final Accountability Report, 114; Kimi Klein, e-mail message to Mark Rawitsch, April 18, 2006; Warren Harada, e-mail messages to Mark Rawitsch, August 6 and 27, 2007.

14. Quotations from Sumi Harada, interview by Mark Rawitsch, February 24, 1982; Dr. Harold Harada, interview by Mark Rawitsch, July 23, 2000. "Application for Private Employment by Relocation Center Resident," April 6, 1944, WRA, Harold Harada File.

15. Quotations from Mine Harada Kido, interview by Mark Rawitsch, January 17, 1982. Rosalind Uno, in Mark Rawitsch's interview with Rosalind Uno, Wally Kido, Kimi Klein, Naomi Harada, Dr. Ken Harada, and Paul Harada, October 29, 2005.

16. Quotation from Dr. Harold Harada, interview by Mark Rawitsch, July 23, 2000.

17. "Notification of Death, 1944"; untitled Funeral Division record, January 30 to February 12, 1944, WRA, Shiashi Harry [Jukichi] Harada File; "Funeral Rites for Hikoharu Shimamoto, J. Harada Slated," *Topaz Times*, February 3, 1944. Quotations from Yoshizo Harada, in Yoshizo and Sumiye Harada, letter to Sumi and Shige Harada, January 31, 1944, Harada Family Archival Collection; Claud H. Pratt, letter to Clarke and Harold Harada, February 6, 1944, WRA, Shiashi Harry [Jukichi] Harada File. "List of Pall Bearers, Honorary Pall Bearers, Ushers, and Services for Funeral of J. Harada," February 6, 1944; "Receipt for Urn," February 12, 1944, WRA, Shiashi Harry [Jukichi] Harada File; "Veteran of 1898 War Dies in Topaz," undated newspaper clipping, no original source, Harada Family Archival Collection; "Japanese-American Internee Data File, 1942–1945: Jiryu Fujii, 13579A"; "George S. Kaneko, 12692A"; "Risaburo Inaba, 09146A"; "Yasuichi Teshima, 24027B," http://aad.archives.gov/aad/series-description.jsp?s=623 (accessed November 19, 2010); Sumi Harada, interview by Mark Rawitsch, February 24, 1982; Mine Harada Kido, interview by Mark Rawitsch, January 17, 1982; Dr. Harold Harada, interview by Mark Rawitsch, July 23, 2000; "Weather Report," *Topaz Times*, February 8, 1944. Quotations from the Reverend M. Ohmura, letter to Sumi Harada and Family, February 10, 1944, Harada Family Archival Collection; "Story of a Typical Pioneer

Issei," *Pacific Citizen*, February 19, 1944; Central Utah Final Accountability Report, 26. See *okoden* contribution notes, record of contributions and expressions of sympathy from Poston friends, family, and acquaintances, Harada Family Archival Collection.

CHAPTER 17: QUESTIONS OF LOYALTY

1. "Application for Leave Assistance Grant," May 6, 1944, WRA, Sumi Harada File.

2. Quotations from "Application for Leave Clearance," March 1, 1943, WRA, Sumi Harada File.

3. Sandra C. Taylor, *Jewel of the Desert: Japanese American Internment at Topaz* (Berkeley: University of California Press, 1993), 147–154.

4. Quotations from [WRA Questionnaire, first page missing], February 20, 1943, WRA, Dr. Masa Atsu Harada File. M. A. Harada, MD, letter to Edward M. Joyce, March 10, 1945; Edward M. Joyce, letter to Dr. M. A. Harada, May 23, 1945, WRA, Dr. Masa Atsu Harada File.

5. "Application for Leave Clearance," February 16, 1943, WRA, Dr. Yoshizo Harada File; "Statement of United States Citizen of Japanese Ancestry," February 18, 1943, WRA, Harold Harada File; Dr. Ken Morrison Harada, in Mark Rawitsch's interview with Rosalind Uno, Wally Kido, Kimi Klein, Naomi Harada, Dr. Ken Harada, and Paul Harada, October 29, 2005.

6. Quotation from Dr. Harold Harada, interview by Mark Rawitsch, July 22, 2000.

7. "Government," *Topaz Times*, October 28, 1942; "Election Returns Revealed," *Topaz Times*, December 30, 1942; "New Councilmen," *Topaz Times*, January 13, 1943; "Wedding," *Topaz Times*, February 10, 1942; "Statement of United States Citizen of Japanese Ancestry," February 22, 1943, WRA, Clark Harada File; Clark Harada, [unsigned] letter to Local Board 73, Alameda County, February 21, 1944, Harada Family Archival Collection.

8. Quotations from "Resident Committee Forwards Resolution to Washington," *Topaz Times*, February 15, 1943; "Text of Resolution," *Topaz Times*, February 15, 1943; "Message on Loyalty Sent Dillon Myer," *Topaz Times*, February 17, 1943. Taylor, *Jewel of the Desert*, 149. See "Residents, Not War Dept., Hold Answer, Says Myer," *Topaz Times*, February 16, 1943; "Committee of 33 Prepares Statement," *Topaz Times*, February 19, 1943; "War Dept. Answers Resolution," *Topaz Times*, February 19, 1943.

9. Quotations from "Residents, Not War Dept., Hold Answer, Says Myer," *Topaz Times*, February 16, 1943.

10. Quotation from "War Dept. Answers Resolution," *Topaz Times*, February 19, 1943.

11. Quotation from Clark Harada, [unsigned] letter to Local Board 70, Alameda County, April 28, 1944, Harada Family Archival Collection.

12. Quotation from Saburo Kido, "Timely Topics; Heart Mountain Fair Play Group," *Pacific Citizen*, March 25, 1944. See also Saburo Kido, communication to unknown recipient, April 3, 1944, Archives of the Japanese American Citizens League, cited in Research Report Prepared for Presidential Select Committee on JACL Resolution #7 (also known as "The Lim Report"), submitted in 1990 by Deborah K. Lim, footnotes 261 and 244; Muller, *Free to Die*, 93.

13. Dr. Harold Harada, interview by Mark Rawitsch, July 22, 2000; "Citizen's Indefinite Leave," April 27, 1944, WRA, Harold Harada File; "Application for Leave Assistance Grant," May 6, 1944; [office contact record], May 23 through August 23, 1945; "Union Pacific Railroad Company Form 1584," May 18, 1944, WRA, Sumi Harada File; Central Utah Final Accountability Report, 27; "Leaves," *Topaz Times*, May 27, 1944; Roy Hashimura, interview by Wally Kido, December 7, 2006; Hosokawa, *JACL*, 219.

14. [Multiple medical records], January to July 1944, WRA, Clark Harada File. Quotations from M. Mack, "Mr. Clark Harada Seen, Interview Date: 10/9/44"; J. Hugh Turner, letter to Leah K. Dickinson, October 19, 1944, WRA, Clark Harada File.

15. Quotation from Taylor, *Jewel of the Desert*, 101–102. Joseph R. Byerly, letter to Project Director, War Relocation Center, Topaz, Utah, October 14, 1944, WRA, Clark Harada File. Quotation from L. T. Hoffman, letter to Lt. Col. Joseph R. Byerly, October 19, 1944, WRA, Clark Harada File. "Harada Clark Kohei—20607—Topaz" [chronology of activity], October 3, 1944, to October 31, 1945, WRA, Clark Harada File; Harold Harada, letters to Sumi Harada, [various dates] October 1944, Harada Family Archival Collection; "Citizen's Indefinite Leave," November 1, 1944, WRA, Clark Harada File; Central Utah Final Accountability Report, 26.

CHAPTER 18: IT'S UP TO YOU, MEDIC

1. Quotation from Dr. Harold Harada, interview by Mark Rawitsch, July 22, 2000. "Citizen's Indefinite Leave," April 27, 1944; Charles F. Ernst letter to Shigetaka Harold Harada, Physical Examination for Selective Service, April 6, 1944; "Application for Leave Assistance Grant," April 25, 1944, WRA, Harold Harada File; Central Utah Final Accountability Report, 29.

2. Quotation from Dr. Harold Harada, interview by Mark Rawitsch, July 22, 2000. See also "The Hawaii Nisei Project," University of Hawaii, interview with Ronald Oba, F Company, 442nd Regimental Combat Team, about his time in the south of France, http://nisei.hawaii.edu/object/io_1160630804875.html (accessed September 29, 2007); Dr. Harold Harada, undated draft of a presentation about his wartime experiences, circa 1995, Harada Family Archival Collection.

3. Quotation from Dr. Harold Harada, interview by Mark Rawitsch, July 22, 2000.

4. Ibid.

5. Ibid.

6. Quotation from Dr. Harold Harada, interview by Mark Rawitsch, July 23, 2000.

7. Ibid.

8. Ben H. Tamashiro, "From Pearl Harbor to the Po; the Congressional Medal of Honor: Sadao Munemori," *The Hawaii Herald*, March 15, 1985, "The Hawaii Nisei Project," http://nisei.hawaii.edu/object/io_1160630804875.html (accessed November 12, 2010); Daniel K. Inouye, "MOH Citation for Daniel K. Inouye," Home of Heroes, http://www.homeofheroes.com/moh/citations_1942_nisei/inouye.html (accessed November 12, 2010).

9. Quotations from "A Tour of the Harada House"; Dr. Harold Harada, interview by Mark Rawitsch, July 22–23, 2000. David T. Yamada and Oral History Committee, Mon-

terey Peninsula Japanese American Citizens League, *The Japanese of the Monterey Peninsula: Their History and Legacy 1895–1995* (Monterey, CA: Monterey Peninsula Japanese American Citizens League, 1995), 233–238; "Breaking the Silence after 50 Years; American Soldiers of Japanese Descent," *Monterey County Herald*, November 3, 1996; Jessa Forte Netting, "Beyond Barbed Wire: Encore! Encore!" *Monterey County Herald*, May 12, 2000; Obituary of Setsuyo Sumida, *Monterey County Herald*, June 24, 1972; Masayo Umezawa Duus, *Unlikely Liberators: The Men of the 100th and 442nd*, trans. Peter Duus (Honolulu: University of Hawaii Press, 1983), 29, 121–122.

10. Quotation from Dr. Harold Harada, interview by Mark Rawitsch, July 22, 2000. Duus, *Unlikely Liberators*, 217.

11. Quotation from Dr. Harold Harada, interview by Mark Rawitsch, July 23, 2000.

12. Harold Harada, letter to Sumi Harada, April 30, 1945, Harada Family Archival Collection.

CHAPTER 19: HOME

1. Quotation from Sumi Harada, interview by Mark Rawitsch, December 13, 1976.

2. "Office Contact Record," May 23, [1945?], to August 23, 1945, WRA, Sumi Harada File. Quotation from Sumi Harada, interview by Mark Rawitsch, December 13, 1976. See also Charles Kikuchi's report of his December 1944 interviews with Sumi Harada in Chicago, in which he described a deeply embittered and pessimistic Sumi as having "strong emotional feelings" about the losses of the incarceration and her Chicago resettlement experiences. "Her over-aggressiveness is merely a cover-up for inner feelings of insecurity and it definitely is a defense mechanism," Kikuchi wrote in his "Evacuation & Resettlement Study," December 22, 1944, Case History #60, CH-60 "Shimako Shibata" [pseudonym for Sumi Harada], in BANC MSS 67/14C, Reel 079, Frame 0327, Folder T1.989, Bancroft Library, University of California, Berkeley.

3. Quotation from Paul Bailey, *City in the Sun* (Los Angeles: Westernlore Press, 1971), 204.

4. Quotations from United States Department of the Interior, War Relocation Authority of the United States Department of the Interior Publications, *People in Motion: The Postwar Adjustment of the Evacuated Japanese Americans* (Washington, DC: Government Printing Office, 1947), 65–66; June Nakamura, interview with JARRP, n.d., 5. Duus, *Unlikely Liberators*, 234; Taylor, *Jewel of the Desert*, 211, 268–269; quotation from Edwin C. Hiroto, interview with JARRP, January 26, 1976, 5; see also H. Yashida, interview with JARRP, n.d., 13; H. Nakajima, "Japanese Telephone and Business Directory of Southern California," Los Angeles, No. 25, 1936, 28–29, and No. 34, 1955, 136–141.

5. Hikaru Iwasaki, photographer, War Relocation Authority Photographs of Japanese-American Evacuation and Resettlement, "Reverend Masayoshi Ohmura at 3195 14th Street, Riverside, California," September 7, 1945, Bancroft Library, University of California, Berkeley. See also Lane Ryo Hirabayashi with Kenichiro Shimada, photographs by Hikaru Carl Iwasaki, *Japanese American Resettlement through the Lens: Hikaru Carl Iwasaki and the WRA's Photographic Section, 1943–1945* (Boulder: University Press of Colorado, 2009). "Office Contact Record," May 23, [1945?], to August 23, 1945; "Shipping

Order, Trans-Continental Freight Service," August 23, 1945; "Request for Transportation of Property," August 28, 1945, WRA, Sumi Harada File.

6. Sumi Harada, in discussion with Mark Rawitsch, January 10, 1977.

7. The old potted houseplant was still in the Haradas' dining room when I first visited Sumi in 1976. She explained its history after I spotted it in a family photograph from the 1930s.

8. Quotation from Sumi Harada, interview by Mark Rawitsch, February 24, 1982. "Japanese-American Internee Data File: Haruto Shimazu, No. 34085D," http://aad .archives.gov/aad/series-description.jsp?s=623 (accessed November 19, 2010); "California Deaths, 1940–1997, Haruto Shimazu," September 8, 1926, to October 31, 1965, Ancestry.com, http://vitals.rootsweb.ancestry.com/ca/death/search.cgi (accessed March 20, 2008).

9. "Japanese-American Internee Data File: Takanabe [Family], No. 34102A–G," http://aad.archives.gov/aad/series-description.jsp?s=623 (accessed November 19, 2010).

10. Quotation from Sumi Harada, interview by Mark Rawitsch, February 24, 1982. Japanese-American Internee Data File, "Kobayashi [Family], No. 34087A–F"; "Mayeda [Family], No. 31224A–G"; "Sam Ogawa, No. 40 68A," http://aad.archives .gov/aad/series-description.jsp?s=623 (accessed November 19, 2010).

11. Quotations from Sumi Harada, interview by Mark Rawitsch, February 24, 1982; downstairs bathroom towel sign, Harada House, Harada Family Artifact Collection.

12. Quotations from Roy Hashimura, interview by Wally Kido, December 1, 2006, and January 23, 2007. Wally Kido, e-mail messages to Mark Rawitsch, October 17 and November 27, 2007; quotation from Kimi Klein in Mark Rawitsch's interview with Rosalind Uno, Wally Kido, Kimi Klein, Naomi Harada, Dr. Ken Harada, and Paul Harada, October 29, 2005. Warren Harada, e-mail messages to Mark Rawitsch, November 20, 21, 2006.

13. Sumi Harada, interview by Mark Rawitsch, February 24, 1982; visits to the Harada House with Sumi Harada, 1976–1983, and Dr. Harold Harada, July 21–23, 2000, and April 19, 2001; Naomi Harada, "Naomi Elaine Harada, Social Studies, Period VI" (school report), circa 1965–1966, 5.

14. Sumi Harada, in discussion with Mark Rawitsch, January 24, 1977; Riverside City Directory, 1937; "Japanese-American Internee Data File: Teshima [Family], No. 24027A–D"; "Harry T. Teshima, No. 40 82A"; "John Teshima, No. 33220A," http:// aad.archives.gov/aad/series-description.jsp?s=623 (accessed November 19, 2010). "Dr. Teshima to Return," *Topaz Times*, March 2, 1944; "Dr. Teshima," *Topaz Times*, April 1, 1944; [multiple medical records], January–July 1944, WRA Clark Harada File.

15. Olivewood Cemetery memorial service photograph negatives, Civic Cut Rate Drugs envelope no. 10882, August 2, 1948; Olivewood Cemetery memorial service photographs, Kimi Klein Collection File, Harada Family Archival Collection; Olivewood Memorial Park Records.

EPILOGUE: SUMI'S HOUSE

1. Quotation from Rosalind Uno in author's interview with Rosalind Uno, Wally Kido, Kimi Klein, Naomi Harada, Dr. Ken Harada, and Paul Harada, October 29, 2005.

2. Toshi Nagamori Ito, *Memoirs of Toshi Ito: U.S.A. Concentration Camp Inmate, War Bride, Mother of Chrisie and Judge Lance Ito* (Bloomington, IN: Author House, 2009), 2–3, 9, 11, 27, 60–66.

3. Quotations from Sumi Harada, interview by Mark Rawitsch, December 13, 1976.

4. Quotations from Sumi Harada, interview by Mark Rawitsch, February 24, 1982.

5. Ibid.

6. Quotation from Sumi Harada, interview by Mark Rawitsch, December 13, 1976.

7. Quotation from Mine Harada Kido, interview by Mark Rawitsch, January 17, 1982.

8. Kris Lovekin, "Japan-Bound Teens Learn How to Be Polite with Their Feet," *Riverside Press-Enterprise*, July 23, 1993; "Japanese Return to Poston after 40 Years," *Parker Pioneer* (Parker, AZ), February 21, 1985; Charles Hillinger, "A Nation Apologizes; Japanese Restaurateur Was Denied Citizenship, but His Home Is Being Declared a Landmark," *Los Angeles Times*, August 18, 1991; Raymond Smith, "Four Will Be Honored as Women of Achievement," *Riverside Press-Enterprise*, August 17, 1995; Gene Ghiotto, "Four Women Honored for Courage, Strength," *Riverside Press-Enterprise*, September 15, 1995.

9. Quotation from Sumi Harada, "Autumn," circa 1950–1960?, Harada Family Archival Collection.

10. Quotation from "A Tour of the Harada House."

11. Quotations from Mine Harada Kido, interview by Mark Rawitsch, January 17, 1982; Clark Harada, interview by Mark Rawitsch, January 31, 1977; Dr. Harold Harada, interview by Mark Rawitsch, July 22, 2000. Final quotation from Sumi Harada, interview by Mark Rawitsch, December 13, 1976. See also "Neo-Nazi Demonstration in Riverside Spurs Confrontations," *Riverside Press-Enterprise*, October 24, 2009; Robert Faturechi, "Neo-Nazis Protest at Riverside Synagogue," *Los Angeles Times*, December 20, 2009.

AFTERWORD

Acknowledgments. I thank Mark Rawitsch, Lynn Voorheis, and Kevin Hallaran for their comments on an earlier draft of this afterword. They are not, of course, responsible for any errors that remain.

1. California Cultural and Historical Endowment (CCHE) Planning Grant Application, submitted January 1, 2006. NHL Harada House Preservation Project Funding has been provided, in part, by the California Cultural and Historical Endowment.

2. Two questions that come to mind are, how typical were the Haradas? and how typical is the Harada House itself? It is hard to say because there is no other documented case of this kind, or at this level of detail, presently on the record. My own sense is that in many ways, for a family of its time and of its class and religious orientation, the Haradas were a bit more successful than many but otherwise not strikingly different.

3. Books and essays by Yuji Ichioka remain a critically important source for understanding the worldview of the pre-war Issei, or first-generation Japanese immigrant. Readers may wish to start with Ichioka's classic study, *Issei: The World of the First-Generation Japanese, 1885–1924* (New York: Free Press, 1988).

4. Interestingly enough, detailed studies of the Japanese house in English go back at least to Edward S. Morse, *Japanese Homes and Their Surroundings* (Tokyo: Tuttle Publishing, 1972), which was originally published in 1886.

5. For a still useful, if not uncriticized, delineation of how the *ie* permeated Japanese social organization writ large, see Nakane Chie, *Japanese Society* (Berkeley: University of California Press, 1972).

6. For treatment of the passage and impact of the California Alien Land Law, see Rawitsch's excellent discussion, *supra*.

7. It is convenient to differentiate the idea of the house, as a physical entity providing shelter and a space for dwelling, from "home." Although also meaning "dwelling," the roots of the word "home" in Old Norse—*heimr*—include the connotation of "world."

8. This division parallels a Deleuzian approach to house/home as an assemblage: that is, an entity that is at once material, an object, set in time and space, but also layered with meanings and signs. So a home is a house, a thing, but it also has qualities, expressions, and affects, which in turn have their own specific speeds and densities. My primary debt, in terms of conjecturing the application of Deleuze to the understanding of house/home, is apparent: see J. Macgregor Wise, "Home: Territory and Identity," in *Animations (of Deleuze and Guattari)*, ed. Jennifer Daryl Slack (New York: Peter Lang, 2009), 107–127.

9. The phrase "diffuse, enduring solidarity" is borrowed from the work of anthropologist David M. Schneider; see Schneider's *American Kinship: A Cultural Account* (Chicago: University of Chicago Press, 1968).

10. Wise, "Home," 107–127.

11. In his Deleuzian-inspired commentary on the house, J. Macgregor Wise references the material/machinic, as well as the semiotic/enunciated. I have added a third dimension, in hopes of capturing the tacit as well as the kinesic—both significant, as well as unarticulated.

12. John Embree, *Acculturation among the Japanese of Kona, Hawaii*, American Anthropological Association Memoirs 59 (Menasha, WI: American Anthropological Association, 1941), in terms of Hawaii, and Kazuo Ito, *Issei: A History of Japanese Immigrants in North America* (Seattle: Executive Committee for Publication of Issei, 1973), in terms of the US mainland, are two of the very few students of early Japanese America to describe the physical features of the Issei living arrangements. After reading Rawitsch's account and retrospectively examining the available literature, I was struck by the paucity of data about all aspects of Issei-Nisei households. The one exception to this rule is Sylvia Yanagisako's detailed account of Japanese American family ideology in Seattle, especially in regard to the gendered duties of Nisei children vis-à-vis care for elderly parents and inheritance decisions. See Sylvia J. Yanagisako, *Transforming the Past: Kinship and Tradition among Japanese Americans* (Stanford, CA: Stanford University Press, 1985).

13. Cardinality in the positioning of certain furniture was a common Issei practice. If displayed in the house, for example, the body of a deceased relative was laid out with the head facing north; therefore, by tradition, living persons would never be given a bed with its "head" pointed in this direction. Perhaps the Haradas' Christian beliefs inhibited them from reproducing this practice in Riverside. Also, Rawitsch does not mention the bath or bathing practices among the Haradas. Certainly the typical American bathroom does not

lend itself to communal bathing practices, but even Sansei can remember bathing with one or the other parent as a young child, perhaps along with young siblings, at least when they were small enough to fit into the Western-style tub. These intimate details are things that can certainly be filled in through ethnographic interviews or literary accounts, given the foundation that *The House on Lemon Street* offers.

14. On the Japanese concepts of *uchi* and *soto*, see two books by Takie Sugiyama Lebra: *Japanese Patterns of Behavior* (Honolulu: University of Hawaiʻi Press, 1986) and *Japanese Self in Cultural Logic* (Honolulu: University of Hawaiʻi Press, 2004).

15. Tetsuden Kashima, "Japanese American Internees Return, 1945–1955: Readjustment and Social Amnesia," *Phylon* 41, no. 2 (1980): 107–115.

Glossary of
Japanese Terms

AICHI JONJO SIHAN GAKKO. Aichi Prefectural Lower Normal College, alma mater of Jukichi Harada, late 1890s.

AICHI-KEN. Japanese prefecture and ancestral home of the Harada and Indo families, near the city of Nagoya on Honshu Island in central Japan.

DAIKON. In Japanese, "large root"; Japanese white radish.

DASHI. Soup base or cooking stock consisting of water, edible kelp, and dried fish flakes.

EDO PERIOD. Japanese historical period from 1603 to 1868; political era known as the Tokugawa Shogunate, established by the shogun Tokugawa Ieyasu.

GAKKO (or Odaka Gakko). District school.

GUN (as in "Chita-gun"). Japanese administrative division; district.

HAIKU. An unrhymed Japanese poem recording the essence of a moment.

HAKUJIN. White person.

HAN (as in "Kiriya-han"). Ancient feudal domain; administrative division or fief of feudal lords of Japan.

IKEBANA. Art of flower arranging.

ISSEI. Japanese term used in North America, South America, and Australia to specify the Japanese people first to immigrate from their homeland in Japan. Their children born in the new country are referred to as "Nisei," second generation; their grandchildren are "Sansei," third generation. The terms are based on the numbers "one, two, three" (*ichi, ni, san*) in the Japanese language.

KAKITSUBATA. Rabbit-ear iris; signature flower of Aichi prefecture.

KAMITOKU (as in "Kamitoku Room" at the Harada House). A room in the Harada House described by Dr. Harold Harada as the "hair-combing room." According to Eiichiro Azuma, Alan Charles Kors Term Associate Professor of History and Asian American Studies at the University of Pennsylvania, "There is no common Japanese term 'kamitoku' . . . In Japanese, 'combing one's hair' is 'kami wo toku,' and if the expression is shortened, it is 'kamitoku,' though it sounds awkward [to a Japanese speaker]. Nisei often do this, and come up with the terms that occasionally baffle Japanese folks. It is possible that 'kamitoku-room' is an example of [a] Nisei's flexible use of what they consider 'Japanese words.'"

KARIYA JONJO SHOGAKKO. Elementary school in the town of Kariya, Japan, circa late 1890s.

KEN (as in "Aichi-ken"). Japanese administrative division; prefecture.

KIBEI. Term used in the 1940s to describe American citizens born of immigrant Japanese parents who had received their education in Japan and later returned to live in the United States.

KIMONO. Traditional cloth garment worn in different styles and fabrics by women, men, and children.

KOI (or "nishikigoi"). Domesticated varieties of the common carp fish known for their colorful markings.

KOMBU. Edible kelp or "seaweed" common in Japanese cooking.

KOSEKI. Family history register.

KYOKU CHOKUGO. Japanese Imperial Rescript on Education, 1890.

MEIJI PERIOD. Japanese historical period also known as the Meiji Era, 1868–1912, beginning with the restoration of the emperor after the overthrow of the Tokugawa Shogunate at the end of the Edo Period.

MISO. Seasoning paste made of fermented soybeans and/or rice.

NIHONMACHI. In the original Japanese, literally "Japan town" or "Japan street"; term used to describe a major Japanese community in the United States, such as the neighborhood in San Francisco also known today as "Japantown"; also used to refer to historical Japanese communities in Southeast and East Asia.

NIKKEI. Japanese immigrant or a descendant thereof who is not a citizen of Japan; also "the Nikkei community," a broadly defined community of those with Japanese ancestry living outside Japan.

NISEI. Japanese term used in North America, South America, and Australia to specify the children of the immigrant Issei (see also *Issei*); the earliest generation of Japanese family members born in the United States of America.

NOBORI. Military banner used to identify battlefield troops; later used to describe a ceremonial carp fish or koi windsock banner.

OFURO. Water bath in a steep-sided wooden bathtub.

OKAZU. Side dish to accompany rice or noodles typically made from fish, meat, vegetables, or tofu.

OKODEN. Traditional practice of giving a monetary condolence gift.

RONIN. Lordless samurai, one whose feudal lord had been deprived of his territory.

SAMURAI. Warrior; member of the feudal military aristocracy.

SAN (as in "Harada-san" or "Nakamura-san"). Title of respect added to a name.

SASHIMI. Food item consisting of very fresh, thinly sliced raw fish or other fresh seafood.

SENSEI. Title used to address teachers, professors, and other professionals.

SHAKUHACHI. Bamboo flute.

SHI (as in "Kumamura-shi"). Japanese municipality; administrative division like a city.

SHIBAI. In the original Japanese, literally a "play" or a "dramatic performance."

"SHI KATA GANAI." Japanese phrase meaning "it can't be helped" or "nothing can be done about it"; used to describe the ability to maintain dignity in the face of unavoidable injustice or tragedy, especially when circumstances are beyond individual control.

SHOGAKKO. Elementary school.

SHOGUN. Hereditary military ruler and governing leader of Japan.

SHOYU. Soy sauce condiment produced with fermented soya beans and wheat.

SUKIYAKI. One-pot meal with thinly sliced beef and vegetables.

TENPO. Japanese era from 1830 through 1844.

TERIYAKI. Cooking technique in which foods are grilled or broiled in a sweet soy sauce.

TOKUGAWA SHOGUNATE. Feudal regime established by Tokugawa Ieyasu and ruled by the shoguns of the Tokugawa family from 1603 to 1868, when it was abolished during the Meiji Restoration.

TSUKEMONO. Pickled vegetables often served as a side dish.

TSUNAMI. A large, often destructive ocean wave produced by an undersea earthquake, subsidence, or volcanic eruption.

UKIYO-E. Genre of Japanese wood-block prints or paintings produced in the seventeenth to twentieth centuries.

BIBLIOGRAPHY

Aoki, Keith. "No Right to Own? The Early Twentieth-Century 'Alien Land Laws' as a Prelude to Internment." *Boston College Law Review* (1998): 37–72.

"Asian American Riverside." University of California, Riverside. http://aar.ucr.edu (accessed 2007–2009).

Attorney General Records. Sacramento: California State Archives, 1915–1925.

Bailey, Paul. *City in the Sun*. Los Angeles: Westernlore Press, 1971.

Bangarth, Stephanie. *Voices Raised in Protest: Defending North American Citizens of Japanese Ancestry, 1942–49*. Vancouver: UBC Press, 2008.

Bauerlein, Mark. "The Tactical Life of Booker T. Washington." *The Chronicle of Higher Education: The Chronicle Review* 50, no. 14 (November 28, 2003). http://chronicle.com/article/The-Tactical-Life-of-Booker-T/29240 (accessed December 17, 2010).

Bean, Walton. *California: An Interpretive History*. New York: McGraw-Hill, 1978.

Beasley, W. G. *The Modern History of Japan*. New York: Harcourt School, 1963.

"Before Board of Special Inquiry, Port of San Francisco, Cal., October 27, 1904, #455." National Archives and Records Administration, October 1904.

"The Booker T. Washington Papers, Open Book Edition, Vol. 13: 1914–15." History Cooperative, University of Illinois Press. http://www.historycooperative.org/ (accessed April 6, 2008).

Brown, John, Jr., and James Boyd. *History of San Bernardino and Riverside Counties*. Vol. 2. Chicago: Lewis Publishing Company, 1922.

Browning, Oscar. The Papers of Oscar Browning, OB. Cambridge: King's College Archive Centre, 1879–1912.

Buell, Raymond Leslie. "The Development of the Anti-Japanese Agitation in the United States." *Political Science Quarterly* 37 (December 1922): 605–638; and 38 (March 1923): 57–81. http://dx.doi.org/10.2307/2142539.

Burton, Jeffery F., Mary M. Farrell, Florence B. Lord, and Richard W. Lord. "Confinement and Ethnicity: An Overview of World War II Japanese American Relocation Sites." Western Archeological and Conservation Center, National Park Service, US Department of the Interior. 1999 (rev. July 2000). http://www.nps.gov/history/history/online_books/anthropology74/ (accessed March 17, 2007).

California Attorney General. "Biennial Report of the Attorney General of the State of California, 1916–1918." Sacramento, 1919.

California Attorney General. "California Land Title Association, 38th Anniversary Conference." *Proceedings.* Sacramento, 1944.

"California Births, 1905–1995, Riverside County." Family Tree Legends. http://www.familytreelegends.com (accessed May 18, 2008).

"California Deaths, 1940–1997." Ancestry.com. http://vitals.rootsweb.ancestry.com/ca/death/search.cgi (accessed March 20, 2008).

California Department of Parks and Recreation, Office of Historic Preservation. "Five Views: An Ethnic Historic Site Survey for California, Japanese Americans in California." December 1988. www.nps.gov/history/history/online_books/5views/5views.htm (accessed March 15, 2009).

"California Passenger and Crew Lists, 1893–1957, *Gaelic*, 18 June 1903." Ancestry.com. June 18, 1903. www.ancestry.com (accessed May 8, 2009).

Canadian Passenger Lists, 1865–1935, *Princess Victoria*. August 4, 1905. www.ancestry.com (accessed May 8, 2009).

Catalogue of the Birds in the British Museum, Volume 23. London: British Museum, 1894.

"Cemetery Records." 1900–1950. Olivewood Memorial Park, Riverside, CA.

Chang, Gordon H. *Morning Glory, Evening Shadow: Yamato Ichihashi and His Internment Writings, 1942–1945.* Stanford, CA: Stanford University Press, 1996.

Chuman, Frank. *The Bamboo People: The Law and Japanese Americans.* Del Mar, CA: Publisher's Inc., 1976.

"Civil War Pension Index, 1861–1934." National Archives and Records Administration, Washington, DC.

Clancey, Gregory. *Earthquake Nation: The Cultural Politics of Japanese Seismicity, 1868–1930.* Berkeley: University of California Press, 2006.

Clerk of the Superior Court, Riverside Civil Files C-114, 7736–7809. 7751. *The People of California v. Jukichi Harada.* Riverside Superior Court, Riverside, CA, 1916–1918.

Crewdson, Wilson. *The Dawn of Western Influence in Japan.* London: Japan Society, 1903.

Crewdson, Wilson. *Japan Our Ally.* London: Macmillan, 1915.

Crewdson, Wilson. *The Textiles of Old Japan.* Transactions and Proceedings of the Japan Society, XI. London: Japan Society, 1914.

Daniels, Roger. *The Politics of Prejudice: The Anti-Japanese Movement in California and the Struggle for Japanese Exclusion.* Glouster, MA: Peter Smith, 1966.

Directory of the National Society of the Daughters of the American Revolution. Washington, DC: National Society of the Daughters of the American Revolution, 1911.

Duus, Masayo Umezawa. *Unlikely Liberators: The Men of the 100th and 442nd.* Honolulu: University of Hawai'i Press, 1983.

Estes, Matthew T., and Donald H. Estes. "Hot Enough to Melt Iron: The San Diego Nikkei Experience 1942–1946." *Journal of San Diego History* 42, no. 3 (Summer 1996): 126–173.

"Executive Order 9066." Japanese American Internment Curriculum. http://bss.sfsu.edu/internment/executiorder9066.html (accessed April 16, 2009).

Foster, Sandys Birket. *The Pedigree of Wilson of High Wray and Kendal and the Families Connected with Them.* Washington, DC: Printed for private circulation by W. H. and L. Collingridge, 1871.

Fourteenth Census of the United States, State Compendium, California, Statistics of Population, Occupations, Agriculture, Irrigation, Drainage, Manufacturers, and Mines and Quarries for the State, Coun. Washington, DC: Department of Commerce, Bureau of the Census, 1920.

Fry, Edward. *Theodore Waterhouse, 1838–1891: Notes of His Life and Extracts from His Letters and Papers.* London: Chiswick Press, Charles Wittingham and Company, 1894.

Gale, Zona. *Frank Miller of Mission Inn.* New York: D. Appleton-Century Company, 1938.

General Catalogue of Bates College and Cobb Divinity School, 1863–1915. Lewiston, ME: Bates College, 1915.

Girdner, Audrie, and Anne Loftis. *The Great Betrayal: The Evacuation of the Japanese-Americans during World War II.* London: Macmillan, 1969.

Gulick, Sidney L. *Should Congress Enact Special Laws Affecting Japanese?* New York: National Committee on American Japanese Relations, 1922.

Harada Family Archival Collection. ca. 1890–2005. Riverside, CA: Riverside Metropolitan Museum.

Harada Family Koseki Records. Trans. Kayo Kaname Levenson and Takashi Oda. Aichi Prefecture, Japan, 2005.

Harada, Naomi. School report: Naomi Elaine Harada, Social Studies, Period VI. Culver City, CA, ca. 1965–1966.

Harper, Franklin, ed. *Who's Who in the Pacific Coast: A Biographical Compilation of Notable Living Contemporaries West of the Rocky Mountains.* Los Angeles: Harper Publishing Company, 1913.

"The Hawai'i Nisei Story: Americans of Japanese Ancestry during World War II." The Hawaii Nisei Project. http://nisei.hawaii.edu/page/home (accessed September 29, 2007).

Hichborn, Franklin. *Story of the Session of the California Legislature of 1909.* San Francisco: Press of the James H. Barry Co., 1909.

Hill, Kimi Kodani. *Topaz Moon: Chiura Obata's Art of the Internment.* Berkeley, CA: Heyday Books, 2000.

Hillenbrand, Laura. *Seabiscuit: An American Legend.* New York: Random House, 2001.

Hirabayashi, Lane Ryo, Kenichiro Shimada, and Hikaru Carl Iwasaki. *Japanese American Resettlement through the Lens: Hikaru Carl Iwasaki and the WRA's Photographic Section, 1943–1945.* Boulder: University Press of Colorado, 2009.

Hiram Johnson Papers. The Bancroft Library, University of California, Berkeley.

History of Sherman Indian Museum. http://www.shermanindianmuseum.org (accessed February 11, 2008).

Hitchborn, Franklin. *Story of the Session of the California Legislature of 1911*. San Francisco: Press of the James H. Barry Co., 1911.

Holmes, Elmer Wallace. *History of Riverside County, California with Biographical Sketches*. Los Angeles: Historic Record Company, 1912.

Hosokawa, Bill. *JACL: In Quest of Justice*. New York: William Morrow and Company, 1982.

Hosokawa, Bill. *Nisei: The Quiet Americans*. Boulder: University Press of Colorado, 2002.

Hotta-Lister, Ayako. *The Japan-British Exhibition of 1910: Gateway to the Island Empire of the East*. Richmond, Surrey: Curzon Press, 1999.

In the Superior Court of the State of California In and For the County of Riverside, The People of the State of California, Plaintiff vs. Jukirchi [sic] Harada, Defendant. Reporter's Transcript. 7751. Riverside Superior Court, May 28–29, 1918.

Index to Official Records, Grantees and Plaintiffs 1914–1917, A–L, Riverside County 7. Riverside County, Riverside, CA.

"Individual Records." United States War Relocation Authority. Washington, DC: National Archives and Records Administration, 1942–1945.

Indo Family Koseki Records. Trans. Kayo Kaname Levenson and Takashi Oda. Aichi Prefecture, Japan, 2005.

Iseda, Gyosuke. *Frank Miller*. Printed in Japanese, 1928.

Ito, Toshi Nagamori. *Memoirs of Toshi Ito: U.S.A. Concentration Camp Inmate, War Bride, Mother of Chrisie and Judge Lance Ito*. Bloomington, IN: Author House, 2009.

"Japan Occupation Essays: Albert O. Nakazawa." The National Japanese American Veterans Council. http://www.njavc.org (accessed February 11, 2007).

Japanese American Evacuation and Resettlement Records. 1930–1974. The Bancroft Library, University of California, Berkeley.

Japanese Americans in Riverside Research Project. 1890–1980. University of California, Riverside.

The Japanese Association of the Pacific Northwest. *Japanese Immigration: Exposition of Its Real Status*. Seattle: The Japanese Association of the Pacific Northwest, 1907.

Japanese Consulate. *Documental History of Law Cases Affecting Japanese in the United States, 1916–1924*. San Francisco: Consulate General of Japan, 1925.

Japanese Immigration: Hearings before the Committee on Immigration and Naturalization, House of Representatives, Sixty-Sixth Congress, Second Session, July 12, 13, and 14, 1920, Part I, Hearings at San Francisco and Sacramento, California. Washington, DC: Government Printing Office, 1921.

"Japanese-American Internee Data File, 1942–1945." US National Archives and Records Administration. http://aad.archives.gov/aad/fielded-search.jsp?dt=2003&cat=WR26&tf=F&bc=,sl (accessed November 19, 2010).

Kachi, Teruko Okada. *The Treaty of 1911 and the Immigration and Alien Land Law Issue between the United States and Japan 1911–1913*. New York: Arno Press, 1978.

King's College Cambridge, Annual Report. 1918. King's College, Cambridge, England.

Kirby, Edward J. "Subversive Activities at War Relocation Centers." Federal Bureau of Investigation, File No. 100-4483 (declassified). January 9, 1943. US National Archives and Records Administration, Washington, DC.

Kitano, Harry. *Japanese Americans: The Evolution of a Subculture.* Englewood Cliffs, NJ: Prentice-Hall, 1969.

Klotz, Esther. *The Mission Inn: Its History and Artifacts.* Riverside, CA: Rubidoux Printing, 1981.

Konvitz, Milton R. *The Alien and the Asiatic in American Law.* Ithaca, NY: Cornell University Press, 1946.

Kumamoto, J. "Ethnic Minorities in Riverside." Museum Lecture Series. Riverside Metropolitan Museum, Riverside, CA.

Lang, Robert, ed. *The Birth of a Nation: D. W. Griffith, Director.* New Brunswick, NJ: Rutgers University Press, 1994.

Lawton, Harry W. "Chronological History of Chinese Pioneers in Riverside and the Southern California Citrus Belt." In *Wong Ho Leun: An American Chinatown.* San Diego, CA: Great Basin Foundation, 1987.

Lawton, Harry W. "Riverside's First Chinatown and the Boom of the Eighties." In *Wong Ho Leun: An American Chinatown.* San Diego, CA: Great Basin Foundation, 1987.

Lim, Deborah K. "Meeting with Governor Olson, Research Report Prepared for Presidential Select Committee on JACL Resolution #7." 1990. http://www.resisters .com/study/LimPartICID.htm#ID3 (accessed November 7, 2010).

Lincicome, Mark E. *Principle, Praxis, and the Politics of Educational Reform in Meiji Japan.* Honolulu: University of Hawai'i Press, 1995.

"List or Manifest of Alien Passengers for the U.S. Immigration Officer at Port of Arrival, S.S. *Doric*, October 1904." October 1904. National Archives and Records Administration, Washington, DC.

Maine Historical Society. Maine Memory Network. http://www.mainememory.net (accessed March 17, 2008).

Marcella Craft Collection. Archival collection. Riverside Metropolitan Museum, Riverside, CA.

Mermilliod, Jennifer. "3643 University Avenue, Jackson Building." Historic building report. Riverside, CA: Riverside Metropolitan Museum, ca. 2004.

Miguel Estudillo Papers. The Bancroft Library, University of California, Berkeley.

Miller, Frank A. Collection of Material Relating to Riverside and the Mission Inn, 1920–1940. The Bancroft Library, University of California, Berkeley.

Modell, John. *The Economics and Politics of Racial Accommodation: The Japanese of Los Angeles, 1900–1942.* Urbana: University of Illinois Press, 1977.

"MOH Citation for Daniel Inouye." Home of Heroes. http://www.homeofheroes.com /moh/citations_1942_nisei/inouye.html (accessed November 12, 2010).

Moses, H. Vincent, and Brenda Buller Focht. *Life in Little Gom-Benn: Chinese Immigrant Society in Riverside, 1885–1930.* Riverside, CA: Riverside Museum Press, 1991.

Muller, Eric L. *Free to Die for Their Country: The Story of the Japanese American Draft Resisters in World War II.* Chicago: University of Chicago Press, 2003.

Muller, Eric L. "A Penny for Their Thoughts: Draft Resistance at the Poston Relocation Center." *Law and Contemporary Problems* 68 (Spring 2005): 119–157.

"Muster Roll of the Officers and Crew of the United States Steamer *Grant* for the Month of July 1898." July 1898. National Archives and Records Administration, Washington, DC.

"Muster Roll of the USS *Solace*." December 1900–March 1901. National Archives and Records Administration, Washington, DC.

"The Night President Teddy Roosevelt Invited Booker T. Washington to Dinner." *Journal of Blacks in Higher Education* 35 (Spring 2002): 24–25.

Okubo, Mine. *Citizen 13660*. Seattle: University of Washington Press, 1983.

Patterson, Thomas W. *A Colony for California: Riverside's First Hundred Years*. Riverside, CA: Press-Enterprise Company, 1971.

Pendleton, Robert, and Patrick McSherry. "The U.S. Revenue Cutter Service in the Spanish American War." Spanish American War Centennial. http://www.spanamwar.com/USRCS.htm (accessed December 10, 2007).

Raven, Shelly. "Red Paper and Varnished Ducks: Subjective Images of Riverside's Chinatown." In *Wong Ho Leun: An American Chinatown*. San Diego, CA: Great Basin Foundation, 1987.

Rawitsch, Mark H. "Japanese American Relocation: Educational Patterns and Community Receptivity." Seminar paper. Riverside: University of California, 1976.

Rawitsch, Mark Howland. "No Other Place: Japanese American Pioneers in a Southern California Neighborhood." Riverside: University of California, Department of History, 1983.

Record of Common Council, vol. 16. 1918. Riverside City Hall Archives, Riverside, CA.

Register of Members of King's College Cambridge, 1797–1925. King's College, Cambridge, England.

Riddell, Patricia, and Leslie Bacha. "Riverside's Chinatown: A Study of the Past." Seminar paper. June 13, 1974. University of California, Riverside.

Riverside Polytechnic High School. "The 1938 Orange and Green, Riverside Polytechnic High School." Riverside, CA: Riverside Polytechnic High School, 1938.

Riverside School Records, Riverside Polytechnic High School. 1919–1960. Riverside Municipal Archives, Riverside, CA.

Robinson, Greg. *A Tragedy of Democracy: Japanese Confinement in North America*. New York: Columbia University Press, 2009.

Roosevelt, Franklin D. "Day of Infamy Speech." December 8, 1941. http://www.radiochemistry.org/history/video/fdr_infamy.html (accessed November 7, 2010).

Russo, Kurt. "The Harada House." Research paper. Riverside: University of California, Riverside, 2006.

Sanchez, Nellie Van de Grift. *The Life of Mrs. Robert Louis Stevenson*. New York: Charles Scribner's Sons, 1925.

Santa Fe Trailways. "Grand Canyon and the Indian Empire." Brochure. University of Arizona Libraries, ca. 1940. http://www.library.arizona.edu/exhibits/pams/pdfs/75grtrai.pdf (accessed August 12, 2009).

Smith, Bradford. *Americans from Japan*. Philadelphia: Lippincott, 1948.

Smith, Eugene R., ed. *The Gospel in All Lands*. New York: Missionary Society of the Methodist Episcopal Church, 1901.

Spicer, Edward H., Asael T. Hansen, Katherine Luomala, and Marvin K. Opler. *Impounded People: Japanese-Americans in the Relocation Centers*. Tucson: University of Arizona Press, 1969.

Starr, Kevin. *Americans and the California Dream, 1850–1915*. Oxford: Oxford University Press, 1973.

Starr, Kevin. *Inventing the Dream: California through the Progressive Era*. Oxford: Oxford University Press, 1985.

Starr, Kevin. *Material Dreams: Southern California through the 1920s*. Oxford: Oxford University Press, 1990.

Strange, Edward F. *The Colour Prints of Hiroshige*. London: Cassell and Company, 1925.

Strong, Edward K., Jr. *The Second-Generation Japanese Problem*. Stanford, CA: Stanford University Press, 1934.

Taylor, Sandra C. *Jewel of the Desert: Japanese American Internment at Topaz*. Berkeley: University of California Press, 1993.

"Thirteenth Census of the United States Taken in the Year 1910, Volume II, Population 1910, Reports by States with Statistics for Counties, Cities and Other Civil Divisions, Alabama–Montana." Thirteenth Census of the United States Taken in the Year 1910. Washington, DC: Department of Commerce, Bureau of the Census, 1910.

Transactions and Proceedings of the Japan Society. Vol. XXVII. London: Japan Society of London, 1941.

Tsurumi, E. Patricia. "Meiji Primary School Language and Ethics Textbooks: Old Values for a New Society?" *Modern Asian Studies* 8, no. 2 (1974): 247–261.

The Universalist Register: Containing the Statistics of the Church, with an Almanac for 1875. Boston: Universalist Publishing House, 1875.

US Army, Western Defense Command and Fourth Army. *Final Report: Japanese Evacuation from the West Coast 1942*. Washington, DC: Government Printing Office, 1943.

"USS *Solace* Log, Volumes 5 and 6." January–March 1901. National Archives and Records Administration, Washington, DC.

"USS *Solace*, Record of the Miscellaneous of the Day." February–March 1901. National Archives and Records Administration, Washington, DC.

"Vandegrift Genealogy, Generation 10, 573 Nellie Frances Vandegrift and 574 Clara Josephine Vandegrift." Ancestry.com. http://www.ancestry.com/browse/bookview .aspx?dbid=26012&iid=dvm_GenMono006771-001 (accessed October 29, 2009).

Vickery, Joyce Carter. *Defending Eden: New Mexican Pioneers in Southern California 1830–1890*. Riverside: Department of History, University of California Riverside, and the Riverside Museum Press, 1977.

War Agency Liquidation Unit, US Department of the Interior, Division of Budget and Administrative Management. *People in Motion: The Postwar Adjustment of the Evacuated Japanese Americans*. Washington, DC: Government Printing Office, 1947.

War Relocation Authority. "Central Utah Final Accountability Report." United States War Relocation Authority, October 1945.

"War Relocation Authority Photographs of Japanese-American Evacuation and Resettlement, 1942–1945." The Bancroft Library, University of California, Berkeley.

Waswo, Ann. *Modern Japanese Society 1868–1994*. Oxford: Oxford University Press, 1996.

Wattawa, Gayle, ed. *Inlandia: A Literary Journey through California's Inland Empire*. Santa Clara, CA: Santa Clara University and Heyday Books, 2006.

Wong, Morrison G. "The Japanese in Riverside, 1890–1945: A Special Case in Race Relations." PhD diss., University of California, Riverside, 1977.

Woolley, John T., and Gerhard Peters. "37—Executive Order 9102 Establishing the War Relocation Authority." The American Presidency Project, March 18, 1942. http://www.presidency.ucsb.edu/ws/index.php?pid=16239 (accessed November 7, 2010).

Yamada, David T., and Oral History Committee, Monterey Peninsula Japanese American Citizens League. *The Japanese of the Monterey Peninsula: Their History and Legacy 1895–1995*. Monterey, CA: Monterey Peninsula Japanese American Citizens League, 1995.

Zentmyer, George Aubrey, ed. *The Lighted Cross: The First 100 Years of Riverside's First Church 1872–1972*. Riverside, CA: First Congregational Church, 1972.

Index

US Open Door Policy, 113
US State Department, 116
US Supreme Court, 2, 30, 31, 32, 134–35
United States v. Wong Kim Ark, 31
University of California, Riverside, 151, 308
Uno, Edison, 299, 308
Uno, Rosalind "Michan" Kido, 162, 165, 187–88, *234,* 239, 284, 299; at Poston, 204, 219, 220
Urquhart, Annie, 86, 137
Urquhart, A. George, 86, 137; Harada house purchase, 95, 96, 97
Ushijima, Kinji (George Shima): at House Committee hearings, 131–32; house purchase by, 36–38

Vancouver, 26
Van de Grift, Clara, 84, 91, 92
Van de Grift, Clara Josephine, 85, 160
Van de Grift, Frances "Fanny." *See* Stevenson, Frances Van de Grift
Van de Grift, Jacob "Jake," 8, 10, 12, 84, 160; family of, 91–92; and Harada house purchase, 95, 96–97, 125; as real estate broker, 92–93
Van de Grift, Nellie. *See* Sanchez, Nellie Van de Grift
Van de Grift, Nellie Frances, 84, 92
Velzy, Dwight, 122
Villegas, Ysmael, 313
Voting rights, 31

Walerga Assembly Center, 202
Wang Foo Shun, 53
War Relocation Authority (WRA), 185, 199, 207, 243, 271; Sumi Harada's requests of, 268–69; on loyalty statement, 248–49
Warren, Earl, 213
Wartime Civil Control Administration (WCCA), 184–85, 201, 204
Washington, Booker T., 9, 78, 79–80, *81,* 90
Washington, D.C., 286–87
Washington Restaurant, 2, 8, 148, 179; customers, 157–58; during Great Depression, 149–51; Jukichi Harada's ownership of, 69–72, 114, 138–39
Watanabe, Tetsui, 208
Watanabe family, 228
Watari, Kikugiru, 93

Waterhouse, Alfred, 55
Waterhouse, Edwin, 55
Waterhouse, Theodore, 55–56
WCCA. *See* Wartime Civil Control Administration
Webb, Ulysses S., 11, 35; on alien landownership, 100–102, 103, 105; anti-Japanese sentiment, 38, 213; communication with Noble, 94, 124; and Harada lawsuit, 110, 112, 115–18, 126, 127; *People of California v. Jukichi Harada,* 39, 343(n28); and Hayayo Yano case, 133–34
Webb v. O'Brien, 134
WeHara, Russell Hisao, 189, 207
Westerfield, Mike, 99, 152
Western Defense Command, 168, 169
White supremacy, 89–90
Williams, Althea B., 206
Wilson, Florence, 84
Wilson, G. Stanley, 84
Wilson, Woodrow, 35–36, 111, 132
Winslow, Hubert, 21
Wong, Charles, 43
Wong, Morrison "Morri," 288
Wong Kim Ark, 31
Workingmen's Party, 30
World War I, 128, 163; race relations during, 112–13, 129, 31(n19); US entry into, 111–12
World War II: California during, 172–73; 100th Battalion action in, 253–65; Japanese Americans during, 170–71, 173–74, 323–24; relocation, 4, 169–70, 288; US entry into, 166–68; West Coast defense, 168–69
WRA. *See* War Relocation Authority

Yamamoto, Harry, 212
Yamamoto, Ignatius Elmer, *217*
Yamauchi, Paul, 230
Yano, Hayayo, 133–34
Yano, Tetsubumi, 133
Yasui, Minoru, 184
Yokohama Specie Bank, 116
Yonemura family, 151
Yoshida, Morizo, 53
Yoshimori, Chiye. *See* Harada, Chiye Yoshimori
Yost, Israel, 261–62
Yuma County, 222